DUDE LIT

EMILY HIND

DUDE LIT

Mexican Men Writing and Performing Competence, 1955–2012

TUCSON

The University of Arizona Press
www.uapress.arizona.edu

We respectfully acknowledge the University of Arizona is on the land and territories of Indigenous peoples. Today, Arizona is home to twenty-two federally recognized tribes, with Tucson being home to the O'odham and the Yaqui. The university strives to build sustainable relationships with sovereign Native Nations and Indigenous communities through education offerings, partnerships, and community service.

First paperback edition published 2025

ISBN-13: 978-0-8165-3926-0 (cloth)
ISBN-13: 978-0-8165-5700-4 (paper)
ISBN-13: 978-0-8165-3989-5 (ebook)

Cover design by Leigh McDonald
Cover photo: *Glass Men* by J-F Vergel © 2018

Publication of this book is made possible in part by funding from the University of Florida College of Liberal Arts and Sciences and Center for the Humanities and the Public Sphere (Rothman Endowment).

Library of Congress Cataloging-in-Publication Data
Names: Hind, Emily, author.
Title: Dude lit : Mexican men writing and performing competence, 1955–2012 / Emily Hind.
Description: Tucson : The University of Arizona Press, 2019. | Includes bibliographical references and index.
Identifiers: LCCN 2018043114 | ISBN 9780816539260 (cloth : alk. paper)
Subjects: LCSH: Mexican literature—Male authors—History and criticism. | Male authors, Mexican—20th century. | Sexism and literature—Mexico. | Anti-feminism—Mexico. | Mexican literature—20th century—History and criticism. | Masculinity in literature. | Sex discrimination in literature.
Classification: LCC PQ7134.M44 H56 2019 | DDC 860.9/92860972—dc23 LC record available at https://lccn.loc.gov/2018043114

Printed in the United States of America
♾ This paper meets the requirements of ANSI/NISO Z39.48-1992 (Permanence of Paper).

For Holden Mellott-Hind

CONTENTS

ACKNOWLEDGMENTS

I owe this book, some eight years in the making, to the encouragement and collaboration of innumerable friends and colleagues. The following list is necessarily abbreviated, and I apologize for the omissions.

Thanks to my writing group, which met virtually at 6:30 a.m., six days a week, for years. In order of seniority of membership, the other members are John Waldron, Rebecca Janzen, Carmen Serrano, and Carolyn Fornoff. John Waldron graciously read horrible drafts. Rebecca Janzen was the best apartment-mate and soul supporter one could have in Mexico City. Rebecca and John never doubted that I would finish this book. I can't thank them enough for that faith.

Heartful gratitude to Elissa Rashkin, for so much I can't begin to explain. *Thank you.*

Thanks to Susanne Igler, for helping me at such a crucial stage in my early career development. I am still reaping the benefits of that support.

To all the writers, and even a film director and individuals of other professions, who over the years have sat for an interview with me: I can't name you all because that would be ridiculous, but you know who you are, and every time that you forget who I am, I can only smile. A special thanks to Mauricio Carrera, Miguel Sabido, Sergio Mondragón, and Martha Domínguez Cuevas for talking to me in July 2016 about their experiences with the Centro Mexicano de Escritores. Although I did not explicitly cite all the interviews, they certainly influenced my thinking.

The College of Arts and Sciences at the University of Florida supported this project with the Humanities Scholarship Enhancement Fund. A Fulbright grant allowed me a semester at the Universidad Veracruzana in Xalapa, Veracruz, and was instrumental for my research. With the Fulbright award, I had uninterrupted time to write early versions of *Dude Lit*, to find new materials, and to talk with Mexican graduate students and colleagues. I am grateful for the outstanding friendship and guidance in Xalapa provided by Esther Hernández Palacios and Leticia Mora Perdomo, and many others at that wonderful university. I also thank Jackal Tanelorn and Tim McBride for the excellent Fulbright experience. The Center for the Humanities in the Public Sphere at the University of Florida provided a five-day catered writing retreat that oversaw the correction of one last version of the manuscript.

Thanks to Narciso Rojas Moreno for his expert help at the Archive for the Centro Mexicano de Escritores. Thanks also to Julieta Rivas Guerrero and to the wonderful staff at the various libraries and archives that have been so useful over the years, especially the archives at the Coordinación Nacional de Literatura and at the Cineteca Nacional, and the libraries at the University of Wyoming and the University of Florida.

An ongoing thanks to colleagues and former students at the Universidad Iberoamericana. (I love to see your published work, and I love it when you say hello!)

Thank you to another key group of supporters: Ilana Luna, Sara Potter, Cheyla Samuelson, and Amanda Peterson. You are all wonderful academics and tremendous sources of inspiration.

As always, orientation from Patricia Vega and Gabriela Cano remains key to my understanding of Mexico.

Thanks to the University of California Mexicanistas, who are a second family to anyone fortunate enough to hang with them. I am especially indebted to Sara Poot-Herrera, Jacobo Sefamí (and Sally Sefamí!), and Viviane Mahieux.

Thank you to Ignacio Sánchez Prado, who continues to support my career through deep friendship. In that same spirit, I thank Debra Castillo and Beth Jörgensen, who have been fundamental to my well-being from the start and have written all too many letters of recommendation. Nothing can repay my debts to the above trio of supporters, and I count myself lucky to rely on such selfless collegiality. I am pleased to add a new debt of thanks to Kenneth Kidd, colleague extraordinaire.

For my pleasant daily work life, I thank the Center for Latin American Studies and the Department of Spanish and Portuguese Studies at the

University of Florida. Across many disciplines and centers at the University of Florida, I thank in no particular order the all-star lineup of colleagues: Sophia Krzys Accord, Gillian Lord, M. Elizabeth (Libby) Ginway, Efráin Barradas, Jorge Valdés Kroff, Phil Williams, Victoria Condor-Williams, Barbara Mennel, Maya Stanfield-Mazzi, Susan Paulson, Tace Hedrick, Mary Risner, Paul Losch, Margarita Vargas Betancourt, Terry Harpold, Aaron Broadwell, Hélène Huet, Sean Trainor, Luis Álvarez Castro, Martín Sorbille, David Pharies, Kathy Dwyer-Navajas, Víctor Jordán, Sherrie Nunn, Maira Gutiérrez Rascón, Jennifer Wooten, Jessica Aaron, Ximena Moors, Shifra Armon, Aaron Broadwell, Leah Rosenberg, Laurie Taylor, Tanya Saunders, Heather Vrana, Rosana Rosende, Carol McAuliffe, Jim Cusick, Dan Reboussin, Bess De Farber, Chelsea Dinsmore, Jessie English, Jonathan Dain, Glenn Galloway, Rebecca Hanson, Karen Kainer, Pilar Useche, Nicholas Vargas, Lillian Guerra, Jeffrey Needell, Richard Freeman (in memoriam), Cecilia Suarez, María Coady, Héctor Sandoval, Susana Braylan, Andréa Ferreira, Crystal Marull, Greg Moreland, Charles Perrone, Clara Sotelo, Mary Watt, Bonnie Moradi, Trysh Travis, and many more.

Bernice Lawrence cleans the building where I work, which frees me to sit down and focus at my desk.

Thanks also to (again, in no particular order) Rebecca Biron, Susan Antebi, Cristina Carrasco, David William Foster, Hilda Chacón, Oswaldo Estrada, Robert McKee Irwin, Manuel Gutiérrez, Stephanie Pridgeon, Brian Price, Carolina Rocha, Anna Nogar, Dianna Nieblyski, Pedro Ángel Palou, Eloy Urroz, Jorge Volpi, Laura Gutiérrez, Mayra Santos-Febres, Adela Pineda, Sarah Pollack, Irma Cantú, Linda Egan, José Ramón Ruisánchez Serra, Adrienne Erazo, David Dalton, Fernando Fabio Sánchez, Sam Steinberg, Tamara Williams, Oswaldo Zavala, J. Andrew Brown, Margaret Ewalt, Carmen Boullosa, Karen Chacek, Cristina Rivera Garza, Mario Bellatin, Olivia Consentino,—ay, so many, many people—Leslie Marsh, all the outstanding former students at the University of Florida and previously at the University of Wyoming, Diana Aldrete, Anadeli Bencomo, Rongsong Liu, Abby Hathaway, Kathy Waldron, Nicholas Birns, Rosa Beltrán, Analisa Taylor, Jackie Bixler, Sarah Bowskill, Byron Brauchli, Maricruz Castro Ricalde, Citlalli López, Clara Bargellini, Claudia Sorais Castañeda, Ignacio Corona, Cynthia Tompkins, Sandra Cypess, the Lazy imprint and Ediciones Pereza, Sergio de la Mora, Julie Doring, Elizabeth O'Brien, Emilie Bergmann, Stacey Schlau, Erin Gallo, Eric Sandeen, Nuala Finnegan, Licia Fiol Matta, Ron Friis, Gaëlle Le Calvez, Charles St. Georges, Giovanna Rivero, Stasie Harrington, Rocío Oliver, Alejandra Márquez, Isabel Díaz, Jaime Marroquín,

Kathryn Bodnar, Kristina Garcia, Latina Women's League Gainesville, Jane Elizabeth Lavery, Hongmei Li, Luis Felipe Lomelí, Mary Long, Laura Guerrero Guadarrama, María-Rosa Olivera Williams, Lucía Melgar Palacios, Rafael Acosta, José Ramón Alcántara Mejía, Roberto Sirvent, Amy Reed-Sandoval, Alberto Ribas-Casasayas, Robert McRuer, Roberto Cruz Arzabal, Rogelio Cruz, Bernardo Ruiz, Rolando Romero, Silvia Ruiz Otero, Ana Sabau, Laura Torres Rodríguez, Sophie Esch, Luis Héctor Inclán Cienfuegos, Alysa Schroff, Brigitte Shull, Christina Sisk, Nohemy Solórzano-Thompson, Saúl Sosnowski, Cynthia Steele, Francesca Dennstedt, Stuart Day, Mónica Szurmuk, Elizabeth C. Martínez, Antonio Tenorio Muñoz Cota, Niemh Thornton, Tracy Roberts Camps, Ty West, Sara Uribe, Estela Vieira, Anne Wigger, Carla Faesler, Laury Leite, Mónica Nepote, Pablo Brescia, Frieda Knobloch, Julie Ward, Katherine Karr-Cornejo, Lilia Adriana Pérez Limón, Mayra Fortes, Alison Weber, Aníbal González Pérez, Alma Beaupied, Frederick de Armas, Gloria Vergara, Danny Anderson, Margaret O'Neill, Michaela Schrage-Früh, David Huerta, Andrew Paxman, Héctor Manjarrez, Colleen O'Keefe Muñoz, Tiffany Creegan Miller, Edward Chauca, Vicki Garrett, Christina Soto van der Plas, Stacey Wujcik, Ruth Melville, Horacio Legras, Santiago Vaquera-Vásquez, and so many more.

Thank you to Kristen Buckles at the University of Arizona Press for her interest in the project; Melanie Davis, who writes me emails from Interlibrary Loan; Tania Fleming, who makes everything run smoothly in the Department of Spanish and Portuguese Studies; Ivette Hernández, who works after 5 p.m. and before 9 a.m. on days when I lock my keys in my office; and Patricia Alba for patience. An enormous thanks to Diana Rico.

To the family, including the departed Brian Hind. Thanks to Steven, Annabeth, Jordan, Leslie, Juneau, and River. Thanks to Hannah, Mason, and William. Thanks to Stacey, Christian, Oliver, Tom, Kim, Carlos, Liliana, and Adrian. And to Olivia, Jillian, and Nathan.

Thank you to steadfast friends, Jennifer Mayer and Peter Queal. Thanks to Susan Wamsley, whose friendship since kindergarten has always been an inspiration to me—also thanks to her partner J-F Vergel, whose brilliant photography provided the cover image.

The constant and cheerful support from Jon Mellott is greatly appreciated.

Chapter 6 shares information published in my "Classism, *Gente Decente* and Civil Rights: From Suffrage to Divorce and Privileges in Between" (*Modern Mexican Culture*, ed. Stuart Day [Tucson: University of Arizona Press, 2017], 184–202).

Chapter 7 shares some information with my "Contemplation as Resistance to Ageism, and Its Historical Context: Mexican Writers Carmen Boullosa, Guadalupe Nettel, and María Rivera," in a special issue of *Life Writing*, edited by Margaret O'Neill and Michaela Schrage-Früh, vol. 16, no. 1 (2019).

DUDE LIT

INTRODUCTION

THE SET UP

Querying Originality and Why I Keep Coming Back to Juan Rulfo's *Pedro Páramo*, José Emilio Pacheco's *Las batallas en el desierto*, Guillermo Fadanelli's *Mis mujeres muertas*, and the Archive of the Centro Mexicano de Escritores

---

I realized that . . . Mexico's media industries (as is the case with every other media industry in the world!) had been historically (and, despite major inroads made by women at all levels, still is) dominated by heterosexual men and a cis-gendered male subjectivity that attempted to pass itself off as universal.

—ILANA LUNA

In *Gender Trouble: Feminism and the Subversion of Identity*, Judith Butler claims that roles of masculinity and femininity are fluid. The book you hold in your hands largely, and deliberately, fails to apply that claim. For the purposes of understanding the Mexican literary canon, its twentieth-century stars, and the continued habits among twenty-first-century writers and critics when they reference one another, I have narrowed Butler's grades of fluidity to just two categories of actors: men and women. All manner of sexual and gender orientations reside within these two categories, but first and foremost the figures discussed on the following pages receive treatment as either men or women, which means—among other consequences—that gay men seem to enjoy greater status than most women.

Lest you think my binary approach outdated, I encourage you to contemplate the experience of pregnancy, as I certainly have over the last nine months. I write these sentences while nine months pregnant, an experience that has reinforced my perception that the social world in the first place divides all actors along a binary. Let's set aside the cascade of assumptions triggered by others' beliefs about whether I am carrying a boy or girl and which colors, clothes, toys, and expectations are "appropriate" in each case. After all, the "general public" is hardly the body in which I should seek out sophisticated understanding of newly fluid gender roles, right? However, academe itself, at least in its bureaucratic incarnation, seems not to have changed much since the twentieth century and in some cases may have backslid. Note the all-purpose illness forms I've had to fill out to request the "sick leave" to be used after the baby's birth. The one-size-fits-all approach is not a sign of reduced gender discrimination, but a refusal to accommodate easily the sex that does get pregnant. Note also the absence of uniform *paid* parental leave policy in countries such as the United States and Mexico. The "impersonal" bureaucratic structure makes it clear that the rules are not designed for women's experiences; on the contrary, women's experiences must somehow conform to the impersonal, man-made rules.

At present, my moodier moments leave me paranoid that allowing men the same parental leave as women only adds to the discrimination. (Those of you who know what pregnancy is *really* get it, I know. To everyone else, I'm whining and should buck up. Let me tell you, buddy, when the going gets tough, the tough take a nap under their desks.) It is difficult to imagine a "fair" policy for this state of health. While I don't begrudge anyone in a partnership the phrase "We are pregnant," and while I would extend adopting parents every paid day off that I might get, it's clear to me that only the nonmetaphorically pregnant are dealing with upended habits in every aspect of their lives. Don't get me started on what it's like to have given up travel. (Good-bye spring break 2017 in Mexico City and the Latin American Studies Association conference in Lima!) If you think those changes don't affect work performance, the body-aware approach in this book isn't for you. Except that then *you* are part of the problem, so maybe keep reading.

Obviously, I don't have the solutions to these binary issues. The present compilation of research about how Mexican men performed the role of public intellectual is not a book of suggested quick fixes but rather a manual of what I think of as ongoing bad habits in the literary world that extends to *the* world, usually sheathed in all manner of self-deluded claims of impartiality. My response to the ongoing discrimination is to shift from studying women, as I did in my previous book, *Femmenism and the Mexican Woman Intellectual from Sor Juana to Poniatowska: Boob Lit*, to studying men. I am not alone in this move, and I have to wonder what young scholars like Ilana Luna might choose for their next project. Luna has begun—like so many of us—with an optimistic feminist project: that of "adapting gender" and stepping aside from the male heterosexuality behind canonical Mexican art. Will Luna—in the style of Elissa Rashkin, who followed up her early *Women Filmmakers in Mexico* with a book about the all-men group of Estridentistas—turn next to something along more traditional lines? I would like to imagine us, in a phrase borrowed from Donna Haraway, as "staying with the trouble."

Dude Lit contemplates how Mexican men perform the role of writer in order to convince others of their artistic and intellectual competence. Of course, men's handwringing about the loss in status of (men) writers now that (women and men) authors publish across all sorts of platforms encourages some peers to dismiss my project as out of touch. I counter that the role of writer continues to carry a special weight. In the first place, we still buy writers' books and attend their public appearances. Adults seem to be encouraging new generations to keep the flame: today, more children's books are produced and sold in Mexico than in the last century. Additionally, we still recognize writers and their work as the object of study in university literature and culture departments. A reputation as a "real writer" confers an unusual, almost immortal privilege. Most people will have never read a text by whichever famous writer lends his (or, in the minority of cases, her) name to street signs and conference rooms in Mexico, and yet a famous writer's name persists as the symbol—literally, in Mexico, the *signage*—of intellectual prowess; the writerly rep is as much a superficial aura as the reputation of a fashion model, although in the case of the writer, especially under a certain masculine performance, professional status less predictably fades with age. The call for academic originality that wants to dismiss feminism and pretend that we can move on already reminds me exactly of the notion that literature is "done." The declaration of the need for new topics negates the world as I know it, where sexual harassers, such as Donald Trump, make headlines as well as fortunes.

Clearly, my world is international. *Dude Lit* never means to present a case isolated to Mexico, and to reinforce this point I cite Ramón Castellblanch's letter to the editor of the *New York Times*, which accuses the newspaper of repeating newly elected President Trump's jingoistic misogyny in coverage of Mexican culture.[1] Castellblanch writes:

> Before characterizing Mexican male behavior as exceptional, you might look in the mirror. The United States may have the most sexist head of state in the indus-

> trialized world, and its vice president won't meet with a woman without his wife present. Look at the World Economic Forum's latest Global Gender Gap Report. It shows that the gender gaps of the United States and Mexico are virtually the same. Not only that, but the forum rates the United States behind Mexico in gender equity in terms of both health and political empowerment.

Castellblanch refers to the statistics from the *Global Gender Gap Report* that rank the United States in terms of overall political empowerment for women at position number 73, with a dismal ranking of 82 for the specific score of the number of "women in parliament"; in contrast, the report places Mexico in position 34 for general political empowerment of women, with the number of "women in parliament" score ranking the country at number 6. Mexico also beats the United States in the category of "Health and Survival," with a number 1 ranking; the United States ranks 62 for the same measurement.

But statistics only go so far. *Dude Lit* treats particular case studies and anecdotes more than mathematical data. After all, numbers cannot help me prove some of what I know by force of simple observation: in this latest presidential campaign, things didn't go for Hillary Clinton the way they would have had she been a man. She faced paradoxical battles men never have to engage in, including the accusation that she played "the woman card" and thus benefited from the very status that makes her political life so difficult. In my own case, I play the woman card (because that's the one I have), and as a result I court the accusation of academic unoriginality. It is convenient for the status quo to demand new topics rather than devote sustained attention to an unresolved and festering problem. It benefits the continued existence of the problem of sexism that scholarship itself still seems to split between the two groups that supposedly no longer condition our thinking. I understand how feminist analysis can be viewed as unoriginal when I look across the audience and panelists at events related to gender studies and see women overwhelmingly overrepresented. Would the academic value granted to claims of originality shift if men found themselves wrestling with an ongoing problem of the same magnitude?

To root this complaint in a particular example, I will share that at the 2015 Modern Language Association convention in Vancouver, British Columbia, I attended a panel titled "Gendering the Public Intellectual." Predictably, the MLA panel itself consisted of women and, for something like variety, the always lucid Jack Halberstam. Regardless of the numerically feeble representation of gendered difference, the imbalance between men and women, with a few rebel movers and straddlers, caused me to reaffirm the lingering existence of a connotation. The phrase "gendered public intellectual" really means *woman*. As we already know, "'Gender' is more frequently associated with girls and women, while boys and men are often treated as if they were gender-less" (Dowd, Levit, and McGinley 36). Interestingly, the MLA organizers accurately anticipated an enormous crowd and scheduled the gathering in an outsized space, which, I repeat, contained a startling majority of women attendants.

I left that panel unnerved by the contradiction between the majority of women in the room, on both sides of the presentation table, and one speaker's campaign to petition Wikipedia editors to remove the term *women* from entries on "women writers," "women intellectuals," and the like. I find this struggle for erasure—and its attendant faith in the impersonality of bureaucracy—absolutely exotic. In the Spanish language, expressions indicate gender from the very mention of an *escritora* or *escritor*. Calling a woman writer an *escritor* makes little sense, because at the end of the day, or at least the days that remain for me, she is still not treated as a he. Against the movement emanating from English departments to suppress the tag "women" from encyclopedia entries, I have taken to marking authors in drafts of my syllabi for graduate courses in one color for males and another for females, in order to show myself the balance.

We forget, perhaps, that balance won't exist without efforts to measure and then recalibrate.

After that eerie MLA panel on the "gendering [the woman] public intellectual," I belatedly sat at the desk in my hotel room and attempted to get in touch with the organizer of the group, Kate Flint. I wanted to know her estimate of the audience size. It was then that I discovered Dr. Flint wasn't kidding when she said that her email address had been removed from the public venue by her home institution, the University of Southern California, because of cyberharassment. During her talk, she had mentioned that certain phrases in her research, such as *feminist programming*, managed to unleash the wrath of bots, and owing to the onslaught of email, Flint was no longer a publicly reachable presence on the Internet. Her forced silence and our acquiescence to it risk giving the impression of consent; silencing the predicaments of "women writers" does little to turn the tide. Why are we reluctant to admit that *writer*, like *director*, like *commercial film protagonist*, *CEO*, *president*, *billionaire*, and the term *programmer*, is already—largely—gendered as male? It seems to me a better approach to demand that *men* be placed in front of those terms: *men writers*, *men directors*, *men presidents*, *men programmers*, and so forth. Changing the language by replacing *women* in *women writers* with a blank space does not effectively address the problem; try to email Kate Flint about this debate, and you'll see what I mean.[2] Should third and fourth gendered categories (et cetera) be required because the binary does not hold for everyone? Excellent suggestion! Such fine-tuning strikes me as a method of attaining much-needed visibility for the range of performances actually in practice.

On the most troublesome level, I agree with my critics regarding one fundamental point: the problem of sexism runs in me. Sexism alters my trajectory by way of the deep-seated assumptions I make about myself and others, just as it affects the assumptions that I see my women colleagues making about themselves. Take the nature of academic salaries, which point to a tremendous amount of self-sorting in addition to institutionalized discrimination. In 2016, the institution where I work, the University of Florida, reported that among the top one hundred highest-paid salaried faculty members who work at least three-fourths of the year, excluding those hired by the athletic department, only eight are women and ninety-two are men. Of the top one hundred earners, the highest-ranked woman earns $524,450, or around half as much per year as the highest-ranked man, whose salary stands at $984,759 (Vossler).

It is hard to stop being a woman, but it might be even more self-defeating to accept the role. You are *dama*-ed if you do and *dama*-ed if you don't. Note the Twitter feed #Ropasucia (#Dirtylaundry), which in its beginnings allowed women poets battling systemic discrimination in Mexico, such as Maricela Guerrero, Xitlalitl Rodríguez, and Paula Abramo, to denounce unfair treatment. Coverage from the website i-D reports that in its first installation piece, #Ropasucia gathered the sexist phrases reported on Twitter, had them embroidered on clothes, and hung these on the walls of the Galería Libertad (Freedom Gallery) in Querétaro, Mexico ("La #Ropasucia"). One example from the website, stitched in black thread on a white undershirt with a lace appliqué, reads: "Lo siento, pero creo que la poesía femenina en España no está a la altura de la otra, de la masculina, digamos, aunque tampoco es cosa de diferenciar" (I'm sorry, but I think that feminine poetry in Spain isn't at the level of the other kind, the masculine one, so to speak, although it's not a matter of differentiating either) ("La #Ropasucia"). The title of the show, "Todos los originales serán destruidos" (All originals will be destroyed), may refer to the shameful nature of the messages, but I think it also dovetails with this struggle for originality under a rubric that does not tend to view feminism as original.[3]

Allow me to reassert the point: *Dude Lit* tries not to play the originality game. Instead, I take a look—in multiple chapters from distinct angles—at well-known men writers and at a small sample of literary texts. Two of these texts are often assigned in Mexican schoolwork, Juan Rulfo's classic novel *Pedro Páramo* (1955) and José Emilio Pacheco's celebrated novella *Las batallas en el desierto* (1981). I update this curriculum with Guillermo Fadanelli's oeuvre, particularly *Mis mujeres muertas* (2012), which covers a similar romance theme. The publication dates of *Pedro Páramo*, *Las batallas en el desierto*, and *Mis mujeres muertas* fall at intervals of roughly twenty-five to thirty years, and the writing steadily favors cool autonomy for the men protagonists. In the process of returning once and again to these three novels, I also consult the archives of the Centro Mexicano de Escritores (Mexican Center for Writers), abbreviated CME. Those materials supply a fresh look at the insider patterns of career formation, but I do not mean to impute sexism to the CME alone. Furthermore, the CME did not give all men writers their start. Fadanelli never held a grant from that institution, and Pacheco enjoyed only one year of funding from it, from 1969 to 1970, in contrast to Rulfo's career with the institution as a two-time grant winner and decades-long writing tutor. The CME is only one node in a system of standard discriminatory practice.

Across all these chapters, I aim for a panoramic view of the cultural context that shapes the men's performances. Thus, my study takes into account not just the newspaper publicity and friendship networks, but also court cases, advertisements, personal interviews, an etiquette guide, feature films, and more. Speaking of this context, it is important to remind ourselves how quickly we have come to accept the terms of the cultural shift that has entrenched masculinist privilege while convincing some of us that the project of feminism is finished. Susan Bordo observes that as recently as 1991 in the United States, during the Supreme Court confirmation hearings for Clarence Thomas at which Anita Hill infamously testified, male anatomy represented vocabulary so taboo that U.S. senators could manage a reference only when citing directly from Hill's testimony; even Hill's lawyers preferred the term "private parts," which, incidentally, would still be abbreviated "p.p." (24).

It is challenging to remember that even blatant discrimination requires cautious analysis. From the Anita Hill inquiry to the Bill Clinton–Monica Lewinsky scandal, along with the emergence of the Internet, new press standards arose in the 1990s in the United States, followed by a close parallel in Mexico thanks to cable television and the shift to a more open press under President Ernesto

Zedillo. Other factors that influenced the looser public language included the AIDS crisis and academic work in the realms of queer studies and feminism. The turn toward an explicit aesthetic gives the impression that by exposing sexism to the light of day, feminism has shriveled systemic male privileges into an outdated curiosity. But sexism was never a vampire; it was always practiced in front of all of us. The problems remain, right where they were. This stasis appears in the 2018 Senate hearing that had Christine Blasey Ford testify before an eleven-member all-male Republican panel on the Judiciary Committee. Three of those Republican politicians were also present for Hill's degrading experience. The seeming futility of the twenty-seven-year time lapse made headlines even in the nonacademic press (Friedman). Women still do not benefit from what I explore in the following chapter as a "high and hard" system in the same way that men can build reputations off it. As a result of this contradiction—the lash of originality that favors the "bad boys," my present project is, by definition, *de la verga*—"of the penis" and "of low quality."

The election of President Trump succinctly sums up any further argument that I could advance here on the matter. Feminism is not exhausted; I am.

Now, here is the book. Call it cute if you like.
Go ahead.
Do it.

Oh, and this book is titled *Dude Lit* because I was told that *Dick Lit* is offensive.

PART I

THE CIVIL ENGINEERING OF MACHOS

1

HIGH AND HARD, PROHIBITION AND PERMISSION, BÁRBARO AND CIVILIZADO

Binaries that Support the Genius of Salvador Elizondo, Carlos Fuentes, Guillermo Fadanelli, and Fellows (with a Final Gender Reversal Experiment for José Emilio Pacheco's *Las batallas en el desierto*)

They stake their claim to originality not by asserting uniqueness but by sharing it.
—REBECCA L. WALKOWITZ

Creo que el tema de los géneros, masculino-femenino, ya no es una discusión, al menos para mi generación.
—VIVIAN ABENSHUSHAN

Heriberto Yépez infamously uses his Twitter account to kick up dust. One cultural reporter cited Yépez in her article in *El Universal* that covered complaints about the Mexican poets left out of an anthology published with a governmental subsidy; the last paragraph concludes with Yépez's tweet: "Ahora tu papel @julian_herbert es defender una antología oficial, transa, y lo estás haciendo, atacando a sus críticos" (Now your role @julian_herbert is to defend an official, crooked anthology, and you're doing it, attacking its critics) (Aguilar Sosa, "Antología"). The controversy over this French-language anthology was prolonged and vitriolic, and it seems interesting that amid Yépez's determined demand for independence from the government and for greater inclusion among anthologized writers he would argue that the "best" writers are those we already know: Borges and Rulfo. How did someone like Juan Rulfo end up a "safe" and nearly "saintly" figure? Surely, Yépez will argue that his viewpoint draws on Rulfo's and Borges's texts themselves and not the men's extratextual performances. However, Yépez's contentious Twitter feed categorizing only some talents as respectable hints at influences on his opinion that range far beyond peers' written literary production. As the chapters of *Dude Lit* demonstrate, a given writer's biography—the attendant trajectory of studies, friendships, and professional opportunities—can matter at least as much as the quality of the published work when it comes to building a literary reputation. To admit that people care about more than the texts—that they care about what men writers look like and whom they know and admire—seems risky, because examining superficial, even gossipy, topics can make one seem, well, superficial and gossipy.[1] On the other hand, the largely unacknowledged concern with men authors' looks and networked habits strikes me as a prejudice too powerful to ignore.

Critic Sarah Bowskill tries to reverse engineer the successful trajectories of men writers through her study of literary reviews. The historical record provided by these published assessments allows Bowskill to track an apparent gender bias. The mixed reception of Ángeles Mastretta's *Arráncame la vida* (with two English translations: *Mexican Bolero* and *Tear This Heart Out*) provides an informative contrast to the approving evaluations of works such as Gregorio López y Fuentes's *El indio* (*The Indian*) (1937) and Carlos Fuentes's *La región más transparente* (*Where the Air Is Clear*) (1958). For Bowskill, book reviews do more than build the reputation of a literary text; they determine what the text is about in the first place. Knowledge of the contents of a book seems inevitably informed by one's understanding of the author's identity. Bowskill helps us to see the illusory nature of the ideal that New Critics and many contemporary followers claim to achieve—namely, their avoidance of the "fallacy" of interpreting literature through an author's biography. However, part of the very claim to the professional status of literary critics is that they know the details of an individual author's biographical circumstances. *The personal is* not just *political*, as the feminist motto puts it. For writers struggling to create mutual literary reputations, *The personal is professional.*

Clothes readings surely count, and no less a Mexicanist scholar than Claudio Lomnitz appears to agree with me. In his biography of Ricardo Flores, one of the intellectuals of the Mexican Revolution, Lomnitz pays attention to fashion and notes that Flores's generation "flaunted a kind of youthful dandyism in the face of the glass ceiling presented to them by the establishment" (*The Return* 74, 76). As early as 1892, economically frustrated men students who suffered indignities such as "underemployment and limited chances for status recognition" consequently poured energy into their wardrobes (72). Thus, according to Lomnitz, when a Mexican official banned canes and hats among students, "the sartorial prohibition is as significant as the censorship of reading material" (76).[2]

Given both the radical economic inequality between the rich and the would-be middle class, and given the small percentage of literate citizens, *how* poets and other thinkers wrote was likely as important as *what* they wrote. The proportion of Mexicans who knew how to read barely approached 20 percent by 1910 (Mary Kay Vaughan cited in M. J. Gonzales 526).[3] Thus, one can imagine that in those same years poets were not so much read as seen—viewed on the scene—while writing and chatting in bars and cafés, dressed for artistic success.[4] Access to literature involves more than basic reading skill. L. M. Oliveira notes that today, long after the triumph of post-Revolutionary literacy campaigns, few Mexicans can afford new books. In fact, Oliveira calls the price of a new text "offensive" (149). Oliveira may underestimate somewhat the cost of new novels by major publishing houses in relation to the minimum wage—he says only three days of work buy a book—but at any rate the general point of the difficulty of access remains. Consequently, the image of the writer—who is still seen more than read—matters as much today as when literacy rates were lower. Of course, writers seem to have lost cultural power, and in their stead political scientists and other sorts of professional analysts appear in the media as intellectual experts. Nevertheless, the cachet for writers most powerfully developed in the twentieth century persists.

Which twentieth-century writers proved exceptionally influential for the public notion of the look of a writer? Julián Herbert writes an homage to Carlos Fuentes and describes the well-traveled, foreign-educated son of diplomats, the once-husband of a Mexican movie star, as "el inventor de esa aura dandy-izquierdista-machista-cosmopolita-cábula que los artistas mexicanos solemos usufructuar (incluso contra él)" (the inventor of the dandy-leftist-sexist-cosmopolitan-charmer that we Mexican artists usually exploit [even against him]) ("Mi nombre" 46). Herbert repeats insider wisdom. In an interview conducted by Elena Poniatowska, film star Lola Beltrán reveals much the same impression of Fuentes—and of Octavio Paz. Without bothering to claim a reading habit, Beltrán waxes enthusiastic over Fuentes's and Paz's charms:

> Mira, me fascina Carlos Fuentes, puedo estar con él platicando como lo he estado, tardes enteras. ¡Qué hombre tan atractivo!, ¿verdad? Lo mismo Octavio Paz. Aunque a Fuentes lo conozco desde hace muchísimo tiempo, Octavio Paz me vuelve loca, me encanta su dulzura, hemos volado juntos con su esposa Marie-Jo. Él viaja mucho a lo de sus homenajes que le hacen el mundo entero. (Poniatowska, "Su majestad" 264)

> Look, I love Carlos Fuentes. I can spend time with him chatting like I already have, whole afternoons. What an attractive man, right? The same for Octavio Paz. Although I've known Fuentes for a very long time, Octavio Paz drives me crazy. I love his sweetness. We've flown together with his wife Marie-Jo. He often travels to the tributes that they do for him across the whole world.

Whether Beltrán might have bothered to read any work by Fuentes or Paz may be the wrong question to pose. Fuentes and Paz managed a kind of public presence in a way that contemporary writers cannot.

Importantly, a Mexican authorial reputation is *always* built with the help of women, although they do not usually share its rewards. As a case in point, Poniatowska herself helped to cultivate Fuentes's star aura. In one nostalgic piece, she contrasts Fuentes's elegance with her own clumsiness. At a party at the Italian embassy in Mexico City, Fuentes wears "un *smoking* impecable y una corbatita de mono" (an impeccable tuxedo and tiny bow tie), while she impulsively tries a Carmen Miranda–inspired fruit-adorned outfit, which I will not describe further because it's an embarrassment ("No te vayas" 70). Descriptions of Fuentes's classy style sense never really change, while Poniatowska's outrageous costume suggests the confusion regarding how a woman intellectual should dress. This confusion seems understandable, since the variety of clothing options for women was and continues to be much more varied than for men.

Poniatowska's summary of four canonical literary figures leads us to near uniformity among the men's clothing style. Back in the 1950s and 1960s, she writes, "la literatura mexicana giró en torno a cuatro nombres: Alfonso Reyes, Octavio Paz, Juan Rulfo y Carlos Fuentes" (Mexican literature turned on four names: Alfonso Reyes, Octavio Paz, Juan Rulfo, and Carlos Fuentes) ("No te vayas" 73). Nostalgia may descend upon some of my readers after reviewing that neat list of conservatively dapper dressers with their short haircuts. Picking the "top four" Mexican writers these days might elicit more widely disparate picks; moreover, by now the lists will most likely include a (token) woman. However, today's diversified landscape still has the men authors dressing largely alike, still with similar short haircuts, and still recommending one another.

To show this masculinist mutual reputation project, I cite Fuentes in *Myself with Others* (1988), a memoir that he wrote in English. There, the Mexican literary scene in the 1950s appears anchored between two figures, Alfonso Reyes and Octavio Paz. In order to insert himself between these important men, Fuentes describes personally observing Paz in Paris, without mentioning the poet's wife, playwright and novelist Elena Garro. In fact, he does not mention Garro once in the book. Do critics seem troubled by this omission? Renowned Mexican writer Cristina Rivera Garza takes up *Myself with Others* in terms of the curious fact that Fuentes never translated it, and she cites Jacobo Sefamí's intriguing reaction to this same detail.[5] Neither Rivera Garza nor Sefamí has much to say about the all-male Mexican writers' club of Fuentes's imagination, a patent distortion of the actual scene.[6]

In a kind of implicit scaffolding for men intellectuals' authority, in *Myself with Others* Fuentes presents the women around him largely as anonymous lovers who end up confirming his seductive authority. The weightiest of these details emerges with an almost unbelievably callous anecdote regarding Fuentes and Salvador Elizondo's experience with sex workers in Mexico City:

> We [Elizondo and I] would go to a whorehouse oddly called El Buen Tono, choose a poor Mexican girl who usually said her name was Gladys and she came from Guadalajara, and go to our respective rooms. One time, a horrible scream was heard and Gladys from Guadalajara rushed out, crying and streaming blood. Elizondo, in the climax of love, had slashed her armpit with a razor. (21)

Fuentes skips the expected denouement of counseling the couple and procuring some sort of reparations for the attack by ending the anecdote exactly as I have cited it. Immediately after, in the next paragraph, he shifts to his 1950 trip "to do graduate work in international law at the University of Geneva." Sex work is decriminalized in Mexico, and so this incident of unrepentant violence against a probably unarmed woman matters more here than the ethically tricky matter of paid sex. The reader familiar with the contemporary escalations of violence in Mexico might ask why sex work enjoys zones of tolerance while certain "drugs" remain prohibited. My answer relates to the benefits that Fuentes's and Elizondo's reputations derive from the careful balance between bad boy rule breaking and gentlemanly scholarship. In order to break the laws, said laws must exist in the first place. Conveniently, these standards of justice are often drafted by the very male thinkers who need to violate them in order to prove their simultaneous status as competent rebels.

The *civilizado*'s ability to engage in paid sex—or illicit drug use, as per cocaine users Julián Herbert and Guillermo Fadanelli—without becoming an unredeemed *bárbaro* in admirers' eyes supplies a key concept to the masculine artistic performance. This binary between civilization and barbarity is nothing new, and I borrow the trope, in part, from a canonical nineteenth-century Argentine work, *Facundo: Civilización y barbarie* (1845), by Domingo Faustino Sarmiento. Men writers love to complain about the barbaric; it reinforces their status when they take up the mantle of the civilized *and* when they play the bárbaro rebel.

Of course, long before the nineteenth century, men writers famously staked a civilized reputation on the supposed rejection of the barbaric. From the aftermath of the Conquest, Walter Mignolo glosses the Dominican friar Bartolomé de Las Casas's final section of his *Apologética historia sumaria* (ca. 1552), where the monk classifies four types of barbarians who in various ways, in Mignolo's summary, "'lacked' something in the area of government, knowledge of Latin and alphabetic writing because they lived in [a] state of nature," as well as a fifth category of barbarian who seeks to destroy Christianity (471). My purposes here do not require five types of barbarian; the essential binary suffices. Like Mignolo's overarching point in the article that "there is no modernity without coloniality," I recognize that there is no civilized actor without the barbarian. These two roles characterize alternating movements of a single performance, whether for the civilized Las Casas, who thinks that black slaves might better replace the indigenous slaves of the Americas, or for the enlightened Mignolo himself, who seems to rely mostly on men thinkers without explicitly acknowledging that preference (466).

For example, count the intellectuals credited in Mignolo's argument in the above-cited article on the decolonial: behind this rejection of the linked nature of modernity and coloniality is a roster of men. According to Mignolo, the "groundbreaking formulation" in decolonial work comes from Aníbal Quijano (450), who happens to appear in the first endnote as Mignolo's interlocutor, along with Enrique Dussel, who in the same style debuts on the second page of the article as a fundamental thinker and reappears in the first endnote as Mignolo's intellectual acquaintance (500). The boys' club in this first endnote tallies eight men to three women.[7] I am certain that Mignolo might come to the defense of his article by citing his detailed praise for Gloria Anzaldúa, the gloss for which appears at the bottom of the fortieth page (488)—in a document that wraps up the body of the text on the fifty-second page. Anzaldúa represents a token woman thinker here. Mignolo's relatively isolated use of her *Borderlands* fills out an article containing an extensive bibliography that cites, by my rough tally, no more than fifteen women thinkers alongside some forty men thinkers—including Mignolo himself, with the highest number of works cited (seven titles in total). This imbalance in cited authority does not seem to me to cast the decolonial way of things as exactly "new."[8]

Where Mignolo, I, and other scholars agree is on the point that contemporary times have much to do with the colonial. (And *oh so much more* than these men writers may even suspect.)[9] To name one more example of excellent work that nevertheless seems guilty of what it itself critiques, Sergio Villalobos-Ruminott views contemporary politics in the Americas as an extension of the Conquest and colonization, even as he points out the ridiculousness of the old Argentinean debate between civilization and barbarousness (49). Without delving much into gender studies, Villalobos-Ruminott notes the dynamic between Occidentalism and Orientalism in the binary mirage that splits tame urban from lawless rural behaviors (56). Certainly, the tendency to skip over gender when thinking about what seem to be opposing models of masculinity may inform Villalobos-Ruminott's decision to mention only one woman fiction writer in his text, the Chilean Diamela Eltit. Still, he does recognize major work by Diana Washington Valdez, Sergio González Rodríguez, Charles Bowden, and Rita Laura Segato on the unsolved murders of women on or near the Mexico-U.S. border territories (164).[10] Failing to talk in a sustained manner about gender as an underlying factor in the historic system of violence that perpetuates femicide ends up with a glaring blind spot. While some scholars will argue that if I want to cite gender analysis, then I should read feminism, my point here is that failing to engage gender analysis sufficiently when claiming to talk about issues of social justice results in a repetition of the problem under critique.

Nonetheless, I admire both Villalobos-Ruminott and Mignolo. For instance, I share Villalobos-Ruminott's belief that violence functions as an integral element of the system developed to sustain the Conquest—which, it bears repeating, operates from the beginning in a gendered manner. Thus, Villalobos-Ruminott and I agree that violence emerges as a "performance of the law" (*una performance de la ley*) and that, at the same time, the law functions as a strategy of war (129).[11] According to Villalobos-Ruminott, this performance of the law also appears as a performance of capital (133). I add that this notion of capital is gendered, a point observed by scholars of imperialism such as Revathi Krishnaswamy.[12]

Stepping aside from questions of colonialism, I can update the gender bias in terms of the contemporary version of laissez-faire capitalism—*capitalism* being the term that Mignolo prefers in his article (480–81). I was struck when reading Angus Burgin's history of neoliberalism, *The Great Persuasion*, that nearly all the names in the book, which span a range of philosophers, economists, presidents, academics, and more, are men's. By my probably slightly inaccurate count of the index, some 180 names of men appear, and only 10 women. None of the women named in the index receives as high a number of citations as do the principal male players in the history.[13] Yet, Burgin's history makes a case for the fundamental importance of the economy in defining the meanings of *human*—not just men's—lives within that economy (8). If economic understanding shapes the very notion of community, then an economy driven overwhelmingly by men seems likely to disadvantage women and those who shoulder tasks often traditionally assigned to females. The need to point out this imbalance emerges because the economy operates under the guise of gender neutrality.[14]

Even books that turn away from the term *neoliberal* and elect something more global, like *Expulsions* (2014), a book written by a woman (a Dutch American sociologist named Saskia Sassen, to be precise) that describes in sweeping terms the systemic and subterranean predatory logic in effect today, seem oblivious to gender analysis. Returning to the dominant term in interdisciplinary literature studies, *neoliberal*, it has been argued that the ongoing patriarchal structure of the current social arrangement draws on literary, rather than mathematical, techniques. Ericka Beckman helps me to make this point by articulating the fictional root of neoliberal economic thought: "But what passes as impeccable economic logic today is rooted in a *fiction*, raised to previously unimaginable heights: that natural resources, together with human creativity and labor, 'exist' only so that they might become alienable commodities" (*Capital Fictions* viii). If neoliberal thought is a kind of fiction, and an unsustainable one at that, it may not be a coincidence that precisely the departments that study languages and literatures have suffered defunding under it.

In a related thought, I find it curious that academics continue to take Salvador Elizondo's art seriously, without much critique of his unrepentant confession of spousal abuse in an early autobiography. *Autobiografía precoz* (Premature autobiography) (1966) has Elizondo review the details of his violent attack against his wife, Silvia, the day he left a mental asylum and she told him she had asked her lawyers for a divorce:

> Esta noticia me proporcionó el pretexto para experimentar uno de los más grandes goces que he experimentado en mi vida. Nunca he tenido grandes prejuicios contra el uso de la violencia física contra las mujeres. Hay algo en su condición que la atrae y la desea. Ese día, creo que agoté para siempre todas las posibilidades de ser brutal contra un ser indefenso y mientras me ensañaba de la manera más bestial contra su cuerpo compactado en las actitudes más instintivamente defensivas que pudiera adoptar, experimentaba al mismo tiempo el placer de, mediante la fuerza física, poder aniquilar una concepción del mundo. Sólo tuve la presencia del ánimo, mientras la golpeaba, de notar que sus posturas eran, en cierto modo, idénticas a las que adoptaba cuando hacía el amor. Con esa efusión estaba yo imponiendo, quizá para siempre, mi condición de "macho" sobre sus alambicados conceptos de mujer "emancipada" y estaba yo destruyendo la concepción de "hombre civilizado" que para entonces yo despreciaba y que me avergonzaba. Silvia huyó. Y yo tomé al día siguiente un avión que me llevó otra vez a Nueva York. (72–73)[15]

> This news gave me the excuse to experience one of the greatest pleasures I have ever experienced in my life. I have never had much prejudice against the use of physical violence against women. There is something in their condition that attracts it and desires it. That day, I believe that I exhausted forever all the possibilities of being brutal against a defenseless being, and while I raged mercilessly in the most bestial way against her body compacted in the most instinctively defensive poses she could adopt, I experienced at the same time the pleasure of, through physical force, my ability to annihilate a concept of the world. I only had the presence of spirit, while I was beating her, to note that her postures were, in a way, identical to those she adopted when we would make love. With that outpouring I was imposing, maybe forever, my condition of "macho" over her affected ideas of the "emancipated" woman, and I was destroying the concept of "civilized man" that by then I despised and that shamed me. Silvia fled. And the next day I boarded a plane that carried me back to New York.

Elizondo discusses overtly the civilizado and bárbaro split here and voices his disgust with the civilizado. His self-awareness regarding his participation in barbarity may signify his understanding that the bad boy behavior leads to greater artistic credibility as a genius. My boredom with his *Farabeuf o la crónica de un instante* (*Farabeuf* [or the chronicle of an instant]) (1965) inspires me to wonder whether part of the trouble that neoliberal ideology faces with literary critics stems from its seeming refusal to respect the notion of male literary genius.[16] It's time to rethink that label.

The problem for women writers in this old boy system is that they cannot flip between the roles of the civilizado and the bárbaro and earn the kind of respect enjoyed by men intellectuals such as Elizondo and his brothel companion, Fuentes. Critics aid the writers' transition between the poles of law-creating and law-breaking thinker. For instance, Emmanuel Carballo, in his prologue to the *Autobiographía precoz*, calls the topics chosen by Elizondo and his cohort behind the 1960s magazine *S.nob* "almost virginal," a word choice perhaps inspired by the patriarchal notion of which gender's virginity matters (6). The short-lived literary magazine of 1962, according to Antonio Ortuño's homage to *S.nob*, brought together a "*dream team*" (to quote Ortuño) of the period: Elizondo's coeditors Juan García Ponce and Emilio García Riera, along with a nucleus of collaborators that included Jorge Ibargüengoitia, Tomás Segovia, Álvaro Mutis, José de la Colina, José Luis Cuevas, Alejandro Jodorowosky, and a token woman, Leonora Carrington (Ortuño). Call me paranoid, but the ability to avoid noting that *S.nob* largely gave voice to men surely finds support in a masculinist view, on full display from the beginning of Ortuño's piece, which defends the word *snob* by way of contradicting a woman's bad taste: "Una joven editor, con la que tuve la desgracia de trabajar durante algún tiempo, se quejó una vez de un texto en el que la palabra snob aparecía dos veces en ocho párrafos" (A young woman editor, with whom I had the misfortune to work for a while, complained once about a text in which the word snob appeared twice in eight paragraphs). Elizondo emerges as a genius by implication because of his difference from this gendered, and conveniently anonymous, *editor*.

I imagine that fans of Ortuño and Elizondo will object that I cherry-pick the examples; I respond that if the reader believes Ortuño's choice of a woman protagonist for the brutal action-movie violence of the novel *La fila india* (The Indian [e.g., single-file] row) (2013) makes him a feminist, then I have a gender reversal experiment for you at the end of the present chapter. As for *La fila india*, slapping a woman's name on a character endowed with the male privilege of transforming from civilizado to bárbaro and back again does not mean that women can actually play that dual role in texts not written by men and get away with it. Whether he criticizes the women characters or the women writers,

Ortuño will be there to call them on their bad taste—just as another man was there to play the same role in his day, Emmanuel Carballo.

In the prologue to the first edition of Elizondo's autobiography, the gender politics emerge as Carballo suggests that Elizondo establishes mastery over the following "virginal" topics: "entre otros [temas casi vírgenes] el erotismo, el sadismo, la escatología y los novedosos paraísos artificiales [de las drogas]" (among other [almost virginal topics] eroticism, sadism, eschatology and the new artificial paradises [of drugs]) (*Salvador Elizondo* 6). This language describing sexual and other taboo topics as "virginal" for their novelty puts Elizondo's title in a new light. Could *Autobiografía precoz* play with the echoes of the phrase in Spanish for premature ejaculation, *eyaculación precoz*? (Does expert writing *have* to be so masculinist?) Carlos Fuentes also employs this "virginal" vocabulary nearly a decade before Carballo's prologue, in 1956, for a grant proposal to the Centro Mexicano de Escritores (Mexican Center for Writers).[17] In his search for support to work on *La región más transparente*, Fuentes labels his topics "casi vírgenes en nuestras letras" (almost virginal in our literature) (CME Fuentes 10).

Another instance of this sex-infused language appears in Elizondo's story titled "Anapoyesis" from *Camera lucida* (1983). There, a text that has not been read by anyone but the author is a "poema virgen" (43). Of course, Elizondo's title for the anthology is certainly not "virginal," as it repeats Roland Barthes's title for his meditation on photography, published in 1980. Nevertheless, Elizondo proposes in the fiction "Anapoyesis" the possibility of originality and its explosive energy. In the story, a series of men—in the first place the poet Stéphane Mallarmé, in the second place the mad scientist in search of Mallarmé's *virgin poem*, and in the third place the reporter who narrates the tale—mine the value of originality.

In greater detail, the plot of "Anapoyesis" has Elizondo's fictional Professor Pierre Emile Aubanel, an eccentric applied linguist and professor of thermodynamics, explain to the male reporter-narrator that he has moved into Mallarmé's former home in order to strip undiscovered poems from the wallpaper and run them through his machine, the "anapoyetrón," which, as predicted by Aubanel's theoretical book *Énergie et langage*, registers variations in energy levels (45). The story concludes with the report of Aubanel's death from an explosion, "la anapoyesis" (47). Elizondo delights in the idea that the irrational energy of the poem might literally explode at least one scientist's mind. The all-male lineup of the scientific and literary references, from the tradition of the man detective to the French man poet to the French men professors, sets up a kind of echo chamber in which women's absence implicitly anchors men's genius. Significantly, the larger *Camera lucida* intercalates fictional pieces with the honorary speeches Elizondo delivered upon his induction to two venerable Mexican intellectual institutions, La Academia Mexicana de la Lengua and El Colegio Nacional.

Elizondo's example demonstrates that a man may spend time in an asylum without losing his artistic career or his intellectual reputation. Poniatowska broaches Elizondo's time in the mental hospital during an interview first published in 1971; in the midst of the conversation, she winds up asking him if she is boring him. Elizondo responds by lumping her in the eccentric group with him, thus suggesting that her sanity is on par with his, and he seals the complicity with the masculine offer of alcohol, which he surely knows that she will not accept: "Tú también estás loca, por lo tanto, no. ¿Quieres una cerveza?" (You are crazy too, so no. Do you want a beer?) (Poniatowska, "El más inquietante" 393). Poniatowska turns down the beer and asks point-blank: "Oye Salvador, ¿y tú quieres volver al manicomio?" (Listen Salvador, do you want to go back to the mental hospital?) He responds, "Me da igual" (It's all the same to me) (394).

Elizondo enjoys a peculiarly masculine privilege of playing crazy without also seeming silly, something that Poniatowska cannot pull off successfully. Her Carmen Miranda outfit alongside Fuentes's elegant tuxedo, if you remember the earlier anecdote, makes her look ridiculous and not rebellious. By and large, this bárbaro or bad boy performance is not available to women, because they cannot flip tracks as easily and rejoin the ranks of the expert, responsible, and civilized. Peers do not allow it.

This bárbaro company is rich. For example, Emmanuel Carballo, the author of the prologue for Elizondo's autobiography, unabashedly confesses his own former womanizing habits in a conversation with Rafael Luviano:

> He dejado mi donjuanismo. [. . .] [A]hora vivo con una sola mujer, con ella quiero morir y me sentiría ridículo andar persiguiendo muchachitas de veinte años. Sería lastimoso que un hombre casi calvo, con el cabello semiblanco, con muchos dientes postizos, con problemas de corazón, de azúcar en exceso y que no puede respirar plenamente, se dedicara a enamorar veinteañeras. Para mí, esa parte del mundo se acabó. [. . .] Coincido con Carlos Fuentes: el donjuanismo es lastimoso después de los sesenta. (qtd. in Domínguez Cuevas 89)

> I have abandoned my womanizing. . . . [N]ow I live with just one woman, with her I want to die and I would feel ridiculous chasing after little twenty-year-old girls. It would be pathetic that an almost bald man, with semiwhite hair, with a lot of false teeth, with heart problems, with excess sugar levels, and who can't take a full breath, devoted himself to making twenty-somethings fall in love. For me, that part of the world ended. . . . I agree with Carlos Fuentes: womanizing is pathetic after your sixties.

Carballo never bothers to see his actions from the perspective of one of his female partners, never makes amends. This self-absorption and lack of empathy that leave women anonymous—largely defined, not by name, but by age (and profession, in Fuentes's anecdote)—may translate to a kind of wide-ranging binary that splits the intellectual from the corporeal, the boldly competent and experimental from the silly, and the male from the female. "Literature" itself, like the men who "best" write it, operates as a kind of "high and hard" master, who rejects the "soft and low" and anonymous, commercial lovers.

I say "high" because men's writing is the most canonical; it is *high literature*. I say "hard" because the canon requires expert help to interpret. Of course, *high* also connotes drug-addled delusion, including the idea that some drugs and some texts are reliably "harder" than others. Skill with the manipulation of this culturally determined binary marks the admired male writer.

Alí Chumacero, a little-read poet but at times a much-cited name in the newspapers during his day, provides another excellent example of the respected womanizing Mexican male intellectual. An article for *Excélsior* published in 1997 covers Dionicio Morales's assessment of Chumacero as "inquieto, muy sociable aunque también mal hablado y mujeriego" (restless, very sociable although also foul-mouthed and a womanizer) (Atamoros 55). As Morales remembers fondly, Chumacero made the civilized intellectual act into a more barbarous endeavor through alcohol: "Ejerció [Chumacero] la enseñanza sin corbata, desconoció el aburrimiento. Su método, si podemos hablar de ello, es sencillo: Leo un texto tuyo, luego entonces me invitas un trago; me invitas un trago, luego entonces leo un texto tuyo." (He [Chumacero] practiced teaching without a tie, never knew boredom. His method, if we can call it that, is simple: I read your text, then you invite me for a drink; you invite me for a drink, so then I will read your text.) Morales adds that Chumacero was "pornográfico a medias, porque habla demasiado" (half-pornographic, because he talks too much) (Atamoros 55).

When I read that last quote, I strongly suspected I was reading a woman writer who reported on Morales's comments on Chumacero. Such intuition can be difficult for nonspecialists to trust; after all, Morales gave the quotation, the reporter simply chose to cite it, and at least one editor of undetermined sex approved the quotation. However subtle the example may seem to the untrained eye, the sheer number of examples of this sort of cultural reporting has taught me what Mexicans of one sex and the other allow themselves to observe about authors in public. Men, in the context of calling one another "pornographic," tend to take a more respectful implicit stance toward that particular element of rule-breaking boldness: pornography in that context represents intellectual prowess. Women tend to report on such rule-breaking with the driest of wry touches. In effect, I was right: the homage to Chumacero was covered by Noemí Atamoros.

I mention this intuition largely to rat myself out as to my ability to detect sexism almost by rhythm rather than by any kind of formal rhyme, which implies that I have absorbed the sexist rules. Awareness of sexist nuance and subtly critical responses to it doesn't make me pure; it contaminates me. My times have not changed and sexism has not ended. I am steeped in it and thus continue to track it.

It may not surprise the reader that Chumacero was a great fan of bullfighting, with six reserved spots at the ring, as well as of boxing, according to a report published after the national homage that saw him travel the country at the end of 1996 (Montes García 29).[18] But alcohol over all else tips Chumacero's self-performance toward the masculine—the "white" masculine. Here is Alí Chumacero on his alcohol habit, quoted in 1996 from comments he made at an homage to his life's work:

> Yo soy nayarita, pero viví algunos años en Jalisco y tomaba puro tequila. Ahora ya no puedo porque a la segunda botella me da tos. Pero no importa, puedo beber whisky indefinidamente. Es bueno y sano, además porque no te da eso que los indios babosos llaman cruda. Yo soy de raza blanca y desprecio a los indios canallas que tienen cruda. Hay gente que bebe para paladear la bebida. ¡Esos son pendejos! Hay que beber para emborracharse. El que no se emborracha no tiene nada que hacer en la vida. No conozco ningún abstemio longevo, se mueren pronto. Los bebedores somos eternos. (CME Chumacero 49-1: 23)[19]

> I am from Nayarit, but I lived a few years in Jalisco and I used to drink pure tequila. Now I can't anymore because the second bottle makes me cough. But it

> doesn't matter, I can drink whisky indefinitely. It's good and healthy, also because it doesn't give you what the stupid Indians call a hangover. I am from the white race and I despise the scoundrel Indians who have hangovers. There are people who drink to savor the drink. Those are assholes! You have to drink to get drunk. He who doesn't get drunk doesn't have anything to do in life. I don't know any long-lived teetotaler, because they die early. We drinkers are eternal.

This passage flirts with parody of the macho man and implicates racism as well as drunkenness in the construction of competent intellectual manliness.[20] To drink is to know how to live, intelligently and not like "stupid Indians," according to Chumacero.

Laura Gutiérrez helps me think about the link between bad boy behavior and race, because she takes up a dual Mexico-U.S. perspective. While Gutiérrez quickly desists in the effort to view the "bad girl" angle of performance art by Nao Bustamante, an artist of Chicano political concerns, because the gender reversal makes little sense, the theme allows Gutiérrez to code the bad boy aesthetics as not only strongly gendered but also white and middle-class:

> However, the avant-garde—conceived as a bad-boy (i.e., white bourgeois) aesthetics with its "shock-value" strategy—is often thought to be incompatible with the identity-based cultural production that is often associated with the performative art production of women and/or so-called racial and/or sexual minorities. (*Performing Mexicanidad* 138)

Can bad boy *Mexican* writers be "white"? The answer is, necessarily, of course! What makes a "white" male civilizado is knowing when to cross into the exceptional privileges of the macho bárbaro, and being allowed to do so, which says something about respected violent civilized men, from nineteenth-century president Benito Juárez to . . . , well, truth be told, it *is* difficult to come up with a bad boy among the contemporary Mexican men writers with skin as dark as Juárez's complexion.

Can't we move on? my critics ask impatiently. *Enough with the bulls.*

No. We can't move on. If we could, I think we would have. And as Gutiérrez's binational work can already tell you, it is a mistake to think that only Mexico participates in this binary.

It's not easy to notice what isn't there. No woman won a Nobel Prize in 2016, when bad boy singer Bob Dylan received the literature prize. According to the website maintained by the Nobel Prize organization, 48 women won a Nobel between 1901 and 2016, out of 885 total laureates ("Nobel Prize Facts").[21] Or take the numbers assembled by VIDA: Women in Literary Arts, the U.S. organization. VIDA finds that in English-language periodicals, men review many more books than women. The *London Review of Books* in 2014, for instance, featured 527 men and 151 women among its authors and critics (Abrams). In fact, the *London Review of Books* fails to represent anything resembling steady progress; fourteen fewer books by women appeared among the reviews in 2014 than in 2013 (Abrams). The *New York Review of Books* is not much better, according to VIDA, "with a ratio of 677 men to 242 women" (Abrams). In order to focus on a more optimistic statistic—aside from the gleefully rueful thought of what would happen to these periodicals if women stopped buying them—I note that in December 2016 the New York Metropolitan Opera mounted an opera composed by a woman, Kaija Saariaho, for the first time in over a century. The reasons for the preference for men composers have "little to do with music," according to coverage of the milestone, and instead are a response to the men's superior skills at the composerly performance duties "of self-promotion, of fund-raising, of a kind of confidence that makes others follow instructions" (Gregory). Just the thought of women composers failing to self-promote makes me wish I could type this analysis with even more swagger, but then my bad boy style—with heavy-handed typos that might seem second-bottle-of-whisky inspired—might be mistaken for *cute*.

Although I lack the statistics to prove my suspicion, it will not surprise me if reviews written by men outnumber those by women in Mexican periodicals. Judging by the film reviews that I consult on contemporary movies using the files of the Cineteca Nacional, the ratio of well-established Mexican men to women film critics in Mexican newspapers overwhelmingly tips toward males. The official numbers on employment in the media in Mexico claim that among self-defined professionals, men outnumber women in every branch.[22] The least gender equity is found in the television industry, in which data for 2005 place women at only one-fifth of employees, with 4.8 percent among the highest positions held by women ("Pasos hacia" 10). Of the total economically active population in Mexico for 2006, only 0.69 percent (289,744 people) claimed a profession in arts and entertainment; only one-fourth of those workers were women (70,273). Men outnumber women, to the tune of 87.5 percent, for the professions of composers, singers, musicians, actors, and dancers; the percentage of men drops to 65.4 percent for writers, critics, journalists, and editors. Similar statistics, 66.9 percent, hold for men as painters, sculptors, sketchers, designers, and choreographers. In the group of writers, critics, journalists, and editors, the last two professions predominate, and about a third of those positions are held by women (34.6 percent) ("Pasos hacia" 11).[23]

Claudia Sorais Castañeda G., the same person who pointed me toward the above statistical information, also kindly shared preliminary findings from her thesis on literary prestige and gender in Mexico. She sent me an unpublished excerpt on the composition of judges for the Mexican Aguascalientes Poetry Prize, today one of thirteen Bellas Artes (Fine Arts) literary prizes issued thanks to governmental subsidies. Sorais Castañeda studied fifty years of the award and broke down the information into three periods. When the prize was known as the National Poetry Prize, across twelve rounds of the prize, from 1968 to 1979, with three judges to a panel, thirty-two of those thirty-six judges (nearly 89 percent) were men. In 1980 the Aguascalientes Poetry Prize was incorporated into the Bellas Artes federal system; in this second period, from 1980 to 2000, twenty-one rounds of three-person panels resulted in some lopsided math, now in terms of geography as well as gender: for about a third of the instances, judges were from Mexico City, and 78 percent of the time the judges were men. For 2001, Sorais Castañeda detects a third period, beginning with the creation in that year of the Instituto Nacional de las Mujeres (National Institute for Women) and a corresponding law that required gender parity. From 2001 to 2017, seventeen Aguascalientes poetry prizes were awarded, usually by men; of the ten total women judges during that stage, seven of them (70 percent) were from Mexico City.

The statistics grow still more interesting as Sorais Castañeda contemplates the details. Across the fifty years she studied, her count turns up ninety unique names of judges, thirty-three of whom participated in a minimum of two and a maximum of seven competitions. Those thirty-three repeat judges are twenty-seven men (82 percent) and six women (18 percent). Even more indicative of a lopsided elite that distributed prestige along an insider network, Sorais Castañeda finds that of the fifty prizewinners, thirty had functioned as judges themselves for this same Aguascalientes Poetry Prize. Of that group of thirty winners-cum-judges, six (20 percent) were women and twenty-four (80 percent) men. Among that same group of thirty, fifteen people (four women and eleven men) served more than once as judges. To summarize then, double-role winners/judges participated in the selection of new winners on 28 percent of the 150 possible occasions. Sorais Castañeda concludes, "Quien selecciona, configura" (They who pick, configure).[24]

Before I continue with information on prizes in Mexico, I want to acknowledge that the United States and other influencing countries are never distant from these prejudices. In her study of the creation of the Latin American literary boom, Deborah Cohn provides a list of selected literary works published in translation through the Association of American University Presses program. Cohn gives only a selection of the translations from the 1960s, and in her first table, of the twenty-seven "Latin American" people listed, only two are women (*Latin American Literary* 116–17). In the second table of authors and titles, with information pertaining to the Center for Inter-American Relations translation program, no woman writer appears among the twenty-one authors (172–73).[25] The governmentally funded programs from the United States helped to create the boom as a men-centric phenomenon, to judge from Cohn's data. Sexism is not a *Mexican* problem, but a global one.

Despite governmental publicity to the contrary, Mexico continues to repeat these international macho preferences. Few women won a grant in 2016 from the Mexican governmental subsidy program for artists and intellectuals, the Sistema Nacional de Creadores de Arte (National System of Creators of Art, or SNCA). In the essay category, the lone woman writer who received the prestigious three years of funding to work on her literary endeavors was the poet Tedi López Mills; she appeared alongside six men winners.[26] In the narrative category, the winners were three women—Vivian Mansour, Coral Aguirre, and Guadalupe Nettel—and seventeen men.[27] In the same year, two women poets, Karina Cano and Claudia Posadas, appear next to the nine winning men poets.[28] The jury responsible for this lopsided award pattern was made up of three women writers, Silvia Molina, Carmen Villoro, and Barbara Jacobs, and two men authors, Felipe Garrido and Sergio González Rodríguez ("Resultados" 2016). In other words, don't think that being a woman makes you immune to meting out this sexism.[29]

Not just the prestigious prizes ignore Mexican women writers. A popular culture list published in 2012 in the online magazine *Sin embargo* lists "10 unmistakably Mexican authors" and includes eight men and two women; neither of the latter two are fiction writers, and they occupy the last two spots on the list (Maristain).[30] It's hard to say whether the official lists, such as the Nobel Prize winners and the SNCA grantees, matter more than popular journalism, but it does seem that they give largely the same gender message.

Mutual promotion, in addition to self-promotion, keeps male privilege functional. Take the essays from Guillermo Fadanelli's *Insolencia: Literatura y mundo* (Insolence: literature and world) (2012), where, by my count, 4 women and 115 men appear in the body of the text; the latter range from Albert Camus to Ludwig Wittgenstein. None of the women mentioned are Mexican.[31] The imbalance applies not only to the thinkers Fadanelli references but also to the characters studied. Five women characters appear in total and in one breath: "Julieta Capuleto, Nora [from *A Doll's House*], Madame Bovary, Lady Chatterley, Lady Macbeth" (75). Across the essays Fadanelli takes greater interest in men characters. In the final "Bibliografía para continuar la conversación" (Bibliography to continue the conversation), seventy-two authors appear, only four of whom are women, or 5.56 percent. Again, none of these women is Mexican.[32] Switching to other texts by Fadanelli, I can find the same prejudice. Fadanelli's article "Breve diccionario de autores anómalos" (Brief dictionary of anomalous authors), published in his column "Terlenka" for *El Universal* in 2012, lists twenty-four writers, among whom are two women, neither of them Mexican, which places women at 8.33 percent of the recommendations.[33] Even the acknowledgments for the first edition of the novel *Lodo* (2002) demonstrate inequity in Fadanelli's repertoire of influences: the twenty names include only two women (or 10 percent), Spanish collaborator Teresa Yagüe and the author's sister, Norma J. Fadanelli, although the book does contain a dedication to his longtime partner, Yolanda Martínez.[34]

My positive personal impression of Fadanelli's behavior during our interview (as charming as Fuentes and Paz!) points toward a tricky reason for men intellectuals' success. In addition to the support of their fellow men, they count on the cooperation of women. In fact, women—the younger perhaps the more adamant—sometimes actively defend a sexist system. In order to make this point, I want to compare parallel lives: that of Fadanelli and that of the Mexican woman writer Vivian Abenshushan, who is about twelve years younger than Fadanelli and coincidentally shares with him an apartment building in Mexico City. Just as Fadanelli owns a publishing house, Moho, with his live-in partner, Yolanda Martínez, Abenshushan owns a publishing house, Tumbona, with her live-in partner, Luigi Amara. At least in 2010, when I interviewed her, Abenshushan seemed to hold views regarding women writers that largely agreed with those of Fadanelli. I have observed this pattern in other women writers; by now, her early denial of feminist help may have morphed into acknowledgment that the playing field could use better arbitration. However, during that long-ago interview, I commented to Abenshushan that if I had not decided beforehand to include equal numbers of men and women in my second book of interviews,

I would have included mostly men, because, as a group, they are more visible and more prolific. In response, Abenshushan had this to say:

> Sí. Pero tal vez tampoco haya tantas escritoras que valgan la pena. Es decir, hay que preguntarse también qué tantas escritoras se atreven a publicar. Y entre las que publican quiénes valen la pena, o si valen la pena sólo porque son mujeres. Yo creo que no podemos caer en este juego de cuotas, publicar el libro de una escritora—aunque sea terrible y haya un consenso alrededor de eso—sólo porque es mujer. Eso es nefasto. Pasa en México todo el tiempo. Se lo oigo a muchos críticos literarios, y a muchos académicos: "Aunque sea mala, hay que ponerla porque hace falta una mujer." Entonces eso no ayuda, todo lo contrario, va generando un rechazo y una desconfianza legítimas hacia la literatura escrita por mujeres. Y ni modo, ese espacio se tiene que encontrar por la escritura misma, no por ayudas ni cuotas ni ideas políticamente correctas. (Hind, *Generación XXX* 50)

> Yes. But maybe there are not many worthwhile women writers. That is, one must ask how many women writers dare to publish. And among those who publish, which are worthwhile, or are they worthwhile only because they are women. I think that we cannot fall for this game of quotas, of publishing a woman writer's book—even if it's awful and there is a consensus around that—just because she is a woman. That is disastrous. It happens in Mexico all the time. I hear it from many literary critics, and many academics: "Even if she's bad, you have to put her in because we need a woman." So that doesn't help, on the contrary, it generates a legitimate rejection and mistrust of literature written by women. And what can you do, that space must be found by the writing itself, not with favors or quotas or politically correct ideas.

Some English-language activists agree with Abenshushan on this point of gender tallies, and Erin Belieu, the cofounder of VIDA, told a reporter from the *Guardian*: "Our goal has always been consciousness not quotas" (Abrams). To extrapolate the assumption behind Abenshushan's and Belieu's comments, they hope for acceptance into the grouping of the high and hard by avoiding explicit insistence that one's sex should matter in the assessment of art. The attempt to become one of the guys does not seem to work for long, in my observation.

The ultimately sexist idea that literary writing makes its way in the world without relying on a contextualized writerly performance, and on corresponding socialized reception among also embodied (and embedded) readers, seems to me one of the reasons that the bureaucratic and media systems can be imagined as intrinsically merit based, rather than macho biased. The women writers who initially buy into the anti-quota idea perhaps realize, as they age, that performance does matter.

Making it to the status of an old woman who still writes is no easy feat. Already at this midstage in Abenshushan's career, her partner, the poet and essayist Luigi Amara, publishes more than she. Even though Amara's recent titles outnumber Abenshushan's lifetime production, which in total claims two books of essays, one book of short stories, and one slender biography, Fadanelli outpaces them both, as he has published about a book a year since the early 1990s.[35] Interestingly, none of the three has attracted much attention from academic interviewers. As far as I know, I am the first scholar to publish an interview with Fadanelli in an academic journal, a conversation that appeared in 2016; as of that same year, Amara, like Abenshushan, had appeared in only one book of interviews listed in WorldCat. That book, Óscar Alarcón's *Veintiuno: Charlas con 20 escritores* (Twenty-one: chats with 20 writers) (2012), contains twenty men writers and not a single woman (or 0 percent), by contrast to my project *Generación XXX*, for which I interviewed Abenshushan as one of a cohort of ten women and ten men writers born in the 1970s (50 percent).[36] The widely disparate publishing rates among Amara, Fadanelli, and Abenshushan, along with the sexist nature of at least some of the networks surrounding them, suggests that Abenshushan's early refusal of quotas has backed a rigorous pose that may not ultimately have helped her career as much as she might have liked. Rigor, perhaps because it stems from a tradition that does not favor women, can end up in silence.

Just what sort of perspective does Abenshushan support when she aligns herself with Fadanelli? Consider the latter's most infamous remark, cited—among other instances—in 1998 by Sergio González Rodríguez ("*Barracuda* en Moho" 1). Fadanelli stated in obscene terms that women writers were not worth his time: "No quiero saber nada de escritoras, ojalá les den a todas por el culo, no conozco a una sola capaz de afectar mi sensibilidad" (I don't want to know anything about Mexican women writers. I hope they take it up the ass. I don't know a single one able to affect my sensibility). The phrase "take it up the ass," at least in common circulation, tends to express macho aggression and not exactly gender-neutral liberation. Fadanelli articulates this antipathy for women writers in other forums:

> En cuanto a la presencia de escritoras, creo que siempre ha habido aunque últimamente muchas señoras dejaron de jugar canasta uruguaya para ponerse a leer y a escribir, y esto le ha dado una especie de cariz a la literatura femenina que es parte más de la mercadotecnia que de la realidad. Las escritoras interesantes siguen escasas, las mismas que fueron siempre. (Garza).
>
> As for the presence of women writers, I think they have always been there, but lately many ladies stopped playing Uruguayan canasta in order to start reading and writing, and this has given a kind of look to women's literature that is part of marketing more than of reality. The interesting women writers continue to be scarce, the same as they always were.

No, I did not look up the statistics on Uruguayan canasta, because I see the joke, as much as I resent it. I'll limit myself to citing the humor, because I take the lesson of *Dude Lit*: women have a more difficult time than men straddling this line of the barbarous comedian and civilizing upholder of intellectual and aesthetic standards. Only the likes of Fadanelli get to play *both* feminist and misogynist with these declarations. By 1997, Fadanelli had already seen fit to temper his initial style of remarks; he began to claim that rather than hating women, he feared them. In one conversation, he clarified that while "the feminine world" seduces him, he cannot tolerate "certain women writers" (Mendoza Mociño). This strain of comments proves easy to locate, because Fadanelli repeated them.

When I asked Fadanelli about these stock responses during our interview in 2016, he admitted that his pose was misogynist and that, indeed, he intended that posture as feminist:

> Para mí la literatura femenina no existe, como tampoco la literatura masculina. Existe la literatura y un ser único detrás de ella. [. . .] Fue, el mío [el comentario], un recurso para molestar y acentuar el hecho de que la solidez de una obra literaria no está en el ser hombre, en el ser mujer, sino en cómo se desarrollan, vía el lenguaje, las pasiones o emociones propias e inéditas. Pero me divertí mucho. Además las escritoras se acercaban a mí sin recelo pues comprendían bien el sarcasmo de mis palabras. A mí me gusta reírme a costilla de los demás, como dije antes. Pero bueno, a la postre me acusaron de ser un escritor misógino. Después la acusación se volvió una especie de lugar común. Yo jugaba a representar un personaje y obtenía merecidas repuestas a causa de ello. Decía que yo no odiaba a las mujeres, pero que me causaban temor porque ellas representaban lo otro, lo

> diferente. En fin, creo que eso fue una de los episodios más pintorescos, y a veces un poco absurdos de mi historia pasada, ¿no? Sobre todo porque no era yo el adalid del hombre escritor. Era más bien un burlón, un hombre sarcástico, y si alguien tomó en serio aquella clase de comentarios pues entonces bien que se los mereció. (Hind, "Entrevista" 321–22)

> For me, women's literature does not exist, and neither does men's literature. There is literature and one unique being behind it. . . . It was, mine [my comment], a resource to annoy and accentuate the fact that the strength of a literary work is not in being a man, or in being a woman, but in how it develops, via one's own unpublished language, passions, or emotions. But I had a lot of fun. Besides, the women writers approached me unsuspiciously, since they understood the sarcasm in my words. Personally, I like to laugh at others' expense, as I said before. But hey, ultimately they accused me of being a misogynist writer. Later the accusation became a kind of cliché. I would play at representing a character, and I would elicit well-earned answers because of it. I used to say that I didn't hate women, but that they inspired my fear because they represented the other, the different. In the end, I think that was one of the more colorful, and at times a little absurd, episodes from my past story, no? Above all because I wasn't the champion man writer. I was instead a mocking, sarcastic man, and if someone took those kinds of comments seriously, well then they really deserved it.

The effect of this game is to make me a humorless and uninsightful critic if I reject Fadanelli's misogyny. The most interesting point here turns, not so much on the fact that Fadanelli can base an early and successful career on misogyny, but that women writers do not seem to mind it.

Some academics refuse this flexibility; among the few feminists who will pay attention to Fadanelli in published comments, Diana Palaversich writes scornfully that his stories in *Más alemán que Hitler* (More German than Hitler) (2001) remain indebted to "los esquemas mentales del machismo folclórico latinoamericano que contamina los clichés gastados" (the mental schemes of Latin American folkloric machismo that contaminates worn clichés) (194).[37] While many feminist critics have yet to develop a taste for Fadanelli's games, according to his words above, truly savvy women viewed his stance as *sarcastic*. However, the "joke" of misogyny principally benefits men, who can be seen to *play* the misogynist in a possibly feminist manner. Fadanelli thereby benefits in both directions: as a *serious* man writer who, like the sexists in his audience, rejects women writers and as a *playful* feminist who rejects the distinction between women and men writers. Both postures favor men's careers because neither does much to further the cause of women intellectuals.

Just as a gender-reversal thought experiment, I want to try on Fadanelli's thinking and size it up from the inside out. Here goes . . .

I cannot stand men writers. I don't know a single one capable of affecting my sensibility.

Does that seem funny to you? Or did I just sound like an idiot? What kind of critic can say, "I cannot stand men writers"? A *bad* one, and not a *bad boy* one, that's who. The gender-inverted version of Fadanelli's game sets me up to give a mentally ill declaration of the *SCUM Manifesto* variety. That declaration by Valerie Solanas accompanied her deranged shooting of Andy Warhol, who as a result was temporarily pronounced dead on the operating table at the hospital. Solanas came off as crazy rather than rebelliously serious because, as I have been asserting, women cannot flip between poles of barbarity and civilization—unlike men's examples in the would-be murdering intellectual role, à la David Alfaro Siqueiros and his apparently respectable attempt to assassinate Leon Trotsky. In order to be taken seriously, women authors seem better off, or at least less prone to incarceration, if they support the system that dismisses them.

As a young writer, the non-quota-supporting Abenshushan took Fadanelli seriously enough to review his work and to give him a severe critique, as Fadanelli remembered during our conversation. The topic came up because I reminded him that, as of July 2015, his personal webpage linked to reviews of his writing by Abenshushan, as well as by Guadalupe Nettel, Valeria Luiselli, Brenda Lozano, and Claudia Guillén. Yes, that's *five* women writers who have reviewed Fadanelli's publications and appear on his website. I do not know of any review that he has written of one of these women's work.

The solution to the imbalance seems clear to me: quotas. Can you imagine what would happen if scholars took up a one-year ban on writing, reading, assigning, or buying texts in the relevant academic specialty by or about men writers, men film directors, men presidents, men business owners, men academics, et alia? This proposal is not as crazy as it might sound, given that we already habitually reduce or eliminate women from many projects, such as the Mexican and U.S. presidencies, as well as a majority of the best paid and highest profile jobs. Quotas would combat an obstacle to women's competitiveness, which is that despite the industries that hire women models and women actors, women are simply *seen* less.

For rich data on the gender imbalance and the slow pace of change, I turn to a study of U.S. films, a relevant source given that the most cursory of consultations of the website Box Office Mojo shows that U.S. films dominate among the top grossing films in Mexico.[38] Numbers from 2007 through 2016, excluding 2011, from the Media, Diversity, and Social Change Initiative at the University of Southern California quantify the one hundred top-grossing movies from across a nine-year span and find that of those 900 films, only thirty-four women worked as directors (Smith, Choueiti, and Pieper, "Inequality in 900 Popular Films" 3). In 2016, the number of women writers in film production was a paltry thirty-eight, or 13.2 percent (Smith et al., "Inequality in 900" 3). The academic study inserts an exclamation point to punctuate the slow pace of change: "The prevalence of female speaking characters has not changed meaningfully across the 9 years evaluated. The difference between 2007 and 2016 is only 1.5%!" (6).[39] Quotas might begin to remedy the situation, but in the longer haul other habits would need to change as well. Women would have to become better networked.

In lieu of quotas, men use a strong network to keep themselves gainfully occupied. The networking effect appears in the publicity that men writers give one another, evident throughout the cultural journalism of the twentieth and now twenty-first centuries. For instance, renowned Mexican novelist and poet Fernando del Paso tips toward his male peers in an interview from 1966. There, a thirty-something del Paso sketches out for a reporter the twentieth-century canon of his peers, who all happen to be men, and all of his personal acquaintance:

> Por último, puedo decirte que, para mí, el libro más importante que se ha escrito en México es *Pedro Páramo*. Sí, es un lugar común decirlo, pero hay que hacerlo, Rulfo es la sabiduría. Arreola es la retórica. Carlos Fuentes, el *glamour*. Me tiene fascinado *Farabeuf*, de Salvador Elizondo. Creo en el talento de Juan García Ponce, y en el de José de la Colina, José Emilio Pacheco y Juan Vicente Melo. Pero deben dar más. Como poetas, admiro mucho a Octavio Paz, y después a Francisco Cervantes y a Homero Aridjis. [Jaime] Sabines es un caso de pureza excepcional, con grandes caídas y grandes hallazgos. (qtd. in Domínguez Cuevas, *Los becarios* 295–96)[40]

> Finally, I can tell you, for me, the most important book ever written in Mexico is *Pedro Páramo*. Yes, it's cliché to say it, but you have to do it. Rulfo is wisdom. Arreola is rhetoric. Carlos Fuentes, glamour. *Farabeuf*, by Salvador Elizondo, fas-

> cinates me. I believe in the talent of Juan García Ponce, and in that of José de la Colina, José Emilio Pacheco, and Juan Vicente Melo. But they should give more. As poets, I really admire Octavio Paz, and then Francisco Cervantes and Homero Aridjis. [Jaime] Sabines is a case of exceptional purity, with big blunders and great discoveries.

It bears repeating that this list dates from *1966*. Fifty years later, Rulfo is still considered the author of the most important twentieth-century Mexican novel. Paz earned the Nobel, Julián Herbert's assessment of the most glamorous man in Mexican literature is still Fuentes, and the rest of the names continue to resonate. The fact that Herbert *was not yet born* when del Paso spoke the paragraph above indicates the startling stability of certain assessments of the "best" performances among Mexican writers.

A similarly familiar list of names appears in Carlos Monsiváis's early autobiography, published in 1967, one year after del Paso's comments. There, Monsiváis recognizes the role of seven men, José Emilio Pacheco, Elías Nandino, Rafael Solana, Rubén Salazar Mallén, Alí Chumacero, Paco Zendejas, and Salvador Reyes Nevares, in giving him an early start at the literary magazine *Estaciones* and in related informal conversations (*Carlos Monsiváis* 34). Monsiváis also acknowledges five other male peers published in *Estaciones*: Sergio Pitol, Juan Vicente Melo, Salvador Elizondo, Gustavo Sainz, and Lazlo Moussong. A woman finally figures into these lists when Monsiváis remarks that in 1960 Nancy Cárdenas—in Monsiváis's verb—"gave" him the Yale program on cinema and criticism, apparently so that he could teach for it (36). The young Monsiváis does not mention extending a similar opportunity to a woman. Instead, the list of male literary influences continues to expand without even a token woman.[41] Among many other names, Monsiváis gets around to acknowledging seven key Mexican men: José Vasconcelos, Carlos Pellicer, Jorge Cuesta, Juan José Arreola, Julio Torri, Juan Rulfo, and Octavio Paz (50, 51).

The stability of this list of important authors in Mexico, who are all male, can be seen in a poll conducted of critics and writers (including myself) by *Nexos* in 2007. At the risk of repeating information familiar to the expert, I like to mention that poll because it decided with a highly splintered vote that the three best Mexican novels published in the last thirty years were Fernando del Paso's *Noticias del Imperio* (*News From the Empire*), José Emilio Pacheco's *Las batallas en el desierto* (*Battles in the Desert*), and Juan García Ponce's *Crónica de la intervención* (Chronicle of the intervention). All three writers share certain distinctions, including key early support from the Centro Mexicano de Escritores. Widely admired men's achievements, such as the aforementioned, are not outliers so much as centers; if they are not objectively the *best* texts in aesthetic terms, because such a measurement does not lend itself to objective criteria, these works are certainly the best connected. These fictions caught the interest of friends who were predisposed to view the men's work *not* as, say, romantic clichés, but as a maximum expression of serious concerns. In the case of canonical texts like Rulfo's *Pedro Páramo* and Pacheco's *Las batallas en el desierto*, which revolve around men's violence as well as a heterosexual love story, it is ultimately impossible to know exactly how peers come to decide that the texts represent worthy achievements and not melodramas, or *novelas rosas*.[42]

Indeed, *Dude Lit* operates on the hypothesis that what creates great literature is as much a performance of power and a network of complicit peers as this nebulous concept of *talent*. No less of a feminist than Gloria Steinem agrees and proposes that the equivalent of "chick flick" ought to be "prick flick," an obscene term that courts the accusation of participating in the same macho art that it purports to critique. Steinem's proposal ends up being, in the usual conundrum, *de la verga*.[43]

In order to take a stab at some reasons for men artists' success stories, it proves helpful to think of the "best" or canonical texts, not as residing at the top of the pyramid of aesthetic quality, but as the most connected nodes in a network in which all works exist on a horizontal plane. The lack of vertical orientation in this model means to show that the most interconnected texts do not just happen to be written by men. They reflect friendships among potential equals built on shared assumptions and prejudices, and these commonly held beliefs come to stand for "quality" among the members of the mutual admiration society. The best-connected books also respond to well-connected, or central, figures on that single horizontal plane.

I conclude the present chapter with a thought experiment that imagines the consequences of reversing gender. A revised *Las batallas en el desierto* stars, instead of protagonist Carlitos, a hypothetical Carlita, who falls in love, not with a twenty-eight-year-old single mother, but a father, himself apparently unemployed and tangled in an affair with a major political figure.[44] Carlita interrupts the single father one morning while he is alone at home, still in his robe and in the midst of shaving, and receives for her troubles no more than a chaste kiss. Would this material become as popular for school reading assignments, for decades, as Pacheco's original work did? I think not. For one thing, the plot seems at once overfamiliar as melodrama and strange as dangerous taboo, hardly a moral model for schoolchildren.

Furthermore, the background violence breaks accepted gender codes. If Carlita bloodied the face of her most impoverished schoolmate in response to being called an insulting term for lesbian, the verbal and physical bullying might repel the mainstream audience. Additionally, the gender-reversed tradition of the second family, or *casa chica*, seems frankly unimaginable as an approved text. The idea that Carlita's mother would maintain a semiclandestine second family, without divorcing her first husband, would threaten to swallow the rest of the plot for its scandalous irresponsibility. A two-timing mother who sequesters herself in the basement of her "first" home, teaching herself English rather than investing time with her official husband or with any of her five children, might be seen to display signs of mental illness rather than fulfilling her familial obligations.

In sum, the gender-reversed *Las batallas en el desierto* almost seems an exploration of perversity, rather than an appropriate school lesson. That the original version presents the various zones of male privilege and becomes a school assignment says much about the complicity of the audience in the network of the most connected texts.[45] This complicity protects both men writers' fiction and the circulating anecdotes about their personal lives. The strangeness of the gender reversal plot suggests just how invisible men's privileges can be. What can we see when we stare hard enough at men? The next chapter takes a stab at an answer by looking at the figure of the male intellectual.

2

PUTTING THE GENIUS IN HOMOGENOUS: WHAT DOES AN INTELLECTUAL LOOK LIKE?

Meditations on Naked Men and Censored Drugs, the All-Male Iconografía and Nuevos Escritores (with Examples from Ramón López Velarde, Amado Nervo, José Agustín, Octavio Paz, Carlos Monsiváis, Huberto Batis, and More)

Indeed, one can argue that the term "public intellectual" is redundant in Mexico.

—DEBRA CASTILLO AND STUART DAY

I summon the courage to telephone Octavio Paz. Although more brazen than most people, I am nonetheless nervous. It is like asking to speak to God. I introduce myself, explain as I had in previous letters our interest in doing an extended interview for National Public Radio's series on contemporary literature from Latin America. Before I can finish my explanation, he breaks in sharply. His scorn is searing. Under no circumstances will he participate. The telephone clicks off, leaving me startled, deflated, and confused.

—LOIS R. FISHMAN

Tomabas un taxi y de él descendía Carlos Monsiváis. Subías un elevador y él estaba allí en un rincón observando a todos con una mirada escrutadora y mustia. Ascendías los escalones de una pirámide y en la cima se hallaba sentado Monsiváis en posición de flor de loto. Yo recuerdo habérmelo encontrado en el aeropuerto de Madrid y haber sido presa de una depresión profunda: viajar tan lejos y encontrarte de frente con uno de los Indios Verdes.

—GUILLERMO FADANELLI

Some of the disorienting effects of the gender-reversal thought experiment stem from the tendency to assume that everyone should strive for male privilege. In my most anxious moments, I believe this standard stems from the ongoing slang habits that pose women as a largely nontransferable category and men as a neutral pronoun. In the United States and Mexico, twenty-first-century men and women talk to each other like guys, with supposedly gender-blind language. Women and men call each other the equivalent of "dude" or *güey*—or even *verga* (dick). A kind of paranoia emerges for me with this language, in the tradition of Woody Allen's fear that people were always talking about Jews when they mumbled things like, "Didjew eat? JEW eat" (Allen and Brickman). Like that joke from Allen's *Annie Hall* (1977), I find myself ruminating over possible threats in casual conversation. I think, "*Güey*, this paranoia has something to do with, *dude*, the fact, *bro*, that men are always on our minds, *man*." They are interjections, a kind of universal interlocutor. "The most famous intellectuals, *Dios mío*, are men, *cabrón*, because genius is masculine. *Híjole*, what a problem." And yet I recognize that I might be wrong—*au contraire, mon frère*—and hence the paranoia. After all, anyone can bitch-slap, and now men can call each other "bitches." In both English and Spanish, people are talking more about ovaries as a sign of courage. Still, *balls* or *güevos* in both languages more commonly represent the notion of bravery. And what if this masculinist habit is correct? What if *dude* is really just *anyone*? What if, at base, I am a kind of macho too? What if, at the core of my intellectual performance, I have been trained to be a macho and am thus paid to act like a macho, but only in the civilizado role?

Brené Brown, the best-selling academic specialist in social work, recounts her epiphany on this matter, framed in appropriately aggressive and italicized language: "*Holy shit. I am the patriarchy*" (95). If I may not bring myself to allow men to drop the bárbaro act, in the same way that I won't allow myself to assume it, I can certainly point out some of the ways the otherwise civilizado benefits from the implicit threat of force and rule breaking, which literary critics do not like to admit as an influence on their assessments. One of the most silent of these aspects is a given author's height.

The issue of height might seem to some readers utterly irrelevant. The best meditation I can find on the matter of height comes from one who suffers from a lack of it: Elena Poniatowska. In an interview, she speaks about it, not in terms of gender, but in terms of social class—the very factor that allows a certain group of men like Fuentes and Elizondo to visit a brothel without facing contamination from the lower-class connotations of a *casa de citas*. Poniatowska ends up focusing her remarks on her petite frame, a torturous source of embarrassment for her and motivation to overachieve:

> Sin embargo, le debo a esa inseguridad todo lo que soy; todo lo que he hecho ha sido debido a que nunca creí que cumplía con los requisitos que me exigía la sociedad y el mundo al que pertenecía. En primer lugar, ni siquiera me sentía lo suficientemente alta, soy una mujer chaparrita, mido 1.57 [metros]. En mi familia todas las mujeres miden 1.70, a nadie le faltaban 15 o 20 centímetros, como a mí. Todo esto me producía angustia, sentía que no cumplía con los requisitos físicos de mi familia. Físicamente no destacaba, me sentía una cucaracha fumigada, aunque no puedo decir que fuera una niña fea. (Ascencio 36)

> However, I owe everything that I am to that insecurity; everything that I have done has been because I never thought I fulfilled the requirements that society and the world to which I belonged demanded of me. In the first place, I didn't even feel that I was tall enough, I'm a shorty. I'm 1.57 [meters, or five foot one]. In my family, all the women are 1.70 meters [five foot five]. No one is 15 or 20 centimeters too short, like I am. All that caused me anxiety, I felt that I didn't meet the physical requirements of my family. Physically I didn't stand out. I felt like a sprayed roach, although I can't say that I was an ugly child.

Clearly, Poniatowska's height affects her self-assessment, and one consequence seems to be her ability to play the ingenue or "amateur" during interviews she's conducting in order to disarm her subjects. This game of childlike innocence, undoubtedly facilitated by her scant height, supports her disarming custom of point-blank questions, such as the previously cited one she poses to Elizondo: "Oye Salvador, ¿y tú quieres volver al manicomio?" (Listen Salvador, do you want to go back to the asylum?) ("El más inquietante" 394). Of course, as my reader already knows, Poniatowska's impudent naïveté—coupled with her physically nonthreatening presence—leads to her dismissal, as Elizondo judges her material for the asylum too: "Tú también estás loca" (You are crazy too) (393). Unlike Elizondo, Poniatowska anchors her "crazy" performance in a politely self-restrained act. Despite her pathbreaking efforts in journalism, it is difficult to read her as a bad boy.

Viviane Mahieux helps me to clarify what must seem a paranoid argument to unsympathetic readers—no doubt few among the cynics are petite—when she suggests that the most heterosexual of the twentieth-century masculinist intellectual performances sought disembodiment by assigning embodiment either to the audience or to the object of critique. This principle of disembodiment allows tall people to have their height and ignore it too, which sets up a system of largely unacknowledged prejudice. Mahieux does not base her argument solely on notions of height, however, and she concentrates mostly on men's self-serving claims to disembodiment. Thus, she writes, José Vasconcelos and Octavio Paz established an implicit binary against the majority of unexceptional minds by defining themselves "as pure intellect (disembodied thought), while the masses described came into being through their corporality" (175). In other words, our complicity with Paz's and Vasconcelos's disembodiment coaxes us to pretend that being taller than Poniatowska isn't an immense advantage when it comes to building a writing career.

Mahieux settles on the specific example of Salvador Novo's performance as a contrasting example to that of men like Paz or Vasconcelos because Novo openly, flamboyantly, inhabited his body as part of his claim to aesthetic competence. In fact, Novo embraced this notion of the also embodied masses by way of participation in "the flow of popular publications in the 1920s" (Mahieux 175). That is, even as Novo made use of his superior vocabulary and privileged education, he wrote for truck and taxi drivers—partly in order to cast among that set for likely lovers.[1]

In what could serve as the thesis statement of *Dude Lit*, Mahieux extracts an overarching principle from the gay poet's embodied practice: "An intellectual stance is not about *being*, Novo suggests, it is about *performing*" (165). Mahieux also happens to mention, almost in passing, Novo's considerable height, and it seems probable that Novo appreciated the impression of authority that his tall frame conceded him.[2] Except for a document produced by the FBI that records Elena Garro's estimation of Octavio Paz's height as 5 feet 9 inches (FBI 5), I lack exact measurements for the heights of Mexican men writers—after all, what biographer can be troubled to record such trivia? I have the impression that writers who receive considerable attention over the following pages, such as the bulky José Emilio Pacheco (bulky, at least, when compared to those who are petite) and the former college basketball player Guillermo Fadanelli, were interpreted by others to be relatively tall. Certainly, my impression of both these men when I met them in person was that they stood a great deal taller than I, at my nonthreatening five feet and two inches. My effort to articulate the unspoken but palpable correlation between physical height and literary stature disrupts the pretensions of literary critics who would somehow read "only" the literary text and thereby objectively discover men as the geniuses behind the "best" of them.

An Argentine visual artist has anticipated my suspicion that many successful leaders, in one way or another, look alike. Not writers but presidents inspire *Retratos de poder* (*Portraits of Power*), Alejandro Almaraz's series of portraits that show how, within a national tradition, a given country's leaders resemble one another and represent periods distinguishable by appearance. For each of the countries studied in the series, Almaraz superimposes the images of a succession of its presidents and winds up with a single blurry portrait of presidential power. All the presidents of Mexico from 1867 to 2008 form a coherent image in Almaraz's schema. Over the 150-year span, Almaraz reveals the generalized Mexican president as a light-skinned mustachioed man, mostly with brunette hair, though with some gray peeping through the edges. Almaraz's composite image for the Mexican president appears before a hazy background of books.[3] The connotation of unsmiling contact with books links serious masculine authority to the literary and to the notion of a communal store of knowledge. Along those lines, an art critic for the *New York Times* notes that *Retratos de poder* ends up proposing an aesthetic of power as collective, and not individual or heroic (McCann).

The notion of a composite image of the respected Mexican intellectual provokes my suspicion that something as simple as remembering *not* to smile for the official photo can signal artistic success. Octavio Paz does not smile on the commemorative coin from the 1990s; Juan Rulfo generally appears melancholic in photos; Carlos Monsiváis does not smile in his 2015 wax museum statue in Mexico City. The inverse habit might lead figures to be taken less seriously. Is part of Poniatowska's reputation problem owing to her tendency to smile for the camera? To get a sense of whether women tend to smile more than men when posing for a photo that represents them as authors, I counted up the profile pictures from Martha Domínguez Cuevas's slightly edited version of the winners of a yearlong grant from the Centro Mexicano de Escritores. Of the 234 total winners represented, women make up slightly less than one-third (27.78 percent). Thirteen of the women pictured among the photos, that is, 21.6 percent of them, smile in a way that shows teeth. At the risk of boring my reader, I arrange an approximate list of toothy smilers in alphabetical order:

Ingrid Cabrera Caderwall
Emma Dolujanoff
Gabriela Figueroa

Valentina Gatti
Verónica Ladrón de Guevara
Julieta Lozano Aguirre Beltrán
Graciela Martínez Zalce
Rita Murúa Beltrán
Martha Robles
María del Carmen Sánchez Ambriz
Marcia Torres Sasia
Marianne Toussaint
Ana Cecilia Treviño (Bambi)
Enzia María Verduchi

Only the specialized reader will recognize these names. My point? A teeth-baring smile on a woman who would be an intellectual may predict anonymity. If this correlation seems stupid to you, remember that I never claimed that sexism was sophisticated. It is perhaps the very lack of sophistication that makes some mechanisms of prejudice so difficult to spot; the obvious comes to be taken for granted. Of course, this study of smiles is far from scientific, and exceptions abound. Carlos Fuentes smiles in his profile photo—so the rule of a serious expression equaling a serious reputation remains only an imperfect generalization.

Interestingly, the women grant winners of the Centro Mexicano de Escritores pictured in Domínguez Cuevas's volume who face the camera stiffly or who tilt their heads seductively for a close-up, without smiling, seem relatively more famous and also number thirteen:

Inés Arredondo
Rosa Beltrán
Rosario Castellanos
Nancy Cárdenas
Elsa Cross
Amparo Dávila
Guadalupe Dueñas
Luisa Josefina Hernández
Ángeles Mastretta (at best with a faint smile)
María Luisa Mendoza
Silvia Molina

Aline Petterson
Esther Seligson

Additional cases prove difficult to classify. For example, Julieta Campos smiles faintly but shows no teeth, and Beatriz Espejo bares her teeth but does not turn up the corners of her mouth. Poniatowska looks up as if in surprise at the camera angled behind her; the photographer seems to stand over her, and her twisting posture may explain why her mouth is open and the corners of her mouth uplifted. She looks pleasantly surprised and is more or less smiling (Domínguez Cuevas 302). After tallying these photos, I am tempted never to smile again for any professional photograph, unless I think I can pull off something like Fuentes's movie star smile.

And how to dress for success? That is, I anticipate, the question on my most sympathetic readers' minds: If women writers shouldn't smile, how should they dress? The short answer is that even they don't know. The volume edited by Domínguez Cuevas spans the profile pictures of winners of the Centro Mexicano de Escritores from 1952 through 1997. Whatever the outfit displayed in the profile photo, none of the women wears a suit and tie. In fact, few wear eyeglasses. By my count, only eight of the sixty women pictured wear glasses (13.33 percent), while 43 men of the 148 men pictured do (29 percent). Using jewelry seems like an unadvisable move. None of the men wear visible jewelry, while of the sixty women pictured, thirty-two (53.33 percent) wear visible earrings, and ten (16.67 percent) sport a visible necklace.[4] By contrast, the men seem more homogenous, in a reflection of Almaraz's portrait of power. About 76 percent, or approximately 113 of the men, wear a suit and tie. A personal interview with Martha Domínguez Cuevas led me to understand that she used to instruct the men writers to wear ties for the profile pictures she coordinated. Her care for detail seems plausible.

In response to my question during our interview about whether the men who refused to wear a tie were trying to be rebellious, Domínguez Cuevas said yes. Also in response to my prompt, she dated the increase in refusals to wear a tie to after 1968. The original destination of these profile pictures, at one time at least, was for a newspaper; Domínguez Cuevas recalled that *Excélsior* used to publish the photos thanks to the social page editor "Bambi" (Ana Cecilia Treviño), a former grantee from the Centro Mexicano de Escritores herself, who cooperated with Domínguez Cuevas's desire for publicity. An interesting paradox surfaces here: while the men authors actually *do* lend themselves to a composite image, even after 1968, they nevertheless represent for literary critics the notion of individual stylistic brands, while the lump category of "woman writer" corresponds to figures who dressed with stronger individualism.

Men authors denote aesthetic trajectories unto themselves, though not so much by way of their looks. Homogeneity in appearance among men writers seems to free their academic audience to concentrate on each man's claim to intellectual originality. As I stated in the introduction and will review now that I have more evidence, while critics are usually quick to point out that poet Nervo is *not* Huerta or Pacheco, that novelist Gamboa is *not* Fadanelli or Ortuño, that essayist Paz is *not* Monsiváis or Volpi, the academic tendency is to choose the opposite action with figures as radically disparate as Sor Juana Inés de la Cruz and nearly any woman writer, from Elena Garro to Elena Poniatowska to, say, Guadalupe Nettel. However, reverse engineering this habit is possible. We can, for example, pay attention to the men grantees' superficial conformity in the profile photos for the Centro Mexicano de Escritores and create a composite image of the Dude Writer with a clothes analysis: the men dress quite a bit alike because they play by the same rules, which incidentally set them up to win.

One of those rules conveniently implies that clothes (like heights) don't matter, or they matter only to superficial people, like the women who struggle with the array of decisions facing them regarding makeup, hairstyle, jewelry, heel height, skirt length, pant tightness, cleavage depth, and so forth. The women are *by definition* more original in their performance, and yet somehow their sort of originality doesn't count as an intellectually admirable innovation—or even a factor that "serious" critics should take into account. For men, the achievement of originality occurs largely in peer review, a buddy bias that ought to recast our understanding of the degree to which an alleged rebel male writer strikes out on his own.

Thanks to the barbarous pole, even the fights among men writers seem to pull them together. The generalizable communal male will to individual power has men writers operate among a contentious set of friendship clusters that make up a single, mutually reinforcing unit. These aggressions end up furthering the serious intellectual reputations of, say, Octavio Paz and Carlos Monsiváis, to name the headliners in one exemplary public disagreement, and indicate the mechanism of the power loop that allows a man to play alternate roles between the macho civilizado and the macho bárbaro. This power loop seems built into the very roots of Western civilization, as Myles McDonnell's study

Roman Manliness asserts amid a discussion of the masculine *virtus*, whose essence is aggressive courage; thus, "because the ideal of Roman manliness was belligerent and aggressive . . . it was thought to pose a threat to society," and for this reason "a central element of Roman republican ideology and institutions was that *virtus* be constrained" (71). The ways in which the macho civilizado controls the macho bárbaro should not be confused with the ideal macho, who from some angles isn't even imagined as gendered. I take that observation from the immense amount of research that studies social injustice without thinking much about gender. I mentioned this point in chapter 1 in terms of critique of decolonialism and neoliberalism. Here, I can switch examples and include Giorgio Agamben's notion of the state of exception, which rarely unfolds in contemporary analysis through consciously gendered terms. The state of exception, this notion of suspending the constitution in order to later reinstate it once the danger has been subdued through unlawful behavior on the part of the government, seems to me a familiar trick of patriarchy.

One of the most outstanding habits of sexism regarding this ultimately unexceptional cycle of controlling both sides of the law is that male leaders who have killed someone are rarely described first and foremost as murderers. The bloody records of war-hero presidents such as Benito Juárez, Porfirio Díaz, and Lázaro Cárdenas contrast with the general lack of such personal violence effected by Mexican writers, and yet the one group rides on the reputation of the other, as the backdrop of books suggests in Almaraz's composite portrait of Mexican presidential power.[5] The look of books, as a mere backdrop, expresses a masculinist performance of intellectual mastery that allows the most powerful authoritative men to have it both ways. Every Mexican president can read as an educated macho civilizado, but he usually chooses not to cultivate much literary knowledge, because he must also come across as an unsmilingly serious macho bárbaro in potential. In something of a similar binary, the Mexican male writer usually avoids exercising murderous political power, but his reputation as a macho civilizado nevertheless connotes the flip side of that power, and you just never know when he or his buddy might slash a sex worker with a razor. The bárbaro aspect does not necessarily turn on direct violence; reputational contamination suffices.[6]

A trip to the wax museum helps us to explore the binary of lawbreakers and law makers. When I visited the Mexico City Wax Museum on 6 Londres Street in February 2016, I saw a replica of Benito Juárez posed with his hand on a hardback book—a nondescript tome eerily reminiscent of those in Almaraz's presidential composite image. Thanks to a digital image taken with my phone, I can make out at least part of the title of Benito's book prop: *Apuntamiento de la parte general de derecho penal* (Points regarding the general part of criminal law), which the Internet informs me is written by a man law professor, Celestino Porte-Petit Candaudap, whose work came out in its twelfth edition in 1989. A biographical sketch of Dr. Porte-Petit notes that he founded the very doctoral program in law at the Universidad Veracruzana from which he graduated with said degree (García Ramírez, "Celestino" 217). That power play strikes me as the ultimate macho civilizado move: to found the program that declares one an expert at criminal law. Juárez's historic example shines because he also is credited with founding the state of law that then respects him. It strikes me as curious that I don't know how many men Juárez killed. I cannot find the answer; such tabulations have apparently been viewed as irrelevant.

For clarity on this matter, I turn to Rebecca Biron and her meditation on the advantages of combining "murder and masculinity"; in her book of that title, Biron broadly reads Latin American literature in terms of a contradictory legal aesthetic, which on the one hand condemns murder as unlawful and on the other hand glorifies murder "when personalized and made symbolic of risk and change" (17). This almost indivisible link between gore and glory, between violence and intellectual authority, perhaps identifies the reason why it has proven so useful for a masculinist tradition to insist on the separation of body and mind; only one part of the man commits the crime.[7] Lest my readers quibble with the context of murder by the leader as an avenue to understanding the Mexican male intellectual, please remember that for the most part, women don't kill. This habit of leaving antagonists alive no doubt contributes to women intellectuals' inability to access the bad boy artist act. If women behave in an undisciplined or "immature" manner, they risk being dismissed as crazily incompetent rather than praised as admirably original.

Now, as anticipated in Laura Gutiérrez's imputation of the term *white* to the bad boy, this power loop applies to the United States. Take the uproar from 2016, when, during a lecture at Boston University, eighty-four-year-old male writer Gay Talese, according to a report in the *Guardian*, dismissed a question about women writers who had influenced his style, answering, "None" (Pengelly).[8] Nearly a year before, in a 2015 interview with Jonathan Franzen conducted by Susan Lerner, that male novelist defended his earlier dismissal of Jennifer Weiner, a U.S. woman novelist. Lerner sets up the question carefully, and I want to cite her in order to supply the context:

> Let's talk about women in literature. VIDA confirms that literary journals publish many more pieces by men than women. In *The Kraus Project*, as part of your lament about Amazon's power, you wrote that "literary novelists might be conscripted into Jennifer Weinerish self-promotion." Given that women writers are generally swimming against the current, what are your thoughts about the use of social media by women to promote their work? (Lerner)

Franzen winds his way into a revealingly discriminatory answer by first explaining how "tricky" the topic is, because "there's something about Jennifer Weiner that rubs me the wrong way." The irritation, as best as Franzen can articulate it, has to do with Weiner's habit of short-form tweeting, rather than writing what Franzen terms "her long essay" to make the feminist case; also, Weiner writes "formulaic fiction," which Franzen does not think merits a review in the *New York Times*. In a quick twist of the macho civilizado rule-upholding tactic, Franzen invokes feminism in order to launch this sexist argument: "To me it seems she's freeloading on the legitimate problem of gender bias in the canon, and over the years in the major review organs, to promote herself, basically." After having affirmed the continuing existence of a split between high and low literary forms, interviewer Lerner politely asks, "Have you read any of her books?" Franzen replies "No!" and Lerner politely lets the matter drop: "Okay."

I want to emphasize another macho civilizado strategy on display above, namely the denial of the continued existence of the binary of soft and hard, defined in the Franzen-Lerner conversation as "literary" and "commercial." I thank Lerner for the bold move of recognizing the binary. The academic hullabaloo over the postmodernist wave makes that statement of obvious reality difficult, because the 1990s declared its death. As a result, in the twenty-first century, *every single time* that I bring up a soft and hard binary in a comment after an academic literary presentation, I am told—by men, it must be said—that *we* don't *do that* anymore. (*We* must not refer to a lot of people, in that case.) Forget unfashionable. These critics insist that the association of men writers with high and hard literature is newly *nonexistent*, which sets up an emperor's clothes dilemma. The claimed new fashion looks unnervingly similar to the old, as familiar as a birthday suit. Yet, some critics deny this plainly visible reality of the enduring high and hard divide that has men *still* reaping the benefits of the strongest literary reputations.

The founding of the binary in Mexican letters has to do with a handful of fundamental arbiters, such as Octavio Paz, who not for nothing was rewarded for his good taste with a Nobel. Paz helped to create his own high prestige when he judged as implicitly soft and low such precursors as Amado Nervo and Ramón López Velarde. Early in his career, the Nobel Prize winner interpreted these men's work as *cursi* (corny, kitsch), or in bad taste, and thus he implicitly created a contrasting category of competence for writers like himself (*El camino* 24).[9] According to Paz, for example, only some thirty of López Velarde's texts may be justifiably admired; overall, the latter's oeuvre can lend itself to *fácil entusiasmo* (easy enthusiasm) (*El camino* 10). Paz classifies López Velarde as a poet of beliefs more than ideas and thus implicitly sets up the aesthetic of the sincere and *bonito* (pretty) as tied to a *feeling*, rather than an *act*, of poetry (31).[10] It falls to Paz to write the active poetry, one assumes. The very act of calling a famous precursor's work "bonito" exercises stunning efficiency, as it simultaneously validates Paz and undercuts others without forgetting the existence of a tradition.

Peers often agree with Paz's assessment, even when they apparently mean to defend López Velarde. Here is Sergio Fernández's positive review of López Velarde's poetry, which slides unapologetically from the poet's performance to his pages:

> [S]u sinceridad (no me refiero a la de la poesía, claro, sino a la que refleja en parte su existencia) se da el lujo de hilvanar las dos personas—la poética, la humana—en su obra, [. . .] bien puedo decir que hay un ser de bulto, casi concreto, en cada verso, en cada situación poética; y que, a no dudarlo, tan franco es, tan decisivamente íntegro, que todo lector está tentado a poner la mano en el fuego por su sinceridad, no importa cuán literaria sea. En este sentido es poco mexicano; poco *barroco*. [. . .] Si nos dice "amo" es la verdad. (95)

> [H]is sincerity (I do not mean that of his poetry, of course, but that reflected partly in his existence) takes the luxury of tying together two personas—the poetic, the human—in his work, . . . I can easily say that there is a being in bulk, almost concrete, in every verse, in every poetic situation; and that, without hesitation, he is so frank, so decisively whole, that every reader is tempted to stick a hand in the fire for his sincerity, no matter how literary he is. In this sense López Velarde is not very Mexican, not *baroque*. . . . If he tells us "I love" it's the truth.

The ultimately nonsensical logic of calling the poetry "not very Mexican," ostensibly because it is sincere, shows how literary criticism can come to draw from playbooks of mutually agreed upon, yet somewhat incoherent, terms. The men critics, from a certain angle, arbitrate precisely the problem that López Velarde struggled to overcome—to his successors' benefit—which was the difficulty of being seen as a competent man who was also a poet. Woe to be a pioneer.

Guillermo Sheridan's biography of López Velarde quotes the poet as threatening to abandon his writing because no one took seriously an *abogado poeta* (attorney poet) and he feared losing clients (*Un corazón adicto* 111). In an understandable move that recalls Lomnitz's dandy revolutionaries, López Velarde paid careful attention to his physical appearance; he underscored his performance of poetic and lawyerly competence by choosing formal clothes with an aristocratic flair. He habitually used a fancy coat, the *jaquet*, as remembered by another fancy dresser, Salvador Novo, in an interview with Carballo (Carballo, "Salvador Novo" 240). Similarly, foundational poet Amado Nervo's wardrobe came to include a dandy (*catrín*) coat for special occasions (Mendieta y Nuñez and de Anda 54). One biographer describes the photographs of Nervo dressed for his diplomatic role in Europe; the poet appears "pulcramente vestido como refinado caballero del viejo mundo" (neatly dressed as a refined gentleman of the old world) (Mendieta y Nuñez and de Anda 16). To the more contemporary ear, this image almost dooms Nervo, and yet in his day the look of the sincere gentleman helped to earn him so many admirers that when he died in 1919, at the untimely age of forty-nine, his funeral lasted six months. Organizers planned ceremonies and prepared the trip so that, for the benefit of fans, the body would make its publicly escorted way from Montevideo to Veracruz and then to Mexico City. Nervo's remains lie in the Rotunda of Illustrious Persons (Durán 108).

These wardrobe choices matter. As Monsiváis notes in the case of Nervo, in order to become a visible poet, he had to cultivate an audience; during his times, "No [había] mercado literario, pero sí 'mercado sentimental'" (There [was] no literary market, but only a "sentimental market") (*Yo te bendigo* 92). In that context, according to Monsiváis, Nervo's performance of sentimental sincerity awarded him an otherwise impossible social status as a poet or cultural expert: "Nervo es una celebridad indiscutible" (Nervo is an indisputable celebrity) (92). Status can be had by competently, flashily even, playing the role of poet. This performative dash caused posthumous problems for Nervo, whom twentieth-century peers would deride for his feminized bad taste, but who nevertheless in his day built a wildly popular reputation precisely on "excess," which Monsiváis defines in terms familiar from Paz's derisive understanding of López Velarde: "Nervo elige el exceso (la cursilería)" (Nervo elects excess [kitsch]) (22). Monsiváis cites Alfonso Reyes's phrase *gravísimo peligro* (superlative grave danger) to summarize Nervo's taste for *la cursilería* (33). It is no surprise, given these cool assessments of foundational poets' contributions, that kitsch retains gendered underpinnings.

Noël Valis's book *The Culture of Cursilería*, helpfully subtitled *Bad Taste, Kitsch, and Class in Modern Spain*, helps me to advance the analysis. Valis rescues statements such as Ramón Gómez de la Serna's idea that fin de siècle art and the *cursi* spring from the same source, "the feminine" (233). Interestingly, Valis suggests that a century or more ago in Spain the consumers who supported the cursi aesthetic may have ineffectively attempted to denote financial status: "Indeed, the devastating image of pervasive *cursilería* is transmitted through an economy of transactions based on credit. This association between credit and *cursilería* is fundamental: *lo cursi* represents insufficient cultural credit" (150; italics mine). Cultural credit is exactly what figures like Paz manufacture for themselves by placing figures like Nervo and López Velarde into the category of the cursi, or insufficiently credited. Nervo and López Velarde had already created credit for themselves by dressing the part of knowledgeable, fashionable poets. The extraneous and imaginary nature of this performative credit ends up in more of the same by reinforcing rather than reinventing patriarchal privileges. These habits of a would-be accredited intellectual tie into the customs of the middle class at large. David Graeber's meditation on ingrained reciprocity in polite language speaks to this point and identifies my reader among those who participate in the credit and debt system of everyday good manners:

> The habit of always saying "please" and "thank you" first began to take hold during the commercial revolution of the sixteenth and seventeenth centuries—among those very middle classes who were largely responsible for it. It is the language of bureaus, shops, and offices, and over the course of the last five hundred years it has spread across the world along with them. It is also merely one token of a much larger philosophy, a set of assumptions of what humans are and what they owe one another, that have by now become so deeply ingrained that we cannot see them. (*Debt* 124)

The very invisibility of this pervasive system of debt and credit, evident on the most basic levels of polite language, explains some of the difficulty behind the task of examining the reasons for men's stronger reputations as intellectuals. It also explains the appeal of the bad boy. Artists can manufacture credit by refusing to acknowledge their debts, by shrugging off the niceties, and thereby seeming to claim a different sort of credit for themselves.[11]

It is all too easy to predict that women poets by and large failed to receive honors similar to Nervo's burial in the rotunda or the coolly worded concern from their successors, such as Paz and Monsiváis, because no woman writer was as "good." The most convincing reason that it proves difficult to find a comparable female intellectual peer in the early twentieth century has to do with the accrediting network of men. An anecdote drawn from the world of Mexican visual artists helps to illustrate the power of this network: María Izquierdo lost the opportunity to paint a mural. A book on Izquierdo issued by the Mexican Museo de Arte Moderno (Museum of Modern Art) reproduces facsimiles of the relevant newspaper coverage, as well as an essay by Teresa Arcq, which all explain that in 1945 Izquierdo received the commission to paint the walls of the Governmental Palace in Mexico City, a total of 225 square meters. Male competitor muralists Diego Rivera and David Alfaro Siqueiros successfully pressured the government to cancel her contract, even though Izquierdo had already begun work by erecting the scaffolding and readying the sketches. According to Arcq's piece, Rivera and Siqueiros thought that a woman was incapable of achieving a project of such magnitude. A man's ability to toggle between the role of bullying personality and character-based authority figure gives Rivera and Siqueiros the power to manage Izquierdo's marginalization, which has largely been forgotten in the celebration of what she did accomplish on smaller-scaled canvases. Perhaps we forget that Izquierdo was publicly sidelined because it is easier to think that Rivera and Siqueiros are the *best* muralists, rather than the most aggressive and centrally connected bullies backed by a strong network.[12]

In an equivocal bright spot, Izquierdo did enjoy the posthumous honor of burial in Mexico City's Rotunda of Illustrious Persons, renamed in 2003 with relative hypocrisy in order to occlude its more accurate standing as the Rotunda of Illustrious *Men*. By my vision-numbing count, Izquierdo is one of five women among some 113 males in the pantheon. One reason why women like Izquierdo, Rosario Castellanos, and Ángela Peralta might have gained posthumous honors in the rotunda has to do with their relatively early deaths. Izquierdo died at age fifty-three, writer Rosario Castellanos died at age forty-nine, and stage talent Ángela Peralta died at age thirty-three, which suggests that dying young helps to slide a woman into the category of permanently reputable good character.[13] Of course, an early death is not a solution that I willingly prescribe.

On this matter of irrational discrimination, it seems helpful to turn to another pervasively irrational subject in twentieth- and twenty-first-century practice: drugs. Critics of contemporary Mexican literature understand why my worry about "drugs" is hardly off topic. For newcomers to the scene of state violence, mafioso activity, and artistic reactions, which all, at one level or another, respond to an artificially valuable black market commodity, allow me to cite Avital Ronell's work. Her *Crack Wars* elegantly argues the cultural slide from hard drugs to high literary text. To make the connection, Ronell analyzes the U.S. case against James Joyce's *Ulysses* (1920); that court decision allows us to "consider the degree to which the literary object has itself been treated juridically as a drug" (55). According to Ronell's analysis, "*Ulysses*, whether legally conceived as emetic formula or as aphrodisiac philtre, was in the first place distilled down to its essence as a drug" (55). *Ulysses* winds up in court because the threat of "hard" drugs has to do with the macho bárbaro and the way that the macho civilizado reins him in—and gives him slack. If you are wondering why men still command respect as "high lit" writers, even though supposedly such a category no longer exists, let me point out that in the U.S. courts, drugs are still "hard," even though for years now specialists in the pharmaceutical subject have argued against such divisions.

A more notorious bad boy literary figure surfaces in Ronell's analysis of literature as a drug when she shares key insights on the Manhattan Supreme Court case against William Burroughs's *Naked Lunch* (1959). Ronell notes that the U.S. court uses literary criticism to define the value of a text; this criticism ends up functioning as a "veil" for the artwork that reveals its outlines by covering it. Literature thus depends on critics' performance of something like decency; they are the arbiters, or in terms closer to Ronell's idea, the drapers of the veil. The veilings persist even when it seems that censorship and other prohibitions change. Although critics have argued that drugs are not as obscene as they are portrayed by the minority that stands to profit from prohibition, they have not succeeded in convincing law enforcement; perhaps one reason has to do with the continued aesthetic binaries of high and low, and soft and hard. Some drugs must remain hard in order for bad boy artists to remain high.[14]

I ponder this point through Ronell's assessment of Burroughs's drug-themed text *Naked Lunch* (1959). The court must decide whether *Naked Lunch* is a dangerous, too-hard drug or safe-enough literature. As Ronell sees it:

> The court is not wrong to institute the proximity of hallucination and obscenity as neighboring territorialities, since both put in question the power of literature to veil its insight or to limit its exposure. Literature is most exposed when it stops representing, that is, when it ceases veiling itself with the excess that we commonly call *meaning*. (56–57)

If Burroughs's text cannot take appropriate shape through the veil of criticism, it is mere hallucination and pernicious obscenity. On the one hand, the macho bárbaro reputation *needs* the serious "hard" drugs to be defined as such in order to pull off the serious "hardened" performance. On the other hand, the macho civilizado helps Burroughs's work get out of trouble. Other civilized intellectuals, artists, and academics—other *men*—take Burroughs seriously as an artist and *not* foremost as a drug addict. Drugs don't turn Burroughs into a victim; they make him an importantly rebellious writer. If the drugs that so interested Burroughs were legal, he might not seem as high and hard.

Burroughs later claimed that he would never have become a writer if it hadn't been for that accidental murder of his wife in 1951, whom we might term a "soft and low victim": felled by alcohol, by nonintravenous drug addictions, and by the relationship with drug-using Burroughs. The fact that Burroughs shot and killed his wife, Joan Vollmer, while in Mexico City only adds to his credibility as a bárbaro. Despite prodding from anonymous reviewers for the journal *PMLA*, I did not see much connection between the Beats and Mexican men writers until I started to teach Bernardo (Bef) Fernández's graphic novel about Burroughs, *Uncle Bill* (2014). I am not sure that Bef's text reveals much new information about the admired writer, aside from the autobiographically inspired protagonist's admiration for Burroughs. The fictional Bef admires Burroughs in the first place without having read him; he is interested in the figure who coined the phrase "heavy metal" (33). Consequently, young fictionalized Bef hunts obsessively and patiently for Burroughs's texts—a quest that readers familiar with Mexico's inadequate public library system will understand. Perhaps insight is not what I should demand from *Uncle Bill*, however. Burroughs himself was not insightful regarding Mexico, as Bef notes when he sketches Burroughs descending from the airplane in Mexico City, suitcases in hand, asking ignorantly for the beach: "¿Dónde está la playa?" (145).

In order to avoid repeating the racist comments about Mexicans made by Burroughs himself, I cite Drewey Wayne Gunn, who summarizes Burroughs's assessment of Mexico as a "sinister place" (80). Burroughs may need Mexicans to operate at a distance, as inferior beings, even when they are also his lovers, because he relies on the cachet of "drugs" that become more mysterious by way of association with certain minority groups under racist U.S. viewpoints. Burroughs, in other words, needs Mexicans in order to be a bad boy who can swing to the other pole of civilized thinker thanks to his whiteness. The trick of turning moralist in the midst of a bad boy performance depends on a loop that travels from text to performance and helps to police the zone that recognizes "the proximity of hallucination and obscenity as neighboring territorialities" (Ronell 56). Obscene performance of the hallucinations of white privilege and class exceptionalism, which in their maximum expression appear to allow Burroughs to function above the law, informs hallucinatory text that triggers critics' decision of whether to name it "obscene." Only a white man could pull off this act and have it labeled "genius."

The ferocity of one's foe, and the subject of one's study, can strengthen a reputation as a macho combatant; "hard" drugs and "high" authors make for authoritative reputations. Not all are convinced of the necessity of maintaining this critical authority, however. As Ronell writes, "Clearly, it is as preposterous to be 'for' drugs as it is to take up a position 'against' drugs" (50). She also warns that we never really know what we are talking about when we bring up drugs: "No one has so much as defined drugs, and this is in part because they are non-theorizable" (59). While it may be impossible to think without drugs, which means it is impossible to think soberly at all, much less to think soberly about drugs themselves, we can muse by way of the usual delusions about the gendered nature of this binary. Ronell takes up court cases that concern male writers, but does not take as much interest as I would like in the gender dynamic.[15]

Another student of landmark censorship court cases, the very attorney who argued some of them, Edward de Grazia, also largely fails to contemplate the gender issue. De Grazia's subtitle for his lengthy 1992 censorship history, *The Law of Obscenity and the Assault on Genius*, suggests this unexamined link between "hard," obscenity-tinged, court-riling masculinity and "high" civilization-improving genius. I hope that I am not the only one who just cocked a messily tweezed eyebrow.[16] The gender-attuned reader will note the masculinism of the *genius* rough language. When the violation of polite behavior, whose rules seem nearly inviolable for "professional" women, can raise a man's stock as a possible genius, seemingly any manner of rude and even incoherent cliché can be mistaken for an intelligent, "hard-hitting" contribution. How swear words, along with explicit sexual references and violence, can come to be confused with *ingenious* insight and even originality is exactly the conundrum here. The association of exceptional competence, even genius, with obscenity and other forms of rule breaking neatly links men artists with men critics' areas of expertise as both groups perform the role of men.

Men also operate as censors, a detail that the record does not preserve well. In one example rescued from the strikethroughs and silence, we see the duality of rebelliously "original" writers also curating conservative images for Mexican film in the 1950s and 1960s. Perhaps not surprisingly, Elena Poniatowska serves as a source on this matter. It must have been ironic for her to watch the men's reputations benefit as daring innovators, willing to explore themes of sexuality and political critique in their fiction, even as they restricted such visions in film. It seems logical that decades later she remembers these details. In 2014, Poniatowska gave an interview to Jacobo G. García and another to Carlos Rubio Rossell that included nearly identical statements on Carlos Fuentes's and Juan Rulfo's work in cinema as censors. To García, she commented:

> De hecho, Carlos Fuentes y Juan Rulfo ejercieron de censores del cine. Los dos trabajaban en el Ministerio de Interior y en esa época en México se empezaron a grabar muchas películas y ellos hacían de censores. Si aparecía un perro flaco y pulgoso en escena decían: "Corten la escena. Ese perro denigra a México." Y había que volver a rodar. (García, "Entrevista")[17]

> In fact, Carlos Fuentes and Juan Rulfo worked as film censors. The two worked at the Ministry of the Interior, and in that period in Mexico a lot of films started to be shot, and they operated as censors. If a skinny, flea-ridden dog appeared in the scene they would say: "Cut the scene. That dog denigrates Mexico."

Censorship happened on the other side of the filmmaking process as well, and a specific instance of this peculiar sort of "veiling" shows the connection between the topics of drugs and obscenity. Fernando Fabio Sánchez provides a puzzling case with *El hombre sin rostro* (*The Man without a Face*) (1950), directed by Juan Bustillo Oro: a piece of dialogue was censored in postproduction, rendering the exchange nearly incoherent. As Sánchez summarizes the partially suppressed lines between two characters who try to solve a mystery:

> The conversation [in the film] continues about possible leads on which to follow up and Britel asks, "Do you have any clues?" Juan Carlos responds that he does

> not, and adds, "What more can I do? Isn't it just some deranged guy who kills when he's high on ____________?" (71)

Sánchez observes the enigmatic effects of this censored language: "It is impossible to tell which word has been eliminated." Given that someone can get high on almost anything, the possibilities of what is being referred to seem nearly limitless, which underscores the nearly unlimited confines of "drugs."[18] Fortunately, Bustillo Oro provides commentary on the film, and from that data Sánchez gleans that "the murderer is addicted to a stupefacient, and that he needs to search for the murderer in the places where such substances are typically purchased" (72).[19] Might this place of substance purchase be a bookstore? (Kidding.) My point here is that regardless of the stage at which censorship occurs, whether during the film's shoot or after it has been initially assembled in the cutting room, this sort of editing work helps to preserve the category of the "high and hard." The men, such as Rulfo and Fuentes, who worked in the censorship industry as cooperative critics and outside it as rebellious critics thus supported their own reputations as "serious" artists by reinforcing this very category of "serious," even *dangerous*, art.

Decisions regarding which drugs are hard change over time, and in point of fact, as of May 2007 the U.S.-based Motion Picture Association of America began to take into account the smoking of nicotine for film ratings. As nicotine becomes a "hard" drug, films that employ it can make a claim to high and hard status, "for mature audiences," which suggests that the creators of the film are both more mature and more daring than the run-of-the-mill artist.[20] *Plus ça change* . . . no? You'll convince me that observations of the film censorship in 1950s Mexico no longer apply to dynamics in the contemporary arts when the global justice system changes, and that includes counting in the U.S. Supreme Court at least four women of nine judges and in the Mexican Supreme Court at least five of eleven. (We currently stand at three and two.)[21]

Today, the harder edge defined by factors such as explicit nudity and violence continues to win out in certain art circuits, most visibly perhaps in "art" film, where scenes of profane language and explicit sex that previously would have been restricted to XXX theaters now play in multiplexes. Linda Williams succinctly describes this hard edge in high art as an "international phenomenon of hard-core art cinema" (qtd. in Sánchez Prado, *Screening Neoliberalism* 203). The fact that the Spanish-language films in question are, for the most part, directed by men goes almost without saying, although for the record I cite Ignacio

Sánchez Prado on the issue as regards Mexico: "Mexican cinema faces a troubling absence of successful female directors" (218). The nonsensical nature of the high and hard bias that I am reviewing here is, I hope, clear to the reader. "High" means both not sober *and* respected—a contradictory act that men pull off as a peculiar bad boy privilege and that they sharpen by accusing others of being the opposing example, the soft and low (remember Paz on López Velarde). Women do not enjoy the same leeway; they seem to anchor the category of soft and low, where the derided men artists will join them, though perhaps one rung above the females because these inept men will still be talked about more. Precisely in this way the illogical drug laws serve to protect the binary.

Men become rebels by rejecting the middle class that buys and reads their books and that pays for movie tickets. The book consumers are largely women; the filmgoers are about half women, even though overall these women may have less money and less leisure time than men.[22] The irrationality of the system constituted by the high and hard art circuit hints to me that conscionable academics should drop out of the club that admires the extremely violent, as well as violently pornographic, artworks, which—to judge from my personal experience—if they attract women fans, they do so at least in part by default. If I want to participate in the conversation, I have to see the art that my colleagues think is remarkable. Of course, the problem with pointing out systematic sexism is that I sound like a prude: exactly one of those naysaying middling-class consumers who make bad boy behavior riskily admirable.

Or—worse than a prude—I sound like someone from the twentieth century, before U.S. Supreme Court Justice William J. Brennan Jr. authored the decision stating that material dealing with sex, for example, is protected if it "advocates ideas" or "has literary or scientific or artistic value or any other form of social importance" (qtd. in de Grazia 429). Under that 1973 ruling, in order to trigger legal censorship objections regarding obscenity, works had to be shown to be *utterly* without social importance (de Grazia 465). Law students remember this principle by way of the appropriately aggressive SLAPS mnemonic device: to censor for obscenity, a work must be without "serious literary, artistic, political, or scientific value" ("Miller v. California"). Claiming that a work of masculinist genius is unimportant is by definition impossible; these works are crucially important because they help to sustain a binary that imagines *genius* as male. My goal is not to reverse liberalization, but to examine the uses to which more permissive standards have been put. On that note, it's time to look at naked men—in art, of course.

Possibly, my reader would have guessed that more than 9 percent of males appear partially or fully nude in the one hundred top commercially successful films of the U.S. box office, although that number *is* higher than the percentage of males dressed in revealing attire, which stands at a paltry 5.7 percent—especially paltry compared to 25.9 percent of females seen in sexually revealing attire and 25.6 percent partially or fully naked (Smith, Choueiti, and Pieper, "Inequality in 900" 15). Though the total numbers are still small, there is something trendy about the male nude. Of course, tradition in at least one area has always preferred nudity, as marked by the longtime presence of a nearly naked Christ on the crucifix in Catholic churches, a point that pop star Madonna exploited in the early 1980s when she repeatedly declared her appreciation for crucifixes "because there is a naked man on them" (Guilbert 30). The custom of not sexualizing Christ, along with the scandal that ensues from reversing that tradition, finds its counterpart in secular public space in Mexico City, which teems with statues of wholly naked women.

In evidence of the strangely acceptable female nude even among devout Catholics, in a biography of his father published in 2016, *Examen de mi padre* (Examination of my father), Jorge Volpi relates his dad's obsession with painting miniature, nearly naked women—about the size of lead soldiers—and proudly displaying them in the house for guests:

> Si el sexo era tabú que nunca mencionó siquiera con nosotros, no tenía empacho en presumirnos sus creaciones, algunas en el límite de la pornografía o el S/M, o en exhibir esos procaces cuerpos femeninos, con su profusión de nalgas y senos al aire, frente a cualquier visitante. (79)

> If sex was a taboo that he never mentioned to us, he had no problem showing off his creations for us, some on the edge of pornography or S&M, or to exhibit those tender female bodies, with their profusion of hips and breasts in the air, in front of any visitor.

Somehow, naked women in all sorts of poses failed to trigger Volpi's father's stringent sense of self-censorship on the topic of sexuality. He apparently did not paint naked male figures, and in that vein I admit that without Laura Gutiérrez's help, I could not have named a single male nude statue in public space in Mexico City. Gutiérrez reminded me that since 1976 a small replica of Michelangelo's *David* has stood in the Rio de Janeiro Park of the Colonia Roma, surrounded by spraying water, and today serves as the reunion point for such gatherings as naked protesting bicyclists (personal interview; "Plaza Río de Janeiro").[23]

Given the relative paucity of public images of naked men, you can imagine my surprise at the show held in spring 2014 at the National Museum of Art in Mexico City, *El hombre al desnudo: Dimensiones de la masculinidad a partir de 1800* (*The Naked Man: Dimensions of Masculinity from 1800*). The Mexican exhibition mentions as inspiration a similar endeavor staged in Europe, whose catalog appeared with the title *Nude Men: From 1800 to the Present Day* (2012) (Natter and Leopold). Like the European precedent, the range of art included in the Mexican show begins in 1800, but it goes on to exceed the previous program, thanks to the depictions of contemporary violence in Mexico that employ the male nude. The Mexican show provides evidence to suggest that the male nude has always entertained artists in Mexico and elsewhere; the male nude just doesn't underpin the notion of genius to the same degree that the female nude tends to do.[24]

I caught sight of another exhibit of nude males called *Painting the Revolution*, curated by the Philadelphia Museum of Art in 2016–17, which later moved to the Palace of Fine Arts in Mexico City. That exhibit displayed a page of the second number of the magazine edited by Jaime Torres Bodet, *Contemporáneos: Revista Mexicana de Cultura*, from July 1928, which has the artist who signs as "Lazo" portray a grouping of nude male figures, albeit with just buttocks showing, no genitalia. Visitors unfamiliar with this text discovered the image only thanks to the curators' decision to leave the page open to it, and even in other examples it can require aid to see the naked male. Robert McKee Irwin reminds us that nude male exhibitionism appears in Mexican literature as early as *El Periquillo Sarniento* (*The Mangy Parrot*) (1816), and yet this theme can elude contemporary critics accustomed to the explicit register of today's writers. In fact, Irwin believes that "*El Periquillo* is an ideal resource because it likely features more nude male exhibitionism than any other book of the time, save for those of the Marquis de Sade" (*Mexican Masculinities* 27). Academics' habit of failing to see the nude male suggests to me that the macho civilizado does not always celebrate, and perhaps even rarely takes notice of, arty naked men, perhaps because they are neither traditionally bárbaros nor easily recognizable as model civilizados.

Though censorship standards for Mexican cinema, articulated by Carlos Monsiváis, dominate in the 1940s and 1950s, there is by no means a uniform line that stretches from repressiveness to ever more liberal aesthetics (Monsiváis,

El estado laico 31). The conservative midcentury standards for the big screen reject the more liberal scenes available among live performances by *tiples* (showgirls) in the early decades of the twentieth century in Mexico City, as well as such images as a brief scene of a bare-chested woman in the film *La mujer del puerto* (The woman of the port) (1934), as *rumbera* scholar Laura Gutiérrez notes (Gutiérrez, personal interview). The more restrictive aesthetic of the 1940s, '50s, and '60s came about as entities such as the Roman Catholic Church and La Liga de la Decencia (The League of Decency) were able to control film and later television standards and influence the Mexico City mayor, Ernesto Uruchurtu (1952–66), to shut down the cabaret spaces. This same civic organization also managed to force the sculptor Juan Olagbiel to clothe the bottom part of his *Diana la Cazadora* statue about a year after its debut in 1942.

The 1970s saw a loosening in these standards, as Gutiérrez points out, with such soft-core porn films as *¡Tintorera!* (Tintorera: killer shark) (1977); the standards would tighten again—as they did in the United States in the 1980s—only to relax once more in the 1990s. The Mexican censorship standards were loosened with the most notable speed under Ernesto Zedillo's presidency, from 1994 to 2000, a change that may have been hastened by the racy standards of imported cable television fare from the United States, protected in the home country under decisions like the one expressed by Justice Brennan. Evidently, the shift from censored to permissive material hardly occurs in a straight, or "progressive," chronology that flows only in one constantly improving direction. In fact, the fundamental meaning of our relaxed standards remains unclear.

On that note, Carmen Boullosa advances a helpful, if subtle, metaphor regarding the tides of Mexican women writers' fortunes in Mexico. Boullosa remembers that in the late 1970s and early 1980s, when few women in Mexico were writers, they were understood as nonthreatening oddities, which earned them greater status from male peers: "Cuando las mujeres éramos excepción se nos trataba sí con mucho respeto y admiración" (When we women were an exception, they treated us with a lot of respect and admiration) (Boullosa, personal interview). However, as the decade of the '80s progressed, the increased numbers of women writers turned them from exceptions into men's colleagues: "Entonces ya no había tan buen ojo" (Then there wasn't such a benevolent view).[25] Having experienced this shift, Boullosa proposes that the opening of gender opportunity reflects not so much a wave (*ola*), which following the metaphor would always roll predictably in the same direction onto the same beach, but a current (*onda*), which can shift directions: "Yo creo que son ondas, más que olas. Son ondas. Yo he vivido varias ondas. Yo viví la onda en que ser mujer era un plus, una suma. Y he vivido también que ser mujer es un menos." (I think they are currents, more than waves. They're currents. I've lived through several currents. I lived the current when being a woman was a plus, a something more. And I've lived also when being a woman is a minus.) That framework of shifting currents defends her from colleagues who tell her that her writing of the last decade is not quality work; rather than believe them, she argues that assessments of her writing depend on the mood of the times: "Es que fue una onda y ahora es otra onda" (Back then it was one current and now it's another current).

Taking into account these fickle fortunes, we can ask: Do men lose power under the changes, now that more male characters perform naked onscreen, and offscreen are more often flanked by women colleagues? In 2012, James Wolcott's article in *Vanity Fair* "The Hung and the Restless" cataloged the fashion of showing the penis on the U.S. big screen and suggested that this newly liberal aesthetic reflects something more than pornography; the explicitness hints at a shift in power, because phallic authority is succumbing to "all these actual penises" (207). Wolcott speculates that the graphic portrayal of the penis is causing male power to become "symbolically deflated." Given the largely unchanged power dynamics between the sexes in the art, political, and business worlds, however, it seems more accurate to claim that the power of the phallus is now reserved for a more elite group: a select portion of machos civilizados enjoys the most flexibility in exercising the privilege of flipping back and forth with the bárbaro role.

Nakedness is an unusual pose among Mexican men creators. With some exceptions, the reputation of the artistic genius benefits from working not only with nudes but specifically with the female nude. The point regarding the prevalence of naked women in Mexican art is backed by the images collected in the first volume of Humberto Musacchio's rich anthology *México: 200 años de periodismo cultural* (Mexico: 200 years of cultural journalism), which ends in 1907. Volume 1 displays among the pages of literary magazines an initial proliferation of images featuring the authors themselves, in clothes, and, separately, an imaginative variety of bare-breasted women.[26] The 1907 end date for Musacchio's first volume falls about a decade after the *Revista Moderna* began to feature so insistently among the excerpted material the naked torsos of women, in a sharp contrast to the always-dressed male writers who appear in the same publications. Such naked lady drawings appear, for instance, in 1899 (Musacchio 1:515) and in 1900 (522, 524). The artwork perhaps means to associate the feeling of poetry with the image of the naked woman, an allegory of "beauty" as much as a sign of "male privilege." The rule-testing macho bárbaro can handle the naked woman's form because, for most part in public at least, he remains dressed. Unlike Superman, the macho who flips from bárbaro to civilizado does not even require a change of outfit.

However, on occasion a Mexican male intellectual flaunted his nudity, as is apparent, for example, in personal photographs kept by poet Carlos Pellicer of himself nude (*Carlos Pellicer* 117), shirtless, or otherwise more decorously posed (118–21). Or one can observe near nudity on display in the famous photograph of the painter David Alfaro Siqueiros in his underwear (Debroise 241). No punishment for this nudity seems to affect men. In fact, a selection of Pellicer's photos are reprinted as part of an all-male Iconografía (Iconography) series published by the Fondo de Cultura Económica. The oversized volumes, printed on thick glossy paper, feature biographical timelines and personal photographs of Mexican authors, using the writers' names as titles. The lineup features *Alfonso Reyes* (1989), *Daniel Cosío Villegas* (2001), *Jaime García Terrés* (2003), *Carlos Pellicer* (2003), *Luis Cardoza y Aragón* (2004), *José Vasconcelos* (2010), *Efraín Huerta* (2014), *José Revueltas* (2014), and *Agustín Yáñez* (2014). Despite the relatively recent dates of some of the volumes, the series continues to exclude women.[27]

The Iconografía volumes distract somewhat from my topic of nudity but are worth the slight detour in that these subsidized texts indicate that men authors can solicit and circulate photographs and other artworks of themselves without attracting the accusation of vanity that follows women who behave similarly. Photos helped to reinforce peer networks and public images. Alfonso Reyes's volume shows that he dedicated, by hand, the reverse of a wallet-sized image of himself to José Vasconcelos (69). Another photo shows Reyes and his wife, Manuela, with three- or four-year-old Carlos Fuentes and his parents (130). The familiar network of intellectual authorities emerges in this trade of images, and some decades later, Reyes will write Fuentes a recommendation letter that will help him win a grant from the Centro Mexicano de Escritores.

Beyond the Iconografía texts, other books of photographs preserve a given writer's look. *Octavio Paz, entre la imagen y el nombre* (*Octavio Paz, Between the Image and the Name*) (2010), edited by Rafael Vargas, features the occasionally mediocre work of twelve photographers who capture the poet at various stages in his life, reprinted across sixty-five pages of captions and images. In *Carlos Fuentes y la novela latinoamericana* (Carlos Fuentes and the Latin American Novel), the 2013 book on Fuentes's writing, Daniel Mordzinski contributes around twenty pages of photographs of the writer himself (Fuentes La Roche and Mendoza 89–111). These photographs show Fuentes, at times posing with his wife, Sylvia Lemus, in intimate surroundings; evidently, the photographer benefited from an invitation by the novelist to shoot this record. Though no book exists yet, Carlos Monsiváis requested portraits of himself from photographers such as Héctor García. Monsiváis is not remembered as a vain man, unlike Salvador Novo, about whom no photo book exists either.[28]

The absence of a volume on Novo is curious. In addition to Novo's constant media presence, he collaborated with the midcentury celebrity photographer Simón Flechine, known as "Semo." This Mexico City–based self-billed "fotógrafo de las estrellas" (photographer of the stars), whose brand was a "garantía de originalidad y buen gusto" (guarantee of originality and good taste), shot portraits of Novo's face and hands before the closure of Semo's studio on Antonio Caso in 1963 (Morales Carrillo 62, 83). The lack of a book that would include those and other images of Novo suggests that at least one man has proved the exception to the rule and attracted punishment for a reputation of vanity. In one misstep, Novo may have collaborated with the wrong photographer. Pacheco has already famously linked Semo's work with the feminine. In *Las batallas en el desierto*, a fictional portrait of Mariana taken by Semo plays into notions of women's vanity and Mariana's status as a middle-class consumer, but not a producer. Even though Mexican men authors spread self-images then, fiction by Pacheco attributes this self-curating habit to a woman character.

Though readers today may have been trained to pretend to ignore men authors' images, they constitute an item of trade in themselves. Several twentieth-century Mexican writers recall a boyhood hobby of collecting portraits of successful authors. A biography of Juan Rulfo includes a small photograph of the future novelist's childhood album of admired writers (Vital 116). Likewise, the editor of *sábado*, Huberto Batis, confesses in an interview from 1999 to the same pursuit: "Desde niño empecé a coleccionar fotos de escritores" (Since I was a child I started to collect photos of writers) (Miranda, "Entrevista" 69). At the turn of the millennium, this tradition continued in certain sectors of the public education system; I know because a stationery store in Mexico City sold me perforated sheets of stamped color portraits of famous Mexican writers designed, presumably, for Mexican schoolchildren to place in the appropriate spots of corresponding activity books. These writers were overwhelmingly men.

Of course, I don't need to reach to forgotten collections and tedious homework assignments to find the image of the male author. Though authors' images were absent from the salacious Ediciones Botas covers and many of the art deco book designs from the 1920s and 1930s, around the middle of the twentieth-century writers began to appear on back covers. Bernardo Ruiz relies on lived experience to help me historicize this development, and in a personal email, he remembers:

> Entre las primeras editoriales que reprodujeron en los sesentas en sus colecciones la fotografía del autor estaba la Serie del Volador de Joaquín Mortiz. Asimismo la [B]iblioteca de [N]arrativa que usaba toda la 4a de forros (en la sobrecubierta) para mostrar el rostro del autor. Ésa era la colección favorita de Agustín Yáñez, que no era ni Byron, ni Adonis. [La editorial] Siglo XXI también usó en alguna de sus series de bolsillo estampitas con las fotos de [Alejo] Carpentier, [Carlos] Montemayor, o sus entonces recientes autores.

> Among the first publishing houses in the sixties that reproduced a photograph of the author in its collections was the Serie del Volador, from Joaquín Mortiz. Likewise, the Biblioteca de Narrativa used the back cover to show the face of the author. That was the favorite collection of Agustín Yáñez, who was no Byron, or Adonis. [The publisher] Siglo XXI also used in some of its paperback series little boxes with the photos of [Alejo] Carpentier, [Carlos] Montemayor, or its recent authors at that time.

Ironically, with the current heavy circulation of writers' faces and poses in social media, from stills to videos, their likenesses have for the most part once again disappeared from Mexican book editions.

I want to return to the 1980s for one heavily illustrated forum: the cultural supplement *sábado* for the newspaper *unomásuno*, edited by Huberto Batis. Writer Mauricio Carrera first called my attention to Batis's scandalously illustrated publication. Later, I discovered a blog post by Sandro Cohen that specifies the salacious details in the pages to which Carrera had referred:

> Entre "El diván de sábado," pequeña sección donde Huberto publicaba la foto de alguna escritora o *vedette* que visitara las oficinas del suplemento, posada sobre el desvencijado sofá que allí había; la columna de Andreas der Mond (seudónimo de Andrés de Luna) sobre erótica en todo el mundo; dibujos, fotografías, cartones y demás imágenes de hombres y mujeres en paños menores, o sin paño alguno; el "Desolladero," donde lo más exquisito de la cultura mexicana se ponía a mentarse

> madres, el suplemento *sábado* era todo un escándalo. Y al mismo tiempo era lo más propositivo, crítico, creativo y abierto que había. (Cohen, "Huberto Batis")
>
> Between "The Saturday Divan," the small section where Huberto published the photo of some woman writer or showgirl who happened to visit the offices of the supplement, posed on the rickety sofa that was there; the column by Andreas der Mond (pseudonym for Andrés de Luna) on erotica across the globe, drawings, photographs, cartoons, and other images of men and women in their underthings, or with nothing at all; [and] the "Slayer," where the most exquisite of Mexican culture set up to swear at each other, the *sábado* supplement was a scandal. And at the same time it was the most proactive, critical, creative, and open document that there was.

Cohen informatively titles the blog post, "Huberto Batis, pornotólogo" (Huberto Batis, pornotologist), which nicely summarizes his point. Perhaps the most interesting part of this investigation for me on a personal level is my ability to screen out, entirely, Batis's role as a "pornotologist." Until Carrera referred me to the photos in *sábado*, I had been using the archive of the Centro Mexicano de Escritores, at the Biblioteca Nacional, where intermittently over a period of days I stared at the pages of the supplement and studiously skipped over the nudie pictures, usually found on the back of the newspaper clippings that I examined. The lewd cartoons and tits-and-ass photographs seemed incongruous with the intellectual record that I sought to analyze, and so I mentally blocked out those details, which shows just how hard it can be to *see* a pervasive aesthetic of machismo—precisely because it is both omnipresent and out of bounds. I can't pay attention to *everything* and finish the research for *Dude Lit*.[29] Exactly what my training deems irrelevant, however, ends up being fundamental to authoritative image making.

Batis praises the utility of such nudie illustrations as an appeal to mass literacy: "En *sábado* ocurrió un fenómeno extraordinario, lo empezó a leer la gente más humilde del propio periódico, por ejemplo los obreros, los choferes, los *guaruras*" (In *sábado* an extraordinary phenomenon took place; the lowest-class people at our own newspaper began to read it, for example the manual laborers, the chauffeurs, the bodyguards) (Miranda, "Entrevista" 95). Batis explains that this audience liked the articles and fiction by soft and low writers—to use the terms of my analysis—whom the opposing high and hard group disdained. Precisely this dichotomy reveals that one group reinforces the other. Batis views the debate as a division between those who read front to back, that is, the academics and like-minded intellectual writers, and those who read back to front, that is, everyone else (95). The ultimate effect of these clashing audiences was to cultivate a space for bad boy figures.

In commentary printed in Miranda's book, the likes of Fadanelli appreciate that freedom, along with the uneven quality, that a lack of discrimination encouraged: "El *sábado* de Huberto Batis, me parece un suplemento heterogéneo, y un espacio de libertad creativa como hay pocos en México, donde te puedes encontrar colaboraciones excelentes y artículos malos" (The *sábado* of Huberto Batis seems to me a heterogeneous supplement, and a space for creative freedom like few others in Mexico, where you can find excellent collaborations and bad articles) (212). Similarly, Xavier Velasco comments on the "libertad tremenda" (tremendous freedom) that Batis allowed his wide variety of writers (234). Was this freedom extended to women and the cause of feminism? The answer is complicated, more so than many of Batis's female fans might wish to admit. Rosa Sabugal (or Lulú Uruchurtu, her pen name) aligns herself with unambivalent Batis admirers Fadanelli and Velasco [that is, Fadanelli and Velasco admire Batis]: "Huberto todo lo publicaba, siempre con gran respeto a la libertad de expresión. Él es uno de los pioneros de la democracia" (227). (Huberto published it all, always with a great respect for freedom of expression. He is one of the pioneers of democracy.) (With this sort of democracy, it's less unsettling to survey where we've ended up, isn't it?) By the numbers, women did have greater freedom under Batis. The list of collaborators in the cultural supplement *sábado*, at least as presented in Miranda's commemorative book, lists 44 women out of the 113 names, which means the number of women writers actually reaches 38.9 percent ("Introducción" 22).[30]

Alongside the unusually robust intellectual space that *sábado* offered to women, Batis fostered a strangely exhibitionist aesthetic that imagines bad girls as the tools used by artistic bad boys. Risqué illustrations support male privilege. And to give just one example: a drawing titled *Denisse visita a Batis para disciplinarlo* (Denisse visits Batis to discipline him) by Héctor de la Garza, or "Eko" as the paper knew him, accompanies the "Laberinto de papel" (Paper labyrinth) book section of the supplement. It shows a naked woman with a whip leaning over Batis himself, represented in a larger scale than she is but still powerless because he is in a kind of stockade arrangement, his head sticking up in a vise and his hands trapped (Miranda, "Entrevista" 54). The differently scaled figures indicate that Batis is more powerful; implicitly, this S and M play required his initial consent. Thus, Batis's submission in the cartoon is willing and—by implication of this voluntarism—only temporary. Héctor de la Garza, again as Eko, pens another erotic drawing, this one also rescued for Miranda's book on Batis: *Denisse se peina para sábado* (Denisse fixes her hair for *sábado*). The first of three panels depicts a woman sitting on the floor with her crotch and breasts exposed, wearing high heels and with hair that seems blondish. The second image shows an explosion between her legs that blows her hair straight and up as she plugs her ears. The last panel imagines smoke issuing from her vagina and her long hair relaxed in a kind of Brooke Shields waviness (76). What kind of message did *sábado* construct with this constant peppering of the female form in its pages, in contrast to its less emphatic use of the male nude? Whatever message readers may have received, select women wanted not only to write for the publication but also to appear on Batis's couch, for the photographic section titled, after the featured furniture, "El diván."

Bad boys like Fadanelli and Velasco, it perhaps goes without saying, did not pose for "El diván," much less hike up their pants for more skin exposure in their photographs in the way that women pulled up their skirts.

As the amount of skin the models exposed in the photographs rose, some readers found that the initial erotic edge turned crude. Arturo Azuela risks a reputation as a square when he critiques the tawdriness, but with only mild rebuke, given that objections to this sort of exploitative photography cast one as unable to appreciate intellectually risky art:

> Lo único del suplemento que no me gustó en una época, pero que después se modificó, era que Huberto tenía una propuesta erótica-cultural, erótica-literaria, que se fue transformando, fue decayendo en cosas más pornográficas, perdió su lucidez erótica-lúdica, un aspecto muy atractivo, que ha retomado afortunadamente. (qtd. in Miranda, *Huberto Batis* 200)

> The only thing about the supplement that I did not like in one period, but which later changed, was that Huberto had an erotic-cultural, erotic-literary design, which bit by bit was transformed, started decaying into more pornographic things, [and] lost its erotic-ludic lucidity, a very attractive aspect, which has fortunately returned.

Even as I write these words, I know that a variety of readers will find ridiculous my suspicion of a literary supplement spiked with erotic drawings and photos. In my quick search for a synonym for "prude" (by way of the right-click thesaurus function on Microsoft Word), I discovered that my audience may think of a conscientious objector to the images of *sábado* as not just a "square" but also, the label feared across the centuries, a "pedant." Am I, gasp, a *pedant*? (Remember that term and its synonyms: we'll see the pedant again in chapter 6). In defense of myself, and perhaps of Arturo Azuela as well, I want to point out that the *context* offends me more than any one image. I return to my concern with Fadanelli's misogynist/feminist tactics here: Who really gains the power from ironic feminism?

The bárbaro writer does not enjoy a rough reputation merely on the basis of his consumption of porn. An element of aggression also characterized the heyday of *sábado*. The supplement sponsored, if not instigated, conflictive relationships among its published authors, who, as I already said, included women. These spats took place in the section labeled "Desolladero" ("Slayer" or "Flaying place"). Batis explains to Miranda that he initially wanted a bloodier name, "Despellejadero" (Skinning place), after the Aztecs who skinned cadavers and then wore the skins for a ceremony (Miranda, "Entrevista" 122). The fights arose mostly around male figures such as Octavio Paz, but one mixed-sex conflict pitted Salvador Elizondo against a woman, Patricia Cardona. A court ruling eventually ordered Elizondo to retract his disrespectful statements in the newspaper about Cardona and to apologize to her, in addition to paying a fine of 20,000 pesos. Cardona pardoned Elizondo and accepted the payment, only to have him write, in Batis's words, "una carta muy ingeniosa en la cual volvía a insultar a Patricia Cardona" (a very ingenious letter in which he again insulted Patricia Cardona) (139).

In order to defend this lack of civility, in the interview Batis glosses other, more violent acts by Mexican writers. For instance, he names the duel between Ireneo Paz, Octavio's grandfather, and Santiago Sierra, in which the latter died, and he remembers anecdotes about the poet Salvador Díaz Mirón, the legendary murderer of one unfortunate man in the House of Representatives and another man in La Parroquia café in Veracruz; Batis also remembers that Ignacio Manuel Altamirano almost died of a stab wound provoked by an argument about theater after a play. He mentions these examples to justify the tolerance for aggression in the columns of *sábado*, because, he writes, "si revisamos la historia, *El Desolladero* no es nada, son sólo unos insultitos inofensivos de niños que se injurian" (if we look at history, "El Desolladero" is nothing, just a few inoffensive little slights among children who insult one another) ("Entrevista"

141). Insults hurled among writers, along with the nudie images, contribute to what many collaborators viewed as a maximum expression of freedom and what I view as a masculinist tunnel vision. By the twenty-first century, the vision seems to have narrowed into a dead end, rather than earning public respect in the spotlight.

More illuminating than theories of democracy and subversion are the facts of the finances. In the short term, the state sponsored the experiment. Batis himself recognizes that official support funded this foundational effort to set the high and hard against the soft and low: the Mexican government bought 80 to 90 percent of the ads for *unomásuno*, with private businesses supplying a remaining 10 percent, and newsstand sales and subscriptions accounting for just 2 percent of the revenue (Miranda, "Entrevista" 153). The difference between one category, that of the notoriously restrictive state, and another, that of the allegedly freer private and artistic enterprise, seems complicated here.

To give another complex case, I turn to José Agustín, whose career and stylistics benefit from a twentieth-century understanding that "young" writers are "new." Agustín is about a decade younger than Batis and nearly twenty years older than the likes of Fadanelli and Velasco. Although newer and younger writers came on the scene, Agustín sustained an aura as a pioneering rebel talent. Some of his reputation as a long-lasting "new" writer comes from the decidedly not-new treatment of women, not as peers, but as tools. As just one illustration of this point, I cite images from Batis's *sábado*, printed in 1997 in conjunction with an article entitled "El inicio psicodélico de José Agustín en 1968" (José Agustín's psychedelic beginning in 1968) (Calvillo 22). The text appears on same page as a self-congratulatory ad for *sábado*, bearing an image of a naked woman viewed from behind, with a bull's-eye painted over her buttocks and the superimposed words "Muchos / Veinte / Años / De estos" (Many More / Twenty / Years / Of These) (22).

On the next page, at the top, the supplement offers an image of a young woman dressed as a nun, wearing makeup, baring her breasts, and reclining to show one side of her flanks. In the article, Agustín remembers the censorship prevalent in 1968, when the government controlled not just television but all communication media and judged men's loyalty according to their hair length and pastimes: "En Guadalajara estaba prohibido el cabello largo en los hombres; ser joven, músico, intelectual, artista o estudiante era señal de enemistad con el gobierno y las instituciones" (In Guadalajara long hair on men was forbidden; to be young, a musician, an intellectual, an artist, or a student was a sign of animosity toward the government and its institutions). Agustín has short hair as he recounts that oppression some twenty years later, and we know that the diminished mystique of men's long hair did not ultimately require governmental suppression. Agustín's ultimate lack of contribution to change—I register the stasis in view of the overall results—nonetheless connotes an aura of youthful rebellion. That connotation draws on the surrounding irreverent and sexist materials on the newsprint that reviews his contribution. The appearance of the women, and not of the men, marks a kind of change, and yet the men end up exploiting the reputation of this largely spectral evolution.

Notwithstanding Agustín's status as a "young" and thus edgily rebellious writer supposedly representative of new freedoms—liberties of the sort that *sábado* would inherit and develop—he found success through men's networks. He published his first novel, the precocious *La tumba* (The tomb), written at age sixteen, thanks to Juan José Arreola (Bretón 6). It tests credulity to imagine that Arreola might have mustered the same enthusiasm for a bad girl narrative. The intuitive outcome of the gender reversal experiment warns me that a deliberately slangy and rebellious young woman protagonist written by a slang-using young woman might not have the same appeal for throwback cape-dressing Arreola. Such thematics from a young "new" woman might be seen as self-indulgent.

As he matured, Agustín returned the favor extended him by Arreola, and the "new" writer honored his peer network to the near-total exclusion of women. In an interview from 1979, he reviewed the lectures he gave in Iowa and Denver, which risked becoming "telephone directories" of contemporary creators, who it just so happens were all men authors. Agustín elaborated:

> Creo que hablé de lo principal que ha salido desde 65 para acá: Hablé de las novelas de Salvador Elizondo, posteriormente de la escuela de Elizondo; hablé también por supuesto de toda la obra de Vicente Leñero, mucho; hablé mucho de Jorge Portilla, de Ignacio Solares, de [Ignacio] Betancourt, de Hugo Hiriart, de Gerardo de la Torre, de René Avilés, de Luis Carrión, y también hasta donde yo conocía de gentes más jóvenes, como Juan Villoro por ejemplo. (Molina, "EU es el país" 112)

> I think I spoke about the main work that has come out since '65: I spoke about the novels by Salvador Elizondo, later about Elizondo's school; I also spoke of course about all of Vicente Leñero's work, a lot; I spoke a lot about Jorge Portilla, about Ignacio Solares, about [Ignacio] Betancourt, about Hugo Hiriart, about Gerardo

> de la Torre, about René Avilés, about Luis Carrión, and also as far as I knew about younger folks, like Juan Villoro for example.

Agustín added the name José Revueltas before concluding this all-male list (112). Although wading through these listings may have become tedious for the reader, it bears mentioning that Agustín's application for a grant from the Centro Mexicano de Escritores in 1966 referred to an autobiographical book series of the day that included only men writers. Forthcoming, he wrote, was

> mi *José Agustín*, autobiografía, en la serie Nuevos Escritores Mexicanos del Siglo XX Presentados por Sí Mismos, de Empresas Editoriales (en esta serie han aparecido ya las autobiografías de Gustavo Sainz, Salvador Elizondo y Tomás Mojarro, y aparecerán las de Juan García Ponce, Juan Vicente Melo, Vicente Leñero, José de la Colina, Sergio Pitol, Homero Aridjis, Carlos Monsiváis y Marco Antonio Montes de Oca). (CME Agustín Ramírez 178-2: 138)

> my *José Agustín*, autobiography, in the series of New Mexican Writers of the Twentieth Century Introduced by Themselves, by Empresas Editoriales (in this series autobiographies have already appeared by Gustavo Sainz, Salvador Elizondo and Tomás Mojarro, and forthcoming are those by Juan García Ponce, Juan Vicente Melo, Vicente Leñero, José de la Colina, Sergio Pitol, Homero Aridjis, Carlos Monsiváis and Marco Antonio Montes de Oca).

The all-male line up from the Nuevos Escritores autobiographies anticipates the later all-male Iconografía volumes. The assumptions behind the New Writer series prove so rich that I will return to its example in chapter 6 and the conclusion. For the next chapter, however, I want to register the possibility that perhaps if we do not look carefully enough at women writers nor speak often enough about them, neither do we hear much from fictional women characters. To make that point, the next chapter begins by bringing up the Bechdel test. (I predict an F!)

3

WHAT DOES GENIUS SWEAR BY?

Looking for Answers in the Bechdel Test, the Ladies of Polanco, Mi Góber Precioso, Mexican Supreme Court Cases, the Mexican National Anthem, and Swear Words, Featuring (Among Others) Juan Rulfo, José Emilio Pacheco, Roberto Vallarino, and Guillermo Fadanelli

El lugar de Rulfo es tan singular que debemos decir "aquí están los mejores escritores mexicanos y allá, mucho más allá, está Juan Rulfo."
—DAVID HUERTA

Nunca en mi vida he corregido, ni tachado, ni reescrito nada.
—SALVADOR NOVO

"¿Para eso te pago tanto?"—reclamó Azcárraga—. ¿Pa' que traigas el gafete en los huevos?" Se hizo un silencio aterrador. El Tigre había rugido. Pero el empleado pudo musitar una respuesta. Llevando su mano a la garganta, exclamó: "No, señor, ésos los traigo aquí."
—CLAUDIA FERNÁNDEZ AND ANDREW PAXMAN

The Bechdel test illustrates one reason why men authors can write sad love stories, of the sort found in *Pedro Páramo* and *Las batallas en el desierto*, without being accused of creating chick lit. In one of its variations, the Bechdel test examines whether a work of fiction features at least two women who talk to each other about something other than a man.[1] If we apply the Bechdel test to the most famous Mexican literature written by men, we see that women characters do not tend to speak to one another as often as they speak to men characters or as often as men characters speak to one another. José Emilio Pacheco's novella fails the Bechdel test entirely, and in fact defines Carlitos's anonymous mother largely by her archetypical conservative viewpoint and her unhappiness with Carlitos's father, who maintains a second, secret family. That second, also anonymous, partner suggests women's interchangeability.

In Juan Rulfo's *Pedro Páramo*, Susana San Juan speaks briefly to her domestic assistant Justina, who suffers her employer's anger meekly, at times in silence. In one fragment, Susana swears at her loyal worker: "No te irás de aquí, maldita y condenada Justina. No te irás a ninguna parte porque nunca encontrarás quien te quiera como yo" (Rulfo 2012, 145). ("You won't leave, you perverse and wicked Justina. You're not going anywhere, because you will never find anyone who loves you the way I do") (1994, 88). I suspect that this sort of master-servant conversation fails the Bechdel test in spirit, if not in technical terms. But Justina does, at times, speak; she pledges to remain by her boss's side: "No, no me iré, Susana. No me iré. Bien sabes que estoy aquí para cuidarte. No importa que me hagas renegar, te cuidaré siempre" (145). ("No, I won't leave, Susana. I won't leave. You know I will take care of you. Even though you make me swear that I won't, I will always take care of you") (89). The tangled dependencies of this relationship between Susana and Justina, along with the extremely complicated heterosexual romances that Pedro Páramo undertakes with Susana, Dolores, and many other women characters, suggest that Rulfo is more of a romantic relationship explorer, more of a chick lit writer, than people might have been trained to think.[2]

However, Rulfo's reputation as a high and hard creator probably benefits from Pedro Páramo's avoidance of richly intimate relationships among women. Not only do the women characters in *Pedro Páramo* tend to avoid speaking to one another, many of the wives among them can seem, if not exactly easy to replace, relatively interchangeable. The women seem complicit with the male privilege of infidelity. In the most famous instance of this sort of exchangeability, Rulfo's Dolores Preciado has a girlfriend, Eduviges Dyada, lie down beside Pedro Páramo on their wedding night; Pedro merely falls asleep and doesn't let on if he realizes the switch. Cristina Rivera Garza delights in this nearly consummated trick and views it as a mark of Rulfo's feminism: "El lector se enfrenta, pues, de entrada, a un héroe emasculado y a una mujer 'con ganas'" (The reader confronts, then, from the beginning, an emasculated hero and a woman "in the mood") (*Había mucha* 151). Of course, Eduviges does not find satisfaction on this score, and Pedro wakes up the next day to begin an unending streak of disrespectful treatment of his wife, Dolores, which in the end is not quite as subversive of the *chingón/chingada* (fucker/fucked) binary laid out by Octavio Paz in *El laberinto de la soledad* (*The Labyrinth of Solitude*) (1950) as Rivera Garza's view might propose.

A similar tolerance happens with *Las batallas en el desierto*, as critics examine aspects of popular culture and melodrama in the novella without dismissing the novella itself as a soft text. Carolyn Wolfenzon expertly discusses the influence of melodramatic Mexican cinema on Pacheco's text in the context of a defense of melodrama for its "ideales democratizadores" (democratizing ideals) (49). Ignacio Sánchez Prado reaches much the same conclusion; he views *Las batallas en el desierto*, rather than as an exercise in nostalgia, as a blueprint for developing social consciousness, which sets up possibilities for democracy ("Pacheco" 397). Cynthia Steele's analysis of Pacheco's performance of "democratic, anti-elitist" positioning, by way of his constant rewriting of his poetry and his taking on various forms of pseudonymous attribution, suggests that perhaps Sánchez Prado's assessment takes into account the understanding of Pacheco as humble (Steele 89). Steele is not alone in her opinion, of course. Ronald J. Friis agrees with her point, observing that Pacheco "goes to great lengths to avoid any association with the starlike persona many famous writers attain" (24).

Regardless of the information backing claims of a democratic plot, progressiveness in the novella seems less certain in a gender-sensitive reading.[3] After all, the reader can never be sure where the adult narrator Carlos stands in his assessment of his own status as a bystander to the bullying that the allegedly suicidal Mariana suffers mostly in silence. Mariana justifies Carlos's self-absorbed narrative without dominating it, in the same style of contained and thus convenient disability that affects Susana San Juan's mental state. Pedro Páramo's self-centeredness fuels his ineffective communication with her, and Susana does not really speak much to anyone. Rather than talk to one another, women characters' main function in these celebrated Mexican fictions by men authors seems to be to supply men protagonists with a source of regret, which makes the narratives emotionally poignant with men's pain.

Men's pain? you ask. *What can this be?* As Leslie Jamison's insightful meditation reminds us, *pain* largely coincides with understandings of women writers' themes, particularly if autobiographically inspired. The urge to distance oneself from the pained narrative associated with women creates what Jamison calls a "post-wounded" women's narrative, born of awareness "that 'woundedness' is overdone and overrated. They [the women writers] are wary of melodrama so they stay numb or clever instead" (198). This term *numb*, and more precisely *benumbed*, is the meaning of the prefix *narco-*. Numbness that does not appear to challenge a normative state of comfort fails as a sign of genius, but numbness achieved by breaking the law is cool. How did the numb become *clever*? Jamison does not answer the question. In addition to the various legal prohibitions in play, particularly drug prohibitions, which serve to energize the relevant binaries, I think the key here involves vulnerability. The toughest men characters convert pain into a less personal and less directly articulated experience, in line with the twentieth-century literary goal of showing rather than telling. Ironically, this urge to show rather than tell ends up supporting an aesthetic of extremely explicit art—which, perhaps because of the search for new taboos to break, can be imagined as somehow original.

That is to say, the difference between genius "male" pain and the clichéd "female" pain, as literary peers and critics sort the categories, must relate to those obscenity cases mentioned in the previous chapter as they define the "high and hard." The court-protected right to *genius* pain channels pain in macho style, through explicit language, frank sex, and crude violence, which—apparently—only someone outside the protected bubble of middle-class rules would dare call overly obvious. The more benumbed, even bewildering, the narrative, the cleverer and more challenging it seems thanks to *inarticulate* discourse. Coolness, depicted as a kind of numbed confusion that audiences can take for sophistication, turns otherwise clichéd *chick lit* pain into genius *dude lit* pain. The formula for cool is, in the end, so simple.

Just how hard can this art get? Modernist art inspired the torture of pro-Franco prisoners in Civil War Spain, as Erin Graff Zivin reminds us in her use of data from Slavoj Žižek's *Interrogating the Real* (2005). Graff Zivin does not contemplate gender dynamics in this analysis, although she does explain how modernist art was meant to torture the conservative fighters: "Taking as their inspiration Kandinsky and Klee, Buñuel and Dalí, secret torture chambers were constructed in Barcelona in 1938 that forced Nationalist prisoners to confront dizzying images of colors and shapes, cubes, lines, and spirals," and these visual tricks caused them, according to Žižek, "mental confusion and distress" (Graff Zivin 9). These shared aesthetics put to various ideological ends meant that the Spanish anarchists agreed with fears on the other end of the political spectrum—those of Hitler, for example—that abstract art wielded a destructive power. *This* is the sort of art that winds up in a court case (and later in a museum): when a man does the artwork and comes to the attention of other male authorities because of its edgy power. Never mind that women were there all along, though probably not in any significant number as torturers.[4]

So how original is this abstract art feared and respected by anarchists and Nazis alike? Does modernist work spring from men's modern genius? Apparently not. Caroline Levine reviews the curious case of an artwork named *Bird in Space* (1923–28), by the Romanian sculptor Constantin Brancusi, which faced a tax of 40 percent of its value when customs decided it was a table, household, kitchen, or hospital supply and not artwork (68). In order to establish the arty nature of the piece, its defenders affirmed that the avant-garde "actually repeated elements drawn from a venerable history"; after the authorities agreed with this lesson in art history, according to Levine, "what finally emerged in the courtroom proceedings was a definition of the avant-garde not as a rule-breaker but as a repetitive and self-regulating institution" (72). In essence, the customs court in 1927 had successfully pressured the art world to view itself "as a fellow institution, self-sufficient and coherent, with its own rules and guidelines, its own repetitions and its authorized ruptures from those patterns" (73; see also Stéphanie Giry). The original art found its formative context in conformity.

Or, for a measurement of dubious originality, take the case of the (impossible) love story that becomes canonical. The list of tormented love stories exacerbated by dysfunctional relationship skills includes the texts by Mexican men authors with the most familiar characters and titles: as I have said, Pedro Páramo and Susana San Juan from *Pedro Páramo* by Juan Rulfo, as well as Carlitos and Mariana from *Las batallas en el desierto* by José Emilio Pacheco, but also Carlota and Maximiliano in *Noticias del Imperio* by Fernando del Pasos, and even the Chingón (Fucker) and the Chingada (Fucked) in Paz's *El laberinto de la soledad*.[5] The latter example includes rough language from the characters' very names, which pushes us to think that Paz changes a clichéd story of dysfunctional love and family into high and hard thought.

Rough language conveys serious intention, and it appears even in *Las batallas en el desierto*, when Rosales and Carlitos exchange now-illegal hate speech on the schoolyard grounds. Rosales calls Carlitos and Jim a slang term for homosexuals (*putos*) after seeing them on the playground reading a book together. Carlitos responds to Rosales in kind: "Pásame a tu madre, pinche buey, y verás qué tan puto, indio pendejo" (Hand over your mother, fucking dipshit, and we'll see just how faggy [I am], bastard Indian) (24). *Say what? This novella is assigned school reading?* you ask. Well, yes. How else would one teach dude lit except by assigning it?

Examples of macho language from *Pedro Páramo* take into account the more stringent decency standards of the time, but still include Abundio's exclamatory "¡Váyase mucho al carajo!" (2012, 69) ("The hell you say!") (1994, 7). And Toribio Aldrete's assessment of Pedro Páramo, the *patrón* (boss), in the midst of a comment to Fulgor Sedano: "A usted ni quien le menoscabe lo hombre que es; pero me lleva la rejodida con ese hijo de la rechintola de su patrón" (2012, 95) ("There's no one can doubt your manhood, but I'm fuckin' well fed up with that shit-ass son of your *patrón*") (1994, 34). Because Pedro Páramo himself performs a smoother slide between the poles of clean-mouthed civilizado and foul-mouthed bárbaro, his language is less offensive than that of other men characters in the novel; for instance, he names only kidneys (*riñones*), rather than testicles, as the repository for adult male murderous energy during a conversation about his son (2012, 123).[6] Margaret Sayers Peden translates these *riñones* as "guts," which young Miguel supposedly still lacks, and she has Pedro add for good measure in English, "That [the act of murder] takes balls this big" (1994, 64). For the record, however, Pedro never said "balls." He speaks in a more civilized register that shields his barbarous actions, while the men around him recuperate a masculinity that they otherwise cede to Pedro's authority by using much coarser language.

I don't want to ignore the problem of homophobia and the concomitant prohibition of intimate homosocial bonds that encourage these plots. The terrible bullying evident in *Pedro Páramo* and *Las batallas en el desierto* creates a competitive and thus lonely social landscape, and so the protagonists turn to impossible heterosexual romantic ideals for consolation. Given the excessive expectations placed on the idealized women, naturally Pedro and Carlitos wind up disappointed. These common themes of bullying and unhappy heterosexual love suggest that *Las batallas en el desierto* has more in common with the hopeless politics of *Pedro Páramo* than Pacheco's plot might at first suggest. In fact, the three novels that most interest me in *Dude Lit* all have protagonists who suffer for impossible heterosexual love. Pedro Páramo pines for Susana San Juan; Pacheco's Carlitos longs for Mariana; and Fadanelli's Domingo, of the aptly titled *Mis mujeres muertas* (My dead women) (2012), mourns the loss of his partner, Sara K, as well as his mother.

How did celebrated literary protagonists wind up so lonely? you ask. *And why is isolation an admirable lesson?* The answer has to do with authenticity. Loneliness, admirable when experienced stoically by the rebel, indicates a kind of authentic masculinity, which is bolstered by bad language.

Melissa Mohr's *Holy Shit: A Brief History of Swearing* helps me to link obscenity to the impression of authenticity. Mohr explains the tendency to swear through notions of truth telling. Not just etymology but contemporary social science backs this theory. A 2005 study has social science researchers demonstrate that swearwords "actually do 'increase the believability of statements'" (Mohr 185). In greater detail, Mohr reviews the conclusions of an English-language study that found that "testimony that contained words such as *God damn it, shitty, fucking*, and *asshole* was perceived by test subjects to be more credible than the same testimony minus the swearwords" (185). Adding the historical background, Mohr claims that by the sixteenth and seventeenth centuries, obscene words came to "signify the truth of a statement," and toward the end of the nineteenth century "obscene words began to be used nonliterally, for their emotional charge alone; at this point they completed their transformation into swearwords" (176). In fiction and nonfiction, then, characters such as Rulfo's Pedro and Pacheco's Carlitos and Rosales, as well as the narrator of Paz's essay and people who give sworn testimony, infuse their words with greater *authenticity* by cursing. They also provoke a side effect of in-group intimacy without revealing the crucial vulnerabilities that deep friendship respects, which leaves them socially connected on a superficial level but isolated on a more profound one.

The idea that teamwork friendships gain strength from swearing come from Bronislaw Malinowski, who initially slotted swearword-laced speech into the category of *phatic language*. He viewed the phatic as an allegedly "primitive" custom of men in small-scale non-Western societies, although he notes that even complex civilizations allow men to cooperate by cursing. The phatic does not exchange information so much as build a relationship. Thus, according to Malinowski's racist and classist views, the phatic supplies even civilized men under conditions of duress key homosocial techniques, such as "the binding tissues of words which unites the crew of a ship in bad weather, the verbal concomitants of a company of soldiers in action, the technical language running parallel to some practical work or sporting pursuit" (298). This description makes the men's relationships seem more transactional than companionate.

Importantly, even when not profane, this rough language leads us back to the male body. Take Mohr's interpretation of the translated biblical term *thigh*, as more often than not actually referring to the penis "and/or" testicles (75). Thus, Mohr observes, in Genesis 24, when Abraham makes his servant swear an oath, he ensures the sincerity of this pledge through contact with his genitals: "'Put your hand under my thigh,' he tells the servant, 'and I will make you swear by the Lord, the God of heaven and earth'" (Mohr 73, 75). As Mohr observes, "This is a very old form of swearing, an oath not by God but by Abraham's powerful reproductive organs, which founded the tribe of Israel. Of course the servant has to swear by God as well—Abraham is hedging his bets" (75). Mohr links this early association of male genitalia and sincere promises with the English word *testify*, and although the latter term isn't derived directly from a Latin reference to "balls," "the words share a common ancestor in *testis*." I want to propose that one difference between *literatura rosa* (chick lit) and dude lit has to do with this masculine-favoring bias that interprets rule-setting oaths as of a piece with rule-breaking swearwords: both contain echoes of manly cooperation, of ballsy sincerity, and even of intellectual alacrity or *genius*, all tinged with a connotation of potentially threatening aggression.

Fadanelli gives a good example of phatic speech among Mexican males in *Al final del periférico* (At the end of the beltway) (2016). There, the adult contemporary narrator reminisces about his teenage speech in the 1960s and 1970s as meaningless gab, punctuated by phatic swear words and located within a group of male friends: "Y parloteábamos, ejercíamos el bla bla pendejo bla bla no mames bla bla bla no chingues bla bla bla, acerca de un suceso ocurrido en la mañana. Nadie nos escuchaba" (174). (And we chatted, we exercised the bla bla bla asshole bla bla no fucking way bla bla bla fuck me bla bla bla, about an event from that morning. No one listened to us.) Fadanelli indicates that not the content but the shared stylistics created community among the young men. These swearwords are hardly original for a reason: in an age that prohibits intimate male homosocial friendship and the display of men's sentimental vulnerability, profanity channels a forbidden familiarity.

To explore the existence of the lonely but networked male in a nonliterary Mexican context, I want to review a nonfiction case. When the news broke, this sample twenty-first-century dialogue shocked the nation with its insight regarding homosocial collusion, insight drawn not just from the content but also from the style. A leaked telephone conversation first published in *La Jornada*, in February 2006, recorded the phatic dealings of a businessperson known as the "king of denim" in Mexico, Kamel Nacif Borge, and the governor of the state of Puebla, Mario Marín Torres. The audio recording of this impolite conversation also appears in the documentary *Los demonios del Edén* (The devils of Eden) (2007). In the infamous telephone chat, Nacif Borge and Marín Torres plot against journalist Lydia Cacho, who threatened to expose a child-trafficking ring centered in Cancún. In the conversation meant to deal with this looming exposure, Nacif begins by professing affection for Governor Marín and then launches into more serious matters:

—Mi góber precioso.

—Mi héroe, chingao.

—No, tú eres el héroe de esta película, papá.

—Pues ya ayer le acabé de darle un pinche coscorrón a esta vieja cabrona [Cacho]. Le dije que aquí en Puebla se respeta la ley y no hay impunidad y quien comete un delito se llama delincuente. [. . .] Pero es que nos ha estado jode y jode, así que se lleve su coscorrón y que aprendan otros y otras.

—Ya sé, y es que estos cabrones siguen sacando mamadas y mamadas. (Petrich)

"My precious gov'ner."

"My hero, motherfo."

"No, you're the hero of this movie, Dad."

"Well, yesterday I ended up giving a fucking noogie to that old bitch [Cacho]. I told her that here in Puebla, we respect the law, and there is no more impunity, and he who commits a crime is called a delinquent. . . . But the problem is she's been fucking with us and fucking with us, so she needs to take her noogie and everyone—men and women—must learn."

"I know, and these bastards keep putting out bullshit and more bullshit."

For the outsider unfamiliar with the slang, this wording flirts with incoherence. Terms such as *chingao* (fuck), *cabrona* (bitch), and *pinche* (fucking) can be largely struck from the conversation without changing its hard data, which shows them to be used more for phatic purposes of relationship maintenance than for other communicative processes.

Interestingly, Marín Torres intertwines a politically correct, bureaucratic flourish in the midst of the rough speech. The phrasing of *otros y otras* (other men and other women) reflects inclusive speech of the sort that President Vicente Fox first stylized on a grand scale, to the initial amusement of the country. The politically correct rhetoric along with the distortion of literal meaning when the men agree that "impunity" does not exist and that Cacho is a "delinquent" supply almost hallucinatory rhetoric. Cacho's supposed crime is having reported Nacif's involvement in the sex trafficking of minors; Cacho's research led her to discover the trafficking of children as young as six (*Los demonios del Edén*). For Marín Torres and Nacif Borge, the repetitious nature of the phrases like *jode y jode* (fucking and fucking) and, in a later section of the conversation, *mamadas y mamadas* (blow jobs/stupidity and blow jobs/stupidity), signals that this instance of the macho talk of intimacy and trustworthiness based on implied primitive behavior hinges on hypersexuality.

Pablo Piccato's study *Honor in the Construction of the Mexican Public Sphere* meditates briefly on the legal conflict between Cacho and her harassers, "justified by libel laws that had not changed much since the nineteenth century" (259). In Piccato's summary, Nacif's plan to imprison Cacho, with the help of state authorities and the law, fell flat because of a counterpoising balance of sympathetic social relations. That is, the collusion against Cacho

> failed thanks to the intervention of female prison guards and to the reaction of a public that would no longer bear such abuses. The crimes of *difamación* [libel] and *calumnias* [slander] were finally abrogated in the Federal Penal Code in 2007, and Cacho was able to vindicate herself when the real reason for the judicial harassment carried out against her was identified—her courageous charges of pederasty against several powerful men. A man's reputation no longer justified the silencing of a serious journalist. (259; italics mine)

Although Piccato assures the reader that the libel laws have now changed, the language of reputation remains familiar. Marín Torres and Nacif seem engaged in mutual reinforcement of masculine honor, a most traditional concept, as they agree to solve the problem of silencing Cacho, and I suspect that in legal contexts this matter of honor remains tied to notions of male privilege. Certainly, the helplessness that Nacif displays to his male friends during the leaked conversations helps to keep this issue from devolving into a simplified allegory of good and evil. Amid his friends, Nacif also seems isolated.

Another conversation with Nacif, again published in *La Jornada* and available in the documentary *Los demonios del Edén*, occurs during the same period and changes the interlocutor to male friend and businessperson Hanna Naked Bayeh. Nacif is the first voice and complains,

> —Oye, qué feo me veo en la televisión ¿eh? Qué feo me veo.
> —(Risas.) ¿Ya te viste?

—Puta, viejo, pelón, hijo de puta.
"Hey, how ugly do I look on television, eh? I look so ugly."
(Laughter.) "You've seen yourself?"
"Shit [slut], old, bald, son of a bitch."

The words *puta* (slut) and *hijo de puta* (son of a bitch) function by way of the phatic and are used to seek solidarity with Naked. At the risk of sympathizing unduly with Nacif, I understand his predicament. For a real man, too much worry about appearances could push him out of the bárbaro cool category. His friend must laugh when Nacif suggests his pain, which neither man can take seriously without losing face. Yet the techniques for displaying oneself as a real man depend more on form than on substance. Nacif cannot ignore the fact that anyone watching television may judge him as old and ugly, hardly the image of a vigorous, seducing macho.

I should point out that phatic macho talk appears even in Inquisition records, a point demonstrated by the inquisitorial arrest in 1527 of Rodrigo Rengel, a former captain in Hernán Cortés's army. The historian Javier Villa-Flores describes Rengel at the time of detention, "now a syphilitic old man of eighty," as a man past his prime (37). Rengel's self-defense before the inquisitors' accusation that he encouraged others to blaspheme illustrates the colonial foundation on a claim to masculinity: "By God's body, he who doesn't blaspheme is not a man!" (qtd. in Villa-Flores 37). By the age of eighty, Rengel may not have been able to perform adequately the barbarous threat, and thus the civilized Inquisition officers could safely persecute him. Rengel's "abominable blasphemies" included the chestnut that Mary was not a virgin but a whore (37). The Inquisition took a dim view of this macho talk, at least from the elderly. Rengel, in an ironic parallel with Joan Wallach Scott's French feminists, has "only paradoxes to offer." A real man swears, although this barbarous performance is frowned upon in civilized quarters. Rengel is damned by God if he does blaspheme and damned by his peers if he doesn't. This paradox endures in secular culture, and to this day bureaucratic offices discourage the swearwords that, as Nacif's leaked conversations indicate, actually turn the gears behind the paperwork.

Another trait that contemporary bureaucracy—with its sometimes maddening processes for those who cannot skip the chain of command—shares with prosecutions of blasphemy is class-based discrimination. Talal Asad notes that in the English-language tradition, legal attentions dedicated to blasphemy under common law—the successor to medieval law—took into account the style and context of the blasphemy over content, which meant that "vulgar working-class speech was less protected than the polite speech of the middle and upper classes" (35).[7] The Inquisition case may also reflect an urge to constitute class difference, which hints that Nacif and Marín Torres play at an impolite speech that is not middle or upper class when they speak "authentically" to one another. Hardened bárbaros must not perform the high-class civilizado even if their financial and political power places them within the bounds of the latter.

It is hard to know where polite society gives way to prick behavior when it comes to sayings such as Villa-Flores's wry citation of the axiom "Quien bien jura, bien cree" (He who truly swears, truly believes) (148). Usually only the lower classes would be "caught" using the language associated with the working class. The fact that on the whole Mexicans tend to swear by—or perhaps better put, to establish their sincerity on—the male body, rather than by the Virgin, spoken in the most "vulgar" of terms, suggests what they really believe in: a connection between the civilized and the brutal that rests on manly impoliteness.

What happens when women attempt to appropriate this brute force? Rather than newspaper leaks, I turn now to amateur videos, shot with phone cameras and uploaded to YouTube. Examples of Mexican women behaving barbarously in public are searchable on YouTube via the key words "ladies of Polanco."[8] That sarcastic label applies to a pair of relatively wealthy Mexican women who on one unfortunate evening in Mexico City perform angry authority for the on-duty traffic authorities and the bystanders recording them with smart phones. More specifically, in distinctly lower-class language the "ladies" curse at uniformed police officers in the tony district of Polanco while their peers film them. One "lady" even hits an officer in the face, knocking off his hat. The dialogue proves too garbled to transcribe in full, but the phatic repetitive insults obviously seek to intimidate the officers and build community with would-be fellow aggressors, a tactic that fails because, it would seem, women do not build community in public this way. Instead, a scandal erupted when the video appeared on national news.

The phatic speech unfortunately deploys phrases such as "Pinche puto de mierda. Chinga tu madre pinche asalariado de mierda." (Fucking shitty fag. Fuck your mother, you shitty salaried man.)[9] The idea that earning a salary would place a man in a lower social category smacks of colonial hierarchies that protected a rentier class. In fact, in an almost perfectly colonial culmination of the logic, one of the ladies accuses the poorly paid police of creating the nation's problems: "Por putos como ustedes, a este puto país se lo está cargando la verga, cabrón" (Because of fags like you guys, this fag country is going to hell, bastard).

This last comment elicits murmurs from the bystanders off camera, who are perhaps as surprised as the YouTube viewer that officers who respond nonviolently and almost silently to the women's abuse are held at fault for Mexico's problems. Across additional videos of similar scenes, all ironically labeled with the term *ladies*, the daily abuses that well-to-do women exercise on subordinates fails to gain them any meaningful power among their peers. That is, when these ladies act like machos bárbaros and begin to curse and even strike their interlocutors, onlookers openly disapprove.

Another anecdote that features rough language wielded by a woman appears in L. M. Oliveira's *Árboles de largo invierno* (2016), where he summarizes the story of a human rights–violating shelter in the state of Michoacán. Oliveira quotes the report in the British newspaper the *Independent*, which printed testimony by a nineteen-year-old male. After he was raped by an administrator of the shelter, the victim complained to the main administrator, Rosa Verduzco (known as "Mamá Rosa"), who told him: "No te quejes, cabrón, si eres bien maricón" (Don't complain, bastard, you're a total fag) (169). The bárbaro language serves the purpose of intimidation and complicity in a woman's performance, even if she is not attempting to claim status as an artistic genius. The *Independent* reports on the impressive scale of Mamá Rosa's operations: a raid on a children's shelter on July 15, 2014, saw police rescue 6 babies, 154 girls, 278 boys, 50 women, 109 men, and 10 people whose ages could not be determined owing to their malnutrition (167). The difference between Mamá Rosa and a macho bárbaro may surface in her downfall. Verduzco ineffectively mixed a publicly performed soft and low theme of love for her fellow humans with a behind-the-scenes, high and hard usage of bárbaro projects backed by macho language.[10] It isn't surprising that Verduzco's effort at appropriation of the flip between poles eventually failed. The police proved unwilling to remain complicit with a woman's bárbaro activities, even under the guise of civilizada social contributions.

I can track another timely incursion of females into the realm of privileged male speech thanks to the novelist Luis Felipe Lomelí, who in a personal interview in 2015 imitated for my benefit the young women he hears in Baja California calling one another *verga* (cock):

> En Baja California, uno ve a las morritas de trece años diciéndose una a otra, "¿Y entonces qué verga, ¿qué vergas vamos a hacer, verga?" "No, pues no sé, verga." En el lenguaje el cuerpo femenino sigue estando fuera, pero ya en la participación en la violencia es tal cual.[11]

> In Baja California, you see the thirteen-year-old girls saying to each other, "Then what, dick, what are we going to do, dick?" "No, well, I don't know, dick." In the language, the female body is still excluded, but in participation in violence, they are on par.

Just in case this language is so strange you need a reinterpretation, Lomelí observes that young women gang members in Mexico have adopted the masculinist slang of calling one another a slang term for penis, like the young men do. However, in my wary analysis it remains doubtful that the young women can manage the same flip from the bárbaro to the civilizado act. Personal observation in the streets of Mexico City leads me to believe that women still cannot win superficial allegiances by swearing like the guys. The street scenes of verbal abuse of police officers that I have accidentally witnessed in recent years lead me to believe that onlookers are less likely to pull out their phone and film if a man is the aggressor. Furthermore, it isn't clear what advantage women gain by adopting a macho style of talk based not only in homophobia but also in misogyny.

Why don't the "ladies of Polanco" or Rosa Verduzco or the young women of Baja California develop their own codes for swearing? Perhaps the impediment has to do with teamwork. The very tradition of democracy balances peer acceptance and individual rights, as conformist maleness comes to stand for deserving individuality. The aforementioned historian Joan Wallach Scott famously studies early French feminism in order to articulate the centuries-old "discursive practices of democratic politics that have equated individuality with masculinity" (5).[12] One way for women to enter the equation is through a claim to trauma, or at least so argues Lauren Berlant. In addition to the "classic model" of democracy, in which each citizen's value is abstract and protected juridically by a cell of national identity regardless of that person's particularities, an alternative model in U.S. nineteenth-century court decisions grounded rights in traumatic experience (Berlant, "Subject" 53). After briefly reviewing the labor, feminist, and antiracist struggles that gave rise to the trauma claim, Berlant rightly points out that a lack of pain will not necessarily indicate the achievement of social justice. Men have not tended to use pain to claim rights, and this model of privileged numbness may explain one reason why most swearing women choose to play the same old game of macho talk, even if they continue to lose at it.

In a relevant decision, in 2013 the Mexican Supreme Court sought to put an end to homophobic phatic practice. Some years after the scandal of Nacif and Marín Torres's foul-mouthed collusion against Cacho, the court ruled that language such as *puñal* (fag) and *maricón* (queer) is illegal according to the principle of hate speech, despite the pervasive nature of these insults: "los términos 'maricones' y 'puñal,' por desgracia se encuentran fuertemente arraigados en el lenguaje cotidiano de la sociedad mexicana" (the terms "queers" and "fag," unfortunately are deeply rooted in the everyday language of Mexican society) (Zaldívar Lelo de Larrea, "Amparo directo" 52). Perhaps in a nod to these deep roots, then, the court's ruling took into account the age-old concept of honor. It seems almost incredible that such terminology, the terms *honor* and *honra*, vocabulary familiar from my studies of Spanish Golden Age theater, remains relevant. The formal curtailing of bad boy speech because of honor strikes me as so unexpected that I review the matter here in greater detail.

The Supreme Court's decision makes the first mention of the word *honor* on page 5, referencing a damaged reputation, and goes on to view the term through the concept of human dignity, as outlined in the first article of the Mexican Constitution (Zaldívar Lelo de Larrea, "Amparo directo" 24).[13] The court's decision reviews the importance of honor in international law in order to justify the reversal of an earlier finding in favor of free speech.[14] This new judgment finding hate speech unconstitutional uses bold print to emphasize the slide from moral qualities to professionalism; that is, the right to honor shelters the good reputation of a person in his "**cualidades morales y profesionales**" (moral and professional qualities) (26).[15] An attack on professional reputation is an attack on honor, which brings the latter term into more familiar contemporary language (26). Professionalism contradicts the long-standing Mexican habit of play, which employs teasing macho bárbaro puns.[16] Instead of turning to professional reputation as it is entangled with the patriarchal history of *honor*, I wonder if a less charged term might be *credit*.[17] In the second half of the twentieth century, credit became available to men and women and thus supplies a more feminist concept than that of honor, which remains tied up in a macho tradition. Whether *honor* or *credit*, women still face a challenge when it comes to wrangling swearwords, even in an academic context.

On this note, I return to Brené Brown's style of conversational scholarly prose, which in 2012 illustrated the conundrum for women academics who would take up penis projects. Brown reviews the advice she gave her research assistants:

> Whenever my graduate students were going to do interviews with men, I told them to prepare for three things; high school stories, sports metaphors, and the

> word *pussy*. If you're thinking that you can't believe I just wrote that, I get it. It's one of my least favorite words. But as a researcher, I know it's important to be honest about what emerged, and that word came up all of the time in the interviews. It didn't matter if the man was eighteen or eighty, if I asked, "What's the shame message?" the answer was "Don't be a pussy." (92)

Brown cites and then apologizes for, shall we say, *manhandling* the English language, all the while merely repeating a term that male interviewees use. This careful rhetoric suggests an update of the how-many-does-it-take-to-screw-in-a-lightbulb joke: How many words does it take for a woman scholar to use the word *pussy*? Just in case you missed it, I quote Brown again: "If you're thinking that you can't believe I just wrote that . . ." (That's eleven words for one mention of *pussy*!) Of course, men do not tend to apologize for swearing. Octavio Paz never blinks at offensive language in *El laberinto de la soledad*, a book of stereotypes that draws on Mexican swearwords, namely derivations of *chingar*, which academics bizarrely continue to cite in good faith. Paz's bad boy language allows him to interpret the macho bárbaro and pose himself as a macho civilizado. By contrast, and as I keep saying, bad boy language can undo a woman's reputation.

In light of the unoriginal nature of phatic language, it is surprising how much reputational stake high and hard men artists put into originality.[18] I have to wonder if the sciences suffer this battle over judgments of originality. Will scientists one day call warnings about climate change "so 1970s"? ("Yes, but now we *really* have a problem." "That's hardly new.") Jokes aside, the ongoing problems suggest that rather than prizing novelty, it might be helpful to get serious about what we think we already know.

It should now seem more obvious than ever that some entities, such as drugs, art, and even the penis itself, can be alternately viewed as hard or soft without actually undergoing a category switch, thanks to the macho bárbaro–macho civilizado loop. Yesterday's rule breaking helps to reset today's norm, which then facilitates the bárbaro act and another round of alleged innovation—not all that original, given the stability of the underlying mechanism, which itself does not operate in a steady progression toward increased liberal standards.[19] Critics, for all their fashionable disdain of the middle class, usually think within the boundaries of that middle. It is extraordinarily difficult for academics to think soberly about the middle class, because we begin the effort already familiar with fiction writers' critiques of middle-class ideals, critiques that are nevertheless usually written from within one section or another of that code of aspirations.

Bad boys, too, launch their critiques from an insider's understanding of the middle-class system, precisely to offend those values. What keeps the middle class from falling apart under all this disdain is not only men's hypocrisy but also women's image as glue, the stuck-in-the-past bourgeois. (The irony that women in pornographic guise are also used to mark the sophisticated cutting edge does not escape me.)

One way to see the bad boy's ultimate compliance is to contemplate the inefficacy of rebellion. Amitav Ghosh observes the failure of the literary novel to confront an issue like climate change; the topic is relegated to the less respected (the soft and low) genre of science fiction. Given this absent confrontation, Ghosh muses, "Is it possible that the arts and literature of this time will one day be remembered not for their daring, nor for the championing of freedom, but rather because of their complicity . . . ?" (121). From the perspective of *Dude Lit*, Ghosh poses an even more apropos question: "Could it be said that the 'stance of unyielding rage against the official order' that the artists and writers of this period adopted was actually, from the perspective of the Anthropocene, a form of collusion?" (121). This possible collusion would relate to literary critics' inability to think beyond the middle class, the class apparently not troubled by the slip between the macho civilizado and the macho bárbaro. To think beyond the middle class probably implies, on one level or another, an overthrow of the very category of "Mexican literature."

Lawrence James alludes to the difficulty of escaping middle-class presumptions and yet retaining current disciplinary boundaries when he writes that "some might say" the middle class created modern Britain in its own image (1). James reminds us that the pursuit of the "Liberal Arts" themselves is perhaps necessarily coached by middle-class aspirations (57). If literary critics can't think in the absence of nationality or the middle class, because these factors condition paid academic thought on literature in the same inescapable way that "drugs" always affect human cognition, the time has come to think still more carefully about the gendered assumptions that reinforce this intellectual authority.

If you think about the "nonliterary" questions that might seem out of place in academic interviews, some of these structures may become easier to see. In my interview with Guillermo Fadanelli, I tried to shake convention by beginning with the rumors about his alcohol and cocaine use (Hind, "Entrevista" 306). Fadanelli does his best to respect the norms that claim to ignore performance, and he waved off the importance of his drug consumption, while also playing up the theme of solitude. Personal habit is a hard topic to dismiss entirely, however, and near the end of the interview, Fadanelli returned to the subject of drugs and intertwined it with his performance of authorial duties during his last trip to Buenos Aires:

> [C]onecté cocaína en el Bosque de Palermo a unas cuadras del hotel donde me hospedaba. Eso fue una fortuna. [Se ríe.] Y cumplí con mis obligaciones. Tuve una charla con Enrique Serna y con Sergio González Rodríguez, ambos magníficos escritores. Pero en cuanto era posible volvía a mi cuarto de hotel. O a pasear. Me gusta pasear solo y observar. (325)

> I scored cocaine in the Bosque de Palermo a few blocks from the hotel where I was staying. That was a stroke of fortune. [He laughs.] And I fulfilled my obligations. I had a talk with Enrique Serna and Sergio González Rodríguez, both wonderful writers. But to the degree possible I kept returning to my hotel room. Or to take a walk. I like to walk alone and observe.

The slang for scoring illicit drugs, "connecting" in Spanish, followed by the mention of his men literary friends, suggests the social nature of buying an illicit product and of appearing on a book tour—all the while in the context of comments that downplay the significance of drug use and literary friendships. The social/antisocial natures of this loop recall the two poles of the macho act, the civilizado who cooperatively engages with colleagues and the bárbaro who indulges a destructive "hard" habit; here the two poles find a balancing point with the moments of intellectual seclusion. Indeed, without the two permissible modes of the civilizado and the bárbaro act, a moment of seclusion at a conference could be interpreted by unsympathetic peers as a "lack of personality."

By supporting the illicit drug trade, Fadanelli funds a network of profit that sooner or later depends on barbarous violence, which only strengthens the perceived need for the macho civilizado. The same self-interested loop might also be found in conflicts over pollution, another "great derangement," to repeat Ghosh's memorable phrasing. There is no better case for a civilizado lawmaker than a bárbaro's wish to contaminate. I am not, of course, claiming that no women are involved in debates on drug trafficking or environmental matters. I am instead looking at the balance of power and noting that, on the whole, these hypocrisies at present benefit men in leadership roles.

I cannot name a single Mexican woman writer who makes public her taste for cocaine. In fact, the gender-reversal experiment of imagining a cocaine-using

Mexican woman writer proves so difficult that the effort ends up helping me see the mechanism of the bad boy role. Because we are so accustomed to looking at male murderers—whether presidents like Juárez and Díaz or writers like Ireneo Paz and William Burroughs—and calling them "leaders" or "experts" of one sort or another, it becomes difficult to see that this process of legitimation makes men into winners while obscuring the very conditions of their success. The middle class and its polite rules coached by the "Liberal Arts" seem tepid and unoriginal in the absence of the bárbaro loop.

In a related thought, Mexican official culture almost never uses the phrase "veteran of war" and instead prefers "hero," as evident in the phrase *héroe de la patria* (national hero). As per Biron's formulation regarding "murder and masculinity," the freedom of the masculine to operate as if outside the law triggers the moments when that performance is most circumscribed by the law: no one is more a criminal than a murderer (17). No murderer can enjoy that ultimate criminal status without laws that prohibit the act, and most of the laws are written by precisely the gender that violates them. The hero language appears in the Mexican national anthem, which insists, at the end of the first stanza: "el cielo / un soldado en cada hijo te dio" (the heavens / gave you a soldier in every son); here, the overwhelmingly male act of murder is naturalized as part of the very fabric of nationalism. I am not the only one to comment on the masculinism of Mexican nationality. As Héctor Domínguez Ruvalcaba reminds us, "In the literature and cinema of the postrevolutionary period, representations of men form the core of the discourse that constructs the national imagery" (77). This masculinism of the post-Revolutionary period, which in historical labels has now transitioned to such terms as the neoliberal and the *alternancia*, continues today in what might be considered a very long twentieth century.

Stepping outside the discipline of literature, I borrow an idea from the social sciences and wonder about the power of *priming* here, a concept that refers to the effects that unconsciously absorbed information exerts on behavior.[20] While ongoing replication efforts question some social scientists' conclusions on priming (see Harris et al.), the concept nevertheless supplies a useful tool for literary analysis. Literary critics do not require peer-reviewed findings of statistical significance in order to appreciate the possible accuracy of a theory on the influence of language cues. Thus, as a literary critic I can freely hypothesize a "patriarchy effect," a theory impossible to test under the conditions in which we live—in the same way that a true test of a "nationalism effect" or "middle-class effect" or "capitalism effect" also seems highly unlikely to be conducted under laboratory conditions of controlled presence and absence. My hypothesized "patriarchy effect" conditions people to imagine that intellectual authority—upheld by the threat of violence—is gender-coded masculine and both terrifying (bárbaro) and reassuring (civilizado).

I contemplate something like a primed patriarchy effect in Guillermo Fadanelli's use of the lyrics of the national anthem to outrageous effect in the short story "Mi tía Clarita" (My Aunt Clarita), published in *El día que la vea la voy a matar* (The day I see her, I'm going to kill her) (1992). Fadanelli's story imagines a group of inmates in an asylum for people of both sexes; during the narrator's visit to his aunt, an inmate murders her. To avenge that already irreverent act, the other inmates immediately murder the murderer, then offer the bereaved narrator "el pene recién desprendido del asesino" (the murderer's recently detached penis) (40). In a contextual note, I should clarify that at the time of publication Fadanelli's bad boy daring shocked his audience, though today such brutality reflects the everyday Mexican political reality of narcoviolence.

In the conclusion of Fadanelli's early story, which—it bears emphasizing—is set within the guarded confines of sanctioned prescription drug use, the avenging inmates and the narrator sing the Mexican anthem in a moment of simultaneously crazed and fully institutionalized unity. The narrator realizes that his "deber moral" (moral obligation) is to postpone mourning for his aunt and celebrate, a decision that culminates in the communal performance of the anthem. The concluding lines of the story gain power from the reader's relationship with this song, embedded in a deep level of memory:

> Sin pudor alguno comencé a cantar: "Mexicanos al grito de guerra, el acero aprestad y el bridón, y retiemble en su centro la tierra, al sonoro rugir del cañón." Los enfermos al escuchar estrofas tan bellas dejaron de agredirse, abandonaron sus armas y vinieron hasta donde yo me encontraba; me miraban, sus ojos henchidos de esperanza y solidaridad, mientras cantaban al mismo tiempo que yo: "y retiemble en sus centros la tierra, al sonoro rugir al cañón." De pronto, sobrevino algo inesperado, algo que todavía hoy agradezco: la enferma atada a la columna por medio de la camisa de fuerza recuperó el conocimiento al escuchar aquellas notas y haciendo un admirable esfuerzo cantó con nosotros; su voz débil y aguda se escuchó hasta el último rincón del pabellón número doce: "Ciña ¡oh patria!, tus sienes de oliva, de la paz el arcángel divino, que en el cielo tu eterno destino, por el dedo de Dios se escribió." (41–42)

> Without any shame whatsoever, I began to sing: "Mexicans, to the cry of war, prepare the steel and the bridle, and may the earth tremble at its center at the resounding roar of the cannon." The sick people heard these beautiful stanzas, and they stopped attacking one another, they put down their weapons, and they came to where I was; they looked at me, their eyes filled with hope and solidarity, while they sang with me: "and may the earth tremble at its center at the resounding roar of the cannon!" Suddenly, there came something unexpected, something that even today I appreciate: upon hearing those notes the sick woman tied to a column with a straitjacket regained consciousness and in an admirable effort she sang with us; her weak and high-pitched voice could be heard in the farthest corner of pavilion number twelve: "Crown, oh Fatherland!, your brow with olive by the divine archangel of peace, for your eternal destiny was written by the finger of God in heaven."

The absurdity of proposing the curative powers of a violently themed national anthem speaks to the paradoxical bárbaro nature of civilized rituals; even within the estranged humor, Fadanelli gets at the savagery at the heart of the institutional here. War made the system, and a call to war can momentarily pacify the soldier "in every son" who exists in the patriarchal arrangement, including even the "sick woman" tied to a pillar. Through irony, Fadanelli's crude aesthetics stake the narrator's equivocal claim to moral autonomy outside the institutional framework with both a desire to reinstall the civilizado and, at the same time, a resignation to operating as one more of the benumbed bárbaros. This irony is a lonely business, as it makes solidarity and hope seem naïve.

Though I cannot test my theory of the patriarchy effect owing to the overwhelming homogeneity of the priming environment, I can observe the names celebrated in the public architecture that primes me to recognize men over women when choosing honorees. Not just buildings, bridges, streets, professorships, conference rooms, images on the national currency, and so forth, bear the names or likenesses of men, but so do literary prizes, which may affect the probability that the winners are also men. Note that Alfonso Reyes was the first president of the board of the Centro Mexicano de Escritores, which was founded in 1951 largely at the behest of a woman, the U.S. novelist Margaret Shedd. While there is no literary prize in honor of Shedd, Reyes gives his name to an award that former grantees of the Centro won, including Fernando del Paso (2013), José Emilio Pacheco (2004), Juan José Arreola (1995), Jorge Fernández Granados (1989), Alí Chumacero (1986), Rubén Bonifaz Nuño

(1984), and Carlos Fuentes (1979).[21] Some of these figures, in turn, have literary prizes named after them, in a self-replicating effect of the primed environment.

Aside from the Reyes prize, local, national, and international Spanish-language awards for particular literary genres bear the names of José Vasconcelos (essay), Jaime Sabines (poetry), Gilberto Owen (short story and poetry), José Rubén Romero (novel), Juan Ruiz de Alarcón (theater), Mariano Azuela (novel), Juan Rulfo (short story, novella, and photography), José Revueltas (novel and political essay), José Fuentes Mares (one national for theater and another regional for short story, novel, or poetry), Ramón López Velarde (poetry), José Pagés Llego (journalism), Xavier Villaurrutia (any genre), and, of course, many more men writers. A few prizes exist in honor of women authors, such as the Sor Juana, Elena Poniatowska, and Rosario Castellanos awards. The more important the prize, however, the more likely it carries a man's, rather than a woman's, name. Note the prestige of the Miguel de Cervantes prize from Spain, the Rómulo Gallegos prize from Venezuela, even the Nobel and the Pulitzer. Additionally, the awards for film—including self-referential ones—bear names associated with males, as in the case of the U.S. Oscar, the Spanish Goya, and the Mexican Ariel. Except in categories explicitly divided by gender—those of best lead and supporting actors—the winners of these "mixed gender" prizes are usually men, which poses the question whether superior talent, or the best assimilation to the primed idea of an intellectual, or better connectedness, or some combination of all three, scores the triumph.

There are even double-dippers into the same prize. That repetitive success hints that having won one prize sets one up to win another. In the Mexican case, a total of ten of the twenty-seven men who won both a grant from the Centro Mexicano de Escritores and the Xavier Villaurrutia prize actually won *two* grants from the first institution—a relatively unusual feat that among the women grantees only Elsa Cross and Luisa Josefina Hernández managed.[22] Because the archive for the Centro Mexicano de Escritores preserves a wealth of insider data, I can closely examine the trail forged by award winners connected to that institution. It seems significant that grant winners sometimes found success by proposing a text about previous grantees from the same institution. The Centro awarded Alejandro Toledo a grant (1991–92) for the purpose, among other plans, of writing a critical essay on former grant holder Fernando del Paso, tentatively titled "Historia y fantasía de Fernando del Paso" (Fernando del Paso's history and fantasy) (Domínguez Cuevas 387). Del Paso is a prestigious subject, it seems. Former Centro Mexicano de Escritores grant winner Óscar Mata won the National Essay Prize, named for José Revueltas, in 1991 for his book on Fernando del Paso, *Un océano de narraciones* (An ocean of narratives).

Octavio Paz also connotes prestige. Two other grant winners in the same system completed or at least proposed studies on the poet: in 1993 Fernando Vizcáino wrote *Biografía política de Octavio Paz; o, La razón ardiente* (Political biography of Octavio Paz; or, burning reason), and Pura López Colomé successfully pitched a plan for an essay on literature by Octavio Paz, as well as on former grantees José Emilio Pacheco and Marco Antonio Montes de Oca. After earning her grant, Inés Arredondo helped to build other reputations. She wrote about Jorge Cuesta, as did a second grantee from the Centro Mexicano de Escritores, Verónica Volkow, who published *El retrato de Jorge Cuesta* (Portrait of Jorge Cuesta) (2005).

But not all the tributes to Mexican men writers connected to the Centro Mexicano de Escritores are in book form. Centro grantee Héctor Manuel Perea curated Alfonso Reyes's legacy in the form of a traveling exhibit titled *Alfonso Reyes: El sendero entre la vida y la ficción* (The pathway between life and fiction), which circulated from 2006 to 2009 in Europe, Brazil, the United States, Cuba, and Monterrey, Mexico. In reverse chronological order, Miguel Sabido staged a theatrical version of Rulfo's story "Anacleto Morones" before he was accepted to the Centro Mexicano de Escritores. Similar to Sabido's promotion of Rulfo, Juan Tovar, a two-time winner of the prestigious year-long grants from the Centro Mexicano de Escritores, gave a dramatic reading of Rulfo's work *Los encuentros* (The encounters) (1992) and crafted theatrical adaptations of material by Carlos Fuentes and Octavio Paz (CME Tovar 3).[23] As Ronell would say, art becomes visible through this sort of "veiling," as criticism outlines the visible from the otherwise invisible work. Clearly, men writers choose to focus on other men writers, and sometimes women join them. A rule of thumb emerges from the practice of homage: the greatest status is marked by receiving praise from other men; conversely, a large proportion of women supporters indicates lower status. In other words, praise from the group associated with the soft and low indicates a reputation of the soft and low.

Men display some self-awareness regarding this friendship system. Note writer Roberto Vallarino Almada's comments to the press apropos an homage to him in 2001: "Es una cosa de cuates. [. . .] Yo estoy invitando a los participantes: son mis cuates" (It's a buddy thing. . . . I'm inviting the participants: they are my buddies) (M. Fernández). These buddies, as named in the press, consist of six men.[24] Vallarino's homage proves an interesting case, because despite his public comments, a surprising number of women participated in the event. The woman director of the venue Casa Lamm, Claudia Gómez Haro, may have had something to do with this extended guest list.[25] Perhaps more importantly, the large number of women guests, according to the rule of thumb that I have just put forth in this chapter, correctly predicts Vallarino's lower status in the literary world. Indeed, Vallarino is today a forgotten name, although in his heyday he enjoyed two grants from the Centro Mexicano de Escritores, in 1975 and 1977.

Vallarino's bárbaro act lacked an opposing performance of polish, and I find it instructive to review the foul-mouthed autonomy that he performed in the press for the 2001 homage:

> Yo llego al mundo siniestro de la literaturita mexicana y, obviamente, al no pertenecer a un grupo y como soy un salvaje, siempre me la he jugado por el lado de yo soy el último mohicano de la inteligencia y, quítense mariconcitos, y por eso no me ven bien en el medio. Pero yo soy así desde chiquito. La gente que me conoce desde niño, fuera de la literatura, te puede decir que de niño era un cabrón. (M. Fernández)

> I come to the sinister world of Mexican literature and, obviously, by not belonging to a group and since I am a wild man, I have always played it as the last Mohican of intelligence and, move over little fags, and for that reason they don't eye me favorably in the milieu. But I've been like that since I was a little kid. People who knew me as a child, outside of literature, can tell you that since childhood I was a bastard.

The unpolished language—"mariconcitos," "cabrón"—familiar from the analysis of phatic language suggests that Vallarino seeks to talk an insider's game here. His mistake is that the general public is not a group of insiders. The tactic did function for him in other circumstances. To wit, Vallarino got his start in the literary world with an appeal to Octavio Paz. In November 1974, he adapted and directed a reading of Paz's "Piedra de sol" for a performance in Mexico City. Some seven months later, in June 1975, Vallarino was awarded the Diana Moreno Toscano Prize in Lourdes Chumacero's gallery of contemporary art. The jury members who granted the award were a panel of five men: Octavio Paz, Rubén Bonifaz Nuño, Juan José Arreola, José Luis Martínez, and Héctor Azar (CME Vallarino Almada 23).

In his study of the Centro Mexicano de Escritores, Patrick Iber claims that Paz joined the advisory board for the institution "with the hope of counterbalancing those he considered 'professional Mexicanists'" by using his "influence to arrange for his 'cosmopolitan' younger counterparts to be given grants, including Fuentes, and, the previous year, Montes de Oca" (263).[26] Of course, men's admiration for Paz might have influenced the latter's benevolent opinion; that is, Paz may have approved of figures like Fuentes, Montes de Oca, and Vallarino because they admired him. At any rate, for all Vallarino's protests in 2001 about not belonging to any particular literary group, he consistently cultivates a crowd of admired *cuates* (buddies).

The contradiction of a networked loner interests me because it plays both sides: intimate knowledge of a canon and autonomous opinion. In an excellent summary of this tendency to proclaim both independence and connection, Vallarino's second grant proposal to the Centro Mexicano de Escritores competed in the essay category and pitched a book on twentieth-century Mexican poetry. His essay proposal squeezes thirteen men writers' names into one sentence. These figures

> abarcarían desde la obra de Efrén Rebolledo (el primer poeta mexicano que elabora el erotismo) pasando por el Ateneo de la juventud (Torri, Reyes, Vasconcelos) tocando el punto que a mi modo de ver es clave (el grupo de Contemporáneos, del que permanecen injustamente olvidados Cuesta, [Gilberto] Owen, [Bernardo] Ortiz de Montellano y [Enrique] González Rojo) hasta llegar a Octavio Paz, Alí Chumacero, Rubén Bonifaz Nuño, Marco Antonio Montes de Oca y José Emilio Pacheco. (CME Vallarino Almada 50)

> would stretch from Efrén Rebolledo's work (the first Mexican poet who develops eroticism), passing through the Athenaeum of Youth (Torri, Reyes, Vasconcelos) touching on the point that in my view is key (the group of Contemporáneos, from which remain unjustly forgotten Cuesta, [Gilberto] Owen, [Bernardo] Ortiz de Montellano and [Enrique] González Rojo) until we get to Octavio Paz, Alí Chumacero, Rubén Bonifaz Nuño, Marco Antonio Montes de Oca and José Emilio Pacheco.

The success of this application seems logical in view of the name dropping. The ultimate move as a loner expert occurs at the end, when Vallarino closes by citing himself from the first application that he turned in two years earlier

(51).[27] He misspells Mexico in the final line of the letter, writing "Méxuco" (51). It seems likely that an especially sympathetic reading of this application was necessary, and Vallarino's conformist assumptions regarding literary talent helped to smooth the way for peers to view Vallarino himself as competent.[28]

Probably because Vallarino's insistent view that men are the best writers brought him success, he hammered away with that opinion. His tactics exemplify a way to achieve artistic success under conditions of bureaucracy. In a brief essay of three paragraphs, written in June 1977 and titled "José Carlos Becerra y la obra inconclusa" (José Carlos Becerra and his unfinished work), Vallarino judges some of the best Mexican poets to be José Carlos Becerra, Ramón López Velarde, and Jorge Cuesta (CME Vallarino Almada 36). Vallarino presumes that the audience agrees with him and makes no effort to defend the three poets. Rather, their greatness emerges in terms of an alleged disinterest in originality that paradoxically somehow leads to it: "Su obra es un alto ejemplo de los grandes poetas, que nunca han pretendido decir nada nuevo y que por lo mismo lo han dicho" (Their work is a high example of the great poets, who have never intended to say anything new and thus have said it) (36). The contradictory idea that men writers need not worry about originality because it will simply emerge from them hints at the importance of the who's who in the audience. Peers may decide, ultimately, whom to read and cite as original talents. Perhaps even more significant here is the question of incentive for change. Why would men include women as more than token figures (if at all) on lists of the great writers if the all-male list is so mutually beneficial? I still don't have the answer to this question, except to suggest that being out of touch loses one audience even as it retains the insiders.

The chicken-and-egg relationship between connections and talent means that admiring the right people can lead to spending time with the right people; that personal contact can elevate the hanger-on to status as a potential member of the group, which is to say, status as the right person for a job or other opportunity. Knowing the correct boundaries to push comes with this insider status. The next chapter looks at the ever more explicit use of the penis in literature, which allows men to propose it, applaud it, and propose it again in a spiral of high and hard art taken for original.

4

THE PENIS IN LITERATURE (AND AT THE MOVIES)

The *Valer Verga* Paradox (with Brief Appearances by Federico Gamboa, Jorge Cuesta, Rubén Salazar Mallén, Christopher Domínguez Michael, Mario González Suárez, Daniel Sada, Guillermo Fadanelli, Carlos Velázquez, Carlos Reygadas, Gael García Bernal, Etcetera)

Lo que opinaba Carlos Monsiváis, Fuentes o Paz era tomado en cuenta por hombres poderosos, fueran éstos de izquierda o derecha. Yo me considero una especie de anacoreta. . . . Por lo demás, en la televisión ya casi no aparecen escritores.

—GUILLERMO FADANELLI

In Mexican movies, virility is a metonym for Mexicanness, and this manliness is literally larger than life.

—SERGIO DE LA MORA

The history of the penis in Mexican literature is so newly publishable that it seems more like news than literary history: a measure of our times. At the beginning of the twentieth century, a successful style suppressed offensive vocabulary. *Santa* (1903), by Federico Gamboa, found an enormous audience by featuring a sex worker who never employs the word *puta* (slut/whore) (Sandoval 9). Instead, protagonist Santa refers to herself with ellipses; she thinks of herself as "*una* . . ." (a . . .). Gamboa's readers must supply the term *puta*, aided by such contextual cues as the lament "¡No era mujer, no; era una . . . !" (She wasn't a woman, no; she was a . . . !) (Gamboa 26). *Santa* teases the "decent" reader by presenting shocking language through allusion. Remember that when Santa finds herself paralyzed upon entering the brothel for the first time, we must imagine the swearwords employed by the awakening women who speak rudely to the men who spent the night there:

> [L]a casa entera despertó, de manera rara, muy poco a poco, confundidos los cantos con las órdenes a gritos; las risas con los chancleteos sospechosos; [. . .] las carcajadas de hombres con una que otra insolencia, brutal, descarnada, ronca, que salía de una garganta femenina y hendía los aires impúdicamente . . . Santa escuchaba azorada, y su mismo azoramiento fue parte a que no siguiese el primer impulso de escapar y volverse, si no a su casa—porque ya era imposible—siquiera a otra parte donde no se dijesen aquellas cosas. (20)

> [T]he whole house woke up strangely, very slowly, mixing songs with shouted orders; laughter with suspect slapping slippers; . . . the guffaws of men over assorted brutal, stark, hoarse insolence that rose from a female throat and cut through the airs impudently . . . Santa listened, flustered, and her own embarrassment was part of the reason that she didn't follow her first impulse to flee and retrace her tracks, if not to her home—because that was now impossible—then to some other place where they didn't say those things.

The hypocritical word play requires the reader to have some idea of "those things" that Santa might be hearing, but in order to preserve the line between bárbaro and civilizado the audience must pretend, also, to find this material of daily life overly unfamiliar—and inappropriate—but still legible. The text hints at exactly the performance that a male novelist can pull off by crossing between the poles of rule breaker and rule enforcer. Gamboa knew, from personal experience, the sex-trade environment that he describes; his masculinist privilege allows a bárbaro to visit the brothel and then write a civilized text about it.[1]

Irwin's discussion of male sexuality in *Santa* reaches an interesting conclusion; though Santa can control her tongue, men apparently cannot control their penises (*Mexican Masculinities* 112). If the unruly penis is not to be entirely controlled, the literary implication is a possible touch of divinity. This transcendent quality carries through the twentieth century as it becomes acceptable to publish more explicit language. It is worth it to slow down this story and dwell on a period of censorship so that the degree of change is clear. In 1933, Jorge Cuesta's journal *Examen* published selections from the novel *Cariátide* (Caryatid) by

Rubén Salazar Mallén and famously ran afoul of official taste. Salazar Mallén's obscene language set off a censorship campaign concerned with public health, initiated by the journalist José Elguero, who sought to shut down the magazine (Monsiváis, "Jorge Cuesta" 13).

Amusingly, the text that once provoked a scandal for Salazar Mallén and his editor Cuesta proves, in hindsight, to be quite tame. Christopher Domínguez Michael observes,

> Sería difícil, hoy en día, que un estudiante de preparatoria localizara, a simple vista, esas "malas palabras" por las cuales se inculpaba a Cuesta, a *Examen* y a Salazar Mallén. Tras el escándalo público . . . el juez encargado de la instrucción la absolvió. Sin embargo, la revista no volvió a aparecer. ("Prólogo" 29–30)

> It would be difficult for a high school student today to find, at a glance, those "bad words" for which Cuesta, *Examen*, and Salazar Mallén were blamed. After the public scandal . . . the judge charged with the case acquitted it. However, the magazine did not reappear.

Domínguez Michael writes those observations in a prologue to the reprinting of two novellas by Salazar Mallén, published with a governmental subsidy in 2010. The government can safely invest money in Salazar Mallén because, rather than a still-threatening bad boy, his successors' rebellious behavior makes him look like a meek historical curiosity. Indeed, if the "bad words" are hard to spot in the first printed version, a rewritten version of the novel suppresses them entirely.

According to his own explanation, after Salazar Mallén burned the original manuscript for warmth, he rewrote *Cariátide*, cleaning up the language and changing the title to *Camaradas* (Comrades). Domínguez Michael views the changes as for the worse: "Esa reescritura, tal como la consideran todos quienes han comparado *Cariátide* con *Camaradas*, empobreció el texto" (That rewriting, just as everyone who has compared *Cariátide* with *Camaradas* thinks, impoverished the text) ("Prólogo" 31). Still, despite self-censorship, the legend of Salazar Mallén's bad boy act lives on, perhaps because of his hard-drinking performance.[2]

Poniatowska's narrator takes a dim view of Salazar Mallén in *Dos veces única* (Doubly unique) (2015), calling the controversial magazine text "un adelanto grosero de su novela, sin más valor que el de suscitar el escándalo" (a rude preview of his novel, with no more value than that of causing scandal) (172).

Poniatowska, contrary to Domínguez Michael, denies the *grosería*-as-genius equation that justifies the high and hard aesthetic, which for some readers only adds interest to Salazar Mallén's deed. Poniatowska plays the prude here, even if one layer removed thanks to her fiction narrator. This negative judgment effectively represents Salazar Mallén's best reputational interests: the reprimand functions as proof of bad boy status. The macho artists constitute their own biggest problem, but, sadly for Poniatowska's would-be stinging critique, being "big" is a good thing in the masculine world. It's a key component of a "genius" reputation, and only when Salazar Mallén backs down on his own does he become, for Domínguez Michael, even less talented than when being seen to rebel.

What happened to Cuesta, the editor responsible for publishing Salazar Mallén's early piece? Funny you should ask.

The poet and chemist Jorge Cuesta appeared in chapter 3 as the focus of studies by Arredondo and Volkow, and he also figures in Poniatowska's *Dos veces única*.[3] Women may find his example interesting, in part, because of the story of his self-castration. In her historical novel, Poniatowska has Cuesta separate from a dysfunctional marital relationship with Lupe Marín and then announce to friends that he has discovered the chemical equivalent of the fountain of youth, a substance probably known to the rest of the world as LSD (233). Poniatowska coolly describes the scene that brings institutionalization upon a hallucinatory Cuesta, at delusional odds with his own genitalia. She takes up the sequence of events just as a pair of visitors are leaving Cuesta:

> Cuando Víctor y Alicia terminan su visita, Jorge, solo y fuera de sí, toma un picahielo e intenta reventar sus testículos. Luis Arévalo lo encuentra tirado dentro de su propia sangre en la tina. Escandalizado, lo lleva a la clínica del doctor Lavista en Tlalpan. (234)

> When Víctor and Alicia end their visit, Jorge, alone and beside himself, takes an ice pick and tries to burst open his testicles. Luis Arévalo finds him lying in his own blood in the bathtub. Scandalized, he transports him to Dr. Lavista's clinic in Tlalpan.

Cuesta's self-inflicted damage imperiled his ability to interact with the rest of society. He never regained his status as a macho, which proved disastrous for his bid to reassert autonomy. Post-genital mutilation, the bureaucratic system no longer permitted the scientist poet to advocate successfully for himself, despite a well-reasoned letter he wrote to his doctor from institutional confinement, quoted in full in Poniatowska's novel. Even with the evidence of the correctly formatted letter, Cuesta could not make his way back to full status as an independent citizen; his doctors appear to have assumed that no competent intellectual would attack his own genitalia. After it became clear to Cuesta that he had lost the right to be a macho civilizado by way of the damage to his testicles, which ironically are associated at least as much with the ability to act as a full-fledged macho bárbaro, Cuesta committed suicide.[4]

The censorship of the twentieth century discouraged bad language in fiction, which leads to perhaps the most famous example of circumlocution: the infamous sex ed scene from Pacheco's *Las batallas en el desierto*, which has a priest interrogate the protagonist by asking leading questions. The questioning inadvertently teaches Carlitos to try to masturbate, though he proves too physically immature to ejaculate (43). Note the tactful language on the subject: "Llegué a mi casa con ganas de intentar los malos tactos y conseguir el derrame. No lo hice" (I arrived at my house with the urge to try the bad strokes and achieve the spillage. I did not do it) (44). In a less well-known example, because it was not adopted as required reading in Mexican classrooms, the same rather vague language appears in Ricardo Garibay's *Fiera infancia y otros años* (Beastly childhood and other years) (1982).[5] There, Garibay's autobiographically inspired narrator remembers that he did not touch his own skin while bathing: "Me enjabonaba con un estropajo muy áspero, me prohibía sentir mi piel con mis manos" (I soaped myself with a very coarse rag, I did not allow myself to feel my skin with my hands) (86). The penis emerges only implicitly in the next sentence, with the progression to masochism after masturbation: "Cuando adolescente ya me masturbaba, me golpeaba hasta aturdirme o romperme la nariz, como castigo" (By adolescence I masturbated, and I used to hit myself silly or break my own nose, as punishment).

Despite the reticence, Garibay's protagonist in *Fiera infancia y otros años* celebrates prohibited language. Here, he reviews the delights of the verbal crime of "culpas graves," or certain blasphemies:

> Las culpas graves eran las blasfemias, que se colaban hasta el cerebro como si alguien les abriera camino, como si yo las llamara con deleitosa malevolencia. [. . .] La Virgen es puta. Jesús es un impostor, se cuece en los infiernos. Dios es malvado, es injusto y está plagado de mentiras. Con la hostia se introduce en mi

> cuerpo un sexo femenino, abierto y chorreante. Debajo de la cama de mis padres habitan monstruos de colas largos, lisas, viscosas. (86)

> The serious faults were the blasphemies, which marched into my brain as if someone had paved the way for them, as if I had summoned them with delighted malevolence. . . . The Virgin is a slut. Jesus is an imposter, he's cooking in hell. God is evil, unjust, and plagued with lies. With the holy wafer, my body receives the feminine sex, open and dripping. Under my parents' bed live monsters with long tails, smooth, viscous.

To challenge God and other sacred figures through this sexualized language is to reinforce the privileges of the masculine body, intertwining a now profane, now sacred relationship between transcendence and male anatomy. This possible transcendence never goes anywhere, because for all his rebellion, Garibay's protagonist merely follows in his father's footsteps. By the time he enters high school, he has liberated himself from the hypocrisy of the Roman Catholic Church, as well as from his physically abusive father and his downtrodden religious mother, and yet this liberation of skipping church and cutting class for the pool hall and "barrios bajos" (low-class neighborhoods) only repeats the father's choices from a generation earlier: "Estoy haciendo exactamente lo mismo que hizo mi padre y en estos mismos lugares hace cincuenta años" (I'm doing exactly the same as my father did fifty years ago in these same places) (100). This dubious rebellion includes paying for sex, a move already familiar from the nearly eighty years older example of *Santa*. The reader of *Fiera infancia* learns that in the protagonist's youth, the movies cost almost as much as a sex worker; the former is one peso and one of the putas of San Juan de Letrán charged "de uno cincuenta a dos pesos el brinco" (from one fifty to two pesos a round) (119).

Men writers draw on experience not only as clients of sex workers but also as employees tangential to the industry, which allows them to waver once more from bárbaro to civilizado roles. In his autobiography, Garibay remembers leaving his job as an editor for that of inspector of cabarets, which introduced him on an insider basis to a system of generalized corruption (*Cómo se gana* 104). In 1967, Marco Antonio Montes de Oca published an early autobiography in which he remembers his short-lived time as an aide to sex workers in Acapulco: "Pasado algún tiempo, el dueño [del burdel] consideró mis servicios un tanto quiméricos pues consumía en cama de mis 'patronas' la mayor parte del día y la noche" (After a while, the [brothel] owner considered my services a bit chimerical, since

I spent the better part of the day and night in bed with the "boss ladies") (28). In the style of Fuentes's anecdote about Elizondo's violence toward the sex worker in *Myself with Others* (21), Montes de Oca finishes his anecdote abruptly, moving to the next topic without even changing paragraphs: "Luego trabajé repartiendo pan en una bicicleta con sidecar" (Later I worked delivering bread on a bicycle with a sidecar) (28).[6] The implicit message in these texts, that paying for sex is a less momentous experience for men than the degree of literary taboo might suggest, finds explicit articulation by the twenty-first century and upholds the possibility of playing both ends of the binary: the honor of rule breaking and the shame of rule following (and vice versa) helps to foist roles of both bárbaro and civilizado onto a bad boy intellectual.

Starting with the early example of *Santa*, talking about sex work was a hit theme, a tradition that continues. Xavier Velasco's autobiographically inspired novel *La edad de la punzada* (The age of pangs) (2012) repeats something close to Garibay's memories of the rites of maturity with the female sex worker, not to mention the rites of boyhood bullying, but with a key difference: by the twenty-first century, visiting a sex worker no longer presents a definitive gain in manhood. Velasco's protagonist notes that the price for a *brinco* (lay) has risen to 200 pesos (*La edad* 241). Inflation has hit everything but the real value, and protagonist Xavier loses his virginity in a degrading event: "Este palo no vale, me repito" (This fuck doesn't count, I repeat to myself) (243). Instead of becoming a proud nonvirgin, the expected "real man," Xavier laments the transition: "No sé qué me quitaron, pero igual me hace falta" (I don't know what they took from me, but all the same I miss it) (244).[7] By the twenty-first century, literary vocabulary for the penis has expanded vertiginously, and here Velasco differs from the models offered by the likes of Gamboa and Garibay. In Velasco's earlier autobiographical novel *Éste que ves* (This portrait you see) (2007), only a few alternative terms for the penis appear, such as *pipirrucho* and *pipiolera* (equivalents of *peepee*), and the narrator assures us that if only his Catholic upbringing had not made him renounce foul language, he would command much more of the slang (126). What happened between the mysterious circumlocutions of the 1980s and the disenchantment of the twenty-first century?

Before I answer that question with the penis literature of the 1990s, I want to acknowledge a different track in literary history. One alternative novella remains so because Antonio Alatorre chose not to publish it during his lifetime. Homosexual experience is only hinted at in his autobiographically influenced *La migraña* (The migraine) (2012). In the posthumously released text, Alatorre details the protagonist's struggle to accept his body in language that would not have been appropriate in the 1980s and yet seems tame today:

> Me aterra el tamaño de mi sexo, me aterra el vello, me aterra esa voz extraña que desconozco, aunque sale de mi laringe. ¿No he oído decir que ya va siendo hora de que me afeite lo muy poco que hay que afeitar en mi cara? Son cambios encadenados y fatales; no se pueden detener; no hay manera de echar marcha atrás, y esto los hace más aterradores: me arrastran, me estiran, me enronquecen y me desafinan la voz, me hacen salir espinillas que rezuman sueros ligeramente sanguinolentos, me llenan de pelos retorcidos las zonas secretas del vientre y el dulce recoveco de las axilas. ¡Y yo he estado disimulando, haciendo como si nada sucediera! (66–67)

> The size of my sex terrifies me; body hair terrifies me; this strange voice that I don't recognize terrifies me, even though it issues from my larynx. Haven't I heard that it's about time for me to shave the little that should be shaved on my face? These changes are linked and fatal; they can't be stopped; there is no way to turn back, and that makes them terrifying: they drag me, they stretch me, they make me hoarse and crack my voice, they give me pimples that ooze lightly bloody pus, they fill me with twisted hair in the secret zones of my belly and the sweet nook of my armpits. And I have been hiding, pretending that nothing is happening to me!

Here, it seems that Alatorre's church-trained civilizado narrator is afraid of the changes during puberty because they mark the publicly observable emergence of the adult bárbaro. In a lengthy second passage, Alatorre's protagonist finds a moment of solitude in his boys' school run by monks in order to undress alone and study himself in the mirror.[8] Alatorre avoids the word *penis* there, in the tradition of Gamboa, Garibay, and Pacheco, and employs *bulto vivo* (live lump).

Though the publicly heterosexual Alatorre did not dare publish this relatively decorous text, by the time of his death peers had already released homosocial and homosexual material that helps to recalibrate the national decorum. Salvador Novo's explicit *La estatua de sal* (*The Pillar of Salt*) (written in 1945, published in 2008), and later Elías Nandino's memories *Una vida no/velada* (An exposed life) (1986) and *Juntando mis pasos* (Gathering my steps) (2000), treat sexual relations and body parts much more openly than most other texts of their times manage. The heterosexual stories are different.

Where the narratives of homosexual relations tend to emphasize pleasurable choice and frankness, the narratives of heterosexual activity adopt more explicit language without emphasizing the same notion of free will. Mysticism rather than self-control seems to characterize the penis in Mexican literature of the 1990s. In other words, a counterbalance in heterosexual-themed fiction emerges with the loosening of censorship standards: when given free reign, the Mexican men writers of heterosexual plots seem to focus on the protagonist's bodily limitations. This is the civilized swing that creates tension with the bárbaro daring so as to play, still, high and hard.

Because the rebellions of the son end up following those of the father, I don't want to exaggerate the degree of difference among the decades. Still, it proves interesting to review Mario González Suárez's *De la infancia* (On infancy) (1998), which narrates the protagonist's hapless discovery of erections on the same day as his sister's birth, in a repeating time that has the main character experience a second chance at life in order to deal with his father's brutality. Despite the explicit language, ambiguity shades the episode:

> Todo lo descubrimos a fuerza de observar lo que se manifiesta en nuestro cuerpo y en el de otros. El día que nació [mi hermana] Ariadne descubrí que el apéndice que oficialmente sirve para orinar esconde maravillosos placeres e inimaginables culpas: se manda solo, irrumpe como un dios y me gobierna. La primera erección la tuve en el interior del vientre de mi madre. (145–46)

> We all discovered by force of observation what manifested itself in our body and in that of others. The day that [my sister] Ariadne was born I discovered that the appendage that officially served for urinating hid marvelous pleasures and unimaginable guilt: it ordered itself alone, erupting like a god, and it governed me. The first erection I had was inside my mother's womb.

It is not clear whether the protagonist discovers a penis per se or merely the concept of an erection. And while the first erection happened in the womb, the protagonist seems not to remember it until the erect penis erupts "like a god" during this boyhood moment.

The point about dubious free will before the imperious erection reappears in Christopher Domínguez Michael's enigmatic coming-of-age novel from the same decade, *William Pescador* (1997). There, the penis as an "insolent little god" (*diosecillo insolente*) supplies little hope of a pact for salvation (38). Owing to limited space, I edit Domínguez Michael's full two paragraphs on the subject of the discovery of the penis and its indomitable will:

> Trabé amistad con mi pene. Me sorprendió su indiferencia. Lo tocaba y lo estiraba. Guardaba el secreto que empecé a sondear aplicándole cremas para las manos o esas pociones aceitosas de mujer que Milde [su madre] había olvidado. Me saludó con una erección. Esperé esa caudalosa orina blanca que mi esmerada educación sexual me invitaba a presenciar. Aquella baba nunca apareció, y a cambio sufrí las consecuencias irritantes del jabón y de la espuma para afeitar en el prepucio.
>
> El pene crecía. Despertado de su sueño sin memoria por la masturbación infértil, se convirtió en una diosecillo insolente capaz de gobernarse a su capricho. [. . .] Y me resigné a traerlo colgando entre las piernas por el resto de mis días, sometido a sus cambiantes estados de ánimo, a su festiva y venérea existencia. (38)

> I forged a friendship with my penis. It surprised me with its indifference. I touched it and stretched it. It kept the secret that I began to sound out by applying hand lotion or those oily women's potions that Milde [his mother] had forgotten. It saluted me with an erection. I waited for that mighty white urine that my painstaking sexual education had invited me to witness. That spittle never appeared, and instead I suffered the irritating consequences of soap and shaving cream on my foreskin.
>
> The penis grew. Awoken after its sleep without memory by the infertile masturbation, it became an insolent little god capable of governing itself according to its whim. . . . And I resigned myself to wearing it hanging between my legs for the rest of my days, at the mercy of his changing moods, of its festive and venereal existence.

The loosely related incidents that constitute Domínguez Michael's novella suggest that a poetics of the inexplicable apply both to the penis and to indomitable Mexican history. That history seems to rest mainly on the economy, at least to judge from the conclusion. The novel ends with the opening of a gift from the boy's grandfather, the failed fictional Communist Party leader Bob Sachs. The legacy is not much of an heirloom if the boy wanted dignity: "Era la madre de las máscaras. Una hermosa nariz roja de payaso" (66). (It was the mother of all masks. A beautiful red clown nose.)[9] The symbol of a red clown nose as the legacy of the Communist Party based in Atlantic City hints at the entertaining illusions that underpin the quest for more equitable distribution of wealth, always related here in tandem with the theme of the ungovernable male body.

The coincidence that has both Domínguez Michael and González Suárez describe the penis in terms of "god" suggests a relationship of debt and credit that allows nothing to be misspent and nothing to be saved according to any sort of plan; the operations involved are not rational. The result is cyclical crisis that instead of bringing a new era repeats the father's failures—already predicted by the rebellions of authors from Gamboa and Salazar Mallén to Pacheco and Garibay. Rather than a demonstration of mastery, the transition to an adult body—along with awareness of participation in a larger social unit and tradition—brings subordination.

To analyze this hapless, even paradoxically *traditional*, rebellion, I turn once more to Caroline Levine's thoughts in *Forms* (2015), this time regarding Sophocles's power conundrum in *Antigone*. Levine articulates the dramatic impossibility of obeying, simultaneously, the multiple and contradictory forces that constitute patriarchy. "Far from consolidating the powerful hierarchies and showing how well they work in concert," she writes about the Greek play, "it is literally impossible to uphold the father, the gods, the king, masculinity, and the state all at once" (91). Tolerance for contradiction makes the system work, but not everyone elicits sympathy for a necessarily uneven performance. The terms of my study emphasize Antigone's sex. As a woman, Antigone is not allowed to slide from citizen to rebel and back again.[10] A gender-reversal experiment with *Antigone* might be a flop: *of course* a man must choose whom to obey and when to rebel. That decision is his privilege and burden. A woman protagonist adds interest to the story, and the drama of impossible subservience becomes a work of philosophy rather than one of suspenseful plotting because her choice is expected to remain within the confines of the civilized. Levine's overarching point remains compelling, even if *Antigone* would not be as effective with a male protagonist. She writes that power relations "are just as likely to unsettle one another, their collisions as liable to produce gains in odd places as to reinforce given structures of power" (109).

Indeed, the clashing, reversing, and reinforcing energy of the bárbaro-civilizado loop explains how men rebels in literature can end up like their fathers. The Mexican protagonists seem caught in a kind of M. C. Escher–like staircase that has the son moving up and away from his father's model, only to end up back there, generation after generation. All the rebellion does not actually, it would seem, produce a new way, *nor is it supposed to*—or at least that is what I suspect. The explicit turn in Mexican literature is not, in all likelihood, breaking new ground in a manner that might radically change the *forms* of Levine's study, because for the most part the point is not to argue the inferiority of men as compared to the binary opposition presented by women; the artistic point is that men are inferior when compared to an ideal of man not caught in a system of power that sometimes contradicts itself. Domínguez Michael's protagonist, in the ideal case, would receive something other than a clown nose as his inherited economic hope; that legacy does not argue for changing women's positions.

This pessimism finds maximum intensity in Guillermo Fadanelli's work. Along with figures like González Suárez and Domínguez Michael, Fadanelli resorts to explicit language—but more so. In his earliest phase of his bad boy oeuvre, which the reader will recognize from the short story "Mi tía Clarita" discussed in the previous chapter, Fadanelli created a self-denominated *literatura basura* (trash literature), named after the filmmaker John Waters's "trash cinema" example. Like Waters's explicit art, in Fadanelli's initial experiments from the early 1990s, the penis makes explicit and always rude appearances, as in the short story "Mi mamá me mima" (My mother spoils me) from *El día que la vea la voy a matar*.[11] There, the protagonist offends a friend's mother by showing her his penis. The rude narrative never relents, but neither does it go anywhere, and eventually the protagonist pointlessly teases the mother into a fight that has him urinate on her:

> El chorro fue preciso aunque no constante, pues tenía que evadir todos los objetos que la bruja me lanzaba para herirme.
>
> —¡Degenerado! ¡Hijo de la chingada!—me gritaba, plena de cólera. (29)

> The stream was precise although not constant, since I had to evade all the objects that the witch was throwing at me to hurt me.
>
> "Degenerate! Son of a bitch!" she shouted, suffused with rage.

This tale shows Fadanelli's underlying moralist bent, which rejects gentlemanly rules and the mother's self-absorbed authority, but leaves the reader mystified as to the precise nature of the implicit upstanding ethics claim.[12]

Against Novo's happy pleasure in sex in *La estatua de sal*, against Velasco's remorse, against González Suárez's and Domínguez Michael's near transcendence with the unruly, untamed will of the penis, Fadanelli explores male genitalia almost without an eye to the future. His protagonists are not only landlocked in urban spaces but time-locked in an endless present. Breaking the rules for his future-less protagonist is fine as long as it is not done profitably.

Logically then, as Fadanelli's protagonists age, they continue to fail to achieve greater control over their erections, their happiness, or their economic fortunes. For instance, Benito Torrentera, protagonist of *Lodo* (Mud) (2002), laments upon thinking of his new and much younger sex partner,

> Si fuera yo joven o atractivo, no dudo que gastaríamos la mayor parte del día en el sexo. A mi fealdad, además, debe aumentársele otro defecto: el pito se me para sólo una vez cada veinticuatro horas. No hay manera de hacerlo trabajar en horas intermedias. Sin duda poseo un pito dogmático, positivista. (115)

> If I were young or attractive, I don't doubt that we would spend the majority of every day having sex. Besides my ugliness, you have to add another defect: my dick only gets an erection once every twenty-four hours. There is no way to make it work during intermediate times. Doubtless I have a dogmatic, positivistic dick.

By the end of the novel, the "dogmatic dick" has nevertheless aided his entanglement with a much younger woman, whose deeds land the protagonist in jail, accused of a murder he did not commit (although he is not prosecuted for those he did do). The "dogma" of the dick does not include a reliable lesson; its positivism fails the protagonist in the same way that the philosophy failed Mexico. For the good intentions of positivism to work, the system would perhaps require some sort of purity, and Fadanelli's narrative world is based on corruption.

Lodo explores this corrupt system through the aesthetic of masculinist explicitness: "En México la justicia sólo se ejerce cuando una mano poderosa se agarra de su pito poderoso para lanzar un chorro de semen en la dirección deseada" (In Mexico justice only figures into things when a powerful man grabs hold of his powerful dick and launches a squirt of semen in the desired direction) (188). This statement echoes not only Fadanelli's own *literatura basura* but also decades-older precedent, such as a comment delivered by Salvador Novo to Emmanuel Carballo in an interview from 1965: "En México todo sucede acorde con la eyaculación espasmódica de la política" (In Mexico, everything happens according to the spasmodic ejaculation of politics) (Carballo, "Salvador Novo" 241). The fact that Novo said as much nearly forty years before Fadanelli's bad boy writing helps to register the tenor of Fadanelli's rebellion: it does not imagine change. Novo not only issues a similar metaphor for politics, he had already penned an explicit autobiography in 1945 without being able to publish it. Fifty-some years later, during a period of less intense censorship, the loop continued: for the civilizado to exist, the bárbaro must also. Fadanelli's pessimism and apparent disinterest in the sort of originality that claims complex interrogations of the literary tradition prepare us for exactly this continuation. And yet, he can also exploit a representation of "novel" impoliteness. I might term this phenomenon of expedient but false rebellion *static cling* for the inconsequential sparks it throws as it exercises a sticky force of attraction.

By the time he released the autobiographically inspired *Educar a los topos* (Educating the moles) (2006), Fadanelli was using the newly permitted obscene language to reject the would-be allegory of the military school cadets' gossip. That is, the male-genitalia-obsessed schoolboy language grates on Fadanelli's narrator: "Caray, todo en esta maldita escuela se concentraba en los testículos. Los cielos, la tierra, el fuego, la creación entera tenía su origen en esas bolas arrugadas" (Damn, everything in this damned school was concentrated on testicles. The heavens, earth, fire, and the whole of creation had its origin in those wrinkled balls) (147). Note the static cling here: the narrative never tires of the repetitive nature of obscenities, and even as critiques of themselves, they lead to nothing if not more of the same.

This clingy critique occurs when the all-male student body handles the absence of a murdered schoolmate, Aboitis (who himself is rumored to have been molesting room-and-board students), by way of a game of constantly spotting his penis, which stars everywhere as itself and thus leads only to itself, rather than to transcendence:

> La verga de Aboitis se hizo tan famosa como un cómico de televisión y se le encontraba en todas partes, en la olla de lentejas, dibujada en los pizarrones y en los mingitorios; varios mosquetones y carabinas fueron bautizados como las peligrosas vergas de Aboitis y en el comedor no faltaba quien la encontrara en su plato de lentejas o confundida con un hígado de pollo entre el arroz blanco. (158)

> Aboitis's dick became as famous as a comedian on television and was found everywhere, in the pot of lentils, drawn on the chalkboards and in the urinals; several

> muskets and carbines were baptized as Aboitis's dangerous dicks, and in the dining hall there was always someone who found it in his bowl of lentils or mixed in with a chicken liver in the white rice.

Language becomes a kind of nearly *material* reality here that symbolizes little. The above description concludes with an unattributed dialogue that wisecracks with patriotic humor, "Sólo falta que aparezca sobre un nopal, en lugar del águila" (The only thing left is for it to appear on the cactus, in place of the eagle) (158). The spectral play in *Educar a los topos* teases that while the literal is newly permissible, the penis displayed as itself serves no further end than that of a break with decorum, which ensures the stability of the system. Fadanelli's criticism never rises above this superficiality. That is, homophobia and misogyny drive the terms of Fadanelli's critique of masculinism, and thus the reader never abandons the terms of macho discourse.

Interestingly, just as Pacheco's *Las batallas en el desierto* landed on preuniversity assigned reading lists, Fadanelli's *Educar a los topos* and Christopher Domínguez Michael's *William Pescador* appeared in a single volume in the subsidized series 18 para los 18, published by the Fondo de Cultura Económica. Stories of the penis strike judges of pedagogical literature as appropriate tales in ways that stories of the vagina do not.[13] (For more on Fadanelli's pessimism, see chapter 7.)

Across the decades, the men writers echo one another in their various rebellions, and the boy protagonists fail to tame the penis and each time diverge less than they might like from their flawed fathers' examples. Slight differences exist, of course. Unlike the father figure in the novel *La edad de la punzada*, Velasco's autobiographical stand-in doesn't go to jail. Unlike the grandfather in *William Pescador*, Domínguez Michael's self-representation doesn't wear the clown nose. Unlike the father figure in *Educar a los topos*, and later the one in *Al final del periférico*, Fadanelli's fictional doubles do not found families of their own and instead adamantly defend their lack of interest in procreation. However, these rebellions are relatively small.

Before examining Fadanelli's successors in the explicit, I want to pause this exploration of penis literature and contemplate a parallel turn in Mexican film. By the twenty-first century, considering literary history alone proves too narrow, because the movies are entangled in the aesthetic. While most Mexican citizens will not have read the books I mention in the present study, many more will have seen at least one, if not both, of the watershed Mexican films *Amores perros* (*Love's a Bitch*) (dir. Alejandro González Iñárritu, 1999) and *Y tu mamá también*

(*And Your Mother Too*) (dir. Alfonso Cuarón, 2001). In some ways, these hit movies show nothing new. Explicit sex, violence, and language in *Amores perros* pave the way for the explicit sex and nudity in *Y tu mamá también*, a title that, if I may unveil some raw meaning, alludes to the boast "I fucked your mother too." The soundtrack of *Amores perros* includes a Mexican song with rap, "Sí señor," and thus harnesses the aura of rebellion connoted by the group Molotov, known as pioneers in lyrics that foreground swear words, as repeated ad nauseam in songs such as "Puto" (Fag) and "Chinga tu madre" (Fuck your mother).[14]

At the time, at least a few critics rejected the cinematic bad boy art as insufficiently thoughtful. Leonardo García Tsao rolled his eyes at the initial fans of *Y tu mamá también* and "el reflejo condicionado en el público de reír ante la sola mención de una grosería" (the conditioned reflex in the audience to laugh at the mere mention of a swearword). The shocked audience's delight at the new permissiveness largely reflected the thrill of cinematic novelty. But perhaps rightly, García Tsao perceives something less thrilling, less *freeing*, in the new explicitness; for instance, the end of *Y tu mamá también* struck him as tritely moralizing.[15] Still, *Y tu mamá también* entertained mainstream audiences with explicit shots of Gael García Bernal and Diego Luna swimming naked in a dirty pool, masturbating over a clean pool, and having a naked towel fight in a locker room (after Luna's character makes fun of the penis of García Bernal's character). This "real" nudity in the film may have tapped into a search that Sherry Turkle regards as a twenty-first-century obsession: "In our culture of simulation, the notion of authenticity is for us what sex was for the Victorians—threat and obsession, taboo and fascination" (4).[16] If there is one authentic aspect to cinematic make-believe, it is surely the male actor's genitalia.

Yet the authenticity of the penis, for feminists at least, may stake a dubious claim to "serious" art. I want to keep in mind García Tsao's skepticism as I state that across the twenty-first-century history of Mexican cinema, the explicitness only increases, with works such as *Batalla en el cielo* (*Battle in Heaven*) (2005), directed by bad boy auteur Carlos Reygadas, which begins and ends with a close-up of an actual blow job, much like a pornographic film might. Why do critics fail to view *Batalla en el cielo* as a kind of artlessness, given Reygadas's decision to film amateur actors having sex? To what degree do we, the critics, manufacture the civilizado out of the bárbaro by veiling explicit film and literature with academic discussions? Because Reygadas consistently fails at the box office, his work *needs* critical veilings in order to find an audience. Do critics comply with this aesthetic because they want to be edgy bárbaros themselves and thus make their civilized contribution more "hard hitting"?[17] Where do we draw the line between pornographic "real-life" explicitness and intellectually engaging "make-believe" explicitness?[18] The binary is tricky, as one seems to flip into the other, at least for male artists.

The switch happens in spontaneous language and not just curated images. For instance, the celebrated Mexican actor Gael García Bernal, whose fast rise to fame benefited from the explicit films *Amores perros* and *Y tu mamá también*, uses masculinist language to couch his political views. García Bernal comments, in the March 2012 issue of *Gatopardo*, that President Felipe Calderón's effort to use what my peer humanists might call "penis-brained militarism" to control the narcoviolence failed: "Calderón hizo algo de mal tino: no nos incluyó más que como espectadores a la hora que decidió que se iba a agarrar a vergazos contra estos güeyes" (Calderón did something misguided: he did not include us as more than spectators when he decided that he was going to give these dudes a penis whipping) (Osorno, "¿Qué trama?" 101).[19] The *vergazo*, or "penis whipping"—a term derived from the dried bull penis that colonial subjects fashioned into a cow whip—ultimately fails as a satisfactory spectator sport, because there is no reliable safety in a large-scale state of exception. There are no protected sidelines. The use of the masculinist language to talk about masculinism, moreover, may fail to achieve the change—despite the rhetorical claim to authenticity.[20]

Exiting the movie theater and Mexico's celebrity opinions on politics, I return to literature and authors. The latter struggle to outdo nonfictional "penis-brained" violence in the twenty-first century in order to shock the audience. A good example of the turn to the crude appears with Carlos Velázquez, Fadanelli's much less prolific successor. Two of his explicit stories collected in *La marrana negra de la literatura rosa* (The black sow of pink literature) (2010) are setups to an amputated penis. In Velázquez's "El club de las vestidas embarazadas" (The pregnant cross-dressers' club) protagonist Damián somehow ends up joining a self-help club for male cross-dressers who pretend that they are pregnant and during each meeting take care of full-grown men who pretend that they are infants. By the end of this odd narrative, Damián-as-hobbyist-baby lacks a penis: "Damián se desnudó. Su miembro había desaparecido. Se había hecho amputar el pene" (117). (Damián undressed. His member had disappeared. He had had them amputate his penis.) Where Velázquez differs from his predecessors is in his use of a straightforward and choppy language that may discourage a symbolic reading.

Another castration takes place in the Velázquez story "La jota de Bergerac" (Bergerac's fag), again from the *La marrana negra de la literatura rosa*, in which the eponymous Mexican transvestite concludes an act of oral sex with spontaneous revenge on her unfaithful lover. The story concludes with "la jota de Bergerac" taking a self-assigned leadership position in a gay pride parade:

> Protagónica, se incorporó al frente de la marcha. En primer lugar, en el sitio que debía ocupar la reina del Miss Gay. Quiso sacar una pañoleta de su bolsa pero sólo encontró el miembro de Wilmar. No le importó, igual lo agitó en lo alto. Y marchó. Con la frente levantada y el pene ensangrentado en la mano marchó. (65)

> In the protagonist's role, she joined the front of the march. At the head, in the spot that should be occupied by the winning queen Miss Gay. She wanted to take out a kerchief from her bag but only found Wilmar's member. She didn't care, just waved it overhead instead. And she marched. With forehead raised and the bloody penis in hand, she marched.

Velázquez's stories, however far-fetched, seem to beg for a reading of the penis on a literal level, in a way that supposes would-be collective agreement on a commonsensical, dictionary-anchored set of meanings. The resignation of ambitious literary complication, such as allegory, stages a claim to the literal that, I want to restate in no uncertain terms, ultimately fails to break new ground.

Daniel Sada, a more aesthetically ambitious and prolific writer than his fellow northern Mexican Velázquez, reflects upon the narcoviolent context with a torturous castration in the novel *El lenguaje del juego* (The language of the game) (2012). Given the horribly familiar context of the narco, the reader knows from the first threat that character Íñigo is going to lose his penis, regardless of the hope in the tormentor's bargaining ploy: "¡Si no me dices ahora la verdad, te cortaré tu pito junto con tus dos güevos!" (If you don't tell me the truth now, I will cut off your dick together with your two balls!) (172). Truth will not save Íñigo, and I cite the already known progression of the scene in order to show the relative flat-footedness of the writing:

> Filoso movimiento concluyente. Sangre a raudales: ¡claro!, siendo que el miembro estaba ya en el suelo: como un gusano yerto, retorcido. Faltaban los testículos y en eso el hombre torturado externó un alarido que quizá provenía desde el fondo de su alma.

—¡¡¡Mátenme de una vez!!! . . . ¡¡¡Ya no quiero sufrir!!!
¿Qué le iban a hacer caso? (172)

Sharp conclusive movement. Blood streaming: of course! Since the member was already on the ground: like a stiff, twisted worm. The testicles still missing, and in the middle of that the tortured man let out a cry that perhaps came from the bottom of his soul.

"Kill me at once!!! . . . I don't want to suffer anymore!!!

Thinking they would pay attention?

Should this depiction of brutality be counted in the prestigious category that I set up in earlier chapters, that of the high and hard? Sada's use of an urgently familiar sociopolitical crisis continues the resignation before brutality that we saw in Fadanelli's flirtation with failed allegory, with the castration of a dead man's penis in an asylum in "Mi tía Clarita" and a dead boy's member in *Educar a los topos*, and in Velázquez's flatly signifying amputations.[21] The effort to strip out from literature the quality of the literary, that is, to eliminate the "drugs" and the hallucination, seems paradoxical. Appropriately, a contradiction emerges in this literature of penectomy. The castrated characters are "worthless," or, in a similar meaning, "worth dick," almost literal illustrations of the phrase *valer verga* (to be worth dick; to be fucked). Through a maneuver of strange synecdoche, the castrated characters seem to *valer verga* by becoming wholly the part that they no longer have. Men as finally worthless, like the women who are initially worthless, have only paradoxes to suffer in this postcensorship, democratic imaginary.

Do women writers handle these topics of amputation and violence differently?

Certainly, they seem to meditate more explicitly on the issues of metaphor, in the case of Cristina Rivera Garza's castration text *La muerte me da* (Death gives me) (2007), and on the matter of the crude description, as in the translated story by Valeria Luiselli, "Because Night Has Fallen and the Barbarians Have Not Come." There, a female protagonist tires of the *narco*, or the benumbed, by complaining about the explicitness in the news:

The headline reads: FIVE DECAPITATED BODIES FOUND IN TRUNK OF CAR: HEADS MISSING.

Must we say so much? So directly? Say things to the window—that's what our father used to do when he was giving us an order. (142)

Luiselli rejects the plainspoken and thus may also reject the flatly explicit techniques of Velázquez and Sada. In a surprising similarity, given the explicit nature of castration, Rivera Garza's academically inclined novel *La muerte me da* also favors implied and not explicit meanings, at least to the extent that she largely eliminates the gore and shock value that writers like Velázquez and Sada employ—and she ducks the foul-mouthed humor that Fadanelli always manages to insert into his offenses.

But surely one *Mexican woman writer somewhere imitates the macho bad boy style*, you must be thinking.

Possibly such an example appears in *Cuaderno ideal* (Ideal notebook) (2014), where Brenda Lozano's narrator comments on a twenty-four-year-old sociology student at the UNAM, a dead ringer for Marcel Proust, who delivers the following profanity-laced diatribe, though the knowledge that a woman wrote the passage may tempt the reader to interpret the rough talk as not just an unadorned, uncomplicated borrowing of the style but an ironic one. Notably, this example lacks violence: "Pues leí los siete tomos de *En busca del tiempo perdido*. Las siete madres esas, las leí completas. ¿Y sabes qué? Proust es una verga. Es bien chingón el güey. [. . .] Además el güey le dedica un chingo de páginas a todo. Dedica como cincuenta páginas para describir cualquier mamada. Es un chingón ese Proust" (165–66). (Well I read the seven volumes of *In Search of Lost Time*. All seven pieces of the shit, I read them in full. And you know what? Proust is a dick. He is a motherfucker, that dude. . . . Besides, the dude devotes a shitload of pages to everything. He devotes like fifty pages to describe any bullshitty idea. He's a motherfucker, that Proust.)[22] In Lozano's prose, the familiar binary emerges. Proust is *de la verga*, or high and hard, and *of the dick*, because he avoids writing *puras mamadas*, or the soft and low.[23] The "dick tongue," *la lengua de la verga*—so bad it's good—marks the macho cool of the entitled, nontraumatized citizen. This inversion of the would-be insult of calling someone a penis points out that the true offense lies in *not* calling people dicks, because if they aren't dicks, then maybe they aren't *real* men, or worthy individuals with rights to autonomous choice.[24] If men aren't dicks, they will—note yet again the lack of choice—be worth dick, or *valer verga*. If they are dicks, perhaps that penis will revert to some transcendent value, and the men characters will be worth more than nothing.

Overall, women writers such as Luiselli, Rivera Garza, and Lozano, even when they meditate on our violent times, seem to include more cerebral or ironic elements than the men writers I cited. They perhaps understand that the flip from bárbaro to civilizado will not be as easy for women writers, and thus they temper their risks from the beginning with a complaint (Luiselli), deeper intellectual explorations (Rivera Garza), or a hint of ironic citation (Lozano). Owing to performative differences, women writers do not have quite the same relationship to the double meaning of "swearing" (*jurar*) as both telling the truth under oath and using prohibited language.

I wonder if it might be better to reimagine the vocabulary. In the next chapter, I offer something like variety by switching terms from *bárbaro* to *bully*.

PART II

REBELLION AS CONFORMITY

5

BULLYING GAMES

Playing Spot the Token, Locate the Female Helpmate, and Bystanding (with Analysis of Juan Rulfo's *Pedro Páramo*, José Emilio Pacheco's *Las batallas en el desierto*, and the Examples of Juan José Arreola, Juan Rulfo, Antonio Montes de Oca, Sergio Galindo, Ricardo Garibay, Carlos Monsiváis, and More)

Eres inferior a mí; me pelas el prepucio.

—HÉCTOR MANJARREZ, EXPLANATION OF THE INSULT *ME LA PELAS*

En las últimas semanas [Fox] me ha llamado chaparro, mariquita, me ha dicho la vestida, me ha dicho mandilón.

—FRANCISCO LABASTIDA, SPEAKING TO THE PRESS DURING THE 2000 PRESIDENTIAL CAMPAIGN

Where do bullies come from? In linguistic terms, at least, we have an answer: friends. According to Shaheen Shariff's reading of the *Oxford English Dictionary*, the *bully* evolves from *boel*, of the 1600s, meaning "lover of either sex"—for example, one's "beloved" or "brother" (24). By the late 1800s, the term was associated with gangs and referred to tyranny and violence (25). The reverse trajectory occurs in Mexican Spanish, where the former insult *buey* (ox) has transformed into the everyday term *güey* (dude). In addition to defusing the insult, Spanish speakers have adopted the English-language terms *bully* and *bullying*. The Google Ngram Viewer indicates historic high numbers in Spanish for use of the term *bullying* at the turn of the twenty-first century. These patterns that transform *buey* to *güey* and *boel* to *bully* suggest how difficult it is to keep love separate from negative emotions. In the present chapter, I want to think about the dynamics of bullying, mainly through *Las batallas en el desierto* and *Pedro Páramo.*

The U.S. legal scholar Nancy Dowd writes sympathetically of the price that men pay for gender privilege; she links boyhood to manhood through the traumatic experience of bullying: "Men are disproportionately the victims of violence at the hands of other men, violence that is integral to the very definition of masculinity. This definition of what it means to be a man begins with boys and is defined most strongly by bullying" (3). Although Nancy Dowd's book concerns the U.S. cradle-to-grave justice system, her words could apply to Mexico: "A trip to the courthouse in virtually any jurisdiction would suggest that this is a system of boy justice, because of the disproportionately male pattern of children in the system. This pattern links to the similar pattern in the adult criminal justice system" (8).

The reprieves from the bullying violence in prestigious Mexican narrative are few, although as Rulfo's *Pedro Páramo* and Pacheco's *Las batallas en el desierto* show, bullies and victims mean to find respite in romance. Pedro Páramo has Susana's father killed so that he might move her into his house; Carlitos finds out that, at least as gossip has it, Mariana committed suicide to escape the bullying of a politically powerful Mexican lover. Remember in chapter 3 I mentioned Carlitos's foul-mouthed fistfight with Rosales? *Better a bully than the bullied or a bystander be*, Pacheco's protagonist seems to decide. In *Educar a los topos* Fadanelli covers related territory: the unhappy protagonist survives military school by making sure that he is no one else's "slave." Among Fadanelli's adult characters, childhood experiences with bullying may feed into the men's customs of hard drinking and weak friendships.

Because Pacheco delves most deeply into childhood bullying relationships, I want to linger on the pervasive theme of coercion in *Las batallas en el desierto.* The adult Carlos remembers, possibly with pride, his long-ago impartial reaction to his classmates' taunts against the Mexican American student Jim. Instead of joining in, Carlos recalls that he claimed, with high-minded remove, "No soy su juez" (I'm not his judge) (20). The same reserved attitude surfaces with Carlos's memory of the bullying that the Mexican Japanese student Toru endured: "Pensaba en lo que sentiría yo, único mexicano en una escuela de Tokio; y lo que sufriría Toru" (I thought about what I would feel, the only Mexican in a school in Tokyo; and what Toru must suffer) (15). Carlos appears to believe that as a boy he managed to behave in principled fashion. However, a pragmatic manual for educators and parents, *The Bully, the Bullied, and the Bystander*, by Barbara Coloroso, points out that no bystander is innocent; the witness fulfills a key role in the triangular bullying relationship.[1] Although Pacheco's text accepts the "naturalness" of bystander remove, it portrays its permanent trauma. Years after the playground battles, when former classmate Rosales runs into Carlitos, the former ruefully brings up the long-ago bullying of Jim: "Pobre Jim, pobre cuate, tanto que lo fregamos en la escuela. De verdad me arrepiento" (63). (Poor Jim, poor guy, how we used to mess with him at school. Truly I regret it.) Bullying makes an island of every boy, and this lack of functional community on the school grounds probably affects adult behavior.[2]

The "battles in the desert" that reach from the playground to the presidency seem to condition the uncivil society that operates top-down from President Miguel Alemán. If bullying could be successfully eliminated from schools, adult relationships might be unrecognizable. At least, Pacheco's novella provides no clues as to how the resulting humans of a bully-free playground would relate to one another. The saturation of bullying relationships in *Las batallas en el desierto* means that every important character in Pacheco's text seems caught in a bullying triangle. The humiliations to which Carlitos's mother and father subject each other repeat with their eldest son, Héctor, whose violent behavior as a politically active student has him trampling others' human rights and, as a jealous brother, helping drive his sister's boyfriend to suicide. By the end of the novella, Héctor has become the hypocritical conservative head of his own family and may be poised to repeat the father's infidelities. Aside from suicide, there doesn't seem to be an escape from bullying.

Importantly, Coloroso's warnings about children changing roles are echoed in fictional depictions: at first, the binary between the tormented and the tormentor is not especially rigid.[3] True to the social pattern, then, Pacheco's characters experiment with roles only to congeal into one dominant mode. Despite having tried out the bullying role, Carlos seems to become a permanent bystander; by contrast, after enduring betrayals such as that of his two-timing father, Héctor seems likely to have congealed into a bully. Though we never see her as a bully and we only know of her adult behaviors, Mariana must have played the bystander to her lover's abuses of power before taking on the role of victim. The final rigidification of roles conditions the "desert" of adulthood that the children practice during recess. Of special importance is Carlitos's role as bystander, which predicts his alienated distance as an adult narrator from his parents and every other authority mentioned in the text. Carlos narrates without a living sense of the present: he never mentions his adult sexual orientation, his profession, or adult friends. The adoption of a kind of relentless bystander remove matters, because Pacheco is insinuating that radical autonomy and a cool contempt for self and others ensue from Carlitos's youthful experience with humiliation. The strongest lesson occurs after seeking connection and falling in love with the mother of his friend Jim. After a jealous Jim informs the adults of the would-be affair, Carlitos learns the bullying lesson of isolation: he has a public falling out with his parents and his friends, is expelled from school, and is banished to a bedroom alone, no longer sharing a room with a sister. Carlos explains the ostracisms succinctly: "me declararon perverso" (they labeled me perverted) (54).

On this point, Pacheco surely exaggerates the bullying cycle. It violates verisimilitude to think that, amid Carlitos's utterly collapsed childhood social network, he scorned overtures of support from Héctor, who was pleased to share with his little brother the black sheep label. Pacheco makes a point by way of hyperbole: the process of growing up for twentieth-century males demands that boys distance themselves from friends and confidants—an observation supported by school counselor Niobe Way, who writes that boys' alienation is a response to pressure on men to achieve autonomy rather than to sustain relationships (63).[4] Way finds evidence for this pressure in popular U.S. parenting guides that reflect new concern about boys and their social predicament. Although I second Way's complaint that the idea of "maturity" for men is excessively linked to self-sufficiency, there may be more to the story, such as a profitable reputation advantage.

The triangular and isolating relationship of the bully, the bullied, and the bystander feeds into an arrangement that responds to the phrase *structural violence*. That term appears in David Graeber's meditation on bureaucracy, *The Utopia of Rules*, where he discusses "structures that could only be created and maintained by the threat of violence, even if in their ordinary, day-to-day workings, no actual physical violence need take place" (59). This nonviolent social architecture explains widespread bullying. Within the systemic structural violence, the bullied and the bystanders are experts at their roles, which is why no violence need occur for citizens to continue to obey. Perhaps what proves most interesting about this agreement is our inability to think beyond it. Graeber blames our poor imagination on the invisibility of the problem, due to its structural ubiquity: "The main reason that we're unable to notice [these structures], I think, is that the legacy of violence has twisted everything around us" (*Debt* 385).

This inherited pattern of violence no doubt benefits from the image of a genius as a rule breaker who balances knowing the correct techniques and having the right acquaintances with maintaining a certain air of independence from coercion, friendships, and other insinuated influences that would dilute autonomy.

For example, note Pacheco's contemporary Ricardo Garibay and his bullying life performance; aggressive and somewhat isolating relationships with most of his nearly all-male network developed from his activities as a harsh critic of others, a hard drinker, and even at one point an amateur boxer—as he claims in his autobiography *Cómo se gana la vida* (How one earns a living) (1992, 149). Still, Garibay benefited from key friendships, such as that of Agustín Yáñez, who arranged for Garibay's grant at the Centro Mexicano de Escritores, thanks to a review that Garibay had written of Yáñez's novel *Al filo del agua* (*The Edge of the Storm*) (1947) (Garibay, *Cómo se gana* 126). These congenial but nonintimate homosocial alliances provide a certain peace among bullies, although the more powerful the individual man, the more superficial his acquaintanceships become. Garibay also enjoyed friendly, though not intimate, exchanges with the presidents Gustavo Díaz Ordaz and Luis Echeverría. Garibay recalls:

> Andando el 69 y luego el 70, aprendí a estimar a Díaz Ordaz. Lo veía con frecuencia en Los Pinos, iba yo a sus giras por la República. Nunca hubo cercanía o intimidad, las que puede permitir el jefe de Estado, como después sí ocurrió con Echeverría. (277)[5]

> Heading into '69 and then '70, I learned to value Díaz Ordaz. I often saw him in Los Pinos [the Mexican presidential residence]; I went on his tours of the country. There was never closeness or intimacy, of the sort that a head of State can allow, as later there was with Echeverría.

Historically, select Mexican men writers enjoyed a kind of power almost exclusively reserved for the men who ran the country. Some of the men writers actually were politicians themselves, like Vasconcelos, Yáñez, and Sabines. The topic of tepid friendships that connect the most powerful men in a dense network leads me to reckon with the performance of *cool*, a quality that depends on ironical distance and thus—strangely—opposes the sincere tone that public servants traditionally must adopt. I have mentioned the term *cool* in previous chapters, and here I want to explore it carefully. The cool solves the problem of authenticity; a bully and a bystander can perform expert taste by refusing easy sincerity, because the latter facilitates too much vulnerability. Recall the sort of aesthetic inferiority that, in chapter 2, I cited Paz as identifying in López Velarde's poetry, which made Paz the cool expert in command of abstract knowledge against López Velarde's warmly naïve beliefs and operations in the concrete.

Cool writers ought to be the antithesis of well-meaning politicians, according to John Street, who claims that the cool captures "exactly what politicians are not, indeed what they cannot afford to be" (369). It may be that as twentieth-century writers continuously emphasized the cool performance, they posed themselves out of a double career as a politician.[6] Other scholars examine this imbrication of bullies as cool and dutiful characters as stodgily sincere.

Historian Peter Stearns argues convincingly that the cool seems to encourage isolation and an intense relationship with material objects rather than people. He adds, "Cool has become an emotional mantle, sheltering the whole personality from embarrassing excess" (*American Cool* 1).[7] The "emotional mantle" seems especially useful to the performance of masculinity and its claims of invulnerability. To change disciplines without switching topics, I cite evolutionary biologist Geoffrey Miller musing on the same point: "How dull it would be if we realized that . . . 'masculinity' often means little more than low agreeableness, low conscientiousness, and high stability" (185).[8] These three elements of masculinity, that is, low agreeableness, low conscientiousness, and high stability, constitute the cool and help to explain the twinned reputations of the bárbaro and civilizado, or the bully and high-minded bystander roles. These seemingly opposed categories use the same qualities.

I speculate that one reason for the fall from public power in the twenty-first century that Mexican men writers seem to have experienced may center on the incompatibility of the cool critiques and bad boy rebellions and the more reliably sincere performance needed from political commentators and leaders. However, Trump's successful campaign hints that insincere celebrities may now be able to run as antiestablishment figures. A new political role may appear for writers now that the cool has appeared in roles that traditionally required greater sincerity and less self-absorption. Or, it may be that politicians after Trump will lose power as would-be intellectual authorities, just as writers have. Certainly, when Mexican writers also held appointed and elected political office, they sometimes failed to promote writing the way some would have liked.

Marco Antonio Montes de Oca, in an interview from 1994, found fault with artists' double duties as bureaucrats because they failed to push hard enough for artists' benefits.[9] He named men such as Carlos Pellicer, Carlos Chávez, José Vasconcelos, Andrés Henestrosa, and Salvador Novo as examples of creators who worked as competent administrators, but failed to defend the artistic "guild" (*gremio*), despite their moral authority and deep knowledge of the cause (Morales, "Marco Antonio").[10] In the late twentieth century, it was apparently difficult to defend the rebel bárbaro while upholding the public-service civilizado. As I have said, across the decades the combination of official governmental responsibilities and the rebel role of writer ended up in a loss of prestige for the latter. Given the highly visible levels of corruption in Mexican and U.S. governments in the twenty-first century, it can be confusing as to why literary critics are so dismayed by the larger degree of distance that exists now between authors and politicians. While it may be upsetting that authors no longer legitimize corrupt state activity, the shift—however small—might also be seen as an opportunity to exercise a different kind of critique.

Turning from the rough example of Garibay, other performances of these formulaic qualities of low agreeableness, low conscientiousness, and high stability appear with Juan Rulfo and Carlos Monsiváis. For the first case, the researcher will not need to read many interviews before finding that Rulfo attracted negative descriptors from acquaintances, such as *hosco* (gruff).[11] Felipe García Beraza writes that after twenty-eight years of friendship, during their mutual employment at the Centro Mexicano de Escritores, Rulfo turned chatty only when it came to talking about his real and imagined illnesses (136). Martha Domínguez Cuevas tells much the same story; her friendship with Rulfo through the context of the Centro Mexicano de Escritores showed her: "Frente a los desconocidos [Rulfo] era un hombre callado, introvertido. Sin embargo, cuando hablaba con él por teléfono eran conversaciones interminables. Hablaba horas, bajito, casi murmurando" (qtd. in "En sólo dos años"). (In front of strangers he [Rulfo] was a quiet, introverted man. However, when he would speak on the phone the conversations were interminable. He would talk for hours, hushed, almost murmuring.) Such an alternately gruff and self-involved performance by a woman writer might not have been accepted, although Rulfo seemed able to switch tracks and perform as an outgoing humorist when not speaking on the record. Of course, for every statement about Rulfo's humor, at least one exists about his bad moods. One interviewer reports that in four hours of conversation, Rulfo laughed only once, as he joked about his age: "Tengo 58 entrados a 60. Ja. Ja. Ja." (I'm fifty-eight going on sixty. Ha. Ha. Ha.) In that conversation, Rulfo confessed to feeling unhappiness and knowing only two moods, depressed and normal: "Y la mayor parte del tiempo estoy deprimido" (And most of the time I'm depressed) (Reyes Razo 6).[12]

Monsiváis's example demonstrates that heterosexuality is not necessary in the claim to cool writerly masculinity. His recurring moments of aloofness surely would not have allowed him to hold political office in any sustained manner, and his example of trusted authority proves interesting for that reason. In evidence of Monsiváis's gruffness, or low agreeability, Juan Villoro suggests that the writer's sometimes cold personal habits found a counterbalance in a warmer public persona. I witnessed only Monsiváis's chill during one of his twenty-first-century guest visits to the University of California, Irvine, where he spent as little time as possible with the crowd gathered to hear him and he delivered his lecture without smiling.[13]

To add to Villoro's and my testimony, I can cite Elena Poniatowska's multiple anecdotes that portray her good friend Monsiváis as emotionally remote. For instance, after his death in 2010, Poniatowska told the press about the falsetto that Monsiváis would adopt to play the role of his "Aunt María." According to Poniatowska, she called Monsiváis one morning only to have "Aunt María" declare her nephew absent because of a trip to Spain. That afternoon, according to Poniatowska, she came across Monsiváis sitting as usual in the VIPS restaurant on Tlalpan Avenue, near his house in Mexico City. As Poniatowska recounts the perplexing conversation:

> —¿No que habías ido a España?
> —Ya vine. ("*Monsi* después")
>
> "Didn't you go to Spain?"
> "I came back."

Perhaps the most important point about Monsiváis's cool performance is that, in general, women cannot get away with this type of antisocial, masculine behavior *and* build a necessary network of mutually admiring intellectuals. In sociologist Eva Illouz's summation, normative femininity is *cheerful*—the opposite of much of Monsiváis's behavior as his peers recall it (*Cold Intimacies* 3). Only men like Monsiváis can skip the cheerful act without falling out of the network of peers. Like the misogynist/feminist performance that Fadanelli presented in a previous chapter, Monsiváis manages to earn the respect of feminists, thanks to networking skills, without sticking to all the polite rules.

Monsiváis's performance is so emblematic of the cool that it merits closer study. Note that Poniatowska strikes an ambivalent note during a press conference for the anthology of Monsiváis's feminist texts, titled *Misógino feminista* (Misogynous feminist) (2013). There, Poniatowska stated that Monsiváis's very disinterest in his women followers sparked their enthusiasm: "entre más rechazadas, más lo seguimos" (the more rejected, the more we followed him) (Gámez).[14] She repeats this observation in *Sansimonsi* (2013), her children's book about Monsiváis, in which he is represented as a cat and loves only other cats: "Muchos hombres y muchas mujeres decimos: 'Quién fuera gato para que Sansimonsi me quisiera'" (Many men and many women tell ourselves: "Oh to be a cat so that Sansimonsi would love me").[15] When writing for children, it might do to explain Monsiváis as an animal, but for adults, perhaps the better explanation is that Monsiváis performs, to an extreme, a middle-class masculinity. In point of fact, Monsiváis did not drink, curse, or indulge in conspicuous consumption, beyond his collections of books and artful paraphernalia, which leads to the question of how a rule breaker in a bad mood can be seen as cool when he is also upholding middle-class values.[16]

Stephen Bunker's definition of the Mexican cultural (and not just economic) middle class helps me to define their values as hinging on four qualities: "thrift, sobriety, hygiene, and punctuality" (109). These qualities probably influenced Monsiváis's Mexico City neighborhood of Portales to forgive him for his otherwise corrupting ties to powerful people, including the billionaire Carlos Slim.[17] It is commonly known that Slim donated the building in which Monsiváis's museum is housed (Osorno, *Slim* 201). The proper performance of certain middle-class qualities as they intersect with masculinity may allow men writers to be seen to engage in friendships with all sorts of bullies without necessarily tainting themselves.

Further evidence of Monsiváis's impolite image, despite his contact with entities like Televisa, which fellow moralist Fadanelli, for one, refuses to go near, emerges in Monsiváis's perhaps unexpected representation in the Mexico City Wax Museum, a debut given generous coverage in 2013 in the Mexico City newspapers. According to one report, Monsiváis's statue, standing next to that of Octavio Paz, gains authenticity by sporting the deceased writer's own thick-framed glasses and denim jacket, donated by the family (Bucio, "Eternizan" 19).[18] When I visited the wax museum on February 28, 2016, the statue of Paz reported in the article was nowhere to be found. In fact, the only other writer honored with a likeness at the museum was Gabriel García Márquez. Compared to the carefully coiffed women from show business in the museum, Monsiváis's image strikes a remarkable contrast: his thinning Einstein-like white hair, plain denim jacket and beige pants, and solid, square glasses would never work for a female aspirant, although such speculation remains intuitive, since no woman writer save Sor Juana Inés de la Cruz appears there.[19] Certainly, Monsiváis's ordinary "plain-clothes" style, preserved even in effigy, shows that men do not have to dress with virtuoso skill in order to become spectacular attractions. Monsiváis's apparent lack of vanity—a sign of low conscientiousness in an area in which, for intellectuals at least, high conscientiousness can seem frivolous—ends up supporting a middle-class performance of thrift and hygiene, and it may even uphold the masculine act of an emotional containment in stability and disagreeableness. Monsiváis never let fame go to his head, according to the public impression, implicitly supported by the fact that he did not carefully style his hair.

While cases such as the grumpy manner Monsiváis displayed among friends illustrate a legitimate performance of masculinity, it would be incorrect to imagine that this macho act operates in isolation of the feminine. Even though his wax double stands alone in the museum, Monsiváis—the "feminist misogynist"—relied on a team of female helpers. For example, he enjoyed a productive partnership with his mother, Esther Monsiváis, in part because apparently he never learned to type. When the aged Esther could no longer provide crucial typing skills for her son, he replaced her assistance with that of his cousin, Beatriz Sánchez.[20] The latter claims that she never tired of transposing Monsiváis's handwritten texts to the computer. In contrast, I cannot name an example of a Mexican woman writer who always relied on someone else to type her texts. If such a woman exists, she is probably not particularly prolific, unlike Monsiváis and his constant stream of paid production.

But I must tread lightly on the topic of Monsiváis and the bad mood and boring clothes, because I know some women academics near to my heart will not be happy to read any sort of negative view of "Monsi." Reasons for that loyalty materialize in an image from the press surrounding the publication of *Misógino feminista*, which shows eight women and a token man, the event coordinator (Gámez).[21] Out of the many hundreds of photographs that I studied from Mexican newspapers covering Mexican men writers of interest, concentrated in the years 2010–14, I cannot point to another photo with this many women. This photograph hints that a significant number of women receive an invitation to comment when the subject relates to feminism. Moreover, as indicated by the photo op, Monsiváis may be an exception to the rule: a respected man whose "high and hard" reputation nevertheless tolerates relatively large numbers of women participants. This photo leads me to a game for more normative photos that I hope my reader enjoys. I call it "Spot the Token." The "token," of course, refers to the lone woman featured among the men who seems to take on something other than a bystander role.

The photographs that inspired my game of tokenism center on homages to men writers.[22] These images suggest that one way to be coolly autonomous and rebellious, while also appearing suitably grateful and thus making the occasion seem important, is to pick the right peers to honor one—a point that I first broached in chapter 3. To develop this discussion here, I begin with an image of the celebration of José Emilio Pacheco's career during the 2014 Homenaje Nacional, covered in *Excélsior*; the illustrious names listed include "Julio Ortega, Hugo Verani, Darío Jaramillo, Luis García Montero, Rafael Olea Franco, José Luis Martínez, [and] Elena Poniatowska" ("José Emilio Pacheco"). The booby prize goes to my reader who spotted among the seven names that of Elena Poniatowska, the lone woman. Poniatowska is no stranger to the token role. A photograph from 2015, taken in London, features a celebration of Octavio Paz and portrays five men and Poniatowska; thus she anchors events as the token woman on both sides of the Atlantic.[23]

I should mention that twenty-first-century events in the United States lead to sadly successful rounds of the same game. In the early days of the Donald Trump presidency, as Jill Filipovic in the *New York Times* observed, the "all-male photo op" surfaced not as an inadvertent gesture of misogyny but a deliberate appeal to a base of white male voters; relevant images included "a photo of two dozen men sitting around a table."[24] In the same manner, the tendency to feature men over women in photos of events for Mexican intellectuals represents, not a mistake, but a tactic of prestige. In general, the more respected the Mexican writer, the more men will publicly present him, which predicts that women cannot dig themselves out of a reputational hole even with a strong network, if that network comprises mostly women. I cannot overemphasize the importance of this principle: the reputation of the highest among the hardest of writers, such as Nobel Prize winner Paz, is built on the continuing respect of men. In a sidebar announcing a 2014 event to mark Paz's one hundredth birthday, *Excélsior* details the conferences to be attended over multiple days by thirteen figures: Héctor Tajonar, Juan Manuel Garibay, Anthony Stanton, Eduardo Matos Moctezuma, Carmen Gaitán, Martín Soler, Adolfo Castañón,

Jorge Esquinca, Oswaldo Hernández, Manuel Felguérez, Brian Nissan, Arnaldo Coen, and David Huerta (Ávila, "El museo"). The token woman is, of course, Gaitán, the one female among the twelve males.[25]

From a long list of experts on Octavio Paz, announced in an advertisement in 2014 among the leftist-leaning pages of *La Jornada*, only four women appear among the seventeen names of experts: Fabienne Bradu, Adriana de Teresa Ochoa, Helena Dunsmoor, and Guadalupe Nettel ("Colegio de México" 20).[26] The imbalance is even worse, oddly, for a would-be countercurrent book published in 2015. In *Se acabó el centenario: Lecturas críticas en torno a Octavio Paz* (The centennial is over: critical readings around Octavio Paz), edited by Gabriel Wolfson and Jorge Aguilar Mora, only one woman appears among the total of fifteen authors. Maricela Guerrero is listed as the coauthor, with David Rojas, of an article on the technical aspects of the poem "Piedra de sol" (Sun stone); it is the only coauthored article in the collection.[27] Only men's comments are transcribed in the selected answers from the question and answer session. It bears emphasizing that the mechanism in play has men solidify their reputations as intellectuals by talking about men intellectuals, whereas women apparently hope to gain a foothold in this prestigious world by accepting invitations as token representatives of a minority.

To do justice to the general usage of the prestige tactic, I want to play briefly a few more rounds of Spot the Token, this time with publicity in honor of Juan Rulfo, Juan José Arreola, and Sergio Galindo. The website for the Coordinación Nacional de Literatura (National Coordination of Literature) includes a summary of the conference "A propósito de *Pedro Páramo* (1955)" (On *Pedro Páramo* [1955]) and remembers that for the seventy-fifth anniversary of that novel, the celebration concluded with speakers Fernando Benítez, Jorge Ruffinelli, Salvador Elizondo, Carlos Fuentes, Juan José Arreola, and a token woman, Yvette Jiménez de Baéz, "en estricto orden de aparición" (in strict order of appearance) ("El universo").[28] Similarly, an honorary event for Juan José Arreola, as described in the official program planned by the state of Jalisco and the private Casa Lamm Cultural Center, lined up speakers across four gatherings; Arreola himself appeared repeatedly, along with a cast of support that included one woman, Claudia Gómez Haro, the academic director of Casa Lamm, and eleven men (CME Arreola 10-1: 70).[29]

In similar masculinist style, the national ceremony in honor of Sergio Galindo, sponsored by the Instituto Nacional de Bellas Artes (National Institute of Fine Arts, or INBA) in 1993 about a month after Galindo's death, featured four panels that never included more than a token woman on each. The first comprised one woman, Nedda G. de Anhalt, who had written a book on Galindo's work, and two men, speaker Jorge Alberto Manrique and moderator Bernardo Ruiz; the photo of that panel published in *Excélsior* also included the male director of the INBA, Gerardo Estrada (CME Galindo 77-1: 17). The second panel featured three men, and the third panel, four men.[30] The fifth panel included a single woman again, among another four men. Nearly a decade earlier, Mexican writers had held a ceremony to honor Galindo while he was alive to enjoy it. That event included seven invited men panelists and one woman, again the Cuban nationalized as Mexican Nedda G. de Anhalt (Molina, "No fue").[31] About a decade earlier, the invitation to attend Galindo's lecture on the occasion of his joining the Academia Mexicana de la Lengua (Mexican Academy of Language) listed three other men.[32] Winding backward in time shows that the long-standing pattern never varies: a strong network of men over decades supported Galindo's, Rulfo's, and Arreola's prestige. Significantly, women literature teachers, a low prestige job in Mexico, were never in short supply over this period, as far as I know. Though by tradition, the most famous critics in Mexico might be men, the majority of literature academics are probably women.

I could just as well pick other names. Take Marco Antonio Montes de Oca. An homage to him celebrated in 1994 included just a token woman on each panel, setting him up for possible continued high and hard status (Peguero).[33] Certainly, in 2000 his reputation as a macho seemed secure with the all-male lineup of eight guests invited to present *Delante de la luz cantan los pájaros* (In front of the light the birds sing), a collection of Montes de Oca's thirty books of poems in one tome, organized by the INBA and the Fondo de Cultura Económica.[34] I could go on, seemingly infinitely, examining the minutiae of invited speakers at homages to men writers, but I trust that the reader sees the pattern. The corollary to the men-on-men reputation rule assumes that the writer who attracts the most women speakers is a minor figure. Even the most prestigious of women writers—say, Sor Juana Inés de la Cruz—became an official figure largely through men critics' interest in her. Monsiváis, possibly, offers an exception in that women may be invited to comment on him without damaging his status.

The stronger exception to the prestigious peer tactic appears with theater. The stage may provide a special place for the recognition of women, perhaps because of their fundamental importance—a fundamentally *visible* importance—as women actors. Men who worked in theater, such as Salvador Novo and Héctor Azar, appear to name-drop more women than expected. Of course, theater itself may simply be less prestigious than literary genres like novels and poetry. At any rate, women appear in larger numbers as important figures during homages to men directors and playwrights. For example, in 1981, for the thirtieth anniversary of the Centro Mexicano de Escritores, theater specialist Héctor Azar wrote a commemorative piece that mentioned a number of women, including Margaret Shedd and (misspelled) Martha Domínguez. Azar even composed a paragraph that acknowledged ten women who had been given grants through the Centro Mexicano de Escritores: "Emma Dolujanoff, Bambi [Ana Cecilia Treviño], Pilar Campesinos, Elsa Cross, Julieta Campos, Silvia Molina, Guadalupe Dueñas, Amparo Dávila, Dolores Castro, Rosario Castellanos" (Azar, "El Centro" 4). After so many rounds of Spot the Token, it proves almost disconcerting to review this woman-positive list. In his text, Azar also acknowledged the discrimination the women faced, such as from teachers who were not impressed with them.

Nevertheless, press coverage of an homage for Héctor Azar, held in 2000, paid greatest attention to the men attendees. The second paragraph of an article on the matter listed only men who celebrated Azar at the event—five of them—along with their administrative titles: Miguel Limón Rojas, secretary of public education; Rafael Tovar y de Teresa, president of the National Council for Culture and Arts (Conaculta); Gerardo Estrada, general director of the INBA; Juan Ramón de la Fuente, rector of the UNAM; and Víctor Hugo Rascón Banda, president of the General Society for Writers in Mexico (SOGEM) (Hernández, "Homenaje"). The women attendees do not appear in the article until the fourth paragraph, and they are identified as actresses.[35] Women also appear at homages to Salvador Novo's legacy, which may serve as a measure of his second-rate status. A roundtable on Novo's work in theater held in 1994 featured two women and five men, and for the 1990s the presence of two women in the newspaper coverage along with the five expected male authorities points to a diminished reputation.[36] The Mexican cultural television channel 22 attempted to rescue Novo's good name with a biographical documentary, *Adán sin fronteras* (Adam Without Borders) (2004), written by a woman, Isabel Maceiras, but anchored by a male voiceover and men experts. Only three women spoke about Novo, in comparison with the fourteen men who appeared.[37] In a similar and perhaps even more effective documentary effort, *José Emilio Pacheco* (2014), directed by Paulina Lavista with the help of El Colegio Nacional de México, no women were interviewed nor did a woman perform a voiceover narration.[38]

This rule of thumb that the greater the presence of women, the softer and lower the status of the subject leads me to wonder whether Carlos Fuentes's status will hold as the twenty-first century progresses, given that an unusual number of women have participated in relevant volumes of homage. In *Carlos Fuentes y la novela latinoamericana* (Carlos Fuentes and the Latin American novel) (2013), editors Cristina Fuentes La Roche and Rodolfo Mendoza publish twenty-three writers, eight of whom are women.[39] Julio Ortega's collection on Fuentes's work prints nineteen essays, a whopping nine of which are by women (Ortega, *Carlos Fuentes*). By contrast, a commemorative book on Salvador Elizondo published in 2016 gathers fourteen men writers and three women writers (Sándel and Barron, *El libro*); of these three, Vilma Fuentes contributes a single question that Elizondo answers (61), Margo Glantz conducts a brief interview with Elizondo (65–73), and Lucía Zamanillo Noriega co-interviews Elizondo, again only briefly (169–72). Paulina Lavista, Elizondo's second wife, does appear in an interview, split into two parts (Sándel and Barrón, "Los sueños" I and II). Judging from the equivocal power of women to connote the soft and low, my bet is that Elizondo continues to attract attention as a high and hard writer, while Fuentes undergoes critique (and, possibly, devaluation) as a writer who seems to be remembered more for soft and low styles of melodrama.

In defiance of the masculinist photo ops, a curious headline in *Excélsior* announced in 1996: "Martha Robles presentó sola su propio libro" (Martha Robles presented alone her own book) (Idalia). To give some background, I should cite a startling interview from 1993 with Carmen García Bermejo in which Robles expresses a low opinion of her male peers; she states that Mexican literary texts are *intranscendentes* (intranscendent). I know about this interview because Sandro Cohen published a rebuttal accusing Robles of failing to read—you guessed it—an all-male lineup: Octavio Paz, Rubén Bonifaz Nuño, and Carlos Pellicer (Cohen, "Martha Robles").[40] Cohen also drops the name Fernando del Paso, and the argument becomes a kind of dialogue among nonlisteners, as Robles seems to have tired of the all-men system and Cohen insists that an expert would admire major male figures. The missed opportunity for conversation reminds me of Elena Poniatowska's decision to write about Monsiváis as a cat, using the diminutive *gatito* (*Sansimonsi*). This technique will inspire resentment among uncomprehending readers of Poniatowska's "amateur," or feminine, language, while those readers more sympathetic to Poniatowska's battles will note that she merely reapplies the way men talk about *her* in the press as "Elenita." Returning to Robles's solitary book presentation some three years after Cohen's rebuke, I note that her isolation indicates the difficulty of appropriating the techniques of *cuatismo*, the buddy system, that has men network with one another to great mutual success.

If women cannot bully their way into fame, another method of participation is as curators of a man's legacy, or in the terms of the present chapter, as active bystanders. This role brings me to the difference between, say, deceased writers like Novo, and even Arreola, and those like Monsiváis, Paz, Rulfo, and Pacheco.[41] While the first two authors largely lack curators intimately devoted to preserving their good image, the network of (female) friends who surrounded Monsiváis and the widows of Paz, Rulfo, and Pacheco play influential roles in preserving the men's images as something more than successful performers of a gruff mood. Cristina Pacheco, who made the unusual decision for a Mexican woman of taking her husband's last name for professional purposes, appears in the contemporary press in connection with her deceased partner as a sort of intimate, nonacademic authority on him. With a less vocal presence, Marie José Tramini, Octavio Paz's second wife, also surfaces in photographs at select events in commemoration of her husband's legacy. Like Cristina Pacheco, Marie José Paz also assumes her husband's last name in print.[42] Rulfo's wife, Clara Aparicio, has a reputation for managing her husband's predilection for alcohol, and to this day she, along with their children, engages with the media in order to protect Rulfo's reputation and copyrights. Paulina Lavista helps to organize Salvador Elizondo's materials, including his diaries; she gives permission on what to publish and what to keep private, and she facilitated an homage a decade after the writer's death (Aguilar Sosa, "Un asomo" and "Elizondo").

Spot the Token and Locate the Female Helpmate are games that turn excessively predictable after a while, like a round of musical chairs that only allows women to lose a chair each time a partygoer is eliminated. Let's turn over the record, away from this same old song, and contemplate the question of Mexican cool. Is there such a thing? Or am I stuck with U.S. models?

There are certainly Mexican manners, and for that example I will study the *Manual de Carreño*. A Mexican cool would work against those formally codified behaviors, and for evidence of this resistance, I turn to the standby *Las batallas en el desierto* and adult Carlos's cynicism regarding Carlitos's boyhood enthusiasm for U.S. imported foods, appliances, and behaviors. This tension produces something like a "Mexican cool." That coolness views the United States with suspicion as an imperial power and at the same time upholds a distinctly colonial order by adopting the cool it cynically professes to critique. Importantly,

Carlos never explicitly rejects his callousness as a boy toward his poor former classmate Rosales. In response to Rosales's tale of economic woe near the end of the text, Carlitos tells him: "Rosales, de verdad lo siento; pero eso no es asunto mío y no tengo por qué meterme" (Rosales, truly I'm sorry; but that isn't my business and I don't have any reason to get involved) (61). Rosales himself responds to this self-restrained cool with more of the same, although his atrocious table manners cause Carlitos, still playing by Mexican cool that retains one style of colonial order while rejecting the stylings of another empire, to feel revulsion at his former classmate's undisguised hunger. By extrapolating from the critique of the imperial United States and the dejected tone of the conclusion, the reader is perhaps meant to understand that Carlos regrets this callousness. Such an understanding might be part of "Mexican cool," which edges away from the formality of the *Manual de Carreño* and thus can never be formally wrong because it never commits to explicit rules.

For uninitiated readers, I should explain that Manuel Antonio Carreño's etiquette guide continues to circulate among Mexican readers, nearly 150 years after its first appearance in serial form in a newspaper in 1853 and a print edition in 1854 (Enrigue 76). Álvaro Enrigue makes this point about the sales nicely: "No estoy exagerando aquí: el *Manual* de Carreño se ha conseguido siempre en los quioscos y puestos de libros de los mercados de la ciudad de México, en ediciones populares" (I am not exaggerating here: Carreño's *Manual* has always been available in the kiosks and bookstalls of Mexico City markets, in cheap editions) (74).[43] In Pacheco's novella, Carlitos implicitly upholds the formal rules of the Carreño guide, which stipulates, "Nada puede haber más impropio que una discusión acalorada entre padres e hijos" (Nothing can be more inappropriate than a heated discussion between parents and children) (Carreño 116). In only partial opposition to those formal rules, *Las batallas en el desierto* surprises with its ambivalent attitude toward familial relationships.

How does Pacheco's audience consume the *Manual de Carreño* and cool texts like *Las batallas en el desierto* in juxtaposition? The key lies in an international trend toward informalization that still retains faith in self-help books. For more data, I can cite Cas Wouters's *Informalization: Manners and Emotions since 1890*, which examines European and U.S. national histories. These patterns match up relatively well with the Mexican example. Wouters observes that, under the demand for informality, notions such as "'ease' and 'naturalness' gained importance" as "demands for individual authenticity also rose" (92). Pacheco's Carlitos experiences this transition from the formal to the informal, as the following quotation from Wouters helps us see: "The 1960s and 1970s provided almost innumerable examples of challenged authority in combination with a critique of the 'inauthenticity,' 'superficiality,' and 'falsity' of 'icky' old manners" (174). Like the European and U.S. citizens, Mexican readers of Pacheco's novella born in the twentieth century also underwent those changes.

Without the successful process of informalization among Pacheco's audience for the novel, it is difficult to imagine that the narrator Carlos, with his almost merciless critique of his parents, would have found an enthusiastic reception in the school curriculum. Still, much of Pacheco's critique remains implicit, and in this way the 1980s standard for Mexican cool seems to temper the spontaneity imagined under the reign of the informal. My reader is probably already connecting this broader cultural shift with Pacheco's characters' switch to informal grammar, *el tuteo*. Against the association of informality with authenticity, this change does not come "naturally" for all characters. Carlitos defends his family's antiquated habits of formal address in the face of his friend Jim's ridicule of such old-fashioned formality; the reader knows that Jim's informal ways will largely win out.[44] Still, there are no real winners because, as I was pointing out in terms of the Mexican cool, some underlying structures remain.

Peter Stearns, the aforementioned historian of U.S. cool, argues that Wouters's informalization is a mere subcategory of the overall trend toward cool. Stearns cautions us that Wouters's model "overdoes the liberating elements and, still more important, downplays the . . . growing aversion to emotional intensity that such informality requires" (11). Precisely this aversion to intensity explains Carlitos's obedience as well as Carlos's unemotional tone, which shows that Carlitos did learn his parents' lesson: to keep control over his passions, even as he assimilates more informal behaviors and praises the natural. On the one hand, as an adult narrator, Carlos's values coincide with the informal vision of the natural and the authentic, as when he disagrees with his parents' decisions and complains that "el amor es una enfermedad en un mundo en que lo único natural es el odio" (love is a sickness in a world where the only natural thing is hate) (56). On the other hand, on the surface of the plot, Pacheco's text upholds the traditional pedagogical standard of children's obedience to parents. Carlitos's begrudging childhood compliance causes him to stop seeing Mariana, change schools, and consult both the priest and the mental health counselors.

Aside from avoiding heated arguments with his parents, Pacheco's Carlos obeys another of the nineteenth-century set of strictures of the *Manual de*

Carreño: he avoids all mention of his adult body, including any aches, pains, medications, and physical reflexes, such as burping or flatulence. If formality still conditions Pacheco's text, informality will precisely help to justify the new explicitness in his successors' works. This point finds support in a U.S. court case, which Wouters's study cites by way of Kenneth Cmiel's analysis. Obscene language was the issue in *Chaplinksy v. New Hampshire* (1942), "a case in which the defendant was convicted for calling someone a 'damned racketeer' and a 'damned fascist'" (Wouters 174). Ultimately, the U.S. Supreme Court found in favor of the right to use obscenities, which in Wouters's wording of Cmiel's history means that a "legal version" of the larger process of informalization took place: "Free speech gradually won the upper hand over the demand for verbal niceties in civil society" (174). Twenty-first-century Mexican court cases—like the one from 2013 studied in chapter 3—curb some of this liberty at the point of unconstitutional hate speech. The loop of bullying seems built into the very docket of the court system, as the new "naturalness" facilitates tolerance for the behaviors of a bully, which then requires new tests for determining acceptably civilized language. To win at this game, it helps to be seen as coolheaded, even inarticulately so.

Predictably perhaps, alongside all the change, the *Manual de Carreño* remains. Its ubiquitous influence proves hard to measure. In Alatorre's *La migraña* Carreño's manual appeared as a textbook in the seminary; power, even for priests, seemed to issue from knowing one's place in any eventuality (43, 82–83). Born nearly fifty years after Alatorre, Julián Herbert also mentions the *Manual de Carreño* in his autobiographical novel *Canción de tumba* (*Tomb Song*) (2011). In a bizarre juxtaposition, Herbert's narrator claims that his mother recommended he read two books as a teenager: the *Manual de Carreño* and a translation of Norman Mailer's *The Executioner's Song* (1979) (40). This pairing appears to warn that failure to observe proper manners creates the risk of tangling with the disciplinary system. The idea that manners might be more vital than laws when it comes to staying out of trouble reemerges in the mother's policies regarding language in the house. Although she cannot control, for example, her son's illicit drug habit, and although she participates in remunerated sex work, she successfully forbids an assortment of verbal insults, sexualized references to select body parts, and the mention of "drugs" in her household (130–31). There is something not playful about this censorship, designed to inculcate rules of success regardless of the aggressively difficult socioeconomic context that the children must confront.

Another way to think about this aggressive push-pull dynamic between formal and informal custom, which—I reiterate—still rings true with colonial disparities, is to ponder the binary of credit and debt. Notably, the *Manual de Carreño* finds credit problematic. Point 40 in Carreño's section labeled "Reglas diversas" (Assorted rules) explains that credit threatens good manners when the indebted show too much social ambition and assume too much risk:

> Es tan sólo propio de personas vulgares y destituidas de todo sentimiento de moralidad y pundonor el pedir dinero prestado, o hacer compras a crédito en los establecimientos mercantiles o industriales, sin tener la seguridad de pagar oportunamente. La propensión a usar de un lujo superior a aquel que permiten los propios recursos, y el absurdo conato de elevarse sobre la posición que realmente debe ocuparse en la sociedad, son los móviles de esta indigna costumbre. (403)

> It is only typical of vulgar people destitute of all sense of morality and self-respect to borrow money, or buy on credit in mercantile or industrial establishments, without having the certainty of paying promptly. The propensity to use luxury superior to their resources alone, and the absurd attempt to rise above the position that they should really occupy in society, are the motives of this undignified habit.

The idea that in a formal society one does not ask for credit that one cannot immediately pay back and that one should not buy luxury items above one's true income level finds its contradiction in informalization. As appearances of equality benefit from informal manners, so too under informality the notion of worthy credit holders loosened. The U.S. history of credit shows that early in the twentieth century, under more formal manners, credit was seen to mark the user as "immoral or unthrifty" (Hyman, *Debtor Nation* 174).[45] Now, the informal imagines itself to hide social hierarchies, and the aesthetic promotes luxury items, such as designer jeans, that are nearly indistinguishable from the cheaper product.

The story of Mexican credit, like Mexican cool, differs somewhat from its U.S. counterparts. Steven Bunker registers the difficulty of tracing the history of consumer credit in Porfirian Mexico. While sales events caused Mexican department stores to advertise cash-only policies for the duration of the discounts, the rest of the time these businesses allowed for credit in accounting books that are mostly long lost; it is still not known whether stores extended credit only to certain classes of customers (149–50). Though most Mexicans did not perceive any material advantages from it, the Porfiriato managed to improve the banking institution in Mexico. In 1884, Porfirio Díaz's administration began to control the problem with a state-orchestrated merger of the two largest banks to form the Banco Nacional de México (Banamex) (Moreno-Brid and Ros 52). Thus, as indicated by this late date, the early history of banking in Mexico largely centers on the absence of banks in Mexico. Díaz's efforts filled the financial vacuum of the reformed, financially restricted Roman Catholic Church, which had previously served as the main credit lender in Mexico. Before Díaz's initiative, the credit vacuum had been abusively addressed by moneylenders, named *agiotistas*, who even in the early nineteenth century—before the church's forced exit as the national bank—charged the government "exorbitant interest rates sometimes exceeding 300 percent" (Tenenbaum 32).

In harmony with the rules of the *Manual de Carreño*, Diáz's solution of a "semiofficial superbank" continued inner-circle lending privileges: "From 1886 to 1901, 100 percent of all non-government or non-government-guaranteed lending by Banamex went to insiders" (Calomiris and Haber 339, 343). Hence, one of the "logical consequences" of the relatively small number of banks and the pervasive insider lending was scarce credit for the majority of Mexicans, which only worsened with the Mexican Revolution, that economy-shrinking "ten-year period of coups, rebellions, and civil wars" (349). Nonetheless, a close reading of cultural practices intimates that credit was always around. By the 1970s Bunker's cited ads for cash-only sales had largely been replaced by pitches for credit cards, which appeared in the cultural and social sections of Mexican newspapers. For example, in 1972, the cultural section of the newspaper *El Heraldo de México* featured an ad for the Diners Club credit card on the same page as the "Snobissimo" column and an article about the tenth anniversary of the Centro Universitario de Teatro (University Theatre Center) (Diners Club ad).

This subject of debt and credit leads me to notions of personality and character. The utility of studying literature and literary history in respect to these hard-to-quantify subjects keeps getting clearer, even as the topics become more contradictory. I invite the intrepid scholar to follow me to the next thorny chapter, this time on the performance of Mexican character and personality.

6

THE ANTISOCIAL COOL AND PHILANTHROPIC CREDIT

Plus Binaries of Personality and Character, Sprezzatura and Pedantry, the *Manual de Carreño* and *How to Win Friends and Influence People* (with Reflection on Juan José Arreola, Salvador Novo, Juan Rulfo, José Emilio Pacheco, Carlos Monsiváis, Carlos Slim, Et Alia)

Gracias, Garibay. Arrieros somos.

—AGUSTÍN YÁÑEZ TO RICARDO GARIBAY

Yo Tavito no hago mas que pensar en el dia para mí feliz que tu te recibas y eso no lo debes olvidar por nada pues ya estas como quien dice en la puerta y es una gran tonteria que no lo hicieras pero yo creo que si verdad hijito dame ese gusto que yo te vea con tu título de abogado aunque después no ejersas en la carrera.

—JOSEFINA LOZANO DE PAZ (QTD. BY GUILLERMO SHERIDAN)

En las notas de escenografía, Villaurrutia insiste en el "buen gusto" de los muebles y del decorado. ¿Cómo pudo olvidar que el bueno gusto de hoy es lo cursi de mañana?

—OCTAVIO PAZ

Many of the provisions of the current 1917 Constitution may be characterized as "aspirational."

—JORGE A. VARGAS

Remember the U.S. self-help book that dominated sales charts in the early 1990s, *The Seven Habits of Highly Effective People: Restoring the Character Ethic* (1989), by Stephen Covey? The text sold more than 25 million copies and produced an audiobook that became the first to sell more than a million copies (D. Martin). In July 2016 I saw a used copy of *Los siete hábitos de la gente altamente efectiva* for sale on a sidewalk table in Mexico City near Paseo de la Reforma, which tracks the Mexican interest in U.S. self-help books, despite the national complaint about low reading rates. Pacheco's *Las batallas en el desierto* has Carlitos include a related detail: "Mi padre devoraba *Cómo ganar amigos e influir en los negocios*, *El dominio de sí mismo*, *El poder del pensamiento positivo*, y *La vida comienza a los cuarenta*" (My father devoured *How to Win Friends and Influence Business Deals*, *The Control of Oneself*, *The Power of Positive Thinking*, and *Life Begins at Forty*) (51). These guides appear to differ from the *Manual de Carreño* discussed in the previous chapter—and from Covey's book as well—because while the Carreño book follows strict class-based etiquette rules and while Covey wants people to return to reliable upstanding character and not personality behaviors (Covey 185, 187)—the contrasting approach by Dale Carnegie in *How to Win Friends and Influence People* (1936) views personal achievement not through "wealth, status, or power" but by "how well one is liked by others, [and] how well others respond to the roles one is playing" (Susman 200).

The author of these descriptive quotations, cultural historian Warren Susman, studies an earlier installment in this line of thought on personality: a series of self-help books from the *Mental Efficiency Series*, published in 1915 by Funk & Wagnalls, that give advice on personality and advocate for the "quality of being Somebody" (Susman 277). The idea of "being Somebody" does not stress good behavior, as etiquette manuals do, but the power to command attention, which values fame over morals. The Mexican case that most famously approaches this idea actually inverts it. In the 1950s, Octavio Paz's *El laberinto de la soledad* reviewed the social erasure involved in the verb *ningunear* (to make no one), which assigns the low status of "don Nadie" (Sir No One). Paz does not bother to distinguish between character and personality. Rather than Covey's study of great men, Paz and his cohort parse "characterology" in a lament for the character of machos.[1] Still, in the twenty-first century, the goal of being "someone"—along with an implicit binary of personality and character values—does appear in Mexican dialogue. The "chick flick" *Casi divas* (*Almost Divas*) (dir. Issa López 2008) states the driving goal behind the urge to compete for a chance to appear on television as "ser alguien" (to be someone). Yet some of the best-behaved characters in that film choose to remain, as the title warns, *almost* divas (or *almost* whimsical personalities) by electing values of anonymous community service over a quest for fame.

Casi divas and Covey's book show the ongoing debate that poses the virtues of electing character over personality in times that largely seem to prefer the opposite. The aspirational, advice-dispensing tones of the film and self-help book encourage me to suspect that many of the character studies in Mexico, including the main best seller, Paz's *El laberinto de la soledad*, might actually have been an academic form of self-help, interested not so much in raising the fortunes of minority groups, such as women, but rather in preserving a traditional domain of power for men, the very people writing most of the studies, by way of a negative slant that made authority on the subject seem important. The true aim of those studies may have been not to solve a problem but to contemplate it with a knowingly small academic toolkit.

My reader may still not fully understand this binary of character and personality, and to remedy that I need to present the argument that clarified it for me. Susan Cain's *Quiet: The Power of Introverts in a World That Can't Stop Talking* (2012) was released some three decades after Covey's first book, and in the year of his death, to nearly immediate best-seller status. Cain does not acknowledge the precedent of *The Seven Habits*; she works in a different register, with a more polished use of English and a more sophisticated grasp of research. Cain believes that a Culture of Personality benefits from an Extrovert Ideal, which has overtaken the contrasting Culture of Character and its tolerance of introverts. "Quiet," or introverted, people had thrived under the Culture of Character, because "what counted was not so much the impression one made in public as how one behaved in private" (21).[2] Cain refers us to Susman's adjectives to describe the lure of the star personality, which he culled from early U.S. self-help literature; these include "*fascinating, stunning, attractive, magnetic, glowing, masterful, creative, dominant, forceful*" (Susman 277). By contrast, according to Cain, "in the Culture of Character, the ideal self was serious, disciplined, and honorable" (21). Drawing from Susman's model, Cain lists the qualities of character, which include *citizenship*, *duty*, *work*, *golden deeds*, *honor*, *reputation*, *morals*, *manners*, and *integrity* (Cain 23). Cain stimulates me to rethink personality and character in the Mexican tradition, beyond a simple countercurrent to the negative macho characters and the rigid formalities of the *Manual de Carreño*.

Before I complicate things, a citation from the countercurrent would probably enlighten my reader. To wit, an ad from 1928, in *El Universal Ilustrado*, pitches Stacomb hair gel through the question "¿Es usted un hombre a la moderna?" (Are you a man à la modern?) (Stacomb ad). The answer turns on the term *personality*: "En nuestra época el cabello es indicio de la personalidad. Cuidadosamente peinado indica refinamiento y cultura; desgreñado y revuelto acusa negligencia y dejadez" (96). (In our age hair is a sign of personality. Carefully combed, it indicates refinement and culture; unkempt and disheveled it reveals negligence and sloppiness.) The promise of personality coaching stays attractive across the decades, even as the opposing qualities of character are sometimes dusted off to bolster its appeal. In 1969, an ad appeared in the magazine *Mujer de Hoy* (Today's woman), on the reverse of an interview with woman writer María Luisa Mendoza Pilar, that reached in both directions, to character *and* personality. Advertising for Pilar Candel's Personality Course announced "open enrollment" for lessons that range from the Carreño tradition of social etiquette, table manners, and general culture to the Carnegie-personality side of things, with tutoring in psychology, wardrobe, modeling, makeup, and dramatic art (Haro).

Perhaps because character tilted toward the negative in the Mexican tradition, by the 1960s writers generally tended to employ the term *personality* to talk about themselves. The archive for the Centro Mexicano de Escritores includes a winning application letter dated June 10, 1962, by Ulises Carrión, which explains that his goals focus on the development of his personality: "¿Mis fines? Avanzar un paso más en la formación de mi personalidad como hombre y como escritor, y dejar el testimonio escrito de mis fracasos o mis éxitos en esta empresa" (My goals? To advance one more step in the formation of my personality as a man and as a writer, and to leave a written testimony of my failures or my successes in this endeavor) (CME Carrión Bogard 100). Carrión correctly assesses the growing institutional-artistic interest in personality.

The term *character* was nowhere to be found in the boilerplate touting the personalities of Carrión's contemporaries, the "New Writers," published in 1966 and 1967 as part of the all-male autobiographical series Nuevos Escritores Mexicanos del Siglo XX Presentados por Sí Mismos, which I first mentioned in chapter 2. The prefacing material for each autobiography always begins:

> La presente colección se inspira en el propósito de dar a conocer en páginas autobiográficas a la fuerte personalidad de los jóvenes escritores mexicanos del momento. . . . (For examples, see Elizondo, Leñero, Monsiváis, Sainz)

> The present collection is inspired by the goal of promoting in autobiographical pages the strong personality of young Mexican writers of the moment. . . .

This publicity angle breaks with the tenets of New Criticism and insinuates that in order to judge competently these "new writers," we must pay attention to their personalities. Not all writers were happy about that pitch. In his autobiography, Vicente Leñero represents himself in an internal debate about whether he should inform editor Rafael Giménez Siles about his opposition to the literary cult of personality: "yo estoy en contra del culto a la personalidad; yo pienso que son las obras y no los autores lo que debe difundirse" (I am against the cult of personality; I think that the works and not the authors should be publicized) (41).[3]

Notwithstanding these cited examples of personality themes—and the mixed approach anticipated in Pilar Candel's courses and *Casi divas*—twenty-first-century copy sometimes retains the habit of treating the two elements as comfortable juxtapositions. An exceptionally competent exhibit of post-Revolutionary art that I visited at the Philadelphia Museum of Art in January 2017 displayed a plaque that listed the two terms alongside one another: "The Contemporáneos embraced the genre of informal portraiture, which focuses on expressing an individual's personality and character" (*Paint the Revolution*). The Mexican Supreme Court, as I discussed in chapter 3 in regard to the 2013 decision on hate speech, also seems to acknowledge both personality and character when it states that dignity and the rights that follow from it are necessary for individuals to develop "integralmente" (integrally) their "personalidad" (personality). The court's concern for honor, a more character-based term, also alludes to this personality element, and it seems that the court ultimately does not define personality differently from the general notion of character.

Yet, the court might have benefited from splitting the terms into a clear binary. It seems to me that a close cousin of hate speech is the *albur*, the uncouth pun. Carlos Fuentes, in the essay "Tiempo mexicano" (1959), explains the verbal tactic of this genre of dirty pun solely in terms of personality: "El 'albur,' en México, es una operación del lenguaje que consiste en desviar el sentido llano de las palabras a fin de dotarlas de una intención insultante, agresiva, negadora de la personalidad de los interlocutores" (The "albur," in Mexico, is an operation of language that consists in diverting the plain meaning of the words in order to endow them with an insulting, aggressive intention to negate the interlocutors' personalities) (257). The albur can be seen to aid male speakers in switching from a reliably upstanding performance of character in order to give a starring performance of less predictable and flashier personality (and possibly even attributing a stick-in-the-mud reliability of character to the interlocutor)—all without social punishment, until the Supreme Court ruling on hate speech. The albur is a low-class move, and that implied uneducated informality ties into notions of economic power, which brings me to the finances of the binary.

The creditworthiness of honor that the Mexican Supreme Court attributes to personality might pertain more cogently to a discussion of character. As the scholars remind us, stolid "character" performance earned financial credit. Under early twentieth-century U.S. banking practice, *character* constituted one of the four words that began with the letter *C* used to determine whether applicants received a bank loan (Hyman, *Borrow* 58). As historians remind us, before credit checks and credit scores became possible, the key quality of conformity—this aspect of good "character"—affected one's ability to obtain loans.[4] Personality, to the extent that it trades on fascinating and eccentric behavior, damaged creditworthiness because mercurial performance was viewed as a risky investment. (For Mexico's banking history, see the end of the previous chapter.) To Cain's apparent dismay, at some point in the twentieth century, personality became a more bankable form of credit than character. To date this shift, I note that although Susman detects the onset of fame or infamy over good character in U.S. self-help literature as early as the 1920s, he attributes the major rise of personality to the glamorous celebrities of the 1930s, such as movie stars and star athletes (277).[5] Apparently, the improved fortunes of personality spanned the period when the established channels of credit dried up during the Great Depression.

Something like this timeline describes Juan Rulfo's *Pedro Páramo*. José Carlos González Boixó estimates that *Pedro Páramo* begins in 1865 with Pedro's and Susana's births ("Cronología" 181). The beginning of the plot thus falls near the secular reforms that restricted the Catholic Church and hamstrung it as the main credit-issuing institution in the country. Pedro's stinginess stays true to the rural customs, bemoaned in the Porfirian era by foreign would-be capitalists of the Mexican countryside, who complained about the region's "*damned wantlessness*" (Knight 476). His mother and grandmother buy necessities, some on credit, and when the adult Pedro has cash, he hoards it or invests it, sometimes in Catholic indulgences.[6] Because Pedro's rise to power occurs in the vacuum of banking institutions, he *becomes* the main credit holder in town in lieu of the Catholic Church. This institutional nature of Pedro's power explains how he plans to kill off a town: "Me cruzaré de brazos y Comala se morirá de hambre" (2012, 171) ("I will cross my arms and Comala will die of hunger") (1994, 117). History buffs may identify 1927, the likely year of Pedro's death, at least as identified by González Boixó's chronology (182), as the year the Mexican economy stopped growing altogether (Knight 497). In this financial sense, *Pedro Páramo* can be read as an early model for the narco novel and its violent finances of bárbaro personality over civilizado character.[7]

As per the cultural shift over his lifetime, Pedro may start out under a performance of character and find greater success with an unpredictable personality act. He always retains the option to return to rules of character, as per the bárbaro and civilizado slide. Although in some ways this shift from one pole to the other encompasses little more than a change of perspective, Pedro appears to expand his repertoire as he matures; he moves from being an indebted citizen to becoming a credit-holding personality, who can, if it suits him, demand that select others follow the character rules of middle-class ideals. Susana San Juan is perhaps the only person to escape Pedro's hypocritical strategy; she is a temperamental personality, and while she cannot flip back to a character performance, possibly because of poor mental health or perhaps because of the limitations imposed on her gender, Susana can at least defy Pedro precisely by refusing the stable behaviors of character. Susana's madness befits a personality performance concerned with "being Somebody" rather than being a good person, and her diva-like performative whims flummox Pedro.

On the financial side, whether playing by character or personality, Pedro Páramo never pays back his debts; on the contrary, he marries into them by making his creditor, Dolores Preciado, his wife.[8] The credit-extending wife's function in the plot as an *engañada* (the cheated upon) makes her a permanent debt manager who never sees a free-and-clear profit. (Note that Pacheco will repeat Rulfo's pattern neatly with Carlitos's mother and father in *Las batallas en el desierto*.) Dolores (like Carlitos's mother) is stuck with a performance of good or bad character and cannot manage the bully flip to a flashy personality. Dolores appears to be from the state of Jalisco (just as Carlitos's heiress mother in *Las batallas en el desierto* is from Guadalajara), and Rulfo associates a particularly brutal history with this region.[9] To judge from fiction writers' view of the history, the past violence seems to coach an unforgiving character performance among the women.

Interviewer Joseph Sommers draws Rulfo out on this matter by asking, "¿No quiere elaborar un poco la personalidad histórica de esa zona [Jalisco]?" (Don't you want to elaborate a bit on the historical personality of that zone [Jalisco]?). Rulfo answers:

> Sí, porque hay que entender la historia para entender este fanatismo [. . .] Los conquistadores ahí no dejaron ser viviente. Entraron a saco, destruyeron la población indígena, y se establecieron. Toda la región fue colonizada nuevamente por agricultores españoles. [. . .] Entonces los hijos de los pobladores, sus descendientes, siempre se consideraron dueños absolutos. Se oponían a cualquier fuerza que pareciera amenazar su propiedad. De ahí la atmósfera de terquedad, de resentimiento acumulado desde siglos atrás, que es un poco el aire que respira el personaje Pedro Páramo desde su niñez. (Sommers 520)[10]

> Yes, because you have to understand the history to understand this fanaticism. . . . The conquistadors there did not leave anyone alive. They razed it from the start, they destroyed the indigenous population, and they settled there. The whole region was colonized again by the Spanish farmers. . . . So the children of the settlers, their descendants, always considered themselves absolute owners. They opposed any force that seemed to threaten their property. Thus the atmosphere of stubbornness, of accumulated resentment from centuries ago, that is a little bit of the air that Pedro Páramo breathes since his childhood.

The birthright of descending from a particular group of male murderers is imagined as awarding an inalienable right to property. The women who descend from these murderers can trade on this inheritance as a kind of moral superiority born of racism and religious fanaticism, but in fiction at least they cannot control the debt chain—perhaps because the women characters cannot flip from rule-breaking to rule-enforcing performances with peer approval.

An excellent understanding of this chain of debt—though without reflections on the character and personality binary—appears intermittently in Matthew Restall's history of the Conquest and enlivens another small section of David Graeber's world history of debt. In more fanciful terms than Restall's emphasis on the conquistadors' credit-based entrepreneurship, Graeber summarizes the aftermath of the Conquest memorably in terms of a psychology of debt that inspires brutal acts realized upon the hapless peoples converted into slaves—the latter become a kind of living debt marker who can be ruthlessly traded among debtors (*Debt* 318).[11] It comes as no surprise that Rulfo is interested in this cruel history, since Pedro Páramo's methods resemble this original violence. In other chapters, I have already explained the mechanism that lends power to the rule breakers, and here I can add a term to the vocabulary: the *endrogado*. Rulfo's cacique manages to reign over the region by cycling out of his macho bárbaro role when his own chaos threatens to upend his monopoly. The reader who doubts Pedro's role as the civilizado will remember the famous line uttered by Pedro when he explains to the henchman Fulgor, immediately after marrying into his creditor's family and thus turning his own family debt into credit, "La ley de ahora en adelante la vamos a hacer nosotros" (2012, 100) ("From now on we're the law") (1994, 40). By becoming his own creditor in a capitalist system, Pedro Páramo becomes the law: his fascinating personality helps him make others believe in his power, which alternately connotes character-driven authority and integrity, which turns his duped followers like Dolores and his lawyer Gerardo into *engañados* (the tricked). However, a better word than *engañado* for that groupie status is *endrogado*, in the first place because this condition describes Pedro himself, and in the second place because Pedro's notion of justice is not only hallucinatory but also financial. That point leads us to the double meaning of *endrogarse*: both "to fall into debt" and "to get high."

Pacheco actually spells out this dual definition in *Las batallas en el desierto*. Carlos recalls that as a boy he confused a reference to his older brother Héctor's problems: "Cuando escuché que se había endrogado, creía que Héctor debía dinero, pues en mi casa siempre se les llamó drogas a las deudas" (When I heard that he had gotten into drugs, I thought that Héctor owed money, since in my house we always referred to debts as drugs) (52). Debt and drugs, as the verb *endrogarse* hints, lend themselves to similar operations. In point of the mirage-like debt in *Pedro Páramo*, consider the testimony of one of Pedro's victims, which he delivers from purgatory:

> Tenía sangre por todas partes. Y al enderezarme chapotié con mis manos la sangre regada en las piedras. Y era mía. Montonales de sangre. Pero no estaba muerto. Me di cuenta. Supe que don Pedro no tenía intenciones de matarme. Sólo de darme un susto. [. . .] Él no tuvo intenciones de matarme. Me dejó cojo, como ustedes ven, y manco si ustedes quieren. Pero no me mató. Dicen que se me torció un ojo desde entonces, de la mala impresión. Lo cierto es que me volví más hombre. (2012, 136)

> I was covered in blood. And when I tried to get up my hands slipped in the puddles of blood in the rocks. It was my blood. Buckets of blood. But I wasn't dead. I knew that. I knew that don Pedro hadn't meant to kill me. Just give me a scare. . . .

> He left me lame—you can see that—and, sorry to say, without the use of my arm. But he didn't kill me. They say that ever since then I've had one wild eye. From the scare. I tell you, though, it made me more of a man. (1994, 79)

This nameless character almost unbelievably trusts Pedro's lesson in manliness, and even from beyond the grave he praises the experience as helpful in developing strength as a macho bárbaro. The two meanings of endrogado, as indebted and on drugs, describe this victim of bullying, who from the afterlife believes himself capable of taking the lesson of becoming a better bully. It is important to remember that souls do not learn in purgatory; they merely pay back their debt by cleansing their sins. Under the Catholic mythology, Pedro's victims will never come to see things differently, despite a twisted eye and hallucinations of apprenticeship.

Parting from the dynamic of the endrogado then, I can state that Cain hits the bull's-eye when she relates drug use to problems caused by personality cultures, though she overstates the binary when she waxes nostalgic for character arrangements. She does not examine the possibility that character in its most powerful expression revolves around closed circles of privilege, such as exclusive schools and mutual employment opportunities, nor does she acknowledge the idea that this circle of powerful if sometimes *quiet* acquaintanceships comes to reinforce the male preserve of *genius*. To the further detriment of her argument, Cain ignores the performance that alternately elects *between* poles of character and personality. Thus, she never sufficiently reckons with the masculinist privilege that allows a(n) (in)famous Somebody to flip from the bárbaro personality to the civilizado character.

In evidence of their weak interest in gender analysis, neither Susman nor Cain points out the coincidence that personality-driven extroversion, with its unpredictable behaviors often unsuited to a quietly civil workplace, allegedly became prominent just as it became clear that women could do the same work as men. That is, just when increasing numbers of women could work outside the home without damaging their reputations of good character, it became less valuable to do so because personality was coming to new prominence. On the other hand, the domain of conformity and "quiet" in which women who follow traditional gender roles might excel, is somewhat ironically imagined by Cain as under threat—even though stably behaved women in the workplace still fail to receive rewards equal to men's compensation.

Even brilliant Mexicanist scholars sometimes misapprehend the mechanisms of the endrogado, and Jean Franco is on that list. Franco reads *Pedro*

Páramo under the belief that finances corrupt relationships, which backs the notion of character as a performance that needs to be protected against the vagaries of the economy and the trickster professional interests of personality. That is, Franco opines that money, as a corrupting force, subverts the social and moral order in the novel (151). Other academics convincingly refute Franco's operative assumptions, however. As Viviana Zelizer has established in cogent analysis, the "separate spheres" theory of family and finance represents an unrealizable ideal, and in reality money and love always mix. That is, Zelizer makes the point that instead of polluting each other, the spheres of domestic care and financial investment are mutually sustaining (24). To summarize this idea in the terms that I am trying to pull together here, if we are to retain love as an illusion, neither debt nor drugs can be taken out of it. Franco wants to preserve imaginary bounds of good, sober, selfless character in ways that make it easier for the most bárbaro to take advantage of the inevitable condition of the endrogado who loves and credits others.

Women in *Pedro Páramo* (and, for that matter, *Las batallas en el desierto*) are complicit in the masculinist personality-to-character flip because they expect to get paid—and from Zelizer's perspective, rightly so. This expectation is no more corrupt than the entire system is. Dolores never abandons her belief that Pedro will pay; she famously instructs her son, Juan Preciado, to demand compensation from Páramo and thus seems to send Juan to his death: "No vayas a pedirle nada. Exígele lo nuestro. Lo que estuvo obligado a darme y nunca me dio . . . El olvido en que nos tuvo, mi hijo, cóbraselo caro" (2012, 65). ("Don't ask him for anything. Just what is ours. What he should have given me but never did . . . Make him pay, son, for all those years he put us out of his mind") (1994, 3). The quest is delusional because while Dolores supposes that Pedro's debt to her is to her credit, Pedro imagines exactly the opposite: a credit owed to him is now Dolores's balanced account, or at worst, *her* debt. Both characters have a point, but only one will monopolize the resources, and that one will never be a woman for long under this system of masculinist privilege.

Imagining drugs and debts as two parts of the hinged hallucination of masculinism proves exceptionally useful. As I said, *Quiet* anticipates the drug angle. Cain argues that the pressures caused by the rise of personality led to the astonishing mid-twentieth-century success of the prescription medication Miltown. The drug first appeared in 1955 as a remedy for anxiety, and "by 1956 one of every twenty Americans had tried it; by 1960 a third of all prescriptions from U.S. doctors were for Miltown or a similar drug called Equanil" (Cain 29).[12]

Prescription drugs provide a licit, even "secret" weapon for handling the stresses of the personality act.

Why, again, are people performing wild personality if it stresses them? you ask. Because when credit for character vanishes under conditions such as the Great Depression, the notion of a glamorous personality as the means to democratic justice gains traction. Neither character nor personality offers the true key to success, however, which means we are probably in for centuries more of self-help books that argue one or the other without recommending the best trick of cycling between the two, especially under conditions of being a "white" male. Playing only personality risks running afoul of glamour and other magnetic attractions once old age arrives—as I will show near the end of the chapter with Novo's and Arreola's examples. Playing by rules of character alone courts exclusion from the old boys' or insiders' club. If you are wondering whether I am writing a form of academic self-help book that recommends cycling between character and personality as a macho, I have to say that I am no success coach. I deplore the macho flip.

I do think we do well to take a hard look at U.S. prohibitionist policy. Did you know that said policy was inspired by Mexican custom? It's true! Isaac Campos's masterful history of marijuana in Mexico argues that Mexican leaders did not encounter much opposition when they decided to back U.S. prohibition of the plant, because a univocal story line on the dangers of marijuana already existed. From the first evidence of marijuana smoking in Mexico in 1846 to nationwide prohibition in 1920, the "standard" negative descriptions of marijuana's effects "went virtually unchallenged" (Campos 3). In fact, Benjamin Smith goes so far as to claim that U.S. drug policy in the 1930s actually takes its lead from the long-standing Mexican suspicion of substances like marijuana, "underpinned by distinctly Mexican appreciations of race and class" (33). In fact, Smith claims that the influence proved long lasting, into at least the 1970s: "President Nixon's anti-narcotics policies dovetailed with contemporary understandings of Mexican psychologists, criminologists, and commentators" (33).[13]

Mexico is now undoing its prohibitionist laws in tandem with some regions in the United States. In 2014 the same Mexican Supreme Court justice who wrote the previous year's ruling against homophobic hate speech, Arturo Zaldívar Lelo de Larrea, authored a decision that emphasized *play* and *freedom to personality* as legal protections for the individual right to marijuana usage (Zaldívar Lelo de Larrea, "Amparo en revisión" 39). Although this decision defends non-medical ingestion of the drug, the ruling led to the passage of a bill supporting legal medicinal marijuana on December 13, 2016, by the Mexican Senate.[14] In greater detail, the decision in favor of recreational marijuana explains that the four people who brought the suit are protected under Mexican law (termed *ordenamiento mexicano*) and enjoy the fundamental right to the free development of personality; this personality development is derived from the right to dignity and guaranteed in the first article of the Mexican Constitution (Zaldívar Lelo de Larrea, "Amparo en revisión" 32).[15]

Rather than rely on the character-based judicial defense of *honor* as a building block of dignity (as was done in the 2013 decision to outlaw hate speech), the Supreme Court here tacitly agreed that the right to personality overrides the implicit value of moral character, at least to the degree that the latter is implied in the upstanding act of sobriety.[16] This idea seems to want to put an end to the bárbaro and civilizado loop, or the personality and character slide, by making the negatively viewed pole of the binary into a legitimately fun pursuit. In the long run, I have to wonder if by changing the reputation of "drugs," this easing of prohibition might also raise the contemporary status of literature and literary studies. Can a "fun" major and a "useless" academic specialty, as pragmatists dismissively view literature degrees, take on greater prestige if impractical leisure gains a better legal foothold?

Legitimating "drugs" combats the usual silences in ways that can also free endrogados from shame about debt.[17] That is, falling into unmanageable debt and freeing oneself through a mechanism such as declaring bankruptcy forms a parallel with drug shame, whipped up by the "unspeakable" nature of the matter, that finds relief in court-protected drug use. Drug and debt shame have to do with the notion that becoming endrogado results from a lack of character, or an excessive personality.[18]

How will bad boys find proper rebellion, the artistically appropriate kind that fails to make meaningful social equality changes, by way of their use of "drugs," if once-prohibited drugs are already okay? I don't have the answer to that question, but I can cite a sobriety clause that appeared in the late 1990s in the contract that all grantees at the Centro Mexicano de Escritores signed at the beginning of their grant year. Alfredo Carrasco Teja's contract in 1998 included clause number 4, which demanded sobriety:

> Sería motivo de cancelación la beca, la falta de asistencia del Becario sin permiso previo, a dos reuniones consecutivas o presentarse después de haber ingerido bebidas alcohólicas o alguna droga. (CME Carrasco Teja 1)

> Cause for cancellation of the grant would be the Grantee's absence without prior permission from two consecutive meetings or making an appearance after ingesting alcoholic beverages or any drug.

The notion that anyone, ever, anywhere attends a meeting without some sort of "drug" in their system remains odd, but the change in policy proves simply fascinating. As the performance of personality ratchets up—a phenomenon suggested in evidence ranging from boilerplate in the 1960s autobiographies, to Cain's *Quiet*, to the Mexican Supreme Court rulings—the desire for writing students to control personality also increases. This sobriety clause tests the very limits of what it means to perform the role of writer.[19]

Previously, both tutors and grantees at the Centro Mexicano de Escritores had combined drugs such as alcohol with the mentoring and writing process. On the first point I can cite grantee Ricardo Venegas's nostalgic newspaper piece from 2010. Venegas recalls that the (all male) literary advisors sometimes drank with their students and mentions Chumacero as a specific instigator of this practice:

> Probablemente los momentos más placenteros fueron aquellos en los que un brindis suspendía la sesión: Johnnie Walker etiqueta roja para los becarios y etiqueta negra para los maestros. No había reclamos. Estar con ellos y sentirse en el Olimpo de los escritores bastaba; el ambiente en la sala era agradable y relajado. Chumacero habló de Manuel José Othón, bardo potosino que creyó innecesario cualquier vínculo con la capital de la República. (Venegas)

> Probably the most enjoyable moments were those in which a toast suspended the session: Johnnie Walker Red Label for the grantees and Black Label for the teachers. There were no complaints. Being with them and feeling that we were on writers' Olympus was enough; the atmosphere in the room was pleasant and relaxed. Chumacero spoke about Manuel José Othón, the bard from San Luis Potosí who believed that any tie with the capital of the Republic was unnecessary.

The "relaxed and pleasant" atmosphere of alcohol and the social bonding it promotes remains of particular benefit to men, because they can flip between rule-breaking and rule-enforcing roles, or from sober character to lively personality, and find social success in the transition, provided that the peer audience approves. It comes as no coincidence, for readers familiar with chapter 5, that the above quotation is also praising relatively informal behavior.

Women have a harder time with unwritten cool rules and with this alcohol consumption act, in part because a femme can only pretend to be a bad boy and in part because it is difficult for women to look appropriately high-minded when the table has opted for "hard" drinking. Abstinence might be interpreted as unartistic or excessively formal behavior. But drinking too much, facilitated by the discrepant rates of alcohol absorption for women compared to men, puts females at risk for being seen as intellectually incompetent. (I do note that some women writers opt for cultivating a maximum tolerance for alcohol by favoring a hard-drinking habit. I don't think this solution is common.) Clearly, no "final solution" will ever exist, despite such measures as the sobriety clause in the 1990s grant contracts. You would have to be endrogado to believe that anyone can live utterly sober—which Avital Ronell says is impossible—and entirely without a story, which, as Margaret Atwood points out, is a synonym for debt (9). Perhaps rather than legislate the impossible, we should instead attempt to change the connotations of the binary.

Pedro Páramo signals one last point regarding the system of debt, credit, and deliria. In proof of his own participation as an endrogado, Pedro pays an indulgence to the priest Rentería in order to shorten his son Miguel's time in purgatory.[20] Stephen Greenblatt's insight on the purgatorial economy proves extremely interesting here: no money is ever wasted on indulgences, according to the Catholic authorities, because overspending on purgatory payments results in a balance of prayers that is passed on to the next of kin (25). This perfectly immaterial licensing is perhaps the opposite method of the narco (e.g., numbing) economy that Pedro runs, even if Pedro never pays people back in tangible profits either. Everything is wasted under Pedro's secular system of the benumbed that unfeelingly takes all. By comparison with the church's emotionally rich claims of final transcendence, Pedro's economy seems ultimately pointless.

It interests me that other critics appreciate the economy that Rulfo constructs for Pedro's story. One of the main points of admiration for *Pedro Páramo*, in fact, regards the perceived economical nature of the novel. The impetus for that idea may stem in part from the novelist's statements. Rulfo explained how he cut the initial draft of the novel by removing unnecessary passages.[21] The tendency to use Rulfo's words to describe his novel indicates as much about our respectful attitude toward the male writer as it does about the text itself. Moreover, the coincidence between middle-class ideals and the admired qualities of *Pedro Páramo* proves striking: critics describe the novel with synonyms for concepts of thrift, sobriety, timeliness, and cleanliness.[22] Setting aside the praise for the novelistic economy of expression, I note that to call "sober" the delirious narrative of *Pedro Páramo*, as does Juan Pellicer (202), hints that the critic has made up his mind regarding the nature of the text on the basis of elements that are not actually in the text but surround it.

Is it perhaps Pedro Páramo or Rulfo himself who is thrifty, sober, timely, and clean? (Is it shocking that Pedro Páramo could represent middle-class values so faithfully?) Critics who admire an economical text may be influenced by Pedro Páramo's often superficially courteous stinginess. Pedro never appears drunk—and he rarely swears in the text; the narrative of his direct experience omits depictions of him handling guns, nooses, or knives; he never cultivates an interest in athletic prowess, military strategies, games of chance, or pornography. Under conditions of gender reversal, critics might reject a doña Páramo, because she never shows the means of her violence or her talent for it, whether by holding a knife, gun, or noose, or by swearing, or by revealing some sort of athletic prowess and the like. (Remember that the Venezuelan protagonist of *Doña Bárbara* in Rómulo Gallegos's 1929 classic has a motivating backstory of gang rape for her violence.) In the case of *Pedro Páramo*, no more of an explanation for his rage appears than the accidental killing of his father.

As for Rulfo himself, he was famously not always sober; his successful battle with alcohol abuse is well known. (See Barrientos del Monte; Boldy; and Roffé.) And of course, after drying out, Rulfo ran into trouble with thrift; materials available in the Centro Mexicano de Escritores show him complaining of debts at least by 1977, despite the fact that his books left him a profit (Reyes Razo).[23] That detail accurately forecasts the quixotic rather than perfect economy of *Pedro Páramo*. On the one hand, González Boixó's expert materials reveal the contradiction in the timeline for Miguel's death and his ghostly visit to Eduviges, who—oops!—has already killed herself at that point. Yet, in the appendixes to the novel, González Boixó dismisses the importance of that mistake by waving away the need for the very chronology that he takes such great pains to establish: "No puede pedirse a Rulfo, sin embargo, una precisión tan exacta, algo que no nos consta que buscase" (One cannot ask of Rulfo, however, such exact precision, something that we cannot affirm that he sought) ("Cronología" 197). In the introduction, on the other hand, González Boixó praises the clockwork-like mechanics of the novel: *Pedro Páramo* evinces "una estructura minuciosa en la que cada pieza ocupa su preciso lugar" (a minute structure in which each piece occupies its precise place) ("Introducción" 24). The tensions between clockwork precision and ambiguity suggest that González Boixó helps to construct Rulfo's talent even as he claims to study it through readings that actually give Rulfo the benefit of the doubt.[24] Who among us is not an endrogado? (Could the narco problem exist without the cultural middle class?)

Instead of questioning *Pedro Páramo*, many critics extend its seeming economy as a goal for other worthy texts. Rafael Lemus makes part of this point for me when he complains, in a text published in 2008, that efficiency seems to have become a dominant value in literature for young contemporary writers: "Incluso los autores más jóvenes, que no están obligados a saber *cómo hacerlo*, se empeñaban en hacer obras *eficientes*, sin fisuras ni desperfectos, correctamente producidas" (Even the younger authors, who are not required to know *how to do it*, labored to make *efficient* works, without cracks or imperfections, correctly produced) (20). Franco Moretti also ventures a critique of the problems of efficiency when he observes in *The Bourgeois* that "'brute force' may turn out to be more perversely 'efficient' than efficiency itself" (42). By not recognizing some of the values in play in literary criticism that embraces the hallucination of the economical, it seems that critics may hew closer to neoliberal values that they might imagine. High-mindedness, as the bullying triangle from chapter 5 warns, is no guarantee of a bystander's righteousness. On that note, it bears remembering that an antibullying movement swept twenty-first-century Mexico and eventually featured a public-service campaign by Televisa, as well as governmental attention in such platforms as Enrique Peña Nieto's National Plan for Development, and the aforementioned Supreme Court rules against hate speech.[25] Official power has decided that bullying goes too far, which detracts from any possible academic claim on critics' part to special status as a unique ethical force on this front.

If now it is sometimes uncool to bully, what is the proper character and personality performance? Cultural journalism by Yanet Aguilar Sosa helps to answer the question by looking at data from the 1960s. Thus, I backtrack with her to some of the files mentioned at the beginning of the present chapter. In a 2013 review of the Centro's records on Vicente Leñero, Aguilar Sosa called part of the application process a *personality test* (*test de personalidad*) ("Vicente Leñero"). This language hits a sensationalist note, because the institution did not overtly label that step in the application as a personality exam.[26] Still, the gist of Aguilar Sosa's observations reflects the record. The following commentary, excerpted from the archive, rates Leñero's short answers for the literary and personal habits questionnaire; it is dated July 30, 1960, and signed only with the initials E.D.:

> Inteligente. No hay pedantería ni rasgos de autosuficiencia. Más bien modesto. Inhibido. Escasos mecanismos de proyección e identificación. Evidentes elementos de inseguridad que muy probablemente están integrados a un núcleo conflictual más profundo. ("Vicente Leñero)

> Intelligent. There is no pedantry nor traits of self-sufficiency. Rather modest. Inhibited. Few projection and identification mechanisms. Obvious elements of insecurity that very probably are integrated to a deeper conflictual core.

The absence of "pedantry" from Leñero's performance tells us that personality matters for writers, and this grading scale makes me wonder whether on some level all literary opinions also double as tests for "personality." If so, women ought to dread such literature exams. They seem designed to prey on individuals who for reasons coached by social prejudice might be viewed as less expert than the reviewer.

My reader may remember, from the discussion of Batis's *sábado* in chapter 2, that a synonym for prude is *pedant*. In contemplating E.D.'s approval of Leñero's lack of *pedantry* I use this language to help me identify the roots of this cool performance. The sixteenth-century concept of Italian *sprezzatura*, which anticipates the seventeenth-century French *je ne sais quoi*, knows from pedantry.[27] Mario Biagioli's work on the topic guides my thinking. Biagioli analyzes astronomer Galileo Galilei's courtly manners, and by taking into account bodily performance, he convincingly proposes that Galileo's "courtly etiquette and gentlemanly codes of behavior" helped sway an audience to accept his telescopic evidence (73).[28] Sadly for those who want to imitate Galileo, the keys to performing sprezzatura remain under insiders' control. Even the original etiquette manual on the subject imagined sprezzatura as resistant to written instruction (Biagioli 74).

The reader familiar with these debates already knows where I am going with the inverse of this nontransferable genius, but for the uninitiated, I cite Biagioli as he explains that the virtue of sprezzatura

> was routinely opposed to "pedantry," which was seen as the sign of one's technical and therefore low-class background. To be a pedant meant to have dogmatic

> opinions, to be unable to argue as a "free-thinker," to be slave to a philosophical system, to be unable to "play." In short, somebody who sought final causes or was a prisoner to a philosophical system did not display the "intellectual nonchalance" required of a courtly cultural performer. (75)

Only insiders can operate on the inside, in other words, and the rest are stuck with the label of pedants, which from a twentieth-century perspective on the sixteenth, can be understood as alluding to a rule-following performance of character, rather than rebelliously ludic tricks of personality. Fear of being pedantic endures across the centuries. In fact, in the 1960s Emmanuel Carballo uses the term in the prologues for the Nuevos Escritores autobiographies by Leñero and Melo. In his introduction to *Vicente Leñero* (1967) Carballo assesses Leñero's personality at age thirty-three as tending toward introverted intelligence: "Hombre solitario, introvertido, de una timidez que en algo se asemeja a la soberbia, rehúye en la conversación la pedantería y la suficiencia" (A solitary man, introverted, with a shyness that to some extent resembles arrogance, in conversation he shuns pedantry and smugness) (5).

Among the self-aware pages of the biography itself, Leñero presents himself as fearful of pedantry; he makes this worry cool by treating it self-consciously in a heavily metafictional text. That is, not only does Leñero portray himself imagining that he will inform his editor, Giménez Siles, of his disdain for the cult of personality, as I cited, but he also deals with an imagined reply from the editor about accepting the autobiographical project:

> Qué pedante al responder bueno sí, y qué pedante al responder perdone usted pero no. Pedante al hablar y pedante al quedarse callado. A él no le está permitido ni lo uno ni lo otro porque solamente los genios de nuestra literatura nacional [. . .] pueden tomar la decisión que se les antoje, ya que hagan lo que hagan y digan lo que digan seguirán siendo, señores del jurado, eso: genios. (18)
>
> What a pedant when you answer well okay, and what a pedant when you answer sorry sir but no. A pedant when you speak and a pedant when you keep quiet. He [Leñero] isn't allowed one or the other because only the geniuses of our national literature . . . can make whatever decision they feel like, since regardless of whatever they do and whatever they say they will continue being, gentlemen of the jury, just that: geniuses.

Here we have the opposite of the pedantic in mid-century Mexican terms: the self-aware calculation of the risk of pedantry. That is, one escape from the label *pedant* is to claim it, and thus show sprezzatura-like humor. The fictional Leñero explains the technique:

> Si él [Leñero] escribe: soy un pedante, los lectores dirán: no es nada pedante, miren cómo se trata a sí mismo sin ninguna consideración, con lo cual se habrá ganado la simpatía de esa media docena de curiosos lectores, ¡ojalá fueran un millón!: suplica. Y así lo escribe (. . . diciendo que es un pedante consiga producir el efecto contrario, etcétera) otra vez trayendo a colación el mecanismo, juego circular. (29)

> If he [Leñero] writes: I am a pedant, the readers will say: he's not pedantic at all, look how unkindly he treats himself, which will have won the sympathy of that half dozen of curious readers, if only they were a million!: he wishes. And so he writes (. . . saying that he is a pedant can produce the opposite effect, et cetera) once again bringing into it the mechanism, the circular game.

Under this formula, a highly self-conscious self-accusation of pedantry implies its cool inverse. The game of authenticity dizzies me here, as the authentic becomes as coolly ironical as it gets. Is it any wonder writers seem to have talked themselves out of the job of giving authoritative political opinions on television? These men are too cool for school, by more than a sound bite.

Other writers in this period, such as Monsiváis and Montes de Oca, use the same tactic and block the insult by jokingly accusing themselves first of pedantry. The reader cannot take it seriously when Monsiváis explains his youthful embrace of his studious side over his ambition to become a swimmer: "De allí en adelante sería pedante y libresco" (From then on I would be a pedantic bookworm) (*Carlos Monsiváis* 17). Montes de Oca comments that in middle school he became friends with a literary group marked by "obscena pedantería" (obscene pedantry) (*Marco Antonio* 24–25). By contrast, Montes de Oca defines writers Eduardo Lizalde and Salvador Elizondo as brilliant talents: "Él [Lizalde] y Salvador Elizondo son dos genios" (He [Lizalde] and Salvador Elizondo are the two geniuses) (39).[29] The prologue to Montes de Oca's autobiography uses this same language of the pedantic, and Carballo laments the too brief existence of Montes de Oca's early poetry group; the *poeticismo* (poeticism) movement deserved more, he writes, despite the shortcomings of "este ismo entre juvenil y pedante" (this ism between childish and pedantic) (5). The lesson here is that rushing to recognize the pedantic defuses the insult.

My reader may be curious about the identity of Leñero's personality test grader, since "E.D." is clearly not Carballo (E.C.) despite sharing language with him. In July 2016, I talked with Leñero's fellow writer Miguel Sabido, who also enjoyed a grant from the Centro Mexicano de Escritores for 1961–62. He confirmed my suspicion that the initials "E.D." probably correspond to Emma Dolujanoff.[30] Though Sabido may have confused events from more than half a century ago, it seems likely for reasons of proximity and expertise that Dolujanoff was the writer-psychiatrist in charge of evaluating the exams. Her work in assessing the 1961 group, performed in 1960, would have fallen only one year after she finished her second grant with the Centro Mexicano de Escritores. The exam duplicates her masculinist vision of literature as apparent in one of her winning grant proposals, which sought to study, in systematic fashion, men-authored texts as Literature; she planned to "emprender el estudio metódico de la Historia de la Literatura" (undertake the methodical study of the History of Literature) (CME Dolujanoff 16). The 1961 exam for the Centro Mexicano de Escritores required applicants to write about some of the eighteen men authors in a list, from Shakespeare to Tennessee Williams, passing through Dante, Quevedo, Wilde, Faulkner, and Hemingway; no woman writer appears as an option.[31] This list reflects Dolujanoff's plan for her thesis, and she intended to pay special attention to Shakespeare and Dostoyevsky for their "profundo contenido psicológico" (deep psychological content) (CME Dolujanoff 16).

Dolujanoff's likely assessment tools, while exhausted in a flash in the archive, inform us of discriminations usually omitted from the record. Take her negative evaluation of Miguel Sabido's exam, a rejection I preferred not to mention to him some fifty-six years later, as I sat in the living room of his spacious home. On July 30, 1960, the same date as the Leñero document, Dolujanoff probably typed the following "interpretation" (*interpretación*) of Sabido's responses:

> Contesta con sencillez y sin las pretensiones que parecen advertirse en su carta solicitud. Aquí no impresiona como pedante, salvo tal vez en el uso de algún galicismo innecesario y a veces, excesiva firmeza en ciertas opiniones que adquieren casi un tono de sentencia infalible. Ejemplo de esto, cuando manifiesta su opinión acerca de Dickens o cuando dice que "para no caer en lo obvio y escoger a Hamlet o Macbeth," se decide por Porcia. En cuanto a Dickens, puede desde

> luego no gustarle, pero su crítica parece exagerada e injusta. Tal vez sea una "pose de modernismo" la que le impide comprometerse con la ternura y otras cualidades de los personajes de Dickens. Casi seguramente que este exceso es solo un índice de inmadurez en un sujeto inteligente y en mi opinión con muchas posibilidades. (CME Sabido 33–34)[32]
>
> He answers simply and without the pretensions that one seems to note in his application letter. Here he doesn't come off as pedantic, except perhaps in the use of some unnecessary gallicism and at times, excessive firmness in certain opinions that acquire almost a tone of infallible judgment. One example of this, when he expressed his opinion about Dickens or when he says that "to avoid the obvious and pick Hamlet or Macbeth," he elects Portia. Regarding Dickens, you can certainly not like him, but his [Sabido's] criticism seems exaggerated and unfair. Maybe it's a "pose of modernism" that stops him from engaging with the tenderness and other qualities of Dickens's characters. Almost certainly this excess is just one index of immaturity in a subject who is intelligent and in my opinion of much promise.

This evaluation fascinates for its contradictions and vocabulary (*pedante*, *inmadurez*). On the one hand, the unpretentious answers regarding literary taste save Sabido from the dreaded accusation of pedantry. On the other hand, his responses reveal excessive certainty, which appears immature. Obviously, the performance of sprezzatura is no easy task, even for an entitled man. Like Aguilar Sosa's ironic reading of Leñero's file, an irony informed by what we already know of his creative triumphs, I was struck by the amusing contrast between the negative review of Sabido in the archive and the successful television writer he became.

Another quality that tracks literary genius, aka the opposite of the pedantic, is the notion of *malicia* (malice). In the prologue to Salvador Elizondo's autobiography, Carballo writes in 1966 that Elizondo never seems an immature writer because his earliest texts are structured with malicia (9). Similarly, for the prologue to Tomás Mojarro's autobiography, Carballo comments on Mojarro's largely self-taught journey from immaturity to malicia: "Escritor en estado natural cuando inaugura la bibliografía, Mojarro recorre en cinco años la distancia que existe entre la ingenuidad y la malicia, entre la incultura y la actitud contraria" (A writer in a natural state when he inaugurates his bibliography, Mojarro traces in five years the distance that exists between naïveté and malice, between boorishness and the contrary attitude) (5).[33]

That malicia cannot be other than innate or self-taught is a suspicion supported by Danny Anderson's methodical study of the paperwork from the publishing house Joaquín Mortiz. From 1961 to 1973, its manuscript evaluators used malicia as a criterion for the selection of aesthetically edgy texts. Anderson extracts four key elements that define "quality" literature for the Joaquín Mortiz readers: malicia, originality, reader participation, and *oficio* (craft) (22). Anderson views malicia as "perhaps the most crucial of the markers of quality" (24). The term malicia never appears with a formal definition in the reports, although Anderson's understanding is that it relates to "both communicative cunning or narrative instinct," as well as "the ways in which such skill reveals itself in the composition of a text." In other words, malicia evokes vague concepts such as expert craft and "superb intuition about originality" (24). Malicia is probably meant to denote the opposite of writing that is too easy, too pretty (*bonito*) rather than good (*bueno*)—those gendered terms which should ring a bell from chapter 2. The sexist connotations turn nearly explicit when Anderson notes that on the team at work for Joaquín Mortiz, "men greatly outnumbered women as both readers and potential authors" (26). Malicia favors the aggressive and even shocking, the technique of attention getting by breaking the rules, and it makes for a high and hard read, something like Elizondo's *Farabeuf* or Pacheco's *Morirás lejos* (*You Will Die in a Distant Land*) (1967).

How to get at these rumors of gender bias if malicia is never explicitly defined? The prejudices that link the cool and the masculine, as well as the feminine and the pedantic, can be seen, through a game of clumsy lip sync, by citing Susan Fraiman's *Cool Men and the Second Sex* and adding certain synonyms for *cool* and *bad boys*, such as *genius* and *bully*, and by suggesting the synonymous nature of *feminine* and *pedant*. The point is that the substitutions preserve intact the meaning of the paragraph:

> The cool subject [a *genius personality*] identifies with an emergent, precarious masculinity produced in large part by youthful rule breaking. Within this structure of feeling, the feminine [*pedant*] is materialized and hopelessly linked to stasis, tedium, constraint, even domination. Typed as "mothers," women [the *pedants*] become inextricable from a rigid domesticity that bad boys [the *geniuses*] are pledged to resist and overcome. A defining quality of coolness [or *malicia*, *sprezzatura*, and *je ne sais quoi*], then, is that a posture of flamboyant unconventionality [a *magnetic personality*] coexists with highly conventional views of gender—is articulated through them. (xii–xiii)

Perhaps because these terms are so heavily gendered, women cannot move back and forth, from the informal cool to the formal register of character, in the way that men can. Men can "play" by occupying the "light" or "incompetent" side of the binary as merely a joke and not a permanently contaminating experience.

Switching from the pedant, I can find another zone of Mexican bad taste feared by writers in the *naco*. It is easy to overinterpret the racist note in the term *naco*. The insult sounds like the Spanish word for the Totonac tribe, *totonaco*, an indigenous group in central Mexico. However, in contemporary usage, racist aggression is not the primary insult. *Naco* indicates something like the problem of the nouveau riche: an individual who has enough money to make significant consumption choices and yet fails to spend those resources knowledgeably. Though the naco can refer to men or women, I find it significant that Claudio Lomnitz in *Deep Mexico* defines it with a feminine reference: "So, for example, the *naca* is moved by the sofas in her living room and she seeks to preserve their modernizing impact by coating them with plastic." Lomnitz quickly observes, in more gender-neutral terms, "In addition to marking a kind of kitsch, the epithet *naco* also connotes a certain lack of distinction, or at least a lack of hierarchy, between 'high culture' and its popular imitations" (*Deep Mexico* 112).[34] The naco is the opposite of the cool, of sprezzatura, and all the other terms that refer to the unteachable art of edgy behavior.

Conversations with taxi drivers over the summer, in places as diverse as Spain and Mexico, before Trump's win in 2016 helped to persuade me that those whom some view as naco, others call with a straight face, genius; in a gender reversal experiment, it is nearly impossible to imagine a woman pulling off Trump's flip. (Keep in mind that would-be flipping figures like Martha Stewart and Elba Esther Gordillo ended up in prison.)[35] While consumption is viewed negatively when women do it, men with a reputation for genius can get away with it. The consumer-genius—always understood as male—is seen as a benefactor of humanity. With that observation, I want to explore an area of protected shopping mostly exercised by exceptionally privileged men.

One angle that protects a constant shopper, like, say, Carlos Monsiváis—or the nonwriter friend of Monsiváis, Carlos Slim—from a reputation of naco or the pedantic, of bad credit in general, is sheltered status as a philanthropist. This trick of excess deserves close study, not least because as the Mexican state may have become less interested in preserving writers' legacies, philanthropists have stepped in to fill the gap, with nearly indistinguishable results in terms of the quality of project funded and the type of writer picked to receive the benefit.

Jumex money, for instance, has been discussed of late in the cases of woman writer Valeria Luiselli and man writer Juan Villoro (M. Gutiérrez). It seems that when state interest levels off, a private philanthropist continues some support for the arts, an arrangement familiar from the Rockefeller-funded origins of the Centro Mexicano de Escritores.

Think for a moment about the meaning of Monsiváis's book collection. The 27,000-volume personal library remained in his private household until his death, when it was purchased for 13 million pesos by Conaculta, the Mexican governmental fine arts division, at the behest of Monsiváis's woman friend Consuelo Sáizar, and deposited in the José Vasconcelos National Library (Bucio, "Va biblitoeca"). Unlike women's collections of shoes, purses, stuffed animals, and the like (remember the criticism of Daniela Rossell's *Rich and Famous* subjects), a book collection does not receive the same public scorn, because collecting books is not perceived as naco. Monsiváis's collection of nearly two thousand films, along with numerous posters, stills, audience programs, photographs, and autographs, did not elicit negative reactions either when cultural reporters covered the process of cataloging the items that he had not yet donated to the Museo del Estanquillo.

Slim, the aforementioned donor of the Estanquillo museum building, is a multibillionaire and can buy nearly anything he chooses. He also created the Museo Soumaya, located in the posh Polanco neighborhood of the national capital, which lavishly displays the mogul's obsessive interest in the artist Auguste Rodin. Other collections funded by Slim's philanthropy include items related to Salvador Novo, such as his toupees, housed now in an archive. How are Monsiváis and Slim allowed reputations as philanthropists? After all, the act of excessive collecting disrupts the usual flow of capital, not to mention the balance of middle-class propriety.[36] Why is this philanthropy a sign of depth of character and not frivolous personality? The gendered connotations of the philanthropist help us to view Slim's and Monsiváis's holdings as a social investment rather than luxurious self-indulgence.[37] In the way of the conveniently self-serving flip from civilizado to bárbaro, of upstanding character to quirky personality, these men can posit their private collections and personal interests as public goods and thus help to mint the very idea of civilized credit.

Interesting academic work exists on the matter of U.S. philanthropy. Scholarship by Olivier Zunz clarifies that because of its outstanding size, the philanthropic gift operates for "mankind," whereas smaller-scale charity is for the "needy" (10).[38] As Francie Ostrower sums up the convenient trick of outsize donations in *Why the Wealthy Give*, "Philanthropy, in short, allows elites to enjoy the sense that they are making a contribution to society, while defining social benefit on their own terms" (136). In *The Givers* David Callahan makes a similar point. Because almost no oversight exists for philanthropists, giving on a large scale "can be a way of taking" (9). In an example of that idea, I note Carlos Slim's contributions to his own Foundation for the Historic Center, a philanthropic organization that helps to restore an area in the heart of Mexico City, where by October 2007 Slim's family controlled "indirectly" some fifty-six buildings (González G). For the reader new to the subject, I repeat an estimate of Slim's bárbaro fortune: $73 billion in 2013, according to *Forbes* (Haas 107).[39]

I should also stipulate from the start that these elite takers are largely men.[40] By Ostrower's New York–based count, there are fewer wealthy women than men, and those "women occupy an ambivalent position as members of the elite, which combines both power and powerlessness" (69).[41] As predicted from the treatment of wives in *Pedro Páramo* and *Las batallas en el desierto*, whose function at the beginning of the marriage is to extend credit to the businessman and who later find themselves in a compromised position, women seem to have a rougher time turning away from bad credit and poor taste than men.

Thanks to a system devised by the nineteenth-century male captains of industry, the special status of philanthropy earns it a significant tax break.[42] Importantly, in order to qualify as philanthropic, a donation must pertain to a "political-neutral field," which strangely enough in the United States includes gifts to education (Zunz 5). This idea of political neutrality proves, once again, to be a game that favors the performance granted to men. Literary critics know, however, that book collections are not politically neutral. It is precisely Monsiváis's apparent *abundance* of political awareness, supported by the scholarly and thus educational aura of his collections, that strengthens his moral gravitas. By contrast, the apparent *lack* of political consciousness wielded by women who collect items that might be described as "not art," casts them as unaware of the morally questionable origins of their family fortunes, or their proper duty in the world as consumers. The paradox takes my breath away with its efficiency: men are such authorities that they can become, from an institutional perspective, *neutral authorities*, rather than mere political participants. The men authorities seemingly rotate outside the system in order to fix it. Thus, Monsiváis's acquaintanceship with Carlos Slim does not taint him, and thus, Slim stands near Monsiváis. Thus, Mexican presidential power, in Almaraz's composite portrait from chapter 2, poses near books.

The mechanism of philanthropy helps to convert massive wealth into a middle class–conforming appearance of morally upstanding behavior: sober and thrifty—not just because of the donor's clever working of the system for tax benefits but also because resources are invested into the collective future. *But how can someone as fantastically wealthy as Carlos Slim play middle class?* you gasp. Easy: Slim insists on the theme of sobriety when talking about himself and his children: "Diría que soy sobrio y mis hijos también. Por gusto, por convicción, no por disciplina" (J. Martínez, *Los secretos* 68). (I'd say I'm sober and my children too. By preference, by conviction, and not by discipline.)[43] Slim invokes the middle-class value of sobriety to the point that he praises this value as an ideal for institutions as well, as evident in his comments about the state-owned petroleum business, perhaps with an eye to promoting its privatization:

> Entonces lo importante es que Pemex sea una empresa muy eficiente, sobria, muy eficaz, que cree más riqueza y que el fruto de esa riqueza que vaya creando en parte se reinvierta y en parte se redistribuya. (39)

> So it's important that Pemex be very efficient, sober, very effective, that it create more wealth and that the fruit of that wealth that it creates be in part reinvested and in part redistributed.

Again, I note a curious shared territory with the neoliberal and middle-class values, which encourages me to question just how distant literary critics find themselves from the ways and means of neoliberalism, notwithstanding their vociferous disgust with the system. Is our criticism so mired in unacknowledged gender assumptions that it is unable to reckon fairly with the meaning of the literary project under capitalism?

One would never guess that the endrogado could come near Slim's tactics. And yet, he is on the record performing a flipped, decidedly nonsober role. This switch occurs during an interview with Diego Enrique Osorno, who presses Slim on whether he bought the communications monopoly Telmex as an insider favor from then-President Carlos Salinas de Gortari. In reaction to Osorno's question about Salinas's motives for criticizing him in an article, Slim begins to swear. The exchange begins with Osorno's question:

> —Entonces, ¿qué motivación tendría el ex presidente Salinas para sacar este artículo?

—En decir que es un chingón, que él lo hizo todo limpio y que los demás son unos pendejos y sucios, y que Telmex es una mierda.

—¿Eso quiere decir que no hay una relación entre usted y Salinas?

—No, sí lo veo . . . Lo vi el otro día y le dije que decía una bola de mentiras. (Osorno, *Slim* 76)

"So, what motivation might former President Salinas have to publish this article?"

"To say that he is a badass, that he did everything clean and that everyone else is an asshole and dirty, and that Telmex is shit."

"Does that mean that there isn't a relationship between you and Salinas?"

"No, of course I see him . . . I saw him the other day, and I told him that he was spreading a bunch of lies."

The sudden rough language, with terms like *chingón* (badass) and *mierda* (shit) issuing from Slim, marks an agile switch to the bárbaro or bully or personality-rich discourse within an otherwise polite conversation. Slim changes registers partly to match Salinas's perceived failure to play by the rules; the former president broke with gentlemanly courtesy in his impolite criticism of Slim, so the billionaire responds in kind. Furthermore, Slim's swearwords probably aim to establish a phatic bond with Osorno's status as an intrepid northern Mexican male reporter. It tests the imagination to think that Slim would speak this way to a woman reporter.

What happens when a man cannot pull off the transition from bullying personality to civilizado, and gets stuck with the reputation of a *lack of character*? I can name two examples of that predicament: Juan José Arreola and Salvador Novo, who both used outsized personality to pull off glamorously fancy wardrobes and yet, as they aged, began to attract complaints about their ethical faults. They could not successfully use the philanthropist cover to justify some of their excesses, nor could they safely retreat to a conservative middle-class performance. In both cases, something feminine about their approach, familiar from the traditional and glamorous techniques of the "diva-lectuals" whom I studied in *Boob Lit*, ultimately tripped them up.

Novo and Arreola defend their social status as, in the first case, a well-to-do gay man transplanted as a boy to Mexico City by the violence of the Revolution and, in the second case, a financially struggling, self-taught man who came to Mexico City in young adulthood in search of professional opportunity. Novo's homosexuality and Arreola's provincial background and attendant lack of formal education did not initially stand in their way as they staked a claim to intellectual competence through glamorous performance, a technique that worked as long as they remained young looking. When they aged, however, this mystique turned on them. Near the end, Arreola's traditional glamour act coincided with financial instability; Novo's royalist airs only drew public rejection.

I want to review each man's fall in greater detail because these examples prove informative about a no-longer-tolerated bad boy performance. In the case of Arreola, the cape-wearing fiction writer proudly quoted Octavio Paz as having told him, "Eres tan genial y tan cursi como Ramón López Velarde" (You are as charming and as corny as Ramón López Velarde) (qtd. in O. Arreola 239). In contrast to Paz's intellectual lineage, Arreola dropped out of school at age twelve; in contrast to Paz's secularism, Arreola was a fan of the Virgin of Guadalupe, and—like López Velarde—an openly practicing Catholic. To sum up this difference, while Paz, especially after 1968, sometimes shed the suit-and-tie look of his public-servant days, Arreola's wardrobe is most famous for looking *back* in time, to a kind of competence implied by way of aristocratic performance.[44]

Arreola created his own credentials, through performance, and he fell into debt. In 1976, a gossipy conversation with the Mexico City official historian (judging by the date, probably Miguel León Portilla) revealed to the newspaper-reading public that Arreola's tight budget, despite his lucrative employment by the television monopoly Televisa, had him living a nomadic lifestyle:

> También Arreola, quien al parecer gana mucho dinero, se las arregla para gastarlo todo y sigue viviendo como un monje. Hace poco visité la casa de Arreola y noté que ni siquiera posee una cama [. . .]. Arreola duerme en el suelo en una especie de asiento de automóvil que tiende por las noches en casa de una de sus hijas. La pieza está llena de objetos extraños y de cristales. [. . .] Me explicó que paga muchos impuestos, gasta mucho en taxis, que tiene a su servicio diariamente: además ayuda a su familia. [. . .] También esos trajes extraños que se hace son muy caros. Al igual que sus gorras y chalecos. (Palhares 48)

> Also Arreola, who apparently earns a lot of money, manages to spend it all and keeps living like a monk. Not long ago I visited Arreola's house and I noticed that he doesn't even have a bed. . . . Arreola sleeps on the floor on a kind of car seat that he spreads out at night in one of his daughter's homes. The room is full of strange

> objects and crystals. . . . He explained to me that he pays a lot of taxes, he spends a lot on taxis, which are at his beck and call daily: besides he supports his family. . . . Also those strange suits he has made are very expensive. So too his caps and vests.

The matter of Arreola's wobbly finances concerns no few letters in the file on him stored in the Centro Mexicano de Escritores archive. Here we see his struggle with bad credit, which anticipates his fall from public approval.[45]

Luxury items may explain some of Arreola's financial woes; these costly tastes may have served as something like an intellectual credential for the self-taught writer.[46] The unsustainable spending was only part of Arreola's taste for outrageous behavior. Onlookers such as Víctor Villela claimed that on the UNAM campus, Arreola engaged in over-the-top scenes that found complicity with at least one other writer:

> Arreola (con frecuencia envuelto en una capa española) y Rubén Bonifaz Nuño siempre que en la CU [Ciudad Universitaria] se encontraban, se hincaban uno frente al otro (en el punto en que se detectaran con la mirada) y avanzaban de rodillas poco a poco hasta recorrer el espacio que los separaba para finalmente darse un abrazo, ante el azoro de los profesores y de los alumnos que anduviesen por ahí, los que a veces eran una gran cantidad. (CME Arreola 10-1: 49)

> Whenever Arreola (often wrapped in a Spanish cape) and Rubén Bonifaz Nuño came across one another in CU [University City], they knelt one in front of the other (at the point when they detected each other with a look) and advanced on their knees little by little until they crossed the space that separated them to finally embrace, to the embarrassment of the professors and students walking around there, who were sometimes numerous.

Whether the anecdote is true matters less than the memory of personality-rich behavior. This hyperbolic playfulness sets up Arreola's disastrous later-in-life appearance on live television with Mexican pop singer Thalía, in which she accused him of being a "rabo verde" (dirty old man).[47]

The file on Arreola in the archives of the Centro Mexicano de Escritores contains a newspaper article on the topic, which frames the youthful Thalía's comments in the context of a discourse of rebellious authenticity. She calls Arreola "un viejo" (an old man) and criticizes him for having arrived at the program hosted by Verónica Castro, *La movida* (Nightlife), with his zipper down (Quiroz

Arroyo). The article justifies Thalía's own skimpily clothed stage performances as a claim to youth culture. More than public humiliation resulted from Arreola's time on television. Octavio Paz, according to Domínguez Michael, voted in 1972 for Fuentes over Arreola to join El Colegio Nacional, because Paz disapproved of Arreola's entertaining rather than intellectual presence on television (*Octavio Paz* 234).

The same fall from glamour happened to Novo, who starred on television in segments about Mexico City history. Novo used to appear with longtime anchorman Jacobo Zabludovsky on the Friday night newscast *24 Horas*, of the Televisa monopoly, "con evocaciones de la vieja capital" (with tales of the old capital city) (Monsiváis, *Salvador Novo* 186). That friendship would lead to his final humiliation, but first I should review Novo's triumphs. Born almost fifteen years before Arreola, Novo pioneered an outrageous style, which Paz remembers with an intriguing word choice: "Nos azoraban sus corbatas, sus juicios irreverentes, sus zapatos bayos y chatos, su pelo untado de *stacomb*, sus cejas depiladas, sus anglicismos" (We were startled by his ties, his irreverent opinions, his yellowish-cream-colored and short-toed shoes, his hair greased with Stacomb gel, his plucked eyebrows, his Anglicisms) (*Xavier Villaurrutia* 9–10). The verb in that sentence, *azoraban*, is ambiguous: Does Paz mean "startled," or more "alarmed," or full-blown "embarrassed"?

Novo's aristocratic performance, at various stages of his life accomplished with face powder, large rings, plucked eyebrows, bespoke suits, assorted toupees in various colors, and even a cane, may have everything to do with the reason why more onlookers so easily agreed that Novo, but not necessarily Paz or Monsiváis, behaved irresponsibly toward power as he aged. And yet, can we so easily accuse the aging Novo of greater intimacy with Mexican presidential power than Paz enjoyed, to name just one example?[48] Such a binary of Paz's relative integrity against Novo's corruption is the result of reading performance perhaps more than text.

Like Paz, Monsiváis hints at embarrassment over a sixty-something-year-old Novo in an anecdote that documents the latter's attempt to scandalize guests at a party for intellectuals in 1966:

> Novo hace un aparte y se polvea. Me le acerco y le pregunto: "¿Qué pasa, maestro?" Y me responde: "Me gusta provocarlos. Cuando ya se acostumbran a uno, hay que echarle leña al fuego." Y sigue polveándose. (*Salvador Novo* 181)

> Novo steps aside and powders his face. I go up to him and ask: "What's going on, maestro?" And he answers: "I like to provoke them. When they get used to you, you've got to throw more wood on the fire." And he continues powdering himself.

The performative aspect of makeup refuses to accept character-based rules of modesty and sobriety and instead favors a seemingly unpredictable personality-rich act. Onlookers' tolerance for this act ends when the player's youthful sex appeal fades.

Heartbreakingly, perhaps, Novo could see the means of his own undoing: the aging process. As early as 1925, when he was not yet twenty-five years old, he published in *XX poemas* a plucky poem titled "Primera cana" (First gray hair) (Novo, *Material de lectura* 9–10). As the years wore on, of course, Novo did not handle the aging process as gracefully as the relative spunk of "Primera cana" might have predicted. His stylized affinity for the virtues of the past got him into trouble. Ten years after the writer's death, one newspaper article reaffirmed Novo's late-in-life negative reputation by remembering "su incorporación al régimen de Gustavo Díaz Ordaz y su posición pública—lamentable—ante los sangrientos hechos del dos de octubre de 1968" (his membership in Gustavo Díaz Ordaz's regime and his public position—lamentable—regarding the bloody events of October 2, 1968) (Vallarino 137). That comment evokes Novo's public glee after the military takeover of the UNAM campus on September 23, 1968. Mexicans rejected that aristocratic act, and in turn a wounded Novo queried, "¿Pero que no todos sabían que soy un reaccionario?" (But didn't they all know I'm a reactionary?) ("Salvador Novo: Su musa callejera" 141).[49]

His public graces in question, Novo published confessions in the 1970s of his upper-class aspirational and thus middle-class conforming desire to lose weight. For instance, in his newspaper column on May 10, 1972, he admitted his absurd faith in a miracle-promising weight clinic, writing that he had made "la aventada decisión de visitar, al día siguiente esa Clínica que se anuncia tan conveniente, convincente: tantos kilos en tantos días, sin dieta, sin molestias, sin ejercicios ni sacrificios. Garantizados" (Novo, "Cartas"). ([T]he bold decision to visit, the next day, that Clinic that advertises itself as so convenient, convincing: so many kilos in so many days, without a diet, without troubles, without exercises or sacrifices. Guaranteed.) In January 1974, Novo died in a Mexican gastrointestinal hospital ward, apparently from complications due to his weight loss regime.

The hours before his death included the humiliation of being filmed for television without his toupee, makeup, dentures, and wearing only a skimpy hospital gown (Barrera 253). This lamentable exposure was the result of the poet's friendship with Zabludovsky, who had sent his son, a cub reporter, to catch up with Novo during his hospitalization. César Benítez Torres recalls how the younger Zabludovsky caught the poet unprepared:

> Una de las escenas más lamentables que he visto en la TV es aquella en la que el debutante reportero de *24 horas* Abraham Zabludovsky se mete con cámaras y micrófonos hasta el lecho de muerte del que fue Premio Nacional de Literatura, para recoger casi sus últimas palabras. Salvador Novo, con voz cadavérica, alcanzó a gemir algunas frases y después, impotente y vencido, se puso a llorar con angustia y pánico. Ni la cámara, ni el reportero, ni el noticiario, ni la teleaudiencia pudieron respetar esos momentos, sin duda difíciles, de un hombre en agonía. A las pocas horas, el papá del reportero dio la noticia del deceso. ("Salvador Novo y la TV")

> One of the saddest scenes I've seen on TV is the one in which the rookie reporter from *24 Hours* Abraham Zabludovsky entered with cameras and microphones next to the deathbed of he who was the National Literature Prize, to catch his nearly last words. Salvador Novo, with a cadaverous voice, managed to moan a few phrases and then, helpless and defeated, he began to cry with anxiety and panic. Neither the camera, nor the reporter, nor the news show, nor the viewers managed to respect those moments, doubtless difficult ones, of a man in agony. Within a few hours, the father of the reporter broke the news of the death.

Novo's pathetic end strips him of dignity—that necessary underpinning of the character act and justification for sliding to and from a personality performance. Pedro Páramo, while pathologically cruel, never forgoes dignity. Novo lost his grip on it.

One reason why Novo, along with Arreola, may have failed to please fans with his public behavior lies in striking the proper balance. This failure occurred in performance, but not so much in deed. Both men's glamorous acts favored, at the core, democratic values.[50] Arreola tirelessly taught writing to young people and edited their work; Novo left a sizable fortune for scholarships in writing and acting, which helped to fund young artists of the likes of Volpi and Boullosa. Sadly, the scholarship money evaporated under the strain of the fluctuation that devalued the peso in the 1980s—a fact confirmed by Carmen Boullosa in a personal conversation.

This twinned discussion of Arreola and Novo juxtaposes Arreola's troubles with debt and Novo's solid finances and returns me once more to the point that debt and credit are two facets of the same issue. I'd like to offer one last example of debt forged from credit, and credit extracted from debt, thanks to superior performances of authority. I now turn to accreditation matters.

We might think of it as a character-based performance when Rosario Castellanos gains status as an intellectual by way of formal studies: she completed not one but two university degrees, a BA and an MA While Castellanos labors to pay off an intellectual debt that apparently will never release her, men writers of her generation and later can sidestep this formal apprenticeship. Men writers who did *not* finish their degrees include Amado Nervo, Octavio Paz, and José Emilio Pacheco in the field of law; Carlos Monsiváis in economics; Guillermo Fadanelli in engineering; Xavier Velasco in political science and later in literature; and Juan Rulfo in any course of study.[51] Not one of those seven writers finished the university credentialing process. This question of formal educational accreditation is almost wildly unrelated to the success of a twentieth- or twenty-first-century male Mexican artist or intellectual, which shows the power of being seen to wield both the proper personality, which manufactures credit through mirages of superficial, ephemeral change, and to enjoy peers among character-vouching networks, which awards credit on stability.

Ironically, some of these same men participated in a tightening of accreditation processes for the generations that followed them, thereby passing down debts like those Castellanos tried to settle. It is from the very group of men intellectuals who failed to finish their degrees, or took circuitous routes to get them, that institutions such as the Secretariat of Public Education would hire their textbook writers and directors. Alatorre recognizes the influence of friendship over credentials on his career when he confesses that "por puro cariño que me tenía" (out of sheer affection he had for me), Daniel Cosío Villegas wanted to propose Alatorre as a member of El Colegio Nacional, but he ran into the problem of his lack of publications: "por no tener yo en mi currículum ni un pinche libro" (because I didn't have on my CV a single fucking book) (Meyer 135). Alatorre overcame that problem, of course, and enjoyed an illustrious trajectory as a scholar.[52] He and others of his generation ultimately intensified the bureaucratic system, rather than extending the same liberal privileges they received to the generations that followed.

The quality of literary and critical production did not necessarily improve with the increasingly more complex bureaucratic controls, however. Unlike the generations surrounding that of Alatorre, the more contemporary university-trained and fully credentialed Mexican writers tend not to write Latin, Greek, French, and other languages that the older men learned by dint of an education influenced by religious training. Furthermore, the importance of a bullying personality and networking system remained intact. The credentialization process came to mean that nearly everyone looking for a role as an intellectual held more or less the same collection of degrees. Legitimacy had spread to all, which means that people within the cultural space for elite status—the successful bad boys who would move into a character act once personality no longer served them and vice versa—needed to rethink their staked claims to exceptionality.

The next chapter takes on one last tangle of gendered troubles, this time complicated by ageism. I begin by looking at women's tricky need to be seen as both attractively young and artistically mature, and I end with a constrained economic horizon that dooms Fadanelli's characters to immature adulthood.

7

GENDERED AGEISM AND LITERARY DEPRESSION

Age Lies Among Men and Women Writers at the Centro Mexicano de Escritores and Beyond, Prestigious Bad Moods, and Guillermo Fadanelli's Praise for Mediocrity

Él [Salvador Elizondo] y Juan García Ponce, Víctor Flores Olea, Vicente Rojo y yo somos del mismo año. No doy los nombres de las mujeres por discreción y porque siempre me dicen que es un error decir la propia edad.
—ELENA PONIATOWSKA

No se te vaya a ocurrir preguntarme mi edad, no se te vaya a ocurrir . . .
—MARÍA CONESA SPEAKING TO ELENA PONIATOWSKA

Guillermo Fadanelli belongs to perhaps the last generation able to lie about personal age, a possibility now greatly diminished if not vanished thanks to the public data of the information age. The Wikipedia entry on Fadanelli acknowledges the confusion he was able to sow: "sus datos biográficos contemplan distintas fechas de nacimiento que van de 1959 hasta 1965 aunque la real, 1960, no es la que más se repite" (his biographical data include different birthdates that go from 1959 to 1965 although the real one, 1960, isn't the most repeated one). What happens when the bad boy begins to bald and the audience can calculate that he nears sixty years of age? Not much, for two reasons. In the first place, ageism is kinder to men. In the second, bad boys are allowed to exercise the switch in roles from bárbaro to civilizado. An aging man can, if his clothing style has shunned excessive drama and backward-looking refinement, simply revert to playing the correctly civilized. Fadanelli's clothes indicate that he has reworked the flip in his later years. In chronological order and as documented in press photographs, Fadanelli has evolved from dressing all in black to wearing pajamas in public to always sporting Hawaiian shirts to today's more tempered look: sober clothes and, atop his head, throwback fedoras, one of which he wore during the entirety of our interview indoors in his home. Increasing age has encouraged Fadanelli to develop this new role of the more formally dressed civilizado. Sergio Gutiérrez Negrón observes that Fadanelli now balances his act between fulfilling the duties of an established, even institutional writer and keeping up with the demands of an image linked to an irreverent and anarchic "dirty realist" aesthetic (451).

Fadanelli's performance reminds me in some ways of Juan Rulfo's struggles as both a stylistic rebel and a mainstay of an institutional writing scene. Rulfo also told fibs about age, as well as about his birthplace and his education apropos a fictitious certificate in accounting.[1] On his wedding certificate and on his application for the Centro Mexicano de Escritores, Rulfo subtracted a year from his real age. Muckraking biographer Fernando Barrientos del Monte attributes this fib to institutional rules; he claims that from its beginning in 1952, the Centro Mexicano de Escritores considered only writers under age thirty-five, which forced Rulfo to subtract a year (Barrientos del Monte 41). But because Rulfo lied about his age on his marriage certificate, even before filling out the application for the Centro Mexicano de Escritores, I have to question Barrientos del Monte's explanation.[2]

When I ask former Centro grant winners, themselves aged sixty and up, they do not remember the age requirements, so I cannot confirm through them that the early incarnation of the Centro Mexicano de Escritores had an age limit of thirty-five. Not even Martha Domínguez Cuevas could remember clearly whether the Centro screened candidates for age in the early 1950s; she began work there in 1957 and stayed nearly fifty years until the institution closed. Domínguez Cuevas told me she was born in 1930, which makes her twenty-seven when she began work at the Centro—and more than a decade younger than Rulfo and Arreola. When I asked her about Rulfo's age fib, Domínguez Cuevas commented, like many others to whom I put the matter of Rulfo's creative age change, "Yo no le veo gran importancia el quitarse o ponerse un año. Yo no le veo ninguna importancia" (I can't see much importance in subtracting or adding a year. I don't see the importance at all) (personal interview).[3] But this topic does matter.

Rulfo and Fadanelli deserve compassion, though perhaps not complicity, for whatever insecurities drove them to autobiographical fibs and for the resulting tensions those lies may have leveraged.[4] In the larger scheme, their lies indicate the delusional nature of the idea that age presents an objective number and thus guarantees bureaucratic fairness. If age were purely objective, it would be difficult to lie about it, and the negative lash of ageism would affect men and women at the same age. The time has come to examine the meaning of age in the performance of the role of writer, because the twenty-first century has seen the closure of opportunities to lie. Under contemporary rules in the Mexican grant system, "young" writers usually must fall below the threshold age of thirty-five. This means a future Fadanelli or Rulfo will have no recourse once aged out of competition—though Fadanelli never enjoyed an age-graded Mexican grant as a young writer, as far as I know. Rulfo's case especially gives me much to ponder, because he depended on the grants from the Centro to produce the bulk of his oeuvre. Possibly, if paperwork in the mid-twentieth century had been accurate, two of the most storied achievements of Mexican literature, Rulfo's *El llano en llamas* (*The Burning Plain*) (1953) and *Pedro Páramo*, might not have been supported with grants—and thus might not have been completed.

It is impossible to measure the full consequences of today's absent wiggle room with the Mexican federal program Jóvenes Creadores (Young Creatives), which stipulates that the grant-worthy person's age must fall between eighteen and thirty-four. The national Tierra Adentro (Inner Land) program also classifies writers under thirty-five as makers of "young" literature and administers prizes labeled accordingly: Ensayo Joven (Young Essay), Poesía Joven (Young Poetry), Novela Joven (Young Novel), Dramaturgia Joven (Young Theater), Cuento Joven (Young Short Story), and so forth. Once writers age out of the "young" category, they move to other sorts of opportunities, though it isn't clear that a writer can skip the first stage of the age-graded career aids and arrive successfully on the scene as a mature writer. Further evidence of the model that the mature writer imposes is the fact that the fuller titles of the prizes for "young" literature are named for aged men. The awards named Young Essay José Vasconcelos or Young Chronicle Ricardo Garibay or Young Poetry Elías Nandino almost laughably contradict themselves in title by recognizing long-lived men: Vasconcelos died at age seventy-seven, Garibay at seventy-six, and Nandino at ninety-three.[5] And yet perhaps the point of naming "young" prizes for "old" men is to forge intergenerational bonds—a goal probably not well served by emphasizing age differences.

For more thought on this matter of the "young" genre, specifically the category of the young essay, I turn to Ignacio Sánchez Prado's double book review of Valeria Luiselli's *Papeles falsos* (Sidewalks; trans. *False papers*) (2010) and José Israel Carranza's *Las encías de la azafata* (The stewardess's gums) (2010). The paradox of the genre, he writes, has the authors of the young essay speak from a kind of existential medias res and nevertheless manage to articulate personal experience; hence, the genre of the young essay requires a contradictory kind of "madurez vital" (vital maturity) practiced by writers still "en formación" (in development) ("La incesante paradoja" 83). How authors reach full-blown maturity, as *Dude Lit* has been arguing, hangs as much on their extratextual performances as on their texts, and yet Sánchez Prado elides the performative element. In fact, he begins the review with ambivalence about the need to recognize writers' ages at all: "Si ponemos entre paréntesis por un momento la ociosidad de agrupar autores en generaciones, es sin duda de notar el auge que el ensayo ha tenido en escritores nacidos después de 1970" (If we open a parenthetical for a moment for the laziness of grouping authors in generations, it is certainly worth noting the rise that the essay has had among writers born after 1970) (83).

Whether recognizing generational divisions marks a redundant or idle activity or not, critics in the know already tend to think of writers by generation. Age connotes a political message, and these generational groupings can be used to imagine conflicts into or out of existence. I cite age scholar Margaret Morganroth Gullette on the matter, when she argues that the notion of generations supplies a political tool of distraction: "Age, you could say, manages many crises. Silly as this may seem, the constant noise of [generational] blame distracts people from thinking about power, class, or protest. . . ." (*Aged by Culture* 53). The denial of generational literary categories, especially in a context that organizes professional opportunities by age, seems to me an attempt to manage a political crisis by wishing it away. To get a better sense of how expectations for "young" writers have changed, it helps to look more closely at the tradition of rules that brought us to the present moment. To give a spoiler, I advance my finding: the official preference for young writers skews ever younger.

In the late 1970s, writers in the most prestigious category of competition for the Centro Mexicano de Escritores could be as old as forty. Two surviving pamphlets from the late 1970s lay out the rules and list age as the very first of the stipulations. The pamphlet for the 1975–76 grant year distinguishes between those applicants qualified for type A scholarships, awarded to writers "menores de 30 años" (younger than 30 years), and those destined for type B scholarships:

"A quienes, sin haber cumplido aún los 40 años de edad, hayan publicado algún libro o algunas obras de calidad literaria sobresaliente" (Who, without having turned 40 years old yet, have published some book or some works of outstanding literary quality) ("Centro Mexicano de Escritores: Bases" 21). The type B prize awards 10,000 pesos more than the type A. The booklet from 1978–79 increases the prize amounts by 5,000 pesos in each category and leaves the age rules unchanged ("Centro Mexicano de Escritores: XXVII Concurso" 9). Those rules endure with a slight modification, according to a document turned up by a Google search. A web article from 2003 indicates that the category for writers under forty disappeared; according to the disjointed summary of the requirements for that year's grant competition, "Para refrendar su compromiso de apoyar a los jóvenes literatos del país, cuya edad sea menor a 30 años, el cme abre su convocatoria de becas para este año" (To endorse its commitment of supporting the country's literary young people, whose age is under 30 years, the CME opens its call for grants for this year) (Rosales Maldonado).

Though I began by presenting fibs by Fadanelli and Rulfo, more women than men lie about their age for the literary record. As I have been warning, age rules impose a layer of sexism. Gullette warns that "gender always has an age . . . , although theorists rarely notice this" (*Aged by Culture* 160).[6] Women experience ageism about a decade earlier than men, in their forties rather than mid-fifties (Gullette, *Agewise* 4).[7] A photograph from the 1953–54 grant-winning group for the Centro Mexicano de Escritores, which is the year of Rulfo's second grant, shows six writers lined up for the camera. At first glance, the writers might seem to be the same age. The four men, two on each side of the pair of women, wear suits (Héctor Mendoza and Emmanuel Carballo) or a dress jacket and pants with a tie (Jerri Orson and Rulfo). In the middle, Rosario Castellanos wears a shiny sleeveless dress, complete with gloves and a small handbag, and Clementina Díaz y de Ovando seems dressed for colder weather in a three-quarter sleeve suit jacket with matching tweed-like skirt. Both women, in full skirts hemmed below their knees, wear black pumps; they look significantly shorter than the men, even in the heels (Juan Rulfo, Página).

The detail that perhaps does not appear readily to the naked eye is that of those six, not only Rulfo but also Clementina Díaz y de Ovando changed ages for the record. They are the only people in the photo over the age of thirty—by more years than the institution thought.[8] Díaz y de Ovando apparently took four years off her age in the documentation for the Centro Mexicano de

Escritores. Martha Domínguez Cuevas has Díaz y de Ovando's birth year as 1920, but Wikipedia and multiple obituaries date it to 1916 (Domínguez Cuevas 116; "Clementina Díaz y de Ovando"; "Fallece"; Palapa Quijas). At the time that Díaz y de Ovando enjoyed a grant from the Centro, she was actually thirty-seven, although creative mathematics made her thirty-three.

Women helped to reinforce discrimination in more ways than by lying. Margaret Shedd, the founder of the Centro Mexicano de Escritores, whom I introduced in chapter 3, wrote on an evaluation notecard, by hand in English, a compliment that today seems backhanded regarding the merits of applicant Ana Cecilia ("Bambi") Treviño: "Seems to be a very interesting project, and an attractive girl" (CME Treviño 17). The *attractive girl*, according to the information on that same application card, was thirty-two years old.[9] Intriguingly, even this timeline seems suspect: if Treviño were born in 1932, she would have been some sixteen years old when she began work for *Excélsior* in 1948, a date that Domínguez Cuevas reports in her book (402). A Facebook post from 2015 by the Instituto de Investigaciones Bibliográficas (Institute of Bibliographic Research) at the National Library lists Treviño's birth year as 1929, which would make her a more reasonable nineteen years of age when starting work for this mainstream paper. The strict truth matters less here than the possibility of the institutional acceptance of lies as truth. At the same time that people at the Centro cared about age, they seem to have accepted fictions about it, which places the importance of applicants' ages in a paradoxical status.

In the same vein, a winning application for the grant cycle 1966–67 elicited brief opinions handwritten by evaluators on a single notecard headed in typescript: "DAVILA, AMPARO. Edad: 38 años / Divorciada" (CME Dávila 28). The label "divorced" next to Dávila's age on the notecard hints how age can affect expectations for sexual experience and how civil status affects understanding of a gendered performance of age. Incidentally, I do not recall seeing another candidate on the notecards marked as "divorced," and the possible stigma of that adjective helps us understand why some women artists took pains to bury their sexual history. Independently of the Centro Mexicano de Escritores, women writers such as Elena Garro and Nellie Campobello altered their ages and made strategic decisions about the public record on their sexual partners. Garro subtracted a modest three years from her age (as did painter Frida Kahlo), but Nellie Campobello daringly erased an entire decade. Additionally, Garro liked to complain that Octavio Paz married her by force; according to this tale told later in life, Paz ambushed Garro when she was a minor and took her to the court rather than allowing her to attend an academic exam—a story that Domínguez Michael's archival fact-finding debunks (*Octavio Paz* 78–79).

In the Campobello case, Nellie, along with her sister Gloria, simply hushed personal sexual history, including the existence of Nellie's son, born before she moved to Mexico City, who died as a toddler (Tortajada Quiroz 270). As Margarita Tortajada Quiroz wryly observes, the sisters liked to have their sexual freedom and their misogynist stereotypes too: "por un lado ejercieron su sexualidad alejadas de las formas tradicionales y por otro se mantuvieron atadas a éstas y las reivindicaron públicamente (con su exigencia de ser llamadas señoritas, por ejemplo)" (on the one hand they exercised their sexuality far from the traditional forms and on the other hand they remained attached to those and publicly claimed them [with their demand to be addressed as young ladies, for example]) (539). Audience complicity supports the fashion of lying about one's age and sexual history, thereby supporting the women artists' claim to "innocence" along with competence.[10] Staking a claim to intellectual and artistic skill by way of youth presents a tricky balancing act for women. Men have an edge because they can accomplish a double reputation of youth and maturity by way of a younger partner.

In order to have their older age and connote youth too, twentieth-century men artists tended to trade down among partners, which surely contributed to the age pressure women felt.[11] This habit of exchanging a woman partner for someone younger suggests that men artists gained status from lovers' ages. On that note, I cite Max Aub's diary from August 1, 1967, when he marvels at Octavio Paz's second act in life, ostensibly by way of a second marriage to a younger woman: "Octavio Paz, rejuvenecido. ¿Tendrá uno siempre la edad de su mujer?" (qtd. in Domínguez Michael, *Octavio Paz* 291). ("Octavio Paz, rejuvenated. Is one always the same age as one's woman?") Aside from his romantic happiness, Paz's aura of newfound youth may have also benefited from a youthful wardrobe; around 1968 artistic men seem to stop wearing suits and ties as often. That Paz appears dressed down suggests that as long as the style was relatively subdued, older men were allowed to keep up with the trend of "younger" sartorial fashions without seeming to lose dignity. Youthful fashion can be much more difficult for women, and if they follow some trends they court the accusation of failing to dress for their age.

This pattern of achieving maturity and yet connoting youth by way of a junior partner also applies to men's homosexual relationships. A year after Monsiváis's death, *El Universal* informed readers of the author's romantic relationship with the twenty-five-year-old Omar García, referred to as "pareja de Carlos Monsiváis" (Carlos Monsiváis's partner). In an interview from 2011, the bereaved García explored the depth of his commitment to Monsiváis, who required ongoing care before his death at age seventy-two and for whom García had to overcome his repulsion at so many housecats (Piñón, "Entrevista").[12] To give one more example of this freedom allowed to men as they enjoyed profound stability and superficial change simultaneously, as it pleased them, I appreciate Domínguez Cuevas's amused candor when I asked why the archival materials show that writing tutor Carlos Montemayor changed addresses so often: "Carlos Montemayor no cambia de dirección. Cambia de esposas. [Se ríe]." (Carlos Montemayor did not change addresses. He changed wives. [She laughs].) Domínguez Cuevas attributes three marriages to Montemayor, as well as a string of lovers.[13]

Importantly, social class affects a man's ability to attract a series of younger partners, and that caveat brings me again to the fact that age is not an impersonal marker ideal for fair bureaucracy. Marc Augé articulates in an insightful argument that the various facets of class discrimination are imbricated with ageism: "despite the growing average life span, the age at which one becomes old depends upon one's social origin and type of occupation." Ergo, an individual's "relationship to age is an expression of social inequality" (12).

Salvador Elizondo's education and resources must surely have influenced Emmanuel Carballo's impression of the shape-shifting, intermittently "young" writer when the pair first met in 1953: "Tenía [Elizondo] 21 años, y al hablar aparentaba tener 15 o 35—en momentos era más joven que lo joven, en otros sus juicios hacían pensar por personales y exactos que vivía adelantadamente una madurez envidiable" (Elizondo was 21, and when speaking he seemed to be 15 or 35—at moments he was younger than the young, in others his judgments, so personal and exact, made one think that precociously he lived an enviable maturity) ("Prólogo," *Salvador Elizondo* 5). This wildly changing age within the same man, only thirty-three years old when he wrote his autobiography, may have something to do with bad boy maturity, which makes "young literature" a peer- and personality-driven achievement. Who decides which writers are appropriately performing this mature youth? When Carballo wrote the introductions to this series of Nuevos Escritores Mexicanos del Siglo XX Presentados por Sí Mismos, he was thirty-seven years old or so, about four years the senior of the eldest of his subjects, like Elizondo and Vicente Leñero. Carballo's mirage-like implicit claim to critically distanced maturity vis-à-vis his "youthful" subjects also indicates the subjective nature of the enterprise of "youth."

A caveat seems in order here. Despite the cultural influences that I have just taken pains to signal, age is not a category that willful subjects can simply imagine into or out of existence. In some ineluctable ways we *are* our ages. Aiming to alter personal age by too large a degree threatens to change one's very identity; as one scholar observes, "To remove age completely would effectively erase the person" (Fineman 62). And yet, under our current gerontophobia, the final years of the aging process itself threaten to "erase the person" anyway. The stereotypes about the aged are not kind. In the twentieth century, elderly people came to be seen as "inflexible, unadaptable, and out of step with the times, and as inefficient and unproductive workers" (Mintz 10).[14] Additionally, the old were imagined as "frail, fumbling, fussy, forgetful, and asexual" (Schulz and Binstock 2). Have you noticed that at least some of these negative connotations of old age echo those you read in chapter 6 about the artistically unsuccessful: the *pedantic*?

Something about artistic competence in a twentieth-century landscape dominated by men seems to value increasingly an image of youth, which if it is to provide an artistic edge must be performed correctly. Such pressures did not develop suddenly in the midcentury. An advertisement from 1904, in *El Mundo Ilustrado*, hinted that without proper hair care, youths can appear to be old and losers. The pitch for a hair tonic called Petrol del Dr. Torrel, de París (Dr. Torrel's Petrol, of Paris) proclaimed:

> Única preparación que evita la caída prematura del pelo, lo aumenta, suaviza y hermosea, á la vez que le comunica un aroma agradable. EL USO DEL PETROL DEL Dr. Torrel, de París, evita la calvicie prematura, que tanto afea y comunica al hombre el repulsivo aspecto de un joven viejo y ganado. (Petrol del Dr. Torrel)

> Unique formula that prevents premature loss of hair, increases it, smooths and beautifies it, all the while releasing an agreeable aroma. THE USE OF DR. TORREL'S PETROL, of Paris, prevents premature baldness, which really disfigures and communicates to others the repulsive appearance of an old and defeated youth.

This notion of an "old and defeated youth" hints at the cultural tricks surrounding a would-be linear biological aging process; elderly people are the real "old and defeated" in the allusion here, and therefore it becomes grotesque for a young person to look like them. The young should perform youth accurately, because an individual's actual number of years of age is no guarantee of adequate appearance.

As I have pointed out, gender complicates ageism; any given woman writer struggles to convince peers of her proper degree of maturity, which will be devalued as she actually matures into menopause and beyond. The archive on the Centro Mexicano de Escritores preserves the case of Ángeles Mastretta—she whose work received the mixed reviews studied by Bowskill in chapter 1. In the Mastretta file, three notes on separate pieces of paper contemplate the merits of the future best-selling novelist. In one negative comment, Felipe García Beraza wrote, "Como persona va a ser difícil" (As a person she's going to be difficult) (CME Mastretta 64-2). Salvador Elizondo, on a separate notecard, scrawled terse disdain for Mastretta and signed it in large, easily legible, almost block-letter print: "Los lugares comunes en estos libros de mujeres que se sienten adolescentes. Siempre la misma cosa" (CME Mastretta 64-3). (Clichés in these books by women who feel like adolescents. Always the same thing.) This rejection by the mercurial Elizondo is interesting: while he earned a reputation from participating in "new" and therefore "youthful" literature, as well as from masculinist privilege, as I discussed in chapters 1, 2, and 6, he denies the allure of Mastretta's alleged eternal yet false "adolescent" maturity.

In contrast to García Beraza's and Elizondo's naysaying, Rulfo endorsed Mastretta and her implicit "youthfulness."[15] Rulfo's view prevailed, and Mastretta won a writing grant in 1973–74. Her historical romantic novel went on to sell "millions" of copies worldwide (Arráncame). Even though women writers appear in the archive marked by challenges to their maturity, with adjectives such as "difficult" and "adolescent" or the phrase "attractive girl" dotting their application assessments, they seem to take slightly longer than male contemporaries to earn peer recognition. The complexity of women's lives—with the interruptions of childbirth and the time suck of child rearing—may influence this tendency to receive major literary prizes at a later age than male peers. The challenge of maturing youthfully may also affect assessments of their merit.

According to my rough calculations, among the grant-holding members of the Centro Mexicano de Escritores crowd, the average age of recipients of a Xavier Villaurrutia Award is something like 42.74 for men, with the median age of 40. For women, the average age is something like 44, with the median age around 42. According to my nonprofessional mathematical skills and a historical record plagued with inaccuracies, the same phenomenon describes the winning applications to the Centro Mexicano de Escritores: the average and median age for the men admitted to the yearlong grant program falls around 27; for women the average age on winning the first yearlong grant is 29.3, and the median age is 28.[16] The later age at which twentieth-century women writers win awards and grants suggests that if such a trend continues under today's unforgiving age rules, women will face an even trickier performance of maturity than men. While women need to remain younger to avoid the worst of age prejudice, they actually are older when success comes.

Another way to think of these categories of young and old writers and the ways we invent conflict between them employs the metaphor of athletic competitions. Writers themselves sometimes take up the athletic comparison, at least when they are young. Such is the case with Germán Castillo's application to the Centro Mexicano de Escritores in 1964, when he was twenty. Castillo turns in one of the wittiest and briefest packets of the archive, and in the second of two total paragraphs in the cover letter he compares his goal of maturation with athletic training:

> Quiero el brazo del Centro Mexicano de Escritores por escritor y mexicano, quiero caminar así un año más hacia la madurez de oficio. Quiero ser como un atleta al que su nación adiestra y alimenta como muestra clara de respeto. (CME Castillo Macías 13)

> I want the arm of the Centro Mexicano de Escritores because I am a writer and a Mexican. I want to walk like that for one more year toward maturity in the craft. I want to be like the athlete whom the nation trains and nurtures as a clear sign of respect.

The trouble with this athletic comparison, of course, has to do with the lack of agreed-upon measurement for writerly maturity. In athletics, the master's classification divides the younger competitor from the older, largely with the idea of protecting the aged from the superior skills of youth, but it is not clear that young writers are superior to older authors. The narrative of decline that characterizes ageist understandings of older people, as discussed by Gullette (*Aged by Culture* 9), may not actually operate in the same way for writers.[17] Bad boys can sustain a lifetime reputation grounded in youthful rebellion: think of the images of an elderly William Burroughs in the Gap clothing ads or a battered Keith Richards still playing guitar on stage with the Rolling Stones. In the

Mexican case, there are long-lived hard drinkers, such as Rubén Salazar Mallén, who managed to live eight decades, from 1905 to 1986, and Alí Chumacero, who lived nine decades, from 1918 to 2010.

From those examples, we can see that maturity among men writers ends up something of a specter that plays both categories at once: youthful *and* mature, present *and* transcendent, rebellious *and* reliable, official *and* out of the reach of corrupting influences. This flip that can allow writers to occupy both poles of a binary helps us understand the interest in celebrating impossible birthdays. What does age mean when official Mexican publicity marks the one-hundredth birthday in 2014 for Octavio Paz, who died at age eighty-four? What does it mean when birth years of living writers appear on an enormous banner, as they did for a book fair held at Mexico City's Palacio de Minería in 2016, sponsored by the UNAM? Does it matter, as the banner proclaimed, that a writer is ninety years old (Miguel León Portilla), eighty (Angelina Muñiz-Huberman, Mario Vargas Llosa), or seventy (Elsa Cross, Martha Chapa, Hernán Lara Zavala, Mónica Mansour, Francisco Martín Moreno)? Can age really provide a meaningful organizational tool for literary accomplishment? Some of the best guidance I can give for these questions treats age ambiguously, as a here-and-not-here specter.

The spectral nature of youth, for men at least, can last forever. Vicente Leñero, for example, at around the age of thirty-three, has his fictionalized self in the Nuevos Escritores autobiography receive assurances that his boyishness is eternal: "Y usted, amigo Leñero, es y será para siempre un joven promesa; acéptelo con humildad cristiana, no se envanezca: un joven promesa" (21–22). (And you, my friend Leñero, are and will forever be a young promise; accept it with Christian humility. Don't give yourself airs: a young promise.) The entreaty to remain humble sounds a moral warning of responsibility. One of Leñero's peers, José Agustín, earned eternal youthfulness to an even greater degree than Leñero. On the occasion of Augustín's fiftieth birthday, a 1994 headline insists on the legendary early promise: "José Agustín: escritor joven, muchacho eterno" (José Agustín: young writer, eternal boy) (L. E. Ramírez 25). The article begins, "José Agustín ríe al recordar la expresión del crítico estadounidense John Brushwood: '¡Cómo que el escritor más joven de México cumple 50 años!'" (José Agustín laughs as he remembers U.S. critic John Brushwood's exclamation: "How can Mexico's youngest writer turn 50!") (25). The accompanying photograph shows the author surrounded by his three sons, aged twenty-two, twenty, and nineteen—though they are perhaps only temporarily young alongside their permanently youthful father.[18] My reader may think that the Mexican literature of the twentieth century established young writers as never before, but I wager that since youth culture and gendered ageism continue, another eternal boy will emerge for the twenty-first century.

Are you, dear reader, part of the reason these spectral ages occur? Do you hold ageist prejudice? One test might be *Pedro Páramo*. Without using González Boixó's calculations, how old do you imagine Susana San Juan and Pedro Páramo are? Here is Gabriel García Márquez's answer, from an article originally published in 1986:

> Yo siempre había pensado, por pura intuición poética, que cuando Pedro Páramo logró por fin llevar a Susana San Juan a su vasto reino de la Media Luna, ella era ya una mujer de sesenta y dos años. *Pedro Páramo* debía ser unos cinco años mayor que ella. ("Nostalgia de Juan Rulfo")

> I had always thought, out of sheer poetic intuition, that when Pedro Páramo finally managed to take Susana San Juan to his vast kingdom on the Half Moon [ranch], she was already a sixty-two-year-old woman. Pedro Páramo must have been some five years older than she.

Even careful reader García Márquez may err by imagining Pedro as five years older than Susana. González Boixó's chronology estimates that Susana and Pedro were born in the same year, 1865 ("Cronología" 181). Thus, at the time Pedro brings Susana to live with him, they must be around age forty-five. It may disquiet some audiences that Pedro holds such a blazing torch for someone *middle-aged*—despite the fact that he is as well.

Certainly, the age issue kills any cinematic appeal for the plot, according to García Márquez: "Semejante grandeza poética era impensable en el cine. En las salas oscuras, los amores de ancianos no conmueven a nadie" (Such poetic greatness was unthinkable in cinema. In the dark theaters, old people's romances do not move anyone) ("Nostalgia de Juan Rulfo"). If you are thinking that I have broken the rules and changed tracks from Rulfo's and others' authorial performance and illegitimately launched into textual analysis of *Pedro Páramo*, I remind you that the same ideas you use to judge authors and public figures belong to your general toolkit for reading literary characters. In demonstration of our single-mindedness when it comes to ageism, rules about age and romance also affect perceptions of Pacheco's *Las batallas en el desierto*. Critic Saúl Jiménez-Sandoval, in describing

Carlitos's crush on the older Mariana during the aspirational modernity of the Alemán presidency, calls this love "intergeneracional" (intergenerational) and "contraproducente" (counterproductive) (437). Jiménez-Sandoval captures the irony of Carlitos's renunciation of such "counterproductive" love for an older woman; this step can be imagined as a process of "maturation" (439).[19]

Regardless of narrator Carlos's ambivalence, *Las batallas en el desierto* almost certainly buys into the fallen status of becoming an adult under youth culture. As historian Mintz points out, "Adulthood, once regarded as life's pinnacle, has come to be seen by many as a time of stress, remorse, routine, stagnation, and dissatisfaction" (xi).[20] Indeed, critic Beatriz Barrantes-Martín explores an allegory made possible by Pacheco's contraposition of infantile purity and "el México *adulto* corrupto" (the *adult* corrupt Mexico) (30).[21] This notion of adulthood as a disappointing time affects what the reader can understand of Carlos's present moment, which brings me to one method used by Mexican writers to create an impression of seriousness in their fiction.

Cognitive psychologists have found that the human brain pays greater attention to negative than to positive information.[22] Writing from a consistently negative focus likely enhances the seeming importance of a narrative, as per *Pedro Páramo* and *Las batallas en el desierto*.[23] It almost seems unavoidable that adulthood will be presented with negative bias in literature that is taken seriously, given our propensity to focus on and remember unhappy information.

The salience of negative data leads me to mention the overlap between respected literary technique and the symptoms of depression. Twentieth- and twenty-first-century narrative styles that aim to *show* and not *tell* sentiments end up mimicking the cognitive habits of depressed people. In our admiration for such inarticulate technical ploys used to support pessimistic plots, critics may assume that the opposite approach, that of exact vocabulary for emotion, is too easy, a kind of facile storytelling that nongenius writers engage.[24] If the pedantic excessively articulates ideas, cool genius closes off this communication overdrive and tries to place more of the burden of interpretation on the reader. Yet mental health counselors argue that naming emotions with precision can be challenging, especially for men clients (Reiner). In chapter 4, in the context of observing the penis in literature, I noted the tendency for contemporary men writers to publish flat-footed literal narratives. Even that hyperexplained style does not tend to articulate emotion as much as it graphically lays out events.

Other parallels between depressed cognition and prestigious literary technique include what psychological counselors call mind reading, excessively focused rumination, and labeling (see, e.g., Burns 42–43). As regards the last, *labeling*, note that Rulfo's Pedro and Pacheco's Carlos practice this extreme form of overgeneralization in which depressed subjects attach negative labels to themselves and others; in other words, under the sway of overgeneralization, subjects perceive "a single negative event as a never-ending pattern of defeat"—which literary authors might know as a high and hard theme (Burns 42). The literature student might additionally observe that labeling by another name could also be called *characterization*, in the way that mind reading is also the purview of fiction narrators. Another bad habit studied in psychology, *emotional reasoning*, which presumes that "negative emotions accurately reflect the way things really are," also seems intimately related to the ways that lauded twentieth-century narratives establish authority (Burns 42). Furthermore, characters like Pedro and Carlos can be seen to share, in clinical psychological terms, a quality known as "distress intolerance," which has subjects "underestimate their ability to recover from a painful event" (Diener and Biswas-Diener 193).[25]

Precisely these aspects of poor mental health reinforce literary prestige in the face of the most clichéd of topics, like heartbreak or rivalry. In *Las batallas en el desierto*, Pacheco's alienated tone helps to rescue the novella from its citation of the cheesy romantic lyrics of the bolero.[26] Likewise, Pedro Páramo's obsession with Susana San Juan would flirt more directly with the soft and low *novela rosa*—if it weren't for his confused inability to seduce her and otherwise manage his emotions.[27] There is something dangerous in admitting this parallel between prestigious literature and the cognitive consequences of depression, as if I had just reduced all the significant literary complexities to a lack of respect for grief and depression counseling. Still, the overlap between high and hard technique and depressed thinking strikes me as so nearly all-eclipsing that I wonder if risking these observations informs our intelligence more than it insults it.

What are the emotional lessons—the mood models, so to speak—implicit in Pedro's and Carlos's examples? Beyond the broad strokes of love and hate, these texts seem to work off grief and regret. Yet, the naming of shades of grief, and the nuances of regret, as I observed, remains taboo in these narratives. Remember that Pedro claims to feel nothing at key moments. Upon learning of the death of his favorite son, Miguel, Pedro reacts coolly: "No sintió dolor" (2012, 126) ("He felt no sorrow") (1994, 68). He repeats this numbness during his own final moments: apparently, after one of his sons stabs him, Pedro's life bleeds out while he sits in his chair, stonily declaring, "Ésta es mi muerte" (2012, 178) ("This is my death") (1994, 123). As for Pacheco's narrator, Carlos similarly prefers benumbed hopelessness in the face of pain and, for instance, denies his own nostalgia, as per the famous conclusion of the novella: "Se acabó esa ciudad. Terminó aquel país. No hay memoria de México de aquellos años. Y a nadie le importa: de ese horror quién puede tener nostalgia" (67–68). (That city has finished. That country ended. There is no memory of Mexico from those years. And no one cares: for that horror, who could feel nostalgic.) Because the general tone of the novella is nostalgic, this iconic conclusion ends up in a self-undermining authority of alienation. The novella cancels its own sincerity in favor of the cool, in other words, which makes it an authority that is difficult to build on, except in the literary tradition that will continue to write from techniques coached by cool depression.

One major advantage to this stylistic approach is that in addition to conveying an aura of urgency, literary technique that imitates depressed thought makes for consistent novelistic filler. I take that last term, *filler*, from Franco Moretti, whose computer-assisted examination of the novel argues that the genre is formed by narration of the everyday, achieved through emphasis on *regularity* (71). That novelistic rhythm of predictability is accomplished through fillers, which Moretti describes by way of his antecessor Roland Barthes as "weak and parasitic" because they "don't really do much" (71). In the narrative sense, fillers fail to modify the action. From that description, it seems clear that depression and filler share a resistance to new activities in favor of the humdrum. In fact, in *Las batallas en el desierto* Pacheco compresses filler to the degree that even a climactic moment remains consistent with background routines; when Carlitos interrupts Mariana's morning hygiene routine, *nothing happens*: no sex, no commitment, no meal, no future appointment—not even a walk together or a quick game of cards. A kind of violence emerges from this nothingness, and thus Pacheco manages to present the conditions that support structural violence as normative.[28]

Like Pacheco, Rulfo comes up with clever ways of handling filler so that it seems even more negative than the mere routines of the possibly depressed. Double-duty filler has all manner of barbaric ends befalling the characters. A series of grand finales, in other words, serves as background routine, as Rulfo's ghostly chronology allows horrible deaths, rapes, and other coercions to form rhythmic continuations of the same old, same old. Filler in itself, unless it is negative, might not capture our attention as raptly as might be hoped, and here Rulfo takes advantage of another cognitive trick. Psychologists believe that, in addition to negative information, a quality that usually arrests attention is the end of the story (Kahneman 302, 387). The salience we assign to the conclusion of a narrative accounts for part of the success of Rulfo's trick in making depressive patterns at once routine and terrifying; we like his filler because it seems to promise more, as it constantly narrates endings, and bad ones at that. The effect of these various negative and depressive techniques as managed in the literary novel is perhaps to quash hope for "unrealistic" change and to numb us to the ways of structural violence. It can seem irresponsible to do anything but agree with these serious if hopeless novels and their solemn, consistently narrated themes. On that note, I turn to my final subject, Guillermo Fadanelli's oeuvre.

To put it mildly, critics take less interest in Fadanelli's writing than in Rulfo's and Pacheco's oeuvre. Gutiérrez Negrón has already remarked on the anemic academic interest in Fadanelli's work (452).[29] In fact, in November 2016, I received an email from a university student in Mexico who wanted to work with the short story collection *Más alemán que Hitler* and had been told by thesis directors (in the plural) that Fadanelli's writing is "una porquería" (rubbish). I suppress the student's name and institution because I don't want to place this person in hot water; however, I will note that the person's email asks me not if Fadanelli is *good* but if the work is *relevant*. My affirmative answer is predicted by my choice of authors here. In the same way that I ended *Boob Lit* with a chapter on Guadalupe Loaeza, a figure whom serious artists laugh about and yet who sells books by the kilo, I am driven to end *Dude Lit* with a meditation on Fadanelli, who for decades has enjoyed significant space on both the private bookshelves of Mexicans and the bookstores of Mexico. Why in the world would we ignore Fadanelli?

Because he represents the average experience as communicated by filler without the same sorts of tense drama that Rulfo and Pacheco manage to inject into their serious and depressed techniques. Fadanelli does not write a series of conclusions, much less violent endings, into his filler in the way that Rulfo does—nor does Fadanelli mythologize a striver like Pedro Páramo. Fadanelli also avoids the high drama of Pacheco's entitled and yet still depressive Carlos, who has implicitly "made it," thanks to Carlitos's family money, which allowed for a superior education and luxurious international travel, as shown by the scholastic details and holiday plans inserted near the conclusion. If one of Fadanelli's protagonists were to narrate from this type of enabled mobility, a thrill or two over the suddenly expanded horizons might emerge, rather than Carlos's implicit ennui.

Might Fadanelli's complacency with mediocrity without material wealth be a better representation of the spirit of a novel? Do we reject depressing stories, unrelieved by Carlitos's money or Pedro's fame, because they violate the aspirations of the middle class, as accepted implicitly by literary critics? As I have said, the middle class seems so entwined with the endeavor of literature and academic criticism that untangling the imbricated ideals threatens to undo the related professions of author and critic. Thus, I question whether Fadanelli delivers a sufficiently coherent critique of the middle class for its dual (dueling) belief in the rewards owed to good character and the riches due a rule-breaking personality. Does the insufficiency of the critique take root in performance, as well as in the ultimate complacency of the novels? Could Fadanelli's seeming ambivalent stance toward official status curtail the enlightenment he might work on critics' judgment? He refuses to appear on Televisa channels, and yet as I already cited from Gutiérrez Negrón's observations, Fadanelli flirts with institutionalized status. This ambivalence signals to me that the notion that Mexican writers have lost power only because the state no longer supports them is an overstatement of the case. The state continues to support writers, as my brief discussion of the age-graded opportunities signals, and yet something about the power the writers wield in relation to the state has changed.

Fadanelli is distant from some channels of official power and from philanthropic funding, in ways that writers like Paz or Monsiváis were not. Yet Fadanelli does appear regularly in the newspapers through a column that has migrated over the decades from paper to paper. Fadanelli's presence on the literary scene and absence on the academic one leads to intriguing questions. Are *academics* the ones who want to see a writer play out on dramatic scale, in text and performance, a grand dance with the poles of *civilización* and *barbarie*? Is a ringing state endorsement the needed sign of the civilizado talent that legitimizes a bad boy act? To the extent that Fadanelli is already a fixture on the "live" literary scene at book fairs and the like, it bears asking what kind of official state support might make him academically relevant. Equally, we can ask what sort of fine-tuning of his bad boy attitude would merit him more academic studies. Only more questions arise with these musings. Why do we need another bad boy like Burroughs? Why should the state look for another Paz if critics comply in celebrating a ghostly birthday and spectral death anniversary? Do we need another Paz? Regarding the dilemma of the would-be new official writer, it appears that the state has lost the incentive to accept new official authors. Perhaps academics have yet to understand how to incentivize a recasting of that role because we too are reluctant to sanction new ways for writers. The old roles were cast in the twentieth century and can be played by dead people, which suggests that we need to rethink how we determine literary authority and what such authority is supposed to articulate. Fadanelli's key discrepancy with the old rules lies in his refusal to glamorize the mediocre. Possibly because of that last point he loses critical academic interest, which in itself might be his most significant indictment of the system that ignores him.

On other points Fadanelli supports the depressive techniques of prestige that I outlined. Like Pacheco and Rulfo, in his *Mis mujeres muertas*, winner of the Grijalbo Prize 2012, Fadanelli circumvents the "pink" (*rosa*) novel of an interrupted love story by consistently emphasizing the protagonists' narrow focus and repetitive habits. Fadanelli's drunken Domingo, like Rulfo's Pedro and Pacheco's Carlos, engages with ghost women. The deceased Sara K. perforce remains under Domingo's narrative control and lends herself to mind reading and registering Domingo's inconsolable grief: his distress intolerance. Not only is a seemingly unemployed and borderline destitute Domingo coping poorly with the loss of his partner Sara K., he also mourns the death of his mother, Sara Mancini. If Pedro Páramo's anguish over Susana San Juan's death must be shared by the entire community—*or else*—Domingo's pain at the deaths of his partner Sara K. and his mother falls to him to bear in relative isolation, which intensifies the depressive elements without making them more dramatic. No one else suffers Domingo's distress, with the possible exception of the narrative foils, Domingo's brothers.

Siblings Alfredo and Huberto earned graduate degrees in the United States, unlike Domingo's unfinished and presumably local university studies.[30] Nonetheless, rather than academic knowledge, according to Domingo, the lawyer and the doctor talk of little more than their "relations" or the people they know (73–74). The employed and wealthier brothers assign Domingo the seemingly simple task of placing their mother's tombstone on her grave. True to his contrary nature, Domingo cannot complete this task easily, and the span of the novel transpires before the tombstone reaches the cemetery. Domingo praises his own procrastination, arguing for something like the slow food movement translated to decision-making activities:

> —Si fuera por mí, gastaría años en tomar una sola decisión; hasta mover el salero se volvería un motivo de reflexión y de cuidadoso escrutinio. Y así incluso la vida tendría sabor. (154)

> If it were up to me, I would spend years in making a single decision. Just moving the saltshaker would be cause for reflection and cautious scrutiny. And that way even life would have its flavor.

The wording that has Domingo *spend* rather than *pass* the time takes a cue from English; here the passage of time is imagined as a consumption, even a wasteful one. Such a thought would likely never occur to Pedro Páramo, and yet Pedro too winds up in a state of apathy that clings to just one decision: his crossed arms that mean to kill off Comala and avenge Susana's disrespected death. Pacheco's Carlos narrates from such a remote distance from his present-day routine that he too connotes a kind of static energy. Still, only Fadanelli emphatically suggests inactivity as a moral high ground, which ends up in parody.

In contrast to the unusual events and high drama of the heroic quest, even Domingo's encounter with robbers on the way to the cemetery near the end of the novel emerges as a relatively routine event for that particular route in Mexico City. In the rush to analyze seriously, I don't want to pass over the humor that blooms from the incongruous alignment of Domingo's depression and the effort to deliver the tombstone, which Domingo stores—nearly permanently—in his car trunk. For example, laughter ensues from a cantina-set effort to draw a redundant map, as Domingo postpones his mission by sketching a path to the cemetery from memory:

> Domingo trazó una línea tan larga que la hoja no fue suficiente para contenerla, y después otra perpendicular que representaba a la Calzada de los Misterios. Con minúsculas letras de molde anotó el nombre de las avenidas menores y remató con una cruz el sitio donde se encontraba el panteón. Un mapa es necesario en cualquier misión y si hay una cruz en el mapa entonces la Tierra tiene por fin un centro de gravedad. Su memoria tiraba golpes a la manera de un ex campeón anciano y vanidoso, un viejo empeñado en impresionar a las señoritas, a los enemigos de sonrisa socarrona que lo consideraban un ebrio inofensivo. (167–68)

> Domingo drew a line so long that the sheet failed to contain it, and then he drew another perpendicular one that represented the Avenue of Mysteries. With minuscule uppercase letters, he printed the name of the smaller avenues and topped it off with a cross on the site where the cemetery was located. A map is necessary in any mission, and if you have a cross on the map then the Earth has at long last a center of gravity. His memory was throwing punches in the style of a former champion,

> elderly and vain, an old man bent on impressing the ladies, on impressing the enemies with smirking smiles who took him for an inoffensive drunk.

The time spent on quixotic tasks—a map drawn for oneself from memory is unnecessary, after all—sets up a kind of ultraliterary practice. This practice is not centered on splashily original contributions, as the example of the map makes plain, but on something closer to an active reader habit.

I draw that conclusion in part from Domingo's love of literature and his scorn for writers. In some respects, he shares this negativity with his brothers, although they disagree on the particulars. I cite attorney Alfredo's mocking reaction to Domingo's desire to lie to their mother and claim a completed university degree, with honors, in Hispanic literature:

> —¿Letras?—Alfredo rió y su risa se transformó en mueca sorda, la boca abierta, y después la recriminación—: Las letras están hundidas y no tienen ningún valor frente a los números. (77)[31]

> "Literature?" Alfredo laughed, and his laughter transformed itself into a mute grimace, with an open mouth, and then the counterattack: "Literature has failed and has no value compared to numbers."

Not the lie to the mother but the degree in literature seems to offend Alfredo's sensibilities. Although Fadanelli himself has written essays against the moral force that statistics have taken on, it seems possible that his protagonist Domingo may agree on some level with Alfredo on the "failure" of literature.[32] That is, even Domingo may view literature as "done" and no longer open to original contributions—or at least, he views the activity of writing as beneath his dignity, and he "spends" his time, as far as the reader knows, not with contemporary writers but reading translations of nineteenth-century Russian novels, which inspire in him the novelistic fantasy that his mother left him a secret fortune in a bank account (157).

This perspective of Domingo's pessimism regarding the prestige of new writing emerges in a conversation between Domingo and his other brother, Huberto. I will set up Domingo's response by first citing Huberto's critique:

> —Tú habrías podido convertirte en un artista o en un escritor; en un hecho. Es frustrante y doloroso cuando un hombre joven actúa contra sí mismo; pero, bueno, ¿qué carajos vamos a hacer? (102)

> You could have become an artist or a writer; in an accomplishment. It's frustrating and painful when a young man works against himself; but, well, what the hell are we going to do?

Huberto's assessment that Domingo failed to become "an artist or a writer" shows an interesting scorn for the superior role of reader that Domingo will hotly, if only implicitly, defend:

> —¿Un escritor yo?, ¿cómo se te puede ocurrir esa pendejada? ¿Un escritor yo? Soy un hombre solo, ¿no te basta con eso? Los escritores y los poetas usan palabras porque no creen en ellas; son cínicos, pero yo soy una persona ingenua y terminaría escribiendo oraciones o panfletos; estaría peor que ahora. ¿Y quién va a merecerse lo que yo escriba? Nadie, en fin. (102)

> Me, a writer? How could you think something so fucking stupid? Me, a writer? I'm a man, that's all. Isn't that enough for you? Writers and poets use words because they don't believe in them; they are cynical, but I'm a naïve person and I would end up writing prayers or pamphlets; I would be worse off than now. And who deserves what I would write? No one, in the end.

Although some of his bluster may simply protect a paralyzing alcohol habit, it also seems that Domingo does believe in words as an ethical pathway to a meaningful existence. Novels are important as a kind of drug for him that an ethical citizen would not manufacture, but only consume. Through his drug-like use of novels, in tandem with alcohol, he achieves a contemplative state.

Domingo becomes the ultimate novelistic character to the degree that his reading and drinking habits turn him into repetitive and insignificant filler. On a broader scale, Fadanelli admires this "average" quality, and he voiced his respect for nonfictional representations of "mediocrity" in a personal interview:

> Yo soy un amante de la mediocridad en el sentido de mediocridad como *ser que desaparece*. Admiro al mediocre que no levanta la cabeza ni nos daña con su talento, sus grandes ideas o sus deseos de convertirse en un gran hombre. [. . .] Creo que no requerimos de grandes hombres en una época en que la clase media se halla tan adolorida y resquebrajada, tan ausente de instituciones que la representen y al mismo tiempo procuren su bien. (Hind, "Entrevista" 312)[33]

> I am a lover of mediocrity in the sense of mediocrity as *a being who disappears*. I admire the mediocre man who does not raise his head nor harm us with his talent, his big ideas or his desire to become a great man. . . . I think that we don't require great men in an age when the middle class finds itself so injured and broken, so absent from institutions that represent it and at the same time seek its well-being.

The middle class here actually elicits not Fadanelli's disdain for the *naco* but his concern for the average. Unlike some of the bigger names in Mexican literary history, especially Paz, Fadanelli is not prepared to dismiss the tastes of a middling majority—a majority of the mediocre by definition of the very sense of averageness. The perception of a threatened middle class—this class that both can afford to buy books and respects the idea of reading them—may encourage Fadanelli to admire those who live as if in a state of filler: those who can endure a numbing state and persist under the tedium, without resorting to violence or coming into power through a flip to the bárbaro. He writes books in homage to that group, which is certainly not the class to which literary critics aspire to belong, given academics' insistence on study, travel, and other modes of widening horizons.

Fadanelli's attitude here is quite different from the tendency among men artists who complain about bad taste. Through his at times naco characters, Fadanelli does not propose himself as a great writer. He does not ridicule his flawed protagonists in the way that other tastemakers achieved fame through critique. If Paz rails against the "bonito," as I showed in chapter 2, the insouciant case of Monsiváis has him knowingly, often ironically, celebrating kitsch. There is not much room for sincerity in those performances of intellectual authority. What might a sincere appreciation of literature look like? While Fadanelli's later-in-life act may be sincere, an even better image of sincerity emerges in his older fictional characters. Heartfelt middle-classness, of the sort that leads to literary appreciation, is most definitely based on unoriginal taste, to judge from Fadanelli's portrait of the reading fan as a middling man. In *Mis mujeres muertas*, Domingo's immersive reading habit supplies an escapist routine, but precisely that fidelity to the novelistic aesthetic means that he cannot execute any new act quickly, and the filler only strengthens as he stumbles through his days in a radical state of suspension. Domingo nevertheless plays middle class. His pleasure in arriving at the cantina and setting up his reading materials retains a middle-class value of self-cultivation through literature, and perhaps of good hygiene and relative thrift as well. Domingo's habits flout the values of sobriety and punctuality, however, and Fadanelli seems to have something to say here about the nature of drugs and their place in the middle class. The act of contemplation strains the usual middle-class approach to time and related notions of logical efficiency.

The uncertainty of literature in its preference for weighing the possibilities and enjoying a self-imposed routine can defy the pressure to overcome mediocrity and be Somebody (see chapter 6), like some celebrated literary heroes.[34] Fadanelli understands a crucial aspect of the novel in this sense. As he articulates it, narratives based on filler defy memory because "la novela es una digresión consumada" (the novel is a consummated digression) (*Insolencia* 22). This meandering supports Fadanelli's literary aesthetic of forgettable characters and reminds me of his warm view of the antimethodical in the essay *Elogio de la vagancia* (Praise of laziness) (2008). Vivian Abenshushan reviews *Elogio de la vagancia* in terms of the "moral universe" that Fadanelli proposes, in which vagrancy and the vagrant arrive at particular knowledge inaccessible through more systematic means ("Defensa del vividor"). To judge from Fadanelli's defenses of the vagrant in his recent fiction, this revision of middle-class behavior that rejects striving and efficiency is not easily accommodated in twenty-first-century Mexico City. In his plots, Fadanelli stresses this awkward fit by narrowing the vagrant's horizons through economic limitations and confining them within strict boundaries of bureaucracy enforced by the threat of structural violence.[35] The vagrant remains a superior character, because in Fadanelli's city, those who are *not* depressed about surviving in these tight confines of routine and pessimism are wrong somehow: both unconscionable and deluded.

Fadanelli does not suggest solutions; he merely empathizes with the problem. In addition to sticking his characters in a morass of depression so mediocre that it is devoid of grand literary drama, he takes a particular view of the ageing process. Fadanelli's narrators nearly always specify the ages of the main characters. This obsessive interest appears throughout his oeuvre in tandem with a denial of the innocence of childhood or growth in adulthood. That combination limits just how corrupt one of his average-seeming characters can be. It also limits their access to a more positively wielded power. Take the case of one of Fadanelli's four central characters in *¿Te veré en el desayuno?* Bank employee Ulises contemplates his helplessness to authorize credit for an elderly man who needs to buy a refrigerator to keep his medicine cool; the narrator explains: "A sus treinta y siete años era incapaz de solucionar una pendejada como ésa.

Un hombre podía morir sólo porque él no había tenido el talento necesario para ocupar el puesto de mayor altura" (29). (At his thirty-seven years he was incapable of solving fucking bullshit like this. A man could die because he did not have the necessary talent to hold a higher position.) If masculine maturity is defined through autonomy, as per Niobe Way's book cited in chapter 5, then Ulises's impotence denotes immaturity. The narrator's sense of Ulises's oddly immature maturity relates not only to the predicament of a middling class in stasis but also to a conundrum regarding a mature writer amid youth culture.

Fadanelli's consistent views on the predicament of age have his adult characters live out disenchantment in a strangely useless maturity that hints that tensions between mature talent and youthful rebellion are mere fictions of convenience. In the first place, he denies the existence of innocence in a sexual sense for children, male or female, which necessarily casts any "bad boy" rebellions as already knowing and thus doomed to wind up in adult mediocrity. For instance, the narrator of *Educar a los topos* remembers his own relatively unprotected childhood and rejects the idea of children's innocence:

> Como si en verdad existiera algo no apropiado para los niños. ¿Acaso no somos la concreción de un chorro de leche que lanza un pene enloquecido? Como si nuestra sangre no contuviera desde un principio todos los vicios de los padres y sus ancestros. (20)
>
> As if there really existed something inappropriate for children. Are we not the coagulation of a squirt of milk thrown by a crazed penis? As if our blood didn't contain from the beginning all the vices of our parents and their ancestors.

This lack of youthful innocence paves the way for Fadanelli to endow young characters with a driving interest in sexuality, such as the protagonist of *Malacara* (2007), who remembers sexual experiences with his babysitter when she was sixteen and he was six (15). Malacara claims roundabout support from Montaigne regarding a sexual drive that applies even to infants, thanks to a logic of mortality: "Y si tiene [un recién nacido] edad suficiente para morirse tiene edad para acariciar las nalgas de Benita" (And if [a newborn] is old enough to die he's old enough to caress Benita's buttocks) (15).

If young people enjoy some claim to innocence in Fadanelli's oeuvre, they owe it to freedom from political and historical developments. In *Al final del periférico*, Fadanelli specifies this childhood exemption: "Los niños podían quedarse tranquilos porque nadie tendría el descaro de considerarlos sustancia y parte de ningún pasado: los niños no transcurrían en el tiempo" (The children could rest easy because no one would have the nerve to consider them part and parcel of any past: children did not pass through time) (118). Such political innocence counts for little, as all characters are fated to age into complicity, from which there is only endrogado escape—as Domingo knows—in novels and alcohol. To drive home the point that sexuality neither spares nor frees anyone, especially under conditions of oppressive economic pressure, in that same novel the promiscuous teenager Sandra does *not* imagine sex as an achievement of maturity or adulthood; rather that moment might come with her failed attempt to stab her father to death: he lives and she fails to become a murderer. Mediocrity is her apparently ineluctable destiny.

Fadanelli's fiction also denies the potential of intergenerational friendships. Though his older male characters often express sexual desire for adolescents and twenty-somethings, if acted upon, as in *Lodo*, such trysts lead to disaster. In a divergent plot from the prison sentence that concludes *Lodo*, the eponymous protagonist of *Malacara*, a philanderer-cum-teacher, truncates a gender-reversed riff on *Batallas en el desierto* when he exclaims to an eighteen-year-old student who visits his house without an invitation: "Adriana, el protocolo nos hará libres. No vengas a joder a esa hora" (124). (Adriana, protocol will make us free. Do not come to fuck around at this hour.) The switch to "protocol" from the expected phrase "The truth will make us free" shows the limited horizons of these characters' possibilities. Protocol provides the semblance of enlightenment to which the middling characters have access, and that faith in etiquette protects an absolutely middle-class ideal.

Adult women characters in Fadanelli's work also act to quash the possibilities of cross-generational friendship. In *Para ella todo sueña a Frank Pourcel* (For her everything sounds like Frank Pourcel) (1998), a mother tries to convince her daughter to drop a friendship with an older woman, Verena, because of their age difference: "Verena tiene mi edad, hija, no pueden ser amigas dos personas que se llevan veinte años, no tienen los mismos intereses, por favor, no seas romántica" (Verena is my age, daughter, two people can't be friends if twenty years separate them, they don't have the same interests, please, don't be a romantic) (61). It seems important that an aesthetic that celebrates the mediocre would repeat uncritically the expected frown on cross-generational friendships. No wisdom is to be had from adults, in part because the young should not connect with them and in part because the adults cannot grow.

How old is an adult in Fadanelli's fiction? According to "Muebles, de un lugar a otro" (Furniture, from one place to another), a short story published in *Más alemán que Hitler*, adulthood begins after thirty. That is, in response to a character's insistence that she has reached "su edad *adulta*" (her *adult* age), the narrating character strips out the italics and responds coolly: "Sólo tienes veintidós años. En esta época se acostumbra llamar adultos a los que tienen más de treinta" (28). (You're only twenty-two. In this day and age it's customary to call only those who are older than thirty adults.) Attaining adulthood is not much of an achievement, largely because the stagnant national economy contributes to thwarting the characters' individual and even collective importance. Take the frustrations among the characters in *Hotel DF*; for example, Frank Henestrosa thinks that life after age twenty holds no agreeable surprise: "Cuando cumplí 20 años el futuro me tundió con un manazo en la nuca, y me dijo: 'No sonrías, que te espera lo peor'" (When I turned twenty, the future knocked me down with a karate chop to the neck and told me: "Don't smile, the worst is waiting for you") (9). Fadanelli concludes the novel with his character's resignation: "A mi edad, ¿qué puede aprenderse? Soy un hombre maduro y en el cielo las piedras continuarán ardiendo durante millones de años" (290). (At my age, what can be learned? I'm a mature man and up in the sky the rocks will continue burning for millions of years.)[36]

Fadanelli's characters cannot get ahead with financial efforts, because that aspiration is closed to them in an immobile society that nonetheless disturbs the superficial peace with cyclical financial crises. In a final observation, I cannot help noting that Fadanelli's biographical lies about his age may find a novelistic outlet with the ominously named Malacara. That protagonist explains his tortured relationship with his birth year: "Con sólo mirar mi acta de nacimiento cualquiera se convencería de que se trata de un documento anticuado cuyo propietario ha vivido más de tiempo del necesario" (Just looking at my birth certificate, anyone would be convinced that it is an outdated document whose owner has lived longer than necessary) (9). Malacara's solution to this problem is to lie about his age:

> En todo caso, prefiero mentir a un ritmo constante que ceñirme a mi acta de nacimiento o a mi pasaporte [. . .]. Si miento con tanta frecuencia respecto a mi edad crearé tal confusión dentro de mi propio cerebro que con seguridad llegará a desentenderme del asunto. (9)

> In any case I prefer to lie at a steady pace rather than hold myself to my birth certificate or my passport. . . . If I lie often enough about my age I will create so much confusion in my own brain that surely I'll end up distancing myself from the matter.

In Fadanelli's fiction, one reason for fibbing about age is precisely the quixotic nature of contemporary maturity. The characters gain in age while they seem never to fulfill any sort of promise. How could significant growth occur in adulthood if a dominant youth culture insists that the best years are those that come with the least institutional power? Before coming "of age," young people's life is supposed to be sexier, more adventurous, and more intelligent; after coming "of age," maturity connotes a downward slide, leading to mortality.

Is Domingo of *Mis mujeres muertas* mature? Is Fadanelli? I am not sure how to test for appropriate maturity among literary characters and the authors who develop them. If in our traditional rubric, prestigious literature must pass, not the Bechdel test, but a questionnaire aimed at spotting depression, Domingo scores flying colors. However, he largely pales as a bully when compared to Pedro Páramo, and he lacks bystander cool in comparison with Carlitos and the story Carlos tells about him. I'll leave it up to the reader to judge Fadanelli and his characters, and instead opt for posing another question.

Are we so sure that we have set up the proper exam?

In the conclusion, I look at notions of proper writerly maturity with one last case from the archive for the Centro Mexicano de Escritores. If the name Ninett Torres Villarreal rings a bell, you're already cringing.

CONCLUSION

CLOSURES

The Centro Mexicano de Escritores and Ninett Torres Villarreal (with a Final Invitation to Rethink What Sucks)

Your body drops, my breasts. I could have a mammogram and a pedicure at the same time. Do you know what really drops first? The vagina. No one tells . . . The vagina drops first. I woke up about six months ago. [Looks down at her feet.] I went "Why am I wearing a bunny slipper? . . . And why is it gray?"

—JOAN RIVERS

In one last pass through the tangle of opinions regarding writerly maturity, I want to return to the practices of the Centro Mexicano de Escritores.

It seems almost predictable that the Centro would fall into legal trouble once laws regarding discrimination began to change. The precise case happened over a pregnancy. Two years before it closed, the Centro wrestled with an onslaught of negative publicity after retracting a grant awarded to Ninett Torres Villarreal. In 2004, immediately upon learning that her yearlong award had been withdrawn because of her pregnancy, Torres Villarreal promptly acquired legal representation.[1] Domínguez Cuevas, in her capacity as executive secretary, signed a legal document, one of the many contained in the file on Torres Villarreal, which explains at length how the conflict unfolded:

> Los acontecimientos se resumen de la siguiente manera: después de haber sido notificada de haber obtenido la beca que otorga el Centro Mexicano de Escritores [. . .], la joven de 22 años, Torres Villarreal, se presentó en las instalaciones del Centro, previo aviso, para que firmara el contrato por el cual aceptaría las condiciones que el Centro establecía para recibir la beca.

> No obstante, la secretaría del CME, Martha Domínguez, le negó a la becaria la posibilidad de firmar el contrato, debido al avanzado embarazo que reflejaba. Aduciendo que el estado de ingravidez impediría el cumplimiento de las exigencias de la beca, disponibilidad del tiempo y de locación (sobre todo para asistir a las sesiones de taller llevadas a cabo los miércoles de 5 a 7 de la tarde), la señora Martha Domínguez le comunicó a Ninett Torres que consultaría su caso ante el Consejo. (CME Torres Villarreal 5)[2]

> The events can be summarized as follows: after being notified of having obtained the grant awarded by the Mexican Center for Writers . . . , the 22-year-old young woman, Torres Villarreal, arrived on the premises of the Center, as instructed, to sign the contract by which she would accept the conditions that the Center established for the grant.
>
> However, the secretary of the CME, Martha Domínguez, denied the grantee the possibility of signing the contract, due to the advanced pregnancy that she showed. Arguing that the state of pregnancy would prevent compliance with the requirements of the grant, availability of time and location (especially to attend the workshop sessions held on Wednesdays from 5 to 7 in the evening), Mrs. Martha Domínguez told Ninett Torres that she would bring her case to the Council.

Carlos Montemayor agreed with Domínguez Cuevas and withheld the grant. In response to Torres Villarreal's request to attend the first Wednesday meeting, Montemayor refused: the frustrated grant winner testified, "Me dijo que no tenía caso" (He told me there wasn't any point) (15).

The initial decision about Torres Villarreal was eventually reversed by the Mexican justice system. After winning the case, Torres Villarreal joined the Wednesday sessions several months late, for the eighth meeting (Camacho, "Recupera la beca"). In the longer-term aftermath, Torres Villarreal disappeared from the literary scene, and the Centro Mexicano de Escritores closed.[3] If ever a case for the importance of writerly performance hit the papers, it is surely Torres Villarreal's. The documents for the institutional defense ignore the fact that many of the men grantees were married and even had children while holding their grants, a common practice since the very start of the Centro. The defense also leaves out the case of at least one pregnant grantee: Elsa Cross. On January 17, 1972, according to materials preserved in the archive, Cross typed a letter to Felipe García Beraza informing him that she would miss the sessions at the Centro Mexicano de Escritores beginning on January 19 because she was about to give birth. The letter explained that she planned to return "en dos o tres semanas, a lo sumo" (in two or three weeks, maximum) (CME Cross 64). Regardless of the exact date of her return, Cross continued, she pledged to continue work on her writing project. The pregnancy appears to have caused so little consternation among the leaders of the Centro that no other paper regarding it appears in the file, and Cross later won a second full-year grant from 1979–80.

I cite the differing cases of Cross and Torres Villarreal because it is tempting to think that feminism has solved our problems. And yet, it could be that today in some circumstances issues surrounding pregnancy and professional careers have worsened. Could it be that as bureaucratic consciousness of age intensifies, and as adulthood becomes regarded, not as the pinnacle of life, but as a prison sentence, the "problem" of pregnancy deepens for women? Regardless of your answer, the case of Torres Villarreal hints that the supposed "neutrality" of age rules and the "impartiality" of ignoring the body is a crock. In a parallel to David Graeber's work on structural violence and bureaucracy, we could speak here of structural prejudice that works a kind of specifically gendered violence: women operate at a disadvantage within institutions because something about their life performance does not fit. Ignoring this prejudicial structure that jams bodies into molds that do them harm only deepens the problem.

For an optimistic conclusion, I turn to James Schulz and Robert Binstock's suggested fix for ageism: *family policies*. Borrowing this idea of family, I propose that we should tease out our already existing notions of an intellectual family tree, which already proposes colleagues as related. Now we merely need to acknowledge openly our family habit of thinking about writers also as existing within a network, with personal and professional lives that overlap. We are all connected in a family of intellectuals and artists with the habit of awarding, in general, higher status to sons and fathers, uncles and grandfathers, brothers and brothers-in-law; only men can win with bad boy aesthetics that support the bully-to-civilized flip. Family policies and their implications of intergenerational interdependence, as well as their observance of aspirations of the cultural (if not economic) middle class, take us a step in the direction of clamping down on the bullying and its isolations. Just as retirees are not imagined to compete against unemployed or underemployed young people under family policies, women would not push the biological clock by having to place career before child under the more collectively minded arrangements (Schulz and Binstock 235). Family policies fundamentally help us to withdraw from an incorrectly imagined zero-sum game—in the specific context of *Dude Lit*, a winner-take-all game of literary prizes and opportunities. One person's award is not another's oblivion; men can promote women without losing face. Every woman ought to believe that she can promote other women without losing opportunities. As Schulz and Binstock observe, "We should not forget that the beneficiaries of the future would be all of us" (235).

Claims that a canon no longer exists, that differences between high and low literature have been erased, that women can compete equally now, are simply delusional given the ongoing context of prejudice in which literary critics live, read, and publish. If the underlying issues fail to change, the new respect afforded to women writers such as Guadalupe Nettel and Valeria Luiselli will be a short-lived phenomenon, with their fame soon to give way to another token set of younger women writers. Cristina Rivera Garza, Carmen Boullosa, Elena Poniatowska, and others, as they mature, already know to be wary of the longstanding sexism that includes the refusal to allow women to age and gain in intellectual authority the same as men.

But to conclude with a focus not on women but on putting an end to *Dude Lit*, allow me the following recommendations. Admit it when you read performance alongside the published oeuvre. Incorporate thought from gender studies even when you think you don't need it. Make sure you cite women scholars alongside the men, and if you don't, admit that explicitly. Don't pick token women to anchor an anthology, academic study, or panel and call yourself a feminist. And when you publish criticism that focuses almost entirely (or entirely) on men artists and intellectuals, acknowledge that concentration: until things change, the accurate term is *man writer*, not just *writer*. Add the gender nuances that you need if you wish to shade things more finely than the man/woman binary. In your classes, assign women writers in something at least approaching an equal number to the men, if you aren't willing to go whole hog and experiment with a year of only reading and watching women. When you see a panel on "women's issues," go and listen, even if you think that women's issues are not your issues. Family policies mean that we are all in it together.

One more thing: let's rethink the habit of blaming neoliberalism for all our woes. I have spent years now listening to otherwise sharp academics turn to overly broad allegory when they venture their views on politics and economics, especially at conferences during the Q & A. Dividing the world into two camps, good and evil, with the evil side occupied by the neoliberal and the good occupied by a nebulous inverse, hardly represents our maximum effort as literary readers. (On the principle of salient negativity, plus the prestige of depression, see chapter 7.) What if, as professional literary critics, we decide to issue ourselves new credit and get out of this intellectual debt to finances? Reconsidering our place in neoliberalism, as complicit consumers, seems to me a helpful step. We are all laboring under the same system, which means that when we buy books, purchase movie tickets, use the web, attend conference panels, and access other means and ways of cultural production, we are already cooperating with the arrangement that is, allegedly, ruining our profession. We cannot step completely outside this capitalism, no matter how many illegal copies you post on the web for your students. We can change it from the inside, however, which will require more imagination than publishing standards so far encourage.

Admitting our collusion is painful and sets off possibly paranoid repercussions. What if neoliberalism prospers under the very sort of blanket suspicions that literature specialists like to use to cover it? I ask this question because so far our professional unhappiness does not seem to impede the course of this economic policy. Do you remember a time when you did *not* live under this regime? I have never drawn a paycheck in a system other than the neoliberal one that, my colleagues tell me, dominates Mexico and the United States. I'm not saying the headlines don't horrify me. I'm saying that literary critics can do better with the allegories, if that's the rhetoric we prefer. It is my sad suspicion that we collude with our small enrollments and weakening public prominence when we saddle up so haphazardly, with such a lack of sophistication in tools and training, when it comes to riding one of our main hobbyhorses. (And we are the ones who brag about teaching critical analysis!) Most of us are not interdisciplinary; we can read but not publish in another field, which makes us disciplined in literature and curious about the rest.

I realized this limitation when I invited a business ABD student to lecture in my Mexican literature class. While I adamantly disagreed from a literary perspective with his dissertation premise that undoing formal regulations against child labor decreases the demand for child labor, I was thoroughly mystified by the graphs he drew on the white board to support his research. My double-major business students had no problem interpreting the drawings because they have trained in them. My conclusion? There is probably nothing that neoliberalism likes more than having literary critics speak like amateurs. Even as I stepped into the real business world—and not the allegorical neoliberalism of the literary conference—I needed to move my guest lecturer onto my territory and have him read our texts for the day, by Lydia Cacho no less, so that we could engage on more grounds than his chosen terrain.

In order to convince other academics to cross over into lit crit, even as we attempt to visit their stomping grounds—where our shared students have often already made themselves comfortable—it would behoove literary critics to strengthen our discipline. Instead of lawyering up, I am thinking here of "disciplining up," so that we critics hold ourselves accountable to our own high standards of articulate thought issued from concern for social justice. That means trying new moves, such as ducking overly general allegories and examining our own field for sexism, as per *Dude Lit*, as well as incorporating numbers and facts even when they might alter our favorite views. To assign ourselves the amateur role, arguing from mostly a feeling of suspicion, keeps us safely in a collectors' box, to be taken off the shelf when Octavio Paz has another birthday or a colleague from another field needs a "fun" book to round out a syllabus—which is doubly problematic because that contemporary scene still prefers that men star in the discussion. We can change all this if we change.

Still not sure if you belong? Would family policies include you too? If you are reading this book, you are already a member of the family.

Speaking of family, the task of editing *Dude Lit* has taken me past the pregnancy and into the seventh month of my son's life outside the womb. The new responsibilities have afforded me opportunities aplenty to ponder a set of germane insults used in our global patriarchy, which turns on the accusation *You suck!* Similar insults in Spanish include *¡No mames!* (Don't be an ass!) and *¡No seas mamón!* (Don't be stuck up!). When I nudge my baby and coo that he can go ahead and suck, I am struck by the fundamental absurdity of our shared language. How did the act of sucking, with its requisite infant cooperation, wind up with the power to humiliate? Perhaps here is the final lesson, waiting in the beginning of it all. The bullying and barbarism start when we decide that good-natured collaboration—in a word, *interdependence*—especially with one's mother, isn't respectable. But as we have had long occasion to observe, being human and sucking are of a piece, and pretending otherwise sets up a deluded model. It's no disrespect to observe that people suck. Fearing the instinct is where it all goes wrong. Anyway, I'm off now to pick up my son and put in some more hours raising him as a mother-lover. I invite you to become one too.

NOTES

INTRODUCTION

Epigraph: Luna, *Adapting Gender*, xvi.

1. Castellblanch signs the letter as a visiting scholar at the Institution for Research on Labor and Employment, University of California, Berkeley. The *Times* article that spurred his letter covered official publicity efforts to raise awareness of predatory *machista* customs on Mexico City's public transportation system.
2. I am one of those newspaper readers stunned that U.S. Supreme Court Justice Sonia Sotomayor's acknowledgment that she views the world from the angle of her personal experience "could provoke sharp questioning in a confirmation hearing" (Savage). It's worth our time to meditate on the reasons for offense caused by Sotomayor's musing, "I wonder whether by ignoring our differences as women and men of color we do a disservice both to the law and society" (Savage).
3. For a list of some of the phrases collected on the Twitter feed, see the article "#Ropasucia" published in *La Tempestad.*

CHAPTER 1

Epigraphs: Walkowitz, *Born Translated*, 245

I think the issue of gender, male-female, is no longer a debate, at least for my generation.—Abenshushan, in Hind, *La Generación XXX*, 35.

1. Suppressing knowledge of men writers' lives is probably an impossible task in competent criticism, and I point to Christina Soto van der Plas's fine piece on Pacheco's poetry as an example of analysis that avoids all mention of Pacheco's

biography and personal project and yet, by citing Octavio Paz's expert opinion on Pacheco's work, still manages to conjure the specter of Pacheco's social circle and acceptance therein (161).

2. Writers themselves were sometimes reluctant to admit the importance of extratextual performance. Robert McKee Irwin reminds us that the lauded post-Revolutionary "virile" literature never found a clear articulation after the debate sparked over Julio Jiménez Rueda's 1924 article "El afeminamiento de la literatura Mexicana" (The feminization of Mexican literature) (*Mexican Masculinities* 119). Irwin argues that virile writing really has to do with performance: "Jiménez Rueda's attack on literary feminization has less to do with literary style or even with the content of literary production than it does with the perceived effeminacy of certain writers" (120). Sánchez Prado comments that this virile conception of literature plays into conservative notions and is supportive of a throwback to *virreinalista*, or colonial period literature ("Nación y castración" 285–86).
3. From 1895 to 1910 only a small percentage of Mexicans could read; during that period national literacy rates slowly grew from 14.4 percent to 19.7 percent (Vaughan cited in Gonzales 526).
4. Today most Mexicans can read, and UNESCO reports for 2015 a 94.4 percent overall literacy rate, with a 2.2 percent difference between males and females that favors men; apparently, 2015 is the last date for which the UNESCO information is available ("List of Countries").
5. Sefamí, in Rivera Garza's quotation, observes that *Myself with Others* "oddly appeared in English and has not since been translated into Spanish" (Rivera Garza, "Oddly/Curiosamente" 79). According to Rivera Garza, Sefamí views the text as indicative of Fuentes's intellectual status, his sense of humor, and his charisma (77).
6. In *Myself with Others*, Fuentes names an all-male lineup of influences on his writing career, in addition to an enumeration of cities, which gives the impression that the men writers constitute a sort of geography unto themselves: "Neruda, Reyes, Paz; Washington, Santiago de Chile, Buenos Aires, Mexico City, Paris, Geneva; Cervantes, Balzac, Rimbaud, Thomas Mann . . ." (27).
7. For the reader attuned to *Dude Lit* networks, the endnotes prove juicy reading. The second note has Mignolo acknowledging the "participant-members" in a discussion group that informed the article: ten men—eleven counting Mignolo—and four women constitute that roster; the "participant-invited guests," who are all faculty at Duke University, tally four men and one woman.
8. Other token women cited in Mignolo's article include Gayatri Spivak and Rigoberta Menchú. The context in which these names are dropped creates their token status. Spivak appears as the sixth intellectual in a list of five men, Foucault, Lacan, Derrida, Said, and Bhabha (452). Menchú appears next to Anzaldúa's name in a list of six additional men: Waman Poma de Ayala, Mahatma Gandhi, José Carlos Mariátegui, Amilcar Cabral, Aimé Césaire, and Frantz Fanon; Rigoberta Menchú and Gloria Anzaldúa "among others" are the last two names mentioned (452).

9. Sergio González Rodríguez and L. M. Oliveira, as well as novelist Carmen Boullosa, also explore the historical continuity between conquistadors and contemporary Mexican men. In the chronicles of *El hombre sin cabeza* (The headless man) (2009), González Rodríguez proposes that the general conditions of day-to-day life in Mexico correspond to an abject state (160). As predicted by the title, González Rodríguez connects the practice of decapitation in contemporary narcoviolence with customs that date, variously, to the Aztecs, to the Conquest, and to the Independence struggle. Carmen Boullosa achieves much the same point in a brief essay, "Más acá de la nación" (Beyond the nation), where she summarizes the effects of the centuries-old practice of insisting that indigenous peoples speak Spanish and move to Mexico City in order to find work: "Al reproducir día a día la violencia de la Conquista en nuestro modelo social 'mestizo', asfixiábamos al país. Imaginariamente. También prácticamente" (69). (Reproducing day to day the violence of the Conquest in our "mestizo" social model, we asphyxiated the country. Imaginatively. Also practically.)
10. In the analysis, the anonymous raped and murdered women seem to suffer a worse fate than the two cases of torture Villalobos-Ruminott mentions, which are not located on the Mexican border and do not include rape; these cases memorialize the deaths of men: Robert-François Damiens and Fu-Tchu Li (179).
11. Villalobos-Ruminott's exact quotation states that under the historic conquest and colonial pattern of the Americas, founded on violence, "la guerra no aparece como el fin del contrato, sino como una de sus tantas operaciones performativas" (war does not appear as the goal of the contract, but as one of its many performative operations) (129).
12. Krishnaswamy identifies the gendered nature of imperialism and hints at something like the civilized and barbaric modes with the linked phrases "chivalric model of manliness" and "moral superiority": "The cult of masculinity rationalized imperial rule by equating an aggressive, muscular, chivalric model of manliness with racial, national, cultural and moral superiority" (cited in N. Dowd 22–23). Krishnaswamy's quoted text is "The Economy of Colonial Desire," in *The Masculinity Studies Reader*, edited by Rachel Adams and David Savran (Maldan, MA: Blackwell, [2002]), 292–317.
13. These ten women named in Burgin's history are, in alphabetical order, Rosa Friedman, Marie-Thérèse Génin, Rose Wilder Lane, Peggy Noonan, Ayn Rand, Joan Robinson, Anna Schwartz, Margaret Thatcher, Beatrice Webb, and Veronica Wedgwood.
14. This implicit claim to neutrality leads thinkers such as Wendy Brown to launch a critique of neoliberal logic that assumes individual freedom, always ignoring unwaged work and other sorts of family responsibilities: "The [neoliberal economic] story being told, in other words, is not from the perspective of families as ensembles of generic individuals, but from a social positioning long associated with male heads of households" (101).
15. And what might a woman critic say about Elizondo's partner beating? In an article published in 2011, critic Fabienne Bradu reproduces the passage and asks, "¿Qué

juicio cabe? Entre la condena del ser humano y la maestría del escritor, *mon coeur balance*" (What judgment fits? Between the punishment of the human being and the mastery of the writer, *my heart balances*) (193).

16. It is probably no coincidence that his view of erotic pleasure and violence aligns with some fashionable French thinkers' works on similar matters, perhaps most obviously Georges Bataille and Roland Barthes. Elizondo's *Farabeuf*, also reviewed by Villalobos-Ruminott (179), explores precisely the torture by a hundred cuts suffered by Fu-Tchu Li.

17. The English-language name for the organization appears on one website as Mexican Writing Center ("Centro Mexicano de Escritores," *Enciclopedia*). A more faithful translation is the Mexican Center for Writers, which in its earliest years made room for visiting U.S. writers as well.

18. Chumacero's tendency to appear in the context of other men surfaces in another homage, this one held years earlier in honor of the center's thirty-five years; it featured Alí Chumacero with poetry and Juan José Arreola with short story (CME Chumacero 49-1: 41). The 1987 event was sponsored by the Cultural Center for the Department of Finance and Public Credit (Secretaría de Hacienda y Crédito Público). The all-male lineup announced on the card was rounded out with Sergio García Ramírez, president of the Centro Mexicano de Escritores, and Felipe García Beraza as the secretary. Alí Chumacero is a figure around whom, for the most part, women do not appear in newspaper publicity, with the exception of his *compañera* (companion) Lourdes. Chumacero liked girls, however. Another example of the all-male club that surrounds Chumacero's image appears in a quotation from the rector of the University of Guadalajara, José Trinidad Padilla López, speaking on the occasion of presenting a medal for editorial contributions; Padilla López clarifies that Chumacero helped to drive the editing and publication of the first works by Octavio Paz, Carlos Fuentes, Juan Rulfo, Juan José Arreola, and Antonio Alatorre, "entre otros muchos autores que hoy representan la expresión más lograda de la literatura mexicana contemporánea" (among many other writers who today represent the most polished of contemporary Mexican literature) (CME Chumacero 49-1: 86).

19. The remaining bibliographic information on this anonymous clipping from the file on Chumacero in the Fondo Reservado of the Biblioteca Nacional is written by hand: "7-11-96 *Siempre!*"

20. Another article published some days previously in 1996 has Chumacero make similar comments, obviously cited from the same set of remarks, in response to a question about his favorite drink (whisky, because he is too old for tequila) (Camacho Olivares).

21. Fourteen women have won the prize in literature, Gabriela Mistral among them ("Nobel Prize Facts").

22. In general terms, men enjoy a privileged status in the Mexican labor market. According to a poll taken in 2003, in the metropolitan zones of Mexico City,

Guadalajara, and Monterrey, businesses preferred hiring men over women by a ratio of 2 to 1 ("Pasos hacia" 3).

23. The category that marks the biggest gender disparity is musicians, among whom men dominate. The anonymous authors of the report speculate that journalists, like musicians, favor men for reasons of gender stereotypes, such as the notion that men's schedules and freedoms best serve the needs of music tours and late hours, or other sorts of professional travel and public activity ("Pasos hacia" 11).

24. This notion is sobering. If prizewinners exercise outsize influence on the conferral of prizes, the journey to equity is understandably slow. Note the example of the Sistema Nacional de Investigadores (National System of Researchers, SNI), the best funded and most prestigious research status in Mexico. From 1984 to 2016 the total number of women in that group rose from 18 percent to 36 percent, although in 2016 women were only 19 percent in hard sciences and something like 40 or 50 percent in medicine, health sciences, and humanities. These statistics were delivered by the astronomer Irene Cruz-González in 2018 on the occasion of winning a prize named after Sor Juana Inés de la Cruz, a naming habit about which I have more to say in chapter 3 ("Reconoce").

25. Cohn's table 1 lists the two women authors as Elena Garro (with *Recollections of Things to Come*) and the Brazilian Rachel de Queiroz (*The Three Marias*). The twenty-five men writers in table 1 include such names as Juan José Arreola, Adolfo Bioy Casares, Jorge Luis Borges, Daniel Cosío Villegas, Rubén Darío, Sergio Galindo, Martín Luis Guzmán, José Carlos Mariátegui, José Martí, Alfonso Reyes, Juan Rulfo, José Vasconcelos, and Agustín Yáñez (*Latin American Literary* 116–17). In table 2, the all-male lineup includes Octavio Paz, Juan Carlos Onetti, Pablo Neruda, José Lezama Lima, Manuel Puig, Ernesto Sábato, and Severo Sarduy (172–73). Christiane Stallaert notes the tendency to blame translators for weak sales outside of Mexico; in Rulfo's case, for instance, French- and English-language translators were blamed for lukewarm receptions of *Pedro Páramo* (341–44). In line with my study, Stallaert also points out that Rulfo needed a *padrino* (godfather) in order to gain acceptance; she notes that other writers vouched for Rulfo, and highlights the support from Gabriel García Márquez, Jorge Luis Borges, and Juan Carlos Onetti (339); she adds Carlos Fuentes and Octavio Paz as key players in building Rulfo's national reputation (340).

26. In the category of essay, the men winners are Carlos Chimal, Héctor Perea, Fernando Fernández, Gustavo Emilio Rosales, Aurelio Asiain, and Armando González Torres.

27. The men winners in narrative are Dante Medina, Ignacio Padilla, Juan Pablo Villalobos, David Miklos, Eloy Urroz, Orlando Ortiz, Agustín Ramos, Marco Pirelli, Joaquín Armando Chacón, David Toscana, Alain Derbez, Mauricio Carrera, Martín Solares, Francisco Prieto, Gerardo de la Torre, Alberto Chimal, and Mauricio Molina.

28. In the category of poetry, the men winners are Eduardo Milán, Óscar Oliva, Fabio Morábito, Jorge Esquinca, Jorge Ortega, Héctor Carreto, Saúl Ibargeuntias, Josué Ramírez, and Xhander Balaj.

29. The previous year, in 2015, the winners included more women but were chosen by an entirely male jury: Gonzalo Celorio, Eduardo Lizalde, Roberto Frías, Antonio Deltoro, and Antonio Saborit. That all-male panel of judges selected one woman among a total of four essay winners, and for each of the categories narrative and poetry, six women appeared among the thirteen total winners ("Resultados 2015").
30. Journalist Alma Guillermoprieto and political scientist Denise Dresser round out the list of men, who, in order of their ranking, are Jorge Ibargüengoitia, Juan Villoro, Paco Taibo II, Carlos Monsiváis, Juan Rulfo, Rafael Pérez Gay, Alejandro Rosas, and the cartoonist team Jis and Trino.
31. Fadanelli's list of four intellectual women comprises Iris Murdoch (69, 183, etc.), Simone Weil (misspelled as "Simon," 87), Victoria Camps (88, 189), and Madame de Staël (113).
32. Fadanelli lists the following women in this bibliography: Hannah Arendt, Victoria Camps, Murdoch, and Weil. Furthermore, *Insolencia: Literatura y mundo*, like much of Fadanelli's work, includes a dedication that acknowledges only men friends, in this case Leonardo da Jandra and Rafael Pérez Gay.
33. The women whom Fadanelli mentions are Kathy Acker and Virginie Despentes.
34. This habit also appears in unambiguously "soft and low" writers. In his YA novel *Persona normal* (2011), Benito Taibo lauds the act of reading; this relatively unskillful but best-selling book name-drops some 101 authors, of whom 94 are men (197–242). The 7 women are Concepción Company (the editor of the *Diccionario de mexicanismos*), Harper Lee, Toni Morrison, Anne Frank, Santa Teresa de Jesús, Rosa Montero, and Elena Poniatowska. In a follow-up to *Persona normal*, Taibo wrote the similarly themed *Cómplice* (2015), a glorification of reading that features two bookworm protagonists, one a female. In order to emphasize the sudden inclusion of a young woman, Taibo has coprotagonist Isabel search for admirable women protagonists; she rejects all four texts that her teacher suggests as "disappointing," namely, *Madame Bovary* by Flaubert, *Nana* by Zola, *Las damas de las camelias* (*The Lady of the Camellias*) by Dumas, and *Anna Karenina* by Tolstoy (30). Isabel cannot quite identify with Jane Austen's Elizabeth Bennet either (127). Finally, she discovers a YA novel, *Loba* (2013) by Verónica Murguía, a Mexican woman writer, and the case is closed: "Por fin encontré a la protagonista femenina que buscaba" (I finally found the female protagonist I was looking for) (131).
35. Amara's recent titles include books of poetry *Nu)n(ca* (Ne)v(er) (2015), *A pie* (On foot) (2010), *Pasmo* (Astonishment) (2003), and *Envés* (Underside) (2003), plus the books of essays *Historia descabellada de la peluca* (Crazy history of wigs) (2014), *Los disidentes del universo* (The dissidents of the universe) (2013), *La escuela del aburrimiento* (The school of boredom) (2013), *Sombras sueltas* (Loose shadows) (2006), and *El peatón inmóvil* (The immobile pedestrian) (2003), as well as a work of aphorisms and very short texts, *Cuaderno flotante* (Floating notebook) (2012). He has also published two books for children: *Las aventuras de Max y su ojo submarino* (The adventures of Max and his submarine eye) (2007) and *Los calcetines solitarios: Una historia sobre bullying* (The lonely socks: a story about bullying) (2011). Accord-

ing to WorldCat, Abenshushan had no book publications in 2015, 2016, and 2017. In 2014, a reprinting of her collection of short stories *El clan de los insomnes* (The clan of the insomniacs) (2004) appeared, and a collection of essays titled *Escritos para desocupados* (Writings for the unemployed) found a listing in 2013, some three years after she had shared with me the seemingly finalized manuscript. In 2009 Abenshushan released a slim biography of Julio Ramón Ribeyro, and of course in 2007 she published the brilliant collection of essays *Una habitación desordenada* (A messy room).

36. The twenty names listed in Alarcón's *Veintiuno* are Andrés Acosta, Jaime Mesa, Luigi Amara, Guillermo Rubio, Fernando del Paso, Iván Farías, Ricardo Cartas, Paco Ignacio Taibo II, Eduardo Huchín Sosa, Juan Villoro, Rodrigo Durana, Carlos Fuentes, Alberto Chimal, Carlos Reyes Ávila, Xavier Velasco, Mauricio Bares, Mario Bellatin, Óscar de la Borbollo, Leonardo da Jandra, and René Avilés Fabila.
37. For Palaverisch, Fadanelli's sex scenes, in the specific context of the short stories from *Más alemán que Hitler*, break up the narrative rhythm and exist only to provoke and break taboos (200). She adds that although Fadanelli means to reject the morality and ethics of dominant society, his depictions of sex haplessly repeat mainstream machismo (201). Writing about Fadanelli's morals leads to an interesting scholarly mirror. When Héctor Jaimes says of the novel *Lodo* (Mud) (2002) that it shows a contemporary society in which reason, law, and work succumb to passion, corruption, arbitrariness, injustice, and chance, the critic's faith in the first three elements as an ideal strictly separated from the last proves telling (35).
38. For Mexican box office figures, see www.boxofficemojo.com/intl/mexico/yearly/.
39. Interestingly, the numbers show a pattern among the writers and their characters: "Screenwriter gender was related significantly to character gender . . . the presence of a female writer increased the percentage of girls/women on screen in 2016 by 10.6%" (Smith et al., "Inequality in 900" 20). The same lead researchers' study of 700 popular films released from 2007 through 2014 (which also excludes 2011) analyzed 30,835 characters and discovered only about a third of the more than thirty thousand speaking characters were female; in fact, just twenty-one of the one hundred top-grossing films in 2014 "featured a female lead or roughly equal colead." No female actors over forty-five years of age performed a lead or colead role in 2014 (Smith et al., "Inequality in 700" 1). By 2016, that number had improved slightly: in 2015 five women over age forty-five and in 2016 eight women over age forty-five had performed a lead or colead role (Smith et al., "Inequality in 900" 1).
40. The comments appeared in *Siempre*, 8 June 1966.
41. Monsiváis writes that Pitol recommended to him a set of readings other than those Vicente Magdaleno had assigned, including the following eleven men: "Borges, Alfonso Reyes, Faulkner, Dos Passos, Scott Fitzgerald, Nicholas Blake, Thomas Mann, Gide, Hemingway, Nathaniel West, [and] E. M. Forster"; these came to substitute for authors such as Hermann Hesse, Ilya Ehrenburg, "Spaniards," Erskine Caldwell, John Steinbeck, James T. Farrell, Robert Penn Warren, and Evelyn Waugh (*Carlos Monsiváis* 48). Excluding the lump group of "Spaniards,"

eighteen men in total appear in this list. Monsiváis also confesses that he imitates Alfonso Reyes and Salvador Novo (49).

42. For an inevitably truncated though ambitious stab at a comprehensive review of the criticism on Juan Rulfo, as well as the particular endeavor of *Pedro Páramo,* see Gerald Martin. In attempting to survey this vast criticism, the Spanish speaker has an edge. Nuala Finnegan's introduction to an edited volume on Rulfo and visual culture warns, "Of over seventy monographs on the work of Juan Rulfo, the vast majority are in Spanish" (Introduction). For attention to the latest trends, Sánchez Prado provides a relatively comprehensive discussion of the criticism ("Juan Rulfo"). Some of these new trends rehearse a concern for colonialism. Amit Thakkar moves from his book *The Fiction of Juan Rulfo: Irony, Revolution, and Postcolonialism* to a conclusion in a later article, "Irony and the Priest," that mentions the decolonial; Susan Savage Lee looks at neocolonialism in a comparative reading of *Pedro Páramo.* Somewhat along those lines, in the context of thought on transculturation, Lucy Bell offers a helpful review of recent criticism on Rulfo's stylistic elements, with attention to contributions by Walter Mignolo, Adam Sharman, and Evodio Escalante ("Death"). In the context of Rulfo's short stories, Bell recognizes older criticism, by men thinkers, such as William Rowe, Fernando Benítez, Manuel Durán, Jorge Ruffinelli, and Augusto Roa Bastos. In a second article, she picks up on Thakkar's theme of irony and, several years before his article on Barthes's theory of the punctum, reads Rulfo's short stories in those terms, as well as through Benjamin's "shock" experience ("Photography"). For a cogent summary of critical tendencies regarding Pacheco's work and, more specifically, *Las batallas en el desierto,* see Alejandro Zamora. In one update to that body of thought, Michael Dowdy applies ecocriticism to read Pacheco's poetic representations of Mexico City and its problem with smog. In Dowdy's reading, Pacheco deconstructs the polluted Mexico City "from end product (smog) to constitutive processes" (294). In a theme that I will comment on elsewhere, Dowdy cites Mary Docter's idea that Pacheco can "write an original poem entirely from previous texts" (Docter qtd. in Dowdy 295).

43. Steinem meditates on the term *chick flick* and decides that such labels generally disappear for men writers: "Suppose Shakespeare had really been the Dark Lady who some people still think he/she was. I bet most of her plays and all of her sonnets would have been dismissed as ye olde Elizabethan chick lit." She solidifies the point in a statement that summarizes my suspicions: "Indeed, as long as men are taken seriously when they write about the female half of the world—and women are not taken seriously when writing about ourselves, much less about men and public affairs—the list of Great Authors will be more about power than talent, more about opinion than experience" ("Women Have 'Chick Flicks'").

44. I borrow Hugo Verani's distinction between narrator Carlos and protagonist Carlitos to distinguish between the adult and the boy. Additionally, I observe that Mariana's death, which no one can confirm, shows that the plot hinges on sexism until the bitter end. Juan Armando Epple denounces this apparently willful lack of collective memory among Pacheco's secondary characters (41).

45. Florence Moorhead-Rosenberg goes so far as to claim that Carlos's revision of his childhood experience offers "a glimpse of one of the few forms of 'heroic' behavior left to the modern world: the undertaking and simultaneous narration of a scorchingly truthful confrontation with a bleak and better forgotten past in order to understand the nature of one's present" (13). Would the gender-reversed version of the plot strike readers as "heroic"?

CHAPTER 2

Epigraphs: Day and Castillo, "Introduction," 2.

Fishman, "Searching for Juan Rulfo."

You would be taking a taxi and from it would descend Carlos Monsiváis. You would get in an elevator and he would be there in the corner observing everyone with a searching and sorrowful gaze. You would be climbing the steps of a pyramid and on the top you would find Monsiváis seated in a lotus position. I remember having come across him in the Madrid airport and having fallen prey to a deep depression: to travel so far and find yourself in front of one of the Indios Verdes.—Fadanelli, "Monsiváis."

1. As Irwin reminds us, Novo's texts for the magazine *El Chafirete* were meant to help him seduce "the most solidly built of the drivers themselves" ("La pedo" 126).
2. Mahieux writes of Novo, "He truly *is* tall and vigorous" (165).
3. Books seem largely extraneous to a bárbaro's reputation, even if he becomes president. Military figure and sometime nineteenth-century president José Antonio López de Santa Ana "boasted that he had never read a big book and delegated the writing of letters, the composition of speeches, and the fashioning of public manifestos to underlings" (R. Ruiz 66). Present-day tourists who visit dictator Porfirio Diaz's study preserved in el Castillo de Chapultepec, in Mexico City, can observe a quirky plaque that recalls the president's spelling mistakes. The sign clucks that Díaz never bothered to correct these consistent errors. Sebastian Faber reminds us that it was not until the Spanish exiles settled in Mexico City after 1938, when these European academics received substantially better salaries than Mexican university professors, that the latter also began to receive a fatter salary. Faber adds, "In fact they [the Spanish exiles] were the first academics in Mexico to have full-time employment" (18).
4. The numbers for the women who wear noticeable makeup in their profile photo are much higher than the number of women in glasses: about forty-seven of the sixty women pictured wear obvious makeup (78.33 percent).
5. Benito Juárez does not make the 150-year cut of Almaraz's series.
6. Poets Jaime Torres Bodet and Jaime Sabines, along with other Mexican men writers, functioned as politicians in Mexico's political system without ruining their civilized images. Contact with power did not seem to contaminate them in the way it affects women writers' reputations. Think of the consequences for Jesusa Rodríguez, Elena Poniatowska, and Guadalupe Loaeza after they supported the

presidential candidate Andrés Manuel López Obrador for the presidential term 2006–12 that Felipe Calderón won, or Antonieta Rivas Mercado's troubles stemming from her relationship with presidential candidate José Vasconcelos. Women writers do not enjoy men's ability to brush up against power while maintaining an aura of impolite autonomy. Furthermore, women are sometimes subject to the rumor that their male acquaintances slept with them or wrote for them. By contrast, I have never come across the suggestion that Monsiváis (or Pacheco) received favors from Novo because they were lovers. In fact, I have never heard a rumor that Monsiváis (or Pacheco) and Novo were lovers at all. Nevertheless, Monsiváis ghostwrote texts for Novo during his formal employment as Novo's personal secretary—a job that José Emilio Pacheco would later hold. In a personal interview, Miguel Sabido remembers that Monsiváis ghostwrote texts for more people than just Novo: "Escribe [Monsiváis] artículos. No solamente para Novo. Escribe artículos para el Presidente de la República, para ministros [del gobierno]. Es una práctica muy común en todas partes. [. . .] Carlos escribe, tenía el estilo de Novo. Lo tenía muy bien asimilado. Entonces le escribía algunas cosas. ¿Cómo le decía? *Chiquito*. "Oye, Chiquito, escríbeme tal cosa." Yo lo escuchaba porque era asistente [en el teatro] de Salvador Novo y era íntimo de Monsiváis." (He [Monsiváis] wrote articles. Not just for Novo. He wrote articles for the President of the Republic, for ministers [in the government]. It is a very common practice everywhere. . . . Carlos wrote, he had Novo's style. He had assimilated it really well. So he wrote some things for him. What did he used to call him? *Tiny*. "Hey, Tiny, write this thing for me." I would hear him because I was Salvador Novo's [theater] assistant and a close friend to Monsiváis.)

7. Biron's study focuses on crime novels and not detective fiction because of the unsolved nature of so many murders in Latin America (22–23). Her conclusion strikes a note of hope: literary texts that review violence against women encourage the audience to criticize dominant fictions, and thus to question the fictions of masculinity (150).
8. The *Guardian*'s Pengelly covers the story told in part by the *Washington Post*, which quoted a journalist in the Boston audience, Amy Littlefield, as saying that Talese first named the novelist Mary McCarthy as an inspiration before changing his mind: "And then there was a pause and he [Talese] said, 'None. And I'll tell you why.' And he went into this explanation about how educated women don't want to hang out with anti-social people" (McCarthy).
9. John Waldron reminds us that in 1971 President Luis Echeverría made the deceased López Velarde a "national poet" and declared it the "Año de López Velarde" (Year of López Velarde) (49, 62). In 1988, nearly two decades later and after a change in economic policy that swung toward the neoliberal, official celebrations continued to recognize the poet, this time under the justification of the centenary of López Velarde's birth (Waldron 62). Waldron remembers that unlike so many of his contemporaries, López Velarde read only Spanish; this difference certainly sets him

apart from Paz and puts at risk López Velarde's sophistication as Paz might tend to measure it (66).

10. In the same dismissive and possibly competitive vein, in a slim biography Paz describes a man he admired, the Contemporáneo male poet and playwright Xavier Villaurrutia, as privileging feelings over reasoned ideas: "No era un hombre de ideas: era un hombre extraordinariamente inteligente que, por escepticismo, había decidido poner su inteligencia al servicio de su sensibilidad" (He was not a man of ideas: he was an extraordinarily intelligent man who, for reasons of skepticism, had decided to put his intelligence in the service of his sensibility) (*Xavier Villaurrutia* 21).

11. The etymology of the term *credit* derives from the Latin *credo*, or "belief" (Crowston 3). As Crowston reminds us, "credit was also an important theme in discussions of religious faith and the reputation of religious institutions" (37). David Graeber proposes that in the religious context debt exists, *not* to be paid back, but to create community (*Debt*, particularly the first three chapters).

12. Sara Potter's book on the figure of the female muse and Mexican writers remains attuned to the special situation of women visual artists in mid-twentieth-century Mexico. In the context of the International Exhibition of Surrealism in Mexico City in 1940, Potter writes about the curators' somewhat unpredictable decisions regarding women artists: "Curator Wolfgang Paalen included Frida Kahlo even though she repeatedly disavowed any connections between her art and European surrealism; Mexican artist María Izquierdo was excluded despite the fact that both [Antonin] Artaud and Alice Rahon thought highly of Izquierdo's work and considered it to be representative of the Surrealist movement" (79). Potter goes on to note that Remedios Varo did appear in the 1940 exhibition.

13. Two of the five women were older at the time of death: Virginia Fábregas died at age seventy-eight, and Amalia González Caballero at eighty-seven. Interestingly, a high number of these women honored were divorced: Fábregas, Izquierdo, and Castellanos had all managed to escape unhappy marriages without losing their honorable ("illustrious") reputations.

14. Criticism as a hallucination itself declares the existence of genius, in the same way that drug laws invent "hard" drugs. Brian Penrose, in an essay amusingly named "Soft vs. Hard: Why Drugs Are Not Like Eggs," argues that the habit of thinking of illegal drugs as "hard" and licit ones as "soft" is "preposterous." He notes that tobacco and alcohol, both "soft" legal drugs, are more addictive than some "hard" illicit substances, such as LSD, which is not habit-forming, but offers that pesky hallucinatory experience that neighbors on the obscene (164).

15. Ronell's reader is free to see, however, that in the court-backed decisions the men Allen Ginsberg, Henry Miller, William Burroughs, and James Joyce gain a "high lit" reputation from being found legitimately hard—here for obscenities related to the scandal of sex topics, though as Ronell signals, that obscenity inevitably relates to other frightful visions, such as those connoted by "hard" drugs.

16. De Grazia's book covers legal decisions regarding Joyce's *Ulysses*, Ginsberg's *Howl* (1956), and Lenny Bruce's stand-up routines (1960s).
17. See Rubio Rossell, and A. Gutiérrez and Ponce for similar comments by Poniatowska.
18. Nearly any substance can cause a "high," if nearly any substance can be addictive. On this point, Eve Kosofsky Sedgwick follows contemporary logic to its extremes and writes that the discovery of exercise addiction meant that anything could be addictive or, in her more confusing words, "nothing couldn't be [addictive]," that is, "the exercise addict was the limit case for evacuating the concept of addiction, once and for all, of any necessary specificity of substance, bodily effect, or psychological motivation" (584).
19. Sánchez plays up the cuts, citing further mutilated dialogue: "The censored word obviously was considered too vulgar to be included in the videotape release of the film, and it is again censored when Britel responds to Juan Carlos's conjecture by asking if the killer was "on some ___________? Maybe so" (72).
20. Richard Klein's *Cigarettes Are Sublime* wryly observes that late twentieth-century antitobacco efforts present a smoke-and-mirrors campaign, as "the secretary of health castigated cigarette marketing during the very week that the White House chief of staff weakened the clean air bill" (15).
21. The U.S. Supreme Court at the time of my writing includes three women of the nine judges. They are Ruth Bader Ginsberg (b. 1933), Sonia Sotomayor (b. 1954), and Elena Kagan (b. 1960). The Mexican Supreme Court in 2017 included eleven justices, two of whom were women: Margarita Beatriz Luna Ramos (b. 1956) and Norma Lucía Piña Hernández (b. unknown), who replaced Olga Sánchez Cordero (b. 1955) in 2015.
22. To this point, novelist Luis Felipe Lomelí repeated to me the calculation that editors have given him: the majority of readers in Mexico are women (Hind, "El bárbaro" 209). As far as the male-dominated profession of film directing goes, the masculinist slant does not impede women in the United States from buying about half of the movie tickets sold there (Dargis). Similar statistics for the top Mexican commercial draws in the cineplex probably apply. Once at the movies, women may find Laura Mulvey's observations, first published in 1975, about the male gaze in film largely holding true. A related problem exists in television, as again reported for the United States in the *New York Times*: "A recent Directors Guild of America analysis of 277 television series found that women directed only 16 percent of episodes" (M. Dowd).
23. The nude cyclist protest occurred for the sixth time in 2014 ("Mexicanos, ciclistas"). Trading bikes for machetes, the group 400 Pueblos (400 villages/peoples), originating from the state of Veracruz, has used naked or nearly naked protest tactics in Mexico City since 1992. The bare-chested women who join in these protests are much less unusual sights in the megalopolis, thanks to the statuary. Mark Manley works in black and white images to document these protests. See his homepage under the heading "400 Pueblos."

24. The Mexican catalog includes Adolfo Mantilla Osorno's implicit explanation of the absence of naked men in public statuary in Mexico. Depictions of naked men threatened to cast them as women, owing to the "pose of traditional feminine inactivity," and it was not until twentieth-century feminism influenced thinking on the matter that portraits of the nude male became possible beyond the "niche of homosexual art" ("Una genealogía" 50).

25. Furthermore, women such as Ángeles Mastretta and Laura Esquivel wrote the best sellers of the 1980s, most famously *Arráncame la vida* (*Tear This Heart Out*) (1985) and *Como agua para chocolate* (*Like Water for Chocolate*) (1989), respectively, and according to Carmen Boullosa, the men writers resented this literary "massification" (*masificación*). Thus, per Boullosa's understanding of the attitudinal shift, "Entonces ser mujer escritora en México ahora es sinónimo de ser mal escritora. Nos tratan con una displicencia, una grosería, un desprecio que de verdad no merecemos. Y se nos mide a todas por la misma tabla rasa. Todas somos malas" (Boullosa, personal interview). (So to be a woman writer in Mexico is now synonymous with being a bad writer. We are treated with carelessness, rudeness, a contempt that truly we don't deserve. And they measure us with the same blank slate. We are all bad.)

26. The portraits of authors include the following: *El Apuntador* (The note taker) from 1841 shows likenesses of José Joaquín Pesado and Juan Ruíz de Alarcón (Musacchio 1:148, 150). *La Ilustración Mexicana* (Mexican illustration) depicts Juan Cordero in 1851 (213). That same publication devotes a cover to the portrait of Ignacio M. Altamirano in 1893 (439). *El Renacimiento* (The renaissance) in 1869 features portraits of Melesio Morales and Florencio M. del Castillo (267, 273). *El Álbum de la Mujer* (The woman's album) features numerous portraits of men authors: e.g., Juan de Dios Peza in 1884 (342), Manuel Flores in 1885 (350), and Vicente Riva Palacio in 1886 (364). *La Juventud Literaria* (Literary youth) in 1887 shows José Peón y Contreras (366), along with Guillermo Prieto (367), Salvador Díaz Mirón (368), José María Vijil (369), Justo Sierra (370), Manuel Gutiérrez Nájera (379), and Manuel M. González (380). In 1888 it includes José López-Portillo y Rojas (382) and reprints a sketch of a handsome Federico Gamboa (397). In 1890, *Revista de México* (Mexico's magazine) publishes, on the cover, likenesses of Arturo Paz (415) and Manuel J. Othón (423). As for females, opera star Ángela Peralta seems perhaps the most consistently illustrated woman artist. Both trends, that of depicting clothed authors and that of drawing naked women, decline with the second volume, which covers the mid-twentieth century.

27. Some books that feature photos of women authors do exist, though not as part of a series. For example, Elena Garro has been the subject of Patricia Rosas Lopátegui's attentive collection of images, and biographies of Guadalupe Amor and Elena Poniatowska by Michael Schussler include numerous photographs. Poet and governor Griselda Álvarez was the focus of a collection of photographs, issued in 2007 by the Universidad de Colima.

28. One man's reputation bolsters that of another. When La Galería Fundación Héctor García hosted a posthumous homage to Carlos Monsiváis, the images of the writer served to promote the photographer's reputation, and vice versa (Piñón, "Monsiváis" 8). Similarly, Monsiváis, though not included himself in the Iconografía series, participated in the effort by contributing the introduction to the album on Pellicer; José Emilio Pacheco wrote the introduction for the volume on García Terrés, and David Huerta introduced the photographs of Cardoza y Aragón.
29. Of course, Batis also came to publish images of male strippers. In Catalina Miranda's interview with Batis he remembers the surge of interest in male strippers that at one time stole the focus from the women striptease artists. Batis asked one of his writers to cover the story for the lowest-class audience (Miranda, "Entrevista" 95).
30. The forty-four women listed as collaborators with *sábado* are Nedda G. de Anhalt, Sabina Berman, Carmen Boullosa, Ambra Polidori, Rosa Beltrán, Josefina Estrada, Vera Larrosa, Marlene Villatoro, Katya Caso, Margarita Pinto, Pura López Colomé, Fabianne Bradu, Verónica Volkow, Saide Sesín, Roxana Elvridge-Thomas, Claudia Hernández de Valle Arizpe, Mónica Braun, Laura Doriana Vázquez, Vivian Abenshushan, Mary Carmen Sánchez Ambriz, María Luisa Barnés, Gabriela Balderas, Rocío González, Catalina Miranda, Raquel Huerta Nava, Socorro Ortiz Mendieta, Niña Yhared, Claudia Posadas, Fernanda Solórzano, Carolina Luna, Mayra Inzunza, Lucía Rivadeneyra, Claudia Albarrán, Martha Bátiz Zuk, Edmée Pardo, María Fernanda García, Ana Luisa Calvillo, Dolores Corrales Soriano, Mónica Maldonado Yáñez, Laura Linares Palacios, Nuria Armengol, Felisa Santillán Hernández, Ana Ivonne Díaz, and Iris Limón Saquedo.

CHAPTER 3

Epigraphs: Rulfo's place is so singular that we should say "here are the best Mexican writers and over there, way over there, is Juan Rulfo."—Huerta, "La neblina de la literatura."

"Never in my life have I corrected, struck through, or rewritten anything." —Salvador Novo.

"Is that why I pay you so much?" scolded Azcárraga. "For you to put your badge over your balls?" A terrifying silence descended. The Tiger had roared. But the employee managed to mutter a reply. Putting his hand on his throat, he exclaimed, "No, sir, my balls are up here."—Fernández and Paxman, *El Tigre*, 31.

1. The requirement that the two women must be named is sometimes added. The test takes its name from U.S. cartoonist Alison Bechdel, whose comic strip *Dykes to Watch Out For* first appeared in 1985 (Selisker 505). The idea, according to Bechdel, actually came from her friend Liz Wallace (512). Scott Selisker credits Anita Sarkeesian for popularizing the test on her YouTube channel "Feminist Frequency" (506). An Internet site, bechdeltest.com, makes relevant statistics available on more than 6,000 films. Jennifer O'Meara articulates a call for nuance in the context of bechdeltext

.com, which reveals "a certain competitive urge amongst users to find some vindicating dialogue, even if only a single line, which allows a film to pass" (1121).

2. In this sense, Kristine Vanden Berghe's comparison of work and performance by Rulfo and Nellie Campobello proves especially interesting; she notes the coincidence in the use of the diminutive by both authors, for example (311). Though Vanden Berghe does not emphasize the feminine connotations of the diminutive, her readers can easily perceive this angle for themselves. Rather than secular chick lit, Rulfo may model a twisted Christianity, as Patricia Reagan notes in the context of a rich review of the literature. Possibly, *Pedro Páramo* may take up a theme of Christianity through its very failures and absences. In Reagan's ambivalent view, Justina might be a self-sacrificing figure who recalls, however faintly, the notion of the Virgin Mother, as a "surrogate mother" to Susana San Juan, or she could be an "inversion" of Christian roles, as a "non-mother" (Reagan 41).

3. John Waldron's article points toward Pacheco's poetry as the better bet for democratic opening: "The revolutionary potential of poetry is its ability to de-authorize meaning" (60).

4. Graff Zivin does examine the works of one woman writer, Mexican playwright Sabina Berman.

5. In *Mexican Masculinities*, Irwin questions Paz's understanding of homosexuality in *El laberinto de la soledad*. Irwin finds the notion of *chingar* useful to explain the hierarchies that dictate friendship among men in Mexican novels. Irwin adds the synonym *madrugar* (to get up in the wee hours) to the formulaic threat of *chingar* (207). Perhaps because *madrugar* is not an obscene term, critics have chosen to continue to focus on the power of the binary derived from *chingar*.

6. Somewhat related to these kidneys, Rebecca Janzen examines the concept of "bad blood" in *Pedro Páramo* in concert with work by Patrick Dove, Gareth Williams, and Amit Thakkar (55). Janzen's provocative argument holds that "Pedro Páramo, as a sovereign power, has bad blood that perverts weaker characters" (55). Janzen cites the observations of critic Silvia Lorente-Murphy (55). Interestingly, in his comprehensive review of criticism on Juan Rulfo, reprinted in an anthology of 1992, Gerald Martin dismisses Lorente-Murphy's contribution: "Sin embargo, Lorente Murphy [sic] no aporta enfoques novedosos al estudio de Rulfo" (However, Lorente Murphy does not bring novel approaches to the study of Rulfo) (644). Lilia Leticia García Peña's article complements Janzen's research into "bad blood" and explores the trope of stigma through the disappointing son; as a bad son, Pedro merely anticipates the role played later by *his* sons, like Abundio and Miguel, in replacing him (48). Norman Valencia also explores this theme of the troubled son through psychoanalytic theory as brought to bear on the trope of the bad father and the fictitious presence of this same patriarch (see esp. 147–70). To return to Janzen's sources, I note that Gareth Williams views Mexican modernity, "at least up until the economic crisis of 1982," as reliant on a "a *police* project, understood as a permanent coup d'etat" (12). One might say that the critics who critique that police project also, sooner or later, exercise a right of policing, which tends to

keep the "unoriginal" critics (often women) at bay. In this regard, I am especially amused by Keri González's comparison of María Luisa Bombal's *La amortajada* (*The Shrouded Woman*) and Rulfo's style. The article begins with Borges's reaction to Bombal's description of her plot as an impossible project, since it mixes realism with the supernatural (González 89). Borges's policing failed, and González traces Bombal's literary influence through Rulfo and García Márquez.

7. What kind of profession requires curses to get the job done? In tandem with Malinowski's groupings, Villa-Flores notes that, in Rengel's time, the usual swear-word offenders included Spanish soldiers, sailors, and muleteers who supported their activities' masculine qualities by way of "risk taking, sexual assertiveness, and menacing speech" (38). These men did not govern with this language; they completed something closer to menial tasks by way of it.
8. In *The Interior Circuit*, Francisco Goldman discusses the ladies of Polanco imitators. He begins by reviewing the initial case—the one that I discuss—which took place in 2011, with María Vanessa Polo, "a former beauty queen" (175).
9. For a bleeped-out version of the "ladies of Polanco" video, see the coverage anchored by evening newscaster Joaquín López Dóriga ("Las Ladies de Polanco—Noticiero"). Amusingly, the newscaster's name comes up in the audible dialogue of the video when one of the "ladies" shouts that the person filming should send the video to López Dóriga.
10. Jorge Volpi reviews this same scandal and italicizes the term *love* in his summation of Verduzco's performance; he notes the civilized note she struck, over and over, "las extraordinarias dimensiones de su *amor*, como la propia Mamá Rosa no se cansaba de repetir" (the extraordinary dimensions of her *love*, as Mamá Rosa herself never tired of repeating) (129).
11. The published version of the interview does not include this passage because of space restrictions. The section of the conversation that remains appears on pp. 215–16 (Hind, "El bárbaro doctorado").
12. Scott summarizes pre-twentieth-century French feminists' efforts "to refute the prevailing equation of active citizenship with masculinity" (33).
13. The 2013 Supreme Court decision treats a case brought in 2010, when the owner of the newspaper *Síntesis*, Armando Prida Huerta, sued Enrique Núñez Quiroz, from the newspaper *Intolerancia*; both newspapers are located in Puebla. Núñez Quiroz claimed in a column from August 2009 that Prida Huerta was a *puñal* and that *maricones* wrote for him (I. González). Previously, on August 3, 4, 5, 6, 7, 10, 11, and 12, Prida Huerta had reprinted a 2003 column by Erika Rivero Almazán titled "El cerdo hablando de lodo" (The pig talks of mud). In retaliation, on 14 August Núñez Quiroz launched his homophobic accusations in a piece entitled "El ridículo periodístico del siglo" (The journalistic ridiculousness of the century).
14. For example, the Supreme Court document cites Article 11 of the Convención Americana sobre Derechos Humanos (American Convention on Human Rights), ratified by Mexico in 1981, relating to the "Protección de la Honra y de la Dignidad" (Protection of honor and dignity) (Zaldívar Lelo de Larrea, "Amparo directo" 24).

15. The justices go on to elaborate on the point, again all in boldface: **"el juicio crítico o la información divulgada acerca de la conducta profesional o laboral de una persona puede constituir un auténtico ataque a su honor"** (the critical judgment or the information disclosed about the professional or work conduct of a person can constitute an authentic attack on her honor) (Zaldívar Lelo de Larrea, "Amparo directo" 26).
16. One type of aggression seems to link to another. The column that inspired Nuñez Quiroz's hateful retaliation launched, among the accusations of corruption and extortion of politicians, the idea that Rodrigo López Sainz, president of the editorial board of *Intolerancia*, operated as an editor for a child pornography magazine titled *Boys and Toys*, distributed in Central and South America (Zaldívar Lelo de Larrea, "Amparo directo" 4). The column was written by Erika Rivero Almazán.
17. Piccato explains the financial implications of threats to honor in terms of credit: "Crimes against honor undermined this 'power' when they resulted in a loss of credit. From merchants and professionals to bakers and pulque sellers, a stained reputation had a price, even if difficult to quantify; a bankrupt French citizen claimed that 'my *honra* and reputation . . . are the only invaluable goods I possess'" (209; italics mine). Regarding the masculinism of honor, the reader may find it relevant to know that macho duels to the death for honor were not outlawed in Mexico until 1931 (Speckman Guerra 34).
18. Some scholars have already been erecting a defense of the not original. Kenneth Goldsmith describes a "trend among younger writers" who specialize in citation without overt marking of the quoted material, which surely contributes to the unoriginal for more than one reason. He explains that in this iteration of plagiaristic technique, "*context is the new content*" (3). Goldsmith traces a recent history of the acceptance of nonoriginality by way of an article, "The Ecstasy of Influence: A Plagiarism," written by Jonathan Lethem and published in 2007 in *Harper's* (2).
19. Bourgeoisie use of soft drugs hints that if enough of the middle class likes a drug, or a work of art, or some other possibly noxious pharmakon, one can safely bet that it will viewed as soft, as seen in the slow reversals of the U.S. and Mexican laws against marijuana. Axel Klein, amid an argument against the hard and soft distinction for drugs, relates the rise of the public taste for caffeine and sugar to the addictions sanctioned by the middle class (95).
20. A masterful summary of the topic appears in psychologist Daniel Kahneman's award-winning *Thinking, Fast and Slow* (52–53). I heed the warning of Kahneman's thought on the subtle nature of priming: "All this happens without any awareness" (53).
21. Shedd does not receive favorable treatment from some of the grant winners. Luisa Josefina Hernández, the first woman admitted to the Centro Mexicano de Escritores, among the cohort of 1952–53 with Rulfo and Arreola, and the first woman to win a second grant, 1954–55, roundly critiques Shedd. In 1994, Hernández spoke to a newspaper reporter and denigrated Shedd principally for her refusal to recognize the maturity of grantees such as Rulfo and Arreola: "Además, creo que ella

[Shedd] intentó hacer experimentos como de preparatoria gringa en el centro. Pero esto fue imposible, porque ahí había personas que ya publicaban o tenían puestas en escena. En realidad 'los chiquitos' éramos [Enrique] González Rojo y yo. Los demás eran hombres de más de 30 años. Gente con libros, muy aceptados y reconocidos. Entonces no iban a aceptar con facilidad que alguien les dijera: *piensen en un payaso y escriban sobre él.* No se podía enseñar a escribir a quienes ya dominaban el oficio." (Espinosa). (Besides, I think she [Shedd] tried to do experiments as if the center were a gringo high school. But that was impossible, because there you found people who had already published or staged [their work]. In reality, "the little ones" were [Enrique] González Rojo and I. The rest of the men were over 30. People with books, very accepted and recognized. Thus, they were not going to accept easily that someone would tell them: *think of a clown and write about him.* You couldn't teach writing to those who already mastered the profession.)

22. Nine other women won just one grant from the Centro Mexicano de Escritores and eventually the Xavier Villaurrutia prize as well: Inés Arredondo, Carmen Boullosa, Julieta Campos, Rosario Castellanos, Pura López Colomé, Amparo Dávila, Silvia Molina, Elena Poniatowska, and Esther Seligson.
23. The archive reveals that Tovar collaborated with others to adapt Fuentes's novella *Aura* for the opera in 1989 and did the same for Paz's play *La hija de Rapaccini* (*Rapaccini's Daughter*) in 1991 (CME Tovar 8).
24. These six men are Marco Vinicio Barrera, Armando León Bejarano, Rafael Cardona, Alí Chumacero, Manuel Felguérez, and Juan García Ponce.
25. The list of participants includes Arianne Pellicer and Norma Lilia Cruz as poets; Jorge Reyes and Rayito as musicians; and artists Juan Soriano, brothers Alberto and Francisco Castro Leñero, Irma Palacios, Martha Chapa, Teresa Zimbrón, and Carlos Gutiérrez Angulo, "entre otros" (among others) (M. Fernández 6).
26. Ryan Long places the creation of the Centro Mexicano de Escritores into the context of the development of publishing houses (263–64). Although he does not take particular interest in Paz, Long surveys the groupings of important Mexican writers in terms of institutions and publishing outlets and views the 1940s through the 1980s as a period in which authors engaged in "a continuing negotiation about what can be said, how, by whom, and for whom" (264).
27. Vallarino's self-quotation reads, "Si así fuese trataré de encarnar este plan de la forma más auténtica y seria posible" (If such were the case, I would try to incarnate this plan in the most authentic and serious way possible) (CME Vallarino Almada 51). His grant application also includes a paragraph saying that, should time permit, he might add a section on European or English and North American poets whose influence proved decisive in Mexican letters, such as "Valéry, Eliot, Joyce, Supervielle, Borges, etc." (51). Jorge Luis Borges and Jules Supervielle are neither European nor English nor North American, and someone—probably one of the judges on the committee—marked the proposal with blue pen, signaling the erroneous capitalization in Spanish of *European* and *English* on the draft.

28. In this context, I wonder if Carmen Boullosa's many typos in her application to the Centro Mexicano de Escritores might have pulled toward the masculine side of the scale. Perhaps she gave the impression of genius by being too artistically competent to type like an expert office worker (CME Boullosa 50–53).

CHAPTER 4

Epigraphs: What Carlos Monsiváis or Fuentes or Octavio Paz were thinking used to be taken into account by powerful men, whether on the left or the right. I consider myself a kind of recluse. . . . Anyway, writers almost don't appear on television anymore.—Fadanelli, qtd. in Hind, "Entrevista," 326.

Mora, *Cinemachismo*, xiii.

1. Public record contradicts Gamboa's imagined naïveté for Santa. Stephanie Jo Smith's archival work rescues choice words from court testimony in 1920s Yucatán against "the common stereotype of the demure, retiring woman" (113). The difference for a woman who attempts impolite language in official settings may be that the man judge who hears this testimony has likely not been educated to think positively about a woman's attempt to express sincerity through bárbaro language.
2. The enduring bad boy legend may explain why an apparently inferior novel, *Camaradas*, which first appeared in 1959, was reprinted in 1979 with the Catholic publishing house Jus and again in 2010.
3. Cuesta's case lacks documentation and thus forces a reliance on anecdote. Irwin succinctly reviews the rumor that the poet "emasculated himself" before finally hanging himself in the mental institution in which he was confined, on August 13, 1942 ("Legend" 44). In Jesús R. Martínez Malo's telling of events, Cuesta cut his testicles to such a degree that doctors finished the castration by surgical means (32).
4. To get a sense of how bureaucratic existence supplies authority for civilizados who gain even more power from selectively challenging the rules, I turn to anthropologist Emily Wentzell's work in a contemporary Mexican medical clinic. Wentzell records the traumatic prospect of a penectomy through an interview with pseudonymous subject "Johnny Jiménez," whose slated operation allows insight: "He wondered, 'I who liked women so much, what will I do? How will I have relations?' In Spanish, the verb *to have relations* can imply sexual and/or nonsexual social relationships, and it was clear that Johnny also felt the latter to be in jeopardy. His greatest fear was that his male friends would find out and say, 'Jiménez doesn't have a penis.' If this knowledge became public, Johnny feared that he simply would not be able to relate to anyone 'as a man'" (2). Wentzell's research suggests that the real effect of losing the penis is that not even the civilized role is possible—a point perhaps also suggested in Franz Kafka's famous fictional experiment *The Metamorphosis* (1915).
5. In Fadanelli's novel *Hotel DF* (2010), one character remembers that his father began to treat him better after reading *Fiera infancia*, which suggests the novel has a contemporary following, at least among peer authors (19).

6. Montes de Oca and Fuentes are not the only models of such entitled behavior. Take the case of René Avilés Fabila, about whom Ignacio Trejo Fuentes teases that he must censor his anecdotes so that Avilés Fabila's wife does not stop talking to him: "Puedo seguir contando aventuras con el Águila Negra, o Capitán Lujuria, pero eso valdría que Rosario me retirara su valiosa amistad" (I can keep telling stories about the Black Eagle, or Captain Lust, but that would cause Rosario to withdraw her valuable friendship from me) (Trejo Fuentes). When speaking in an interview about the René Avilés Fabila Foundation, in the neighborhood of his youth, Avilés Fabila claims that forty or fifty years earlier beautiful women there used to be the objects of his pursuit; this habit has changed only slightly, as he has moved to a preference for older women: "claro que ahora asedio viejitas pero de todos modos siguen cayendo aunque ya del *Capitán Lujuria* vaya quedando poco" (of course now I chase little old women, but they keep falling anyway even though little is left of *Capitan Lust*) (Garmabella 10-A). In the same vein, José Luis Ontiveros remembers, "René Avilés Fabila resultó un hombre bien parecido, de modales distinguidos, con un aire dandístico, gastrónomo, de amplia conversación, sentido del humor y un gusto casi infalible por las mujeres" (René Avilés Fabila turned out to be a good-looking man, of distinguished manners, with a dandyish, food lover's air, of ample conversation, a sense of humor, and an almost infallible taste for women) (Ontiveros). Roberto Vallarino recalls the importance of alcohol in Avilés Fabila's male friendships: "Nuestros gustos etílicos reforzaron la relación de cuates pasamos a ser 'compañeros de ruta'" (Our alcoholic tastes reinforced our relationship as buddies who became "fellow travelers") (Vallarino Almada). Women may not be Avilés Fabila's "buddies," but they are his fans. In response to a question from interviewer Mary Carmen Sánchez Ambriz about whether most of his readers are women, Avilés Fabila said flirtatiously: "Pienso que sí. Quienes asisten a mis conferencias son mujeres; quienes escriben de mí son mujeres; quienes me piden autógrafos son mujeres; quienes me entrevistan, también, lo cual me encanta" (I think so. Those who attend my lectures are women; those who write to me are women; those who ask for my autograph are women; those who interview me, too, which I love) (Sánchez Ambriz, "Mis lectores" 39). René Avilés Fabila was around sixty-one years old at the time of his conversation with Sánchez Ambriz.

7. Jorge Volpi, in *Examen de mi padre*, narrates a similar experience from a relative distance by describing the sexual habits of his writer friend Eloy Urroz: "A diferencia de mis demás amigos, Eloy no era virgen—como cuenta en una de sus novelas, pertenecía a un medio en el que era normal ser desvirgado por una prostituta—y no paraba de ligar a diestra y siniestra al tiempo que se curtía en una de sus mayores aficiones, la pornografía. [. . .] A lo largo de los siguientes años, Eloy no dejó de perfeccionar sus tácticas, al tiempo que nos adentraba a Ignacio Padilla y a mí en su pasión por las películas pornográficas; a su lado emprendimos sucesivas exploraciones a antros, cines xxx, *burlesques, tables* y prostíbulos, en los que nosotros, a diferencia suya, nos quedábamos paralizados o atónitos" (197). (Unlike my other

friends, Eloy was not a virgin—as he tells it in one of his novels, he belonged to an environment in which it was normal to be deflowered by a prostitute—and he did not stop hooking up left and right while stewing in one of his greatest hobbies, pornography. . . . Throughout the following years, Eloy did not stop perfecting his tactics, at the same time that he led us, Ignacio Padilla and me, into his passion for pornographic films; at his side we undertook successive explorations of dens, triple X cinemas, burlesques, strip clubs, and brothels in which we, unlike he, were paralyzed or astonished.)

8. Alatorre writes, "Con solemnidad teatral y burlona separo del cuerpo los brazos y pongo las palmas de las manos hacia arriba. Curiosamente, de pronto tengo la impresión de que estoy vestido, de que no veo una desnudez, sino un traje, un disfraz. ¡Es tan extraño lo que estoy viendo! ¡Soy tan otro! Es como si la sotana fuera mi piel y esta desnudez fuera una cosa con que me hubiera revestido. ¡Es tan extraño ese bulto vivo que se mueve y palpita por sí solo, que revienta de vida propia y tiembla un poco por la fuerza de la presión que lo mantiene enhiesto, apuntando a lo alto! Y alrededor de él toda esa extensión de mi desnudez" (*La migraña*, 90–91). (With theatrical and sarcastic solemnity, I separate my arms from my body, and I turn the palms of my hands toward the sky. Interestingly, all of a sudden I have the impression that I am dressed, that I don't see nudity, but a suit, a costume. It's so strange, what I'm seeing! I'm so much someone else! It is as if my skin were a priest's robe and this nakedness were a thing that I had used to cover it. It's so strange, this living lump that moves and palpitates on its own, that bursts with its own life and trembles a bit with the force of pressure that keeps it upright, pointing to the peak! And around it all this expanse of my nakedness.)

9. In 2002, Domínguez Michael commented in an interview that he was a member of the Mexican Communist Party until he was twenty years old (León 3).

10. Levine remarks on the privilege necessary for making the different codes work, that is, a seemingly universal heuristic of the sex binary: "And just about anywhere it goes, gender is an organizing principle by which social groups come to be organized in a hierarchy, one high and one low, one wielding power and the other coerced into service" (94). Here, Levine anticipates my interest in high and low, hard and soft artistic reputations and artworks.

11. For a brief introduction to Fadanelli's first literary steps, see Jamie Fudacz (117) or Patricia Isabel Peláez Máximo (55–56). Alice Whitmore also gives an excellent overview of the phenomenon of trash literature and Fadanelli's trajectory; she studies Fadanelli's place in this history as knowingly involved in the consummate contemporary affliction and, in a move that may surprise feminist readers, praises the "sad beauty of Fadanelli's writing, its dark humor and lucid prose" (117). The decision to focus on trash and the environment turns Fadanelli into a praiseworthy writer: "In the midst of all this waste and toxicity, life goes on, life adapts and thrives, always creating in spite of, or in complement to, the decay" (117). Whitmore does not take up the topic of Fadanelli's sexist stance in his writing or as examined in the criticism, an omission that María Paz Oliver duplicates. Paz Oliver, like

Whitmore, writes excellent criticism. Perhaps helpful to explaining this suppression is the all-male context: Paz Oliver writes a chapter on *Lodo* in a book entirely dedicated to men writers; the other figures whose works are examined at length are Roberto Bolaño, Alan Pauls, and Mario Levrero.

12. In his study of *Lodo*, José Ramón Ruisánchez Serra notes that in an early review Christopher Domínguez Michael called Fadanelli a moralist and adds, "Posiblemente no tuviera razón, pero me gusta pensar que ésta es la genealogía del personaje" (He may not have been right, but I like to think that this is the genealogy of the character) ("Literaturas del bien" 80).

13. The texts by Fadanelli and Domínguez Michael were also bundled with a third, Bárbara Jacobs's *Las hojas muertas* (The dead leaves) originally published in 1987. Fadanelli's text in this collection seems destined to spark controversy, if it receives attention at all. Before the 18 para los 18 series, a video on YouTube captured a male physical education teacher yelling at Fadanelli during an open-air conversation in Guadalajara; the teacher complains that Fadanelli's immoral writing corrupts minors' sensibilities. According to Fadanelli's memory of the encounter, Fernando del Paso was seated beside him and mounted a defense of Fadanelli (Hind, "Entrevista" 313–14). As for women writers and the vagina, autobiographical discovery of the vagina appears in Guadalupe Amor's "La solitaria" (The solitary woman) from *Galería de títeres* (Puppet gallery) (1959), which I analyze in *Femmenism* (106). See also Ángeles Mastretta's *Arráncame la vida*, which portrays a married, nonvirgin protagonist who needs a gypsy woman to explain, with euphemisms, how to masturbate, or *sentir*. Finally, see the autobiographically inspired texts released in 2010 and 2011 by Carmen Boullosa and Guadalupe Nettel, respectively. In the essay collection *Cuando me volví mortal* (When I became mortal) (2010), Boullosa writes matter-of-factly about feeling aroused by warm water and a clumsy maternal hand as a child (60, 76). In the autobiographical novel *El cuerpo en que nací* (The body in which I was born) (2011), Guadalupe Nettel's protagonist rubs herself against the railing of a public stairway leading to the apartment building where she lives in Mexico City and continues to do so even after the mother tells her to stop (31–33, 147).

14. For more information, see the documentary *Gimme the Power* (dir. Olallo Rubio, 2012).

15. As García Tsao complains, *Y tu mamá también* concludes with a *moralina* (moral). After the two male leads finally make love to each other, with the excuse of a threesome facilitated by an older woman, they allow their friendship to die.

16. Cynthia Steele reads Pacheco's narrator in *Las batallas en el desierto* as learning to make authenticity a goal (105). Two decades later, the critical opinion shifts. Jessica Lynam dryly notes Carlos's deprecatory attitude toward his own story: "Carlos trivializes the story of his childhood romance with Mariana to assimilate it and be able to tell it in an off-handed, tongue-in-cheek fashion" (58). She describes Carlos's "acerbic cynicism" as "a sort of studied inauthenticity" (58–59).

17. From the relatively implicit sex scenes of *Y tu mamá también* to the explicit *Batalla en el cielo*, Mexican cinema moves to work like *Daniel & Ana* (dir. Michel Franco,

2009), which, not even a decade later, explores an explicit hard-core incest theme. The film leaves little to the imagination as it shows an extortion ring kidnap siblings Daniel and Ana on behalf of a wealthy anonymous patron; the kidnappers medicate the brother with Viagra and have him rape his sister for the video camera, in a scene that viewers of the film watch. A second example of this "hard art" aesthetic is *Los bastardos* (*The Bastards*) (dir. Amat Escalante, 2008), a fictional snuff film that features a pair of killers who end the movie with senseless and gory shootings. Both these films, *Daniel & Ana* and *Los bastardos*, are directed and written by men and trade in a global definition of "high art" as explicit.

18. Sánchez Prado, for one, seems impatient with the critical reviews that legitimate this sort of systematic taboo flaunting as high art. He reviews the case of Carlos Reygadas in skeptical terms: "The fact that he [Reygadas] was awarded the Cannes Film Festival Best Director Award in 2012, a few days after his film *Post Tenebras Lux* was subject to a violently adverse reaction from the audience, embodies well a paradox central to understanding Reygadas, a director whose illegibility and irritating nature [are] precisely the condition of possibility of his impact and genius" (*Screening Neoliberalism* 196). Javier Guerrero, on the other hand, matches one high and hard reputation with another; he quotes an interview with Reygadas to justify the setting of *Japón* (2002) as an appropriation of the view of Hidalgo seen in Rulfo's photos.

19. I borrow the phrase "penis-brained" from fellow academics who, in an analysis published in 1988 apropos of the film *Top Gun* (1986), refer to "penis-brained militarism" (Ryan and Kellner 297).

20. Feminist messages are perhaps also failed by this frank language. In 2017, Sabina Berman published an opinion piece, titled "Pensar con el pene" (Thinking with the penis), that organizes three instances of penis-driven behavior. First, she reviews the case of a recently fired radio personality, Marcelino Perelló, who lost his radio program, *Sentido contrario* (Wrong way), with the National Autonomous University of Mexico (UNAM) after insisting on the air for some twenty minutes, to his female cohost's dismay, that some women like to be raped. Berman notes that rather than a reasoned argument from the head or heart, these pro-rape comments speak from the penis: "Perelló habla por su pene y de su pene y no de mucho más" (Perelló speaks for his penis and from his penis and not about much else). Berman also brings up the case of a Mexican judge, Anuar González Hemadi, who ruled that a young man who stuck two fingers in an underage victim's vagina was not a rapist because he did not feel "deleite" (pleasure) or "lascivia" (lust). That judge, in a circuit court in the state of Veracruz, was promptly suspended for his poor judgment and then sued by a citizen watchdog group (Rosas and Alemán). Finally, Berman notes the third case of a verbal aggressor: he who insists on the Mexican tradition of the *piropo* (catcall) now risks spending the night in jail, at least according to the woman, Tamara de Anda, who put her catcaller there. The details of this story involve de Anda, a journalist and blogger, accompanying a transit police officer and

the taxi driver who called her *guapa* (beautiful) to the Buenavista office of the Juzgado Cívico (Civil Court); the catcaller chose to spend a night in a Mexico City detention center rather than pay the fine for having violated Article 23 of the Civic Culture Law. The event, which de Anda covered in real time on her Twitter account, triggered a series of troll counterstrikes. That aggression on social media landed de Anda in the news again as Internet users from countries like the United States began a custom of falsely declaring her a victim of terrorism ("Trolls Target"). The practice became so frequent that de Anda commented to a reporter, "Every time there is an attack I am sure there will be a few pictures of me around. The last time it happened I knew that a picture was being shared before I knew about the attack" (Wendling and Devlin). As evident in screen shots reproduced in news reports, one of the tweets falsely placing de Anda in London during an attack issued from an account with the self-aware handle "Machitrol Falócrata" (Macho-troll phallocrat) (Saul). With characteristic pluck, de Anda was one of several Mexican public figures who participated in the rollout of the #NoEsDeHombres publicity campaign to raise awareness about harassment of women in Mexico (Deb and Franco). That campaign received coverage in the *New York Times* in response to a "penis seat" on the Mexico City subway, a seat on which no passenger could comfortably sit because of the sculpted penis on the bench (Deb and Franco). That masculine-oriented protest art returns me to my main point: the consistency with which these complaints for and against the penis are framed within the language of the penis shows the elusive nature of alternative language. For another case of harassment, see the trolling that caused U.S. journalist Andrea Noel to leave Mexico ("Trolls Target").

21. To return to cinematic works, the film *Halley* (dir. Sebastián Hofmann, 2012) depicts with an explicit frontal shot the aftermath of a decaying, zombified dead man in Mexico City who has masturbated with disastrous results: his penis has detached. The scene shows the character sitting on the floor of the bathroom and staring down at the darkened space where his organ used to be. I thank Cristina Ruiz-Poveda for bringing this scene to my attention.
22. See also Valeria Luiselli's *La historia de mis dientes* (*The History of My Teeth*) (2013), where she writes about a fictional male character named Gustavo Sánchez Sánchez Carretera and his nighttime erections (72).
23. I translated *mamada* as "bullshit," but in literal terms *mamadas* refers to blow jobs or, even more literally translated from the verb *mamar*, to breastfeeding or suckling.
24. Despite major gains in gay liberation, including same-sex couples' legal right to marry in the United States and, south of the border, a right to civil union in places like Mexico City, it is still possible to sympathize with the spirit of Mark Moss's blanket observation: "Even in these so-called liberated times, if a man does not act manly, his sexuality is held in question. For a young man, nothing is worse than an inquiry on his masculinity" (xv).

CHAPTER 5

Epigraphs: You are inferior to me: you peel my foreskin.—Manjarrez, in *Útil y muy ameno vocabulario para entender a los mexicanos* (Mexico: Grijalbo, 2011), 176.

In the last few weeks, he [Fox] has called me shorty, faggy, he's called me the cross-dresser, he's called me pussy-whipped—Labastida. (For a video recording of the complaint, see, e.g., Aristegui Noticias.)

1. According to Coloroso, the same child can rotate among the roles, although the majority renounce playing the bully or bullied and end up as bystanders (3–4). She perceptively comments on the pervasiveness of this theater of aggression, in which children cannot abandon the bullying triangle when they come home from school, because children do not act out the bullying scripts but rather live them: "They can't go home after a performance and 'get real,' because home is a part of their stage" (5).
2. According to Carlos, playground victim-turned-bully Toru stuck to his taste for bullying: "Nadie volvió a meterse con Toru. Hoy dirige una industria japonesa con cuatro mil esclavos mexicanos" (No one messed with Toru again. Today he heads a Japanese factory with four thousand Mexican slaves) (15). Toru's vocation as a successful tyrant hints at the ways adult men structure their relationships around the dynamics of bullying.
3. Scientific studies have found that the psychological effect of bullying on the victim's side includes "anxiety and depression, impaired concentration, poor self-esteem, and avoidant behavior," and the social scientists affirm that the bullied "are at risk for suicide" (Unnever and Cornell 130). Another academic study notes that in early childhood the roles of aggressor and victim tend to coincide; that is, aggressors attract violence as much as they mete it out (Hanish et al. 132). The authors of the study note that among older youth, the roles rigidify (134). The scientific articles do not express explicit support for Coloroso's proposal that bullying hinges, not on anger or conflict, but on contempt (20).
4. Way developed her expertise from working in the 1980s as a public school counselor in the United States. That time frame coincides with the publication of Pacheco's novella and its early rise to popularity.
5. Such relationships stretch back decades in Mexican literary history. In Revolutionary times, for instance, Ramón López Velarde enjoyed a relationship with presidential power because he served as one of the lawyers for Francisco I. Madero (Sheridan, *Un corazón* 109).
6. Street bases his thinking on definitions of the cool by Dick Pountain and David Robins, who identify three key cool personality traits that prove lethal to democratic political performance: narcissism, ironic detachment, and hedonism. Curiously, Pountain and Robins's book *Cool Rules*, though often cited, is perhaps not the most sophisticated contribution. They associate the antisocial cool with the uncooperative masculine, by way of a pernicious stereotype: "Who can doubt," write Pountain and Robins in an affirmation posed as a question, "that there is

a degree of overlap between our notion of Cool and the 'machismo' of Hispanic cultures, with its emphasis on appearance, male sexual adventurism and flirtation with death, as symbolized in the person of the toreador?" (52).

7. Stearns's history of cool argues that a shift away from the Victorian value of domesticity and toward conspicuous, emotionally charged consumption drives the cool. The cool as the "twentieth-century emotional style" was born in rejection of Victorian affective passion, and it conditioned childhood and adult relationships in favor of relations with material items and "the act of shopping" (*American Cool* 274).
8. Miller refers to the idea in the social sciences of six universal personality traits: O (openness), C (conscientiousness), A (agreeableness), S (stability), E (extroversion), plus G (the general intelligence trait) (G. Miller 153).
9. Montes de Oca won grants from the Centro Mexicano de Escritores for 1955–56 and 1960–61, and among other posts he served as the literary director for the writing school SOGEM (Sociedad General de Escritores de México, or General Society of Writers from Mexico) from 1976 to 1978. He also won the Xavier Villaurrutia prize in 1959, two Guggenheims (1967–68 and 1970–71), and governmental awards such as the FONCA (Fondo Nacional para la Cultura y las Artes, or National Fund for Culture and Arts) grant (1989–90). He served as an emeritus member of SNCA in 1994.
10. Another of these figures is perhaps Sergio Galindo, whose fame might stem from prestigious bureaucratic posts as much as his writing; among other jobs, Galindo served as a cultural attaché to London, an employee in the Public Education Secretariat, and editor of the literary journal *La Palabra y el Hombre*.
11. Steven Boldy, *contra* Poniatowska, describes Rulfo's behavior as hinging on "*socarronería*, a sort of sarcastic sly humour" (3). Yet, in the midst of an outstanding biographical summary, Boldy himself recalls an utter failure to engage Rulfo in conversation in 1981 (25).
12. Barrientos del Monte quotes an interview that has Rulfo attributing his depression to his time at a Catholic boarding school. Rulfo remembers, "Lo único que aprendí fue a deprimirme. Fue una de las épocas en las que me encontré yo más sólo. Y en donde conseguí un estado depresivo que todavía no se me puede curar. [. . .] Antes de eso yo era un niño abierto y alegre, como todos los niños. Y allí me aplacaron bastante" (9). (The only thing I learned was to get depressed. It was one of those periods in which I found myself most alone. And in which I caught a depressive state that I still haven't been able to cure. . . . Before that I was an open and happy boy, like all children. And there they cooled me down considerably.) I do not have perfectly parallel anecdotes about Pacheco, although I was struck by a conversation with critic Juan Bruce-Novoa at a literature conference at the University of California, Irvine, who affirmed as if I had hit on a great truth about Pacheco and the other members of his Medio Siglo generation: they were cool.
13. Villoro's implied meaning here is that only friends knew just how deep Monsiváis's low agreeability traits could run: "Misántropo en la vida privada ("los espero en mi casa para una reunión que comenzará a las 16 horas y acabará a las 16 horas"), era

hipergregario en la vida pública. Llegaba a todas partes con el pelo revuelto por un viento mental y su infaltable chamarra de mezclilla. Era un testigo tan reconocible que la realidad sólo actuaba al enterarse de su llegada" (4). (Misanthrope in his private life ["I'll see you at my house for a meeting that will start at four o'clock and end at four o'clock"], he was hypergregarious in public life. He would arrive everywhere with hair mussed by a mental wind and his inevitable denim jacket. He was such a recognizable witness that reality only functioned after learning of his arrival.)

14. Another article that covers the release of *Misógino feminista* reveals that in his writing, Monsiváis paid relatively little attention to women artists (Sánchez Ambriz, "Con M" 40). At the same event, renowned Mexican feminist and the author of the book's introduction, Marta Lamas, explained the book title: "Él [Monsiváis] decía que era un misógino feminista porque evidentemente para irse de parranda prefería irse con sus cuates hombres y que no fuéramos las mujeres" (He used to say that he was a misogynist feminist because evidently he preferred to go out on the town with his men buddies and that we women not go) (Aguilar Sosa, "Monsi, misógino elegante" E12). If the reader seeks more stories of Monsiváis's capacity for rejection of his admirers, consult Linda Egan, who is experienced when it comes to being rudely ignored by the very subject of her research.

15. Other children's books on men writers show a canon in formation, as the texts introduce young readers to the authors' biographies. Pacheco's daughter, Laura Emilia Pacheco, wrote a children's book about his life, *José Emilio Pacheco: A mares llueve sobre el mar* (It's pouring rain over the the sea) (2014), which is told by a cat. *Crónicas de la infancia* (Chronicles of infancy) (2003), by Vivian Abenshushan, Rodolfo Fonseca, and Gerardo Rod, informs children about Salvador Novo's biography. Juan Abelardo Hernández's *Octavio Paz: El poeta que hiló su tiempo* (Octovio Paz: the poet who wove his time) (2008) and Alberto Ruy Sánchez's *Octavio Paz: Cuenta y canta la historia* (Octavio Paz: telling and singing the story) (2014) do the same for the Nobel laureate. Irene Livas turns in an early example of this genre with her biographical sketch of *Alfonso Reyes para niños* (Alfonso Reyes for kids) (1999). Rafael Barajas's *La princesa Selenita* (The princess Selenita) (2014) tells Poniatowska's life story for young readers.

16. Monsiváis refrained from using swearwords in a habit inherited from his mother, according to Poniatowska ("En recuerdo").

17. Indeed, the residents of his old Portales neighborhood remember Monsiváis, according to one reporter's findings, by way of this very limited glamour: "los habitantes del rumbo no habían leído sus libros, pero lo admiraban porque salía en la televisión, escribía en *TvGuía* y *Notitas Musicales* y no se le habían subido los humos" (the residents of that area had not read his books, but they admired him because he was on television, he wrote for *TV Guide* and *Music Notes*, and he never thought too much of himself) (Avilés). Monsiváis was not alone in his friendship with Slim. No few intellectuals received an invitation to the wedding of Slim's oldest daughter, according to Diego Enrique Osorno, including, in addition

to Monsiváis, the writers Héctor Aguilar Camín and Germán Dehesa and the television magnate Emilio Azcárraga Jean, as well as assorted entertainers and politicians and the cultural functionary Rafael Tovar y de Teresa ("Carlos Slim" 136). Certainly, while Osorno never judges Monsiváis negatively, in his collection of chronicles he criticizes Slim and thus by implication casts doubt on those who dine with him, including some of the billionaire's "favorite writers," such as Carlos Fuentes and Ángeles Mastretta (136).

18. Additional coverage details the memorialized outfit, which seems relatively unremarkable: "un pantalón de gabardina color caqui, camisa azul, cinturón y zapatos cafés, [. . .] una chamarra de mezclilla y unos lentes que pertenecieron al propio Monsiváis" (khaki gabardine trousers, blue shirt, belt and brown shoes, . . . a denim jacket and a pair of glasses that belonged to Monsiváis himself) ("Monsiváis, inmortalizado"). Regarding the author's iconically informal wardrobe, Miguel Reyes Razo wrote in 1978 for *El Universal*: "Carlos Monsiváis—con mezclilla, botines y suéteres resolvió para siempre el problema del '¿qué me queda?'" (Carlos Monsiváis—with denim, boots, and sweaters resolved forever the problem of "what fits me?") (qtd. in Domínguez Cuevas, *Los becarios* 251).

19. Sor Juana sits, unsmiling and gently expressionless, a cross in one hand and a rosary in the other: no desk, no quill, no paper, no book. A nonsmiling Frida Kahlo also appears at the wax museum; she too sits, with a paintbrush in one hand.

20. Monsiváis's image again leads me to wonder whether certain ineptitudes work to the benefit of claims to high and hard genius. Take the bemused reaction in the press in 2010 when Pacheco's pants nearly fell down minutes before he accepted Spain's Cervantes literary prize. Pacheco himself may have set the joking tone, as he reportedly commented "in a good mood" to the Spanish press, "No tenía tirantes, es muy buen argumento contra la vanidad" (I didn't have suspenders, it's a good argument against vanity) (Agencia EFE). The remarkably low conscientiousness that Pacheco demonstrates with his dress code may lead him to raise the expected agreeability level with a joke.

21. The names are Magdalena Galindo, Raquel Serur, Marta Lamas, Carmen Galindo, Sandra Lorenzano, Lilia Rossbach, Elena Poniatowska, Beatriz Sánchez Monsiváis, and José Luis Ibáñez, the event coordinator (Gámez). The coverage notes that three additional women could not attend and sent texts instead: Carmen Boullosa, Sara Sefchovich, and Gabriela Cano.

22. Of course, the game can also be played with written text and no photo. Take the example of an essay by Monsiváis published in 2009. In homage to Pacheco, Monsiváis lists the more established writers who mentored the young Pacheco and Monsiváis: Alí Chumacero, José Luis Martínez, Salvador Novo, Carlos Pellicer, Efráin Huerta, Edmundo Valadés, José Vasoncelos, Octavio Paz, Carlos Fuentes, and Rosario Castellanos—the token woman—appear as the encouraging figures ("José Emilio Pacheco" 93). Incidentally, the prefacing material supports this canon and sets up the piece in competitive terms as written by the best chronicle writer (i.e., Monsiváis) about the best poet (i.e., Pacheco) of a generation.

23. The copy lists the speakers as "Enrique Krauze, Anthony Stanton, Homero Arijidis, Elena Poniatowska," and the British figures "David Brading, Tom Boll, Anthony Rudolf y [and] Richard Berengarten" (Ventura). The ambassador to Mexico for the United Kingdom, Diego Gómez Pickering, inaugurated the event, along with the president of Conaculta, Rafael Tovar y Teresa. Other Mexicans given media recognition at the event include "Enrique Krauze, Juan Villoro, Carmen Boullosa, Jorge Volpi, Tedi López Mills y [and] Valeria Luiseli," which brings the grand total of women at the London celebrations of Octavio Paz and Mexican literature in general to three, out of sixteen names mentioned—not counting the birthday *güey* himself (Ventura).
24. A few days after Filipovic's piece appeared, an editorial against President Trump by Thomas B. Edsall quoted the all-male experts' opinions to back his critique: Steven Nadler, Richard N. Haass, Andrew Bacevich, Charles A. Kupchan, Toby Dalton, David Bell, and Mark Leonard. Edsell also included a paraphrased comment from Warren Christopher, the first secretary of state under Bill Clinton. Nary a token woman appears on either side of the debate. This environment gave way to the widely publicized discontent of the #MeToo movement.
25. A 2014 article in *Milenio* about Octavio Paz's ersatz one-hundredth birthday celebration at the Guadalajara International Book Fair proves especially helpful in this scoring system. In about 226 words, the reporter mentions fifteen men experts and two women authorities who spoke at the event, although not all were called to offer insight about Paz. The all men speakers who either sustained or moderated conversations on Paz were Fernando del Paso, Enrique Krauze, Rafael Tovar y de Teresa, Juan Malpartida, Brian Nissen, Orlando González Esteva, Christopher Domínguez Michael, and Ricardo Cayuela Gally. Two women, Myriam Moscona and Carmen Gaitán, appear toward the end of the brief coverage as participants, not in the festivities for the main man Octavio Paz but for the side attraction of Federico Campbell, who also received attention from Martín Solares, Humberto Masucchio, and Vicente Alfonso ("Concluyen"). In case you're wondering (because it certainly occurred to me), the data available from the World Bank claim that in 2010–14 women made up 51.5 percent of the population in Mexico (World Bank).
26. Anthony Stanton, an academic at El Colegio de México, organized the event, and his name appears twice in the ad, once as organizer and once among the slated speakers. The other men are Aurelio Asiain, Adolfo Castañón, Antonio Deltoro, Jordi Doce, Christopher Domínguez Michael, Paul-Henri Giraud, Víctor Manuel Mendiola, Jorge Monteleone, Alberto Ruy Sánchez, James Valender, Hugo J. Verani, and keynote speaker Eduardo Lizalde ("Colegio de México" 20).
27. The other thirteen names are Jorge Aguilar Mora, Luigi Amara, Víctor Barrera Enderle, Nicolás Cabral, Luis Felipe Fabre, Alejandro Hernández Gálvez, Javier Hernández Quezada, Laurence Le Bouhellec, Leonardo Martínez Carriales, Rubén Medina, Eduardo Millán, Alfonso Montelongo, and Gabriel Wolfson. I have already mentioned David Rojas, coauthor with Marciela Guerrero.
28. For coverage of the sixtieth anniversary of the publication of Rulfo's *Pedro Páramo*, one female reporter cites an all-male list of experts without commenting on the

imbalance: Rafael Olea Franco, Julio Ortega, Jorge Rufinelli, Sergio López Mena, Federico Munguía, and in passing reference, Juan José Arreola (Gámez, "Las interpretaciones" 16). In another piece, a photograph from a 2014 celebration of *Pedro Páramo* features only three pictured men: "los investigadores literarios" (the literary researchers) Víctor Jiménez, Jorge Zepeda, and Alberto Vital (Ávila, "Año, 1954"). Additional names cited include two women, Françoise Perus and Sara Schulz, and four men, Eduardo Subirats, Luiz Ruffiato, Dylan Brennan, and Armando Casa (3).

29. A copy of this official program is in the CME file on Arreola. The men are José Luis Martínez, José María Espinasa, Antonio Alatorre, Mario del Valle, Fernando Díez de Urdanivia, Santiago Genovés, Emmanuel Carballo, René Avilés Fabila, José Agustín, Alejandro Aura, and Fernando del Paso.

30. The second panel included Rafael Ramírez Heredia and Ignacio Trejo, with moderator Agustín Ramos. The third panel featured Alberto Paredes, David Martín del Campo, and Christopher Domínguez Michael, with moderator Miguel Ángel Quemain. A fifth panel included participation by Publio O. Romero, Russell M. Cluff, Jorge de la Luz, and Brianda Domecq, plus moderator Eugenio Aguirre. The grand total for the announced event thus included two women and twelve men, plus the man director of the cultural institution (CME Galindo 12, 17).

31. The seven men panelists are Ignacio Trejo Fuentes, Jorge Alberto Manrique, Felipe Garrido, Luis Arturo Ramos, Álvaro Ruiz Abreu, Eduardo Mejía, and Guillermo Samperio.

32. The three are José Luis Márquez (respondent), Agustín Yáñez (director), and José Ignacio Dávila Garibi (permanent secretary) (CME Galindo 45). Again in 1975, the reception for Galindo upon joining the Academia Mexicana, recognized by the Centro Mexicano de Escritores, was organized by Plácido García Reynoso and Francisco Monterde, with the invitational letter written by Felipe García Beraza, who spoke of "don Sergio Galindo," at that time the general director of the INBA (51).

33. On the panel dedicated to Montes de Oca as a painter, the names are Juan Acha, José Luis Cuevas, Elia Espinosa, Alberto Gutiérrez, Julio César Schara, and the painter himself (Peguero). On the panel dedicated to Montes de Oca's literary production, the names are Víctor Manuel Mendiola, Verónica Volkow, Eduardo Milán, Evodio Escalante, and the poet himself (28). Both were celebrated in the Manuel M. Ponce room of the Palace of Fine Arts (28). Montes de Oca's autobiography, written in 1966, anticipates this homosocial terrain, because he names as influences twenty-three men and only four women (48–50). The list of twenty-three does not repeat key mentors given previous attention, such as Paz, who, in addition to wrangling a grant for Montes de Oca with the Centro Mexicano de Escritores, also helped him publish at the Fondo de Cultura Económica (48). As I discuss in a later chapter, such lists of all-male influences are not unusual. In the same series of autobiographies, Nuevos Escritores, Sergio Pitol in 1966 gives a list of twenty-six men and only three influential women, none Mexican (Marlene Dietrich, María Zambrano, and Edith Sitwell) (44).

34. Aurelio Asiain, Evodio Escalante, Hugo Gutiérrez Vega, Ernesto Lumbreras, Guillermo Sheridan, Alejandro Aura, Julio Trujillo, and Montes de Oca himself. The moderator was Adolfo Castañón.
35. These actresses are Martha Ofelia Galindo, Eloísa Gottdiener, Selma Beraud, and Consuelo Rodríguez, along with actors Gilberto Pérez Gallardo, Alejandro Tommasi, Jorge Galván, and Ernesto Gómez Santa Ana. The directors are Rabindranath Espinosa and Marcela Bourges (Hernández, "Homenaje"). The article also mentions the journalist and novelist María Luisa Mendoza as being present.
36. Fernando Torre Laphan, Kitty de Hoyos, Miguel Córcega, Rosa María Moreno, Luis Gimeno, and Héctor Gómez spoke in a roundtable conversation moderated by José Ramón Enríquez, who was director of the National Center for Theater Research, a center named in honor of a male, the playwright Rodolfo Usigli ("Mesa redonda").
37. The three women are Reyna Barrera López, Jesusa Rodríguez, and Carmen Galindo. The fourteen men are Anthony Stanton, Héctor Anaya, Gonzalo Celorio, Sergio González Rodríguez, Emmanuel Carballo, Miguel Capistrán, Salvador López Antuñano (Novo's cousin), Humberto Guerra, Hugo Gutiérrez Vega, Javier Aranda Luna, Jaime Chabaud, Jacobo Zabludowsky, Salvador Ayala (a waiter at Novo's club La Capilla), and Leonardo Vázquez (the chef at La Capilla).
38. The experts interviewed are Adolfo Castañón, Rafael Olea Franco, Vicente Quirarte, and Armando Ponce.
39. The writers include thirteen Mexican authors, six of whom are women, and ten international authors, two of whom are women. The prologist for the book is a man.
40. The examples of Mexican men writers who only mention other Mexican men writers are numerous. Another case in the Nuevos Escritores autobiographical series is Juan Vicente Melo, who views literature as a man's game, at least from the names he drops. Note Melo's estimation of the best writers in Mexico: "Juan García Ponce escribe en un tono y con un lenguaje totalmente ajenos a los que yo practico. Sin embargo, me importa lo que hace y lo que dice. Creo que después de Octavio Paz y de Tomás Segovia es el mejor ensayista de México" (52). (Juan García Ponce writes in a tone and with a language completely alien to those that I practice. However, what he does and says matters to me. I think that after Octavio Paz and Tomás Segovia, he is Mexico's best essayist.)
41. Unlike Paz, neither Novo's nor Monsiváis's name appears on the wall of honor in the Mexico City federal Congressional building, the Legislative Palace of San Lázaro. For good measure, Novo never received his longed-for burial in the Rotunda of Illustrious Persons, where he wanted to rest among the many poets, such as Ramón López Velarde and Amado Nervo, and the poet-politicians Jaime Torres Bodet and Agustín Yáñez. The reasons for Novo's absence lie in homophobia, at least in Héctor Gómez's explanation (Aguilar Galván 3).
42. See Rafael Vargas's comments regarding the friendship between María García, wife of Héctor García, and "Marie José Paz" (19). In the case of Alí Chumacero, Lourdes failed to outlive her husband, but kept order over him while she lived by

managing his alcohol consumption. Macario Matus, in 1994, recalls visiting Alí in his library at home: "Cuando se anuniaba la tempested etílica, la mano de María de Lourdes despidió a todos" (When the alcoholic storm began to loom, María de Lourdes's hand bid farewell to everyone) (CME Chumascero 49-1: 42).

43. Salvador Oropesa describes Carreño's book as "a brutal choreography that rules every single movement (or lack thereof) that a person must execute twenty-four hours a day to demonstrate to the rest of society that he or she is a gentleman or a lady" (122).

44. Carlitos articulates his family's customs: "No, pues no, a la mía [a mi madre] le hablo de usted; ella también les habla de usted a mis abuelitos. No te burles Jim, no te rías" (28). (No, well, no, I talk to my mother with the formal *usted*; she also talks that way to my grandpa and grandma. Don't make fun of me Jim. Don't laugh.) Representative instances in nonfiction register just how challenging the transition was. For instance, a letter from 1966 that Felipe García Beraza writes on behalf of the Centro Mexicano de Escritores to poet Jaime Sabines shows the administrator hedging his bets: "Estimado Jaime: Probablemente ya no se acuerde usted de mí (pero uso el usted porque lo acostumbramos en aquel entonces)" (Dear Jaime: You probably do not remember me [but I use the formal *usted* because we used to do that back then]) (CME Sabines 60). In the surviving copy of this letter preserved in the archive, the parentheses are penciled into the typewritten carbon copy; thus García Beraza seems to wrestle with his own degree of spontaneity in order to sound the proper tone of respect *and* authenticity.

45. By the end of the 1960s, credit had become a social marker of independence and prosperity in the United States, and those left out, such as middle-class women and working-class African Americans, helped to persuade Congress to pass laws to guarantee impartial access to credit (Hyman, *Debtor Nation* 174).

CHAPTER 6

Epigraphs: Thanks, Garibay. Mule-drivers unite [meaning, "Welcome to the club"].—Yáñez, in Garibay, *Cómo se gana la vida*, 126.

I Tavito can only think about the for me happy day that you graduate and you shouldn't forget that ever because you're as they say at the door and it's very foolish if you don't do it but I think that you will, dear son, give me that satisfaction so that I see you with your lawyer's degree even though later you don't persue [*sic*] the career.—Lozano de Paz, qtd. in Sheridan, "Carta de amor."

In the stage notes, Villaurrutia insists on "good taste" for the furniture and decor. How could he forget that today's good taste is tomorrow's kitsch?—Octavio Paz, from Sheridan, "Carta de amor," using materials held at Princeton University.

Vargas, *Mexican Law*, 12.

1. A good selection of that writing appears in Roger Bartra's anthology *Anatomía del mexicano* (Anatomy of the Mexican) (2002), which evinces Mexicans' tendency to conflate the terms *character* and *personality* and to pay close attention to macho

behaviors. For instance, Santiago Ramírez, in his piece in this anthology, "Psicoanálisis del mestizaje" (Psychoanalysis of the mixed-blood person) (1959), adds to the study of national "caracterología" (characterology) and thinks about bullying, without using that precise term, by advancing the thesis that machismo stems from insecurity (241). Michael Maccoby repeats this line of thought in his essay in the same anthology, "El carácter nacional mexicano" (The national Mexican character) (1967), which is principally interested in the outcome of these frustrated impulses in machos (249–50). Maccoby's article views the Mexican man as tied to his mother, isolated from intimacy with others, and narcissistically protected by a self-image of masculine self-sufficiency and strength. Maccoby reviews the Mexican tradition of characterology and respectfully cites Paz's *El laberinto de la soledad* (251). Yet a third essay in the anthology, "Psicología del mexicano" (Psychology of the Mexican) (1979), by Rogelio Díaz-Guerrero, once again reviews work on Mexican character studies and bemoans their negative focus (287). Díaz-Guerrero's essay, originally titled "Tipos mexicanos," asserts that Mexican children differ from children of other nationalities because they are more likely to believe that fathers should always be obeyed. The children are also more likely to want to grow up to work the same job as their fathers (282–83). No mention is made of their mothers.

2. *Quiet* struck a nerve. Three years after its release, Cain's book was still on the *New York Times'* bestseller list and had sold two million copies worldwide, with translations into thirty-six languages (Quiet Revolution; Holson).
3. Holdover mention of character appears in Juan Vicente Melo's autobiography: "mi padre cree que la fuerza de carácter remedia toda clase de debilidades" (my father thinks that the force of character remedies all manner of weaknesses) (46). Compliant good character ensues, and Melo transforms from a fainting observer in the operating room to a dedicated medical student.
4. A well-known example of the "character" for credit system emerged in an intensive study of Muncie, Indiana, conducted at the end of the 1920s. That study revealed that an excessively idiosyncratic personality incited suspicion and reduced the odds of earning a loan (Carruthers and Ariovich 102).
5. Susman's rambling *Culture as History* reminds us, "One of Raymond Williams' 'keywords,' *personality*, is a modern term" (277). As academic source material, Susman himself draws on David Reisman's *The Lonely Crowd* (1961), which achieved best-seller status despite being an academic work from the field of sociology. Reisman explains that he is not studying personality, but a kind of "'social character' . . . shared among significant social groups" (4). Reisman's text worried about the post–World War II rise of the "other-directed type," an individual who determines goals on the basis of outside peer influence that ranges far beyond the nuclear family, unlike people who employ "tradition-direction" or "inner-direction" (21–22, 25). This type sounds somewhat like the extrovert whom Cain views as dominant in the second half of the twentieth century and today.
6. In line with his hoarding tendencies, Pedro refuses to settle a balance with his attorney, Gerardo, using the excuse of a lack of liquidity: "Tú bien sabes que todo

está invertido. Tierras, animales" (2012, 159). ("You well know that everything I have is tied up. Land, cattle") (1994, 104). Pedro even foists his personal costs onto the lawyer, thus getting by with the cash that Gerardo habitually extracts from his own pocket in order to smooth over the harm caused by Pedro's wild son, Miguel.

7. Cristina Rivera Garza explores this tension of modernity in Rulfo's biography and finds it striking that Jalisco, the region where Rulfo grew up, continues to experience the debts of violence, now under the problem of the narco (*Había mucha neblina* 21).

8. Curiously, in 2015 at the Latin American Studies Association (LASA) conference in San Juan, Puerto Rico, I heard two papers on the links between debt and *Pedro Páramo*. Ericka Beckman and Alberto Ribas-Casasayas are also pursuing this line of thought and have since published on the topic. Beckman's paper, "*Pedro Páramo* and 'Permanent Primitive Accumulation,'" delivered at LASA, finds painstaking development in her article "Unfinished Transitions," which ruminates from a Marxist bent on Rulfo's relationship with debt and development. There, Beckman cites work on *Pedro Páramo* by Ángel Rama, Neil Larsen, Patrick Dove, and Jean Franco. Alberto Ribas-Casasayas reads debt in *Pedro Páramo* through David Graeber, as well as Achille Mbembe's concept of necropolitics, which allows him to interlace the topics of debt and violence with an eye to contemporary Mexican thought, such as that of Irmgard Emmelhainz. Both contributions elaborate excellent, though distinct, meditations on debt in Rulfo's novel.

9. Eduardo Ruiz compares the mother's financial decline and disdainful classist reaction in *Las batallas en el desierto* with another text about the same neighborhood in Mexico City, this one written from an amusingly distinct angle: Luis Zapata's celebrated contribution to gay literature *El vampiro de la Colonia Roma* (The vampire of the Colonia Roma, trans. as *Adonis García: A Picaresque Novel*) (1979).

10. Stefano Brugnolo and Laura Luche explore *Pedro Páramo* as a saga that repeats the "originating trauma" (*trauma originario*) of the Conquest (135); to make that argument, they employ a study of purgatory and Paz's structure of the Chingada from *El laberinto de la soledad*. For his part, Rulfo planned to write a history of the Conquest in the region of Jalisco; he declared in 1982, for example, that "nunca he olvidado mi gran pasión por la historia de México, sobre todo, los siglos XVI y XVII" (I have never forgotten my great passion for Mexican history, above all, the sixteenth and seventeenth centuries) ("Juan Rulfo, Premio Nacional" D-1). Fernando Barrientos del Monte associates Rulfo's interest in writing a history of the Conquest in the region that became Jalisco with part of a television series for Televisora de Occidente, where Rulfo worked from 1960 to 1962 (58). Stephanie Merrim notes this influence of pre-Independence history on Rulfo and reminds us that the last of Rulfo's publications "was a preface to Bernardino de Sahagún's sixteenth-century treatise on pre-Hispanic Mexico," and she observes that his failed novel project, *La cordillera*, was "a novel on eighteenth-century [Jalisco]" (316).

11. At the top of the debt chain, the king needed to remain, in a phrase from the Obama years, too big to fail, and as Graeber remembers, credit woes were in no

short supply at the top (*Debt* 319). Graeber observes the unidirectionality of this debt chain, seeping downward in the social scale, "since Cortés had insisted that the men [under him] be billed for any replacement equipment and medical care they had received during the siege" (317).

12. Cain paraphrases findings from the work of social historian Andrea Tone in order to state that this antianxiety medication "immediately became the fastest-selling pharmaceutical in American history" (29). Unfortunately, I do not have the statistics for Mexican consumption of this drug, but speaking in twenty-first-century terms, Jorge Castañeda notes that, "controlling for GDP per capita, Mexico is probably the most self-medicated society in the world" (xxiv).

13. Campos observes, "By the end of the 1930s, most of the elements necessary for the North American 'War on Drugs' were in place in Mexico and the United States. In 1937, the United States prohibited marijuana on the federal level" (226). Prohibition in Mexico and the United States coincides with antiquated yet ongoing racist attitudes. As David Lenson summarizes, the discriminatory tool of U.S. antidrug legislation "tends to assert the values of one of its subgroups against the others" (25). Despite the racism that works against Mexicans in the north, Mexican attitudes within national borders often reflect similarly racist ideas.

14. This parallel between the decision on antiqueer hate speech and the one in favor of recreational marijuana remains striking. Queer theorists already anticipate the connection between nonsobriety and the queer, as evident in Kane Race's *Pleasure Consuming Medicine: The Queer Politics of Drugs* (2009). Race shows that rules meant to enforce normativity can have precious little to do with the effective protection of public health. Instead, "the status of certain substances as 'illicit' provides an occasion for the state to engage in what can be described as a disciplinary performance of moral sovereignty" (12). Zaldívar articulates these points and explicitly ties in legal battles for queer rights by citing transsexuals' protections to decide sex and gender as an example of the free development of personality ("Amparo en revisión" 35, 36). He also contemplates at length the legal precedents regarding the right to marry and divorce freely (36–38).

15. This concept of freedom to develop personality draws on international agreement, codified in Article 22 of the United Nation's Universal Declaration of Human Rights (Delman). The article declares: "Everyone, as a member of society, has the right to social security and is entitled to realization, through national effort and international co-operation and in accordance with the organization and resources of each State, of the economic, social and cultural rights indispensable for his dignity and the free development of his personality." No further information on what "the free development of personality" might entail appears. Approval of this document took place in December 1948 in Paris, in the UN General Assembly.

16. The four citizens who brought the suit in 2014 asked to use marijuana for recreational but not commercial purposes, arguing against the "indebida restricción de los derechos fundamentales a la identidad personal, propia imagen, libre desarrollo de la personalidad, autodeterminación y libertad individual, todos en relación

con el principio de dignidad humana, así como del derecho a la disposición de la salud" (undue restriction of fundamental rights to personal identity, self-image, free development of personality, self-determination and individual freedom, all in relation to the principle of human dignity, as well as the right to administer their health) (Zaldívar Lelo de Larrea, "Amparo en revisión" 3). The court agreed. Zaldívar stated that the constitution does not protect legal meddling in individuals' lives to achieve "fines perfeccionistas" (perfectionist ends), because "el Estado no puede exigir a las personas que se conduzcan de acuerdo a un determinado modelo de virtud" (the State cannot demand that people behave themselves according to a particular model of virtue) (4). The violence provoked by the international drug trade causes problems for public health, as Zaldívar cited from Article 245, the Ley General de Salud (General Health Law) (45–46). Zaldívar proposed that health information and public-service campaigns provide a more direct and effective protection of public well-being than the indirect method of prohibition (71). For marijuana to become legal for all people in Mexico, the Supreme Court must make the same ruling in a total of five cases; the second of such cases was decided with similar language on April 11, 2018, which ruled in favor of the free development of personality ("Concede Corte amparo").

17. Lenson notes the chilling effect on drug discourse of the Just Say No campaign of the Reagan years, which doubled down on the Nixon-directed support for prohibition: "Drugs are the Unspeakable" (xviii). On this matter, an anecdote recounted by classics scholar D. C. A. Hillman proves informative. During his dissertation defense, Hillman heard the following advice: "Take out the chapter on the ancient world's recreational drug use . . . or fail the exam." (2). According to Hillman, the most vocal member of the committee refuted the conclusion that Romans used recreational drugs with the objection, "They just wouldn't do such a thing" (2).

18. Demands for a kind of character-based virtue cleared the way for the drug-related bullying performance. In the provocatively named *Drugs: America's Holy War*, Arthur Benavie writes that by 1915, in a shift "well under way," the drug addict began to be imagined, not as a "pitiful recluse" or a middle- or upper-class white woman, as had previously been the fashion, but as a "dangerous criminal" or a lower-class urban man, often operating in the underworld (26). The U.S. Supreme Court's Webb decision of 1919 fostered the prohibition ruling still in place today by redefining addicts as having a disciplinary and not a medical problem (27). This point is so important that it bears repetition by way of another source. In *Seeing Drugs*, a history limited to the years 1969 to 1976, Daniel Weimer reiterates the twentieth-century argument regarding the threatening addict as a bully: "Thus a new drug addict profile emerged in the first part of the twentieth century. The typical addict was younger and male. He had not acquired his habit as the result of illness, and he did not belong to the middle or upper class" (25). A magnetic personality as facilitated by rebellious drug use is not permitted to all.

19. Drug consumption is in fact so enmeshed with Mexican understandings of masculinity—in general, and not just for writers—that anthropologist Stanley Brandes

can research a predicament among members of Alcoholics Anonymous (AA): "When [Mexican] men abandon drink radically, as membership in Alcoholics Anonymous requires, they are forced to question their own gender identity. For this reason, . . . much of the therapeutic work [of AA groups] involves testing and manifesting one's manhood" (153). I can also cite the case of an anonymous Mexican hired hit man who in an interview recalls that his abstinence unnerved others, in part because he had used "drugs and used alcohol for practically my whole life" (Bowden and Molloy 134). Implicitly, alcohol use indicated trustworthiness for his employers: "Now, for me, to stop using alcohol and drugs was never a problem. . . . But it was a big problem for my bosses, it was a problem of trust. . . . I would see that they were nervous about me" (162). In U.S. history, masculinity and alcohol are also intertwined; ergo, the double whammy of alcohol prohibition and women's suffrage, in the opinion of one researcher, led U.S. men to make a pilgrimage south of the border, since "both measures threatened traditional male culture" (Merrill 37).

20. As Greenblatt explains, the Catholic Church sold indulgences to the living who hoped that the purchase would reduce the time that the dead spent in purgatory before cleansing their sins and moving to heaven—a process that was inevitable even without the payment that expedited the process (126). Pedro's appreciation for purgatory resurfaces when he overdoes it on the bell ringing for Susana San Juan; according to Greenblatt, the ringing of bells for the dead traditionally constitutes "a call for prayers that would help speed the newly departed soul through its purgatorial torment" (43). When strangers within earshot misunderstand the bell ringing for Susana as a call to carnival, Pedro exacts revenge.

21. That account is so famous that it appears, for instance, in a graphic novel about the creation of *Pedro Páramo* and Rulfo's biography by two Colombian artists, who write that Rulfo's method leaves behind "la historia perfecta" (the perfect story) (Pantoja and Camargo 190).

22. In 2014, Pedro Ángel Palou summarized the tendency to praise Rulfo's sense of narrative economy: "Mucho se ha hablado de la *economía* verbal de la novela de Rulfo" (Much has been said about the verbal *economy* in Rulfo's novel) (95). Palou's friend José Ramón Ruisánchez Serra is one of those critics who take the economical stance. Ruisánchez Serra admires what he calls the internal economy of *Pedro Páramo* and points out one supportive detail: Juan Preciado shares a grave with another character, in an economic relationship of "sobresaturación" (oversaturation) (*Historias* 174). In fact, Ruisánchez Serra thinks of the novel as an "economía renarrativa" (economy of renarration) in which one character can share space with or speak for another (178). In some ways, many uses of the term *economy* to describe the novel fail to converse with one another. It isn't clear that Ruisánchez Serra's idea connects to Julio Ortega's description of *Pedro Páramo* as an exception to the novelistic genre, because Rulfo writes "against the demands of the novel's expansive economy, subtracting from it and representing the world as a lack" (*Transatlantic Translations* 159). Oswaldo Estrada contemplates details in the Rulfian oeuvre,

such as references to water, milk, and alcohol, in terms of scarcity. Patrick Dove uses the language of economy to tie up an argument that otherwise may not have much to do with the economy per se; his rigorous article on *Pedro Páramo* concludes by remarking on "a certain limit within the economy of exchange and recognition that sustains the master discourse" (105). Juan Pellicer writes an article about the "poetic economy" of *Pedro Páramo* and examines the particularly economic use of words in fragment 67, which retells, "in fourteen replicas (like a sonnet)," the years between the consolidation of "Carranzism" in 1915 until the end of the Cristero War in 1929 (197). Pellicer admires the *ahorro* (savings) generated by Rulfo's literary tropes and considers this use an "inmejorable ejemplo de economía poética" (unsurpassable example of the poetic economy) (198). Pellicer's esteem for the novel leads to the final two adjectives of the article, where he praises Rulfo's "poetry" for its "frescura y sobriedad" (freshness and sobriety) (202). Another viewpoint might just as easily argue that the at-times-wordy dialogue in *Pedro Páramo* can be repetitive. The feel of improvised stylistics hinges, not on economical terseness, but on meandering hallucinations, circular nonlinear exchanges, and, in fragment 51, even on stutters. Implicitly writing against this economy, Boullosa observes that "the novel has an astonishing acoustic quality; its dialogues and interior monologues feel improvised, as if the author let the characters speak on their own" ("Dead Souls" 26). Incidentally, Pacheco's work also receives admiration for its perceived brevity. As Cynthia Steele writes in her chapter on *Las batallas en el desierto*, "Pacheco works toward precision, conciseness, the elimination of excess, and understatement" (88).

23. Rulfo comments, "Hoy mis libros alcanzan elevadas tirajes. . . . Sí, gano dinero con mis libros, no el que preciso para vivir, sí el que me permite salir de deudas. Oyó usted bien: dije deudas" (Reyes Razo). (Today my books reach high print runs. . . . Yes, I make money with my books, not the kind I need to live, but the kind that helps me get out of debts. You heard that right: I said debts.)

24. As intimated by the chronological problem with Eduviges's and Miguel's conversation, Rulfo put together the manuscript under a tight deadline. In order to fulfill the conditions of his grant with the Centro Mexicano de Escritores, he turned in a draft marked with handwritten last-minute changes. Understandably, then, the work gives rise to opposing critics' viewpoints of masterful planning and confusing imprecision. For instance, alongside the "clockwork precision" he admires in the novel, González Boixó identifies a contrasting element of ambiguity as a "primordial" characteristic of the novel ("Introducción" 31). To clear up that ambiguity, González Boixó draws on a personal conversation he had with Rulfo in Madrid in 1983, when Rulfo explained two points regarding the novel: first, according to the novelist, Pedro Páramo's son Juan Preciado dies after hallucinating the incestuous brother and sister; and second, Susana San Juan only imagines herself a widow; her deceased husband never existed ("Aclaraciones" 248, 250). Amit Thakkar works to rescue Rulfo from expectations of air-tight chronological order by arguing that "what we are looking for in a political reading of Rulfo's work is not the evocation

of a period but the less precise art of observing a whirlwind of social and ideological conflict which spans the Spanish Empire and a decolonization process which continues to the present day" ("Irony" 215).

25. In the detailed explanation of the proposed "Quality Education," the National Plan for Development refers to "*bullying*," in italicized English, as a phenomenon recently brought to nationwide attention (*Plan Nacional* 61).

26. As Leñero's autobiography indicates, he learned to perform the necessary qualities of a literary personality and won funding from the Centro Mexicano de Escritores in 1961–62 and 1962–63.

27. As for *je ne sais quoi*, Marc Reynebeau points out that this vague "something" defies even onlookers' powers of description (155).

28. Biagioli draws on a number of his peers' work, namely Thomas Kuhn's "tacit knowledge" and Paul Feyerabend's "natural interpretation," as the latter influenced acceptance of Galileo's "way of seeing." Biagioli claims new terrain because, "in their initial formulation, Kuhn's and Feyerabend's categories were still more about minds than bodies" (69).

29. By contrast, Montes de Oca goes on to define terms of mediocrity by citing "señoritos mediocres" (mediocre young gentlemen) who studied medicine in Mexico with the goal of making a profit after graduation (28). Notably, in a statement that may undermine Elizondo's genius for the nonviolent reader, Montes de Oca admits, "Elizondo y yo estuvimos a punto de reñir a golpes en cierta ocasión, todo porque me negué a admitir que él era Dios" (Elizondo and I were on the verge of a fistfight once, all because I refused to admit that he was God) (39).

30. Sabido remembered, "Emma fue psicóloga. Nos hacían una evaluación psicológica para ver si estábamos locos yo creo. Y nos hacían una evaluación de intereses. Me la hizo Felipe García Beraza" (Sabido, personal interview). (Emma was a psychologist. They gave us a psychological evaluation to see if we were crazy or not, I think. And they gave us an evaluation of interests. Mine was done by Felipe García Beraza.) Dolujanoff questioned her ability to evaluate objectively the personality tests. On August 1, 1960, in a letter signed "E. D.," Dolujanoff, presumably, begs off the responsibility of evaluating Homero Aridjis and comments positively on his introverted qualities: "Lo conozco demasiado para intentar una interpretación psicológica. Siempre me ha impresionado como muy modesto y tímido. Me gusta su poesía" (CME Aridjis 86). (I know him too well to try a psychological interpretation. He has always struck me as very modest and shy. I like his poetry.)

31. The complete list of influences includes "Shakespeare, Cervantes, Balzac, Dante, Sofocles [*sic*], Quevedo, Faulkner, Terrencio, Dickens, Camus, Dostoyevski [*sic*], Oscar Wilde, Anatole France, Ibsen, Hemingway, Dos Passos, J. Poncela [Enrique Jardiel Poncela], Tennessee Williams" (CME Sabido 35).

32. Immaturity damages an applicant's chances because it can denote a lack of professional skill. In the initial rejection of Humberto Guzmán for a scholarship, before allowing him one in the years 1970–71, when he was about twenty-two, all three evaluators detected a maturity problem. Rulfo opined, "No escribe del todo mal,

pero todavía su nivel es de concurso escolar" (He doesn't write entirely poorly, but his level is at [that of] a school contest); a middle viewpoint, possibly Felipe García Beraza, agrees, "Me parece interesante, pero inmaduro" (He seems interesting to me, but immature); and the final opinion, in what looks like Salvador Elizondo's handwriting, concurs, "De acuerdo con la calificación" (I agree with the evaluation) (CME Guzmán 65).

33. In today's terms, Heriberto Yépez's malicious Twitter account might form the contemporary equivalent of such literary cunning, although perhaps the form fails the experimental quality that readers sought in the 1960s. The year 2016 continued the long tradition of mutual attacks between writers, largely among men, and figures such as Christopher Domínguez Michael and Heriberto Yépez engaged in a rambling and somewhat nonsensical public argument that lasted for months. Each gained in reputation as they responded to the other's published remarks.

34. For a playful summation of Mexicans' fear of being called *naco*, see Velasco's "La agonía" (65).

35. The men also circle the wagons to protect themselves as parents. Fatherhood troubles experienced by Octavio Paz and Carlos Fuentes are either not mentioned (as tends to be the case with Fuentes) or blamed on the (ex-)wife (in Paz's typical example). For Fuentes's reputation, see Gómez Jiménez; "Carlos Fuentes" in *Wikipedia*; "Muere Natasha Fuentes"; and "Literatura: Muere sorpresivamente." For an exemplary treatment of Paz, see Domínguez Michael, *Octavio Paz*, 323, 474, and 541.

36. Karin Becker Fornäs and her colleagues point out: "Collecting or saving objects, in whatever form it takes, thus disturbs the ordinary chain of consumption" (Fornäs, Bjurström, and Ganetz 106). Shelley Garrigan helpfully explores the difference between a commodity, which creates a shopper selfhood based on earnings and exchanges, and a collection, which disrupts the flow of commodity exchange and instead posits a "'metaphor of production' in which the world is presented as given" (48).

37. If my reader objects to the notion that sober Monsiváis's book collection fails as a possible indicator of luxurious tastes, I note that the country of Chile includes books in the category of taxable items subject to the stiff 19 percent value added tax (Cobin). Chile thinks of books as a luxury item.

38. As Zunz puts it, under these capitalists' investment vision, "American philanthropy would be a capitalist venture in social betterment, not an act of kindness as understood in Christianity" (2). Similarly, Ostrower defines charity as attending to "severe and immediate needs" among the poor, against the larger institutional aims of philanthropy (4).

39. In 2015, Slim, along with the other three wealthiest inhabitants of Mexico, owned fortunes equivalent to about 9 percent of the nation's GDP; Slim's fortune alone equaled almost 6 percent (Tucker).

40. Callahan quotes sociologist Paul Schervish on the subject of "hyperagency," a term meant to describe the ever-more-outsized means and accompanying sense

of philanthropic entitlement among the megawealthy; the extraordinary degree of wealth among the ultrarich has developed globally thanks to what Callahan calls our "New Gilded Age" (40–41).

41. Ostrower juxtaposes the observation that "women are virtually absent from top institutional positions of economic power in the United States" with her finding that among the New York–centered philanthropists she studied, "Married women (75 percent) were far more likely than unmarried women (16.7 percent) to have made a largest gift [the highest category of the study] to culture" (69). The most common recipient of philanthropy among unmarried women was "the social services" (69). Zunz points out the liberal ends that some philanthropists achieved in the United States, from public libraries to desegregated schools.

42. Information on philanthropy in the Mexican context is harder to come by. My librarian colleague Margarita Vargas Betancourt provides an excellent justification. She notes that changes in the Mexican tax code appear in the *Diario Oficial* (Official newspaper), where the modifications are so frequent that even professionals find the pace troubling: "My mother, who was an accountant, checked them on a daily basis. Her conclusion was that the tax code was confusing on purpose."

43. Slim grew up in Mexico City as a second-generation Lebanese Mexican. He received a civil engineering degree in 1961 from the public institution UNAM (Haas 94).

44. Arreola was born some thirty years after López Velarde, and yet the younger writer adopted the throwback look. Arreola linked his clothing taste to his small-town origins; his "second skin" of second-time-around retro fashion, anchored in tastes formed, not in Mexico City, but in small-town Mexico (del Paso 145). This look was meant to connote an earlier, more openly sentimental sensibility, with the "natural" fit of the aesthetics standing in as a sign of Arreola's innate genius.

45. In documents dated from the 1960s, several changes of address in Mexico City hint at a state of upheaval in Arreola's personal life. A letter from Margaret Shedd warns Arreola to show up to work, and other documents show that Arreola's salary from the Centro was transferred as payment of a debt to Antonio Alatorre. Arreola's debt to Alatorre appears in letters like the one dated June 7, 1968, from Felipe García Beraza to Alatorre: "[L]os cheques que el señor Arreola recibirá del Centro Mexicano de Escritores en los próximos meses, estarán a la disposición de usted cada día 15. El cheque mensual es por $1,800.00 [pesos mexicanos]" (CME Arreola 10-3: 159). (The checks that Mr. Arreola will receive from the Mexican Center for Writers in the coming months, will be at your disposition each [month on the] 15th. The monthly check is for $1,800.00 [Mexican pesos].) On July 18, 1968, García Beraza writes again to Alatorre on the matter of the Arreola's debt (158). Alatorre's signature appears on the document, indicating "Recibí cheque" (I received the check) (157). Virtually the same letter on CME letterhead, with the same signatures, reappears with the date September 4, 1968 (153). In a conversation with Jean Meyer, Alatorre says that he went to Princeton to teach for the first time in 1966 (Meyer 138), and from 1953 to 1972, Alatorre directed the Center for Philological Studies at El Colegio de México, so it seems

unlikely that he experienced money problems himself; rather, it was Arreola who suffered the cash crisis. In the end, Arreola's long history of employment, including his election in 1981 to El Colegio Nacional with its lifetime payments, should have lessened his need for loans.

46. Alatorre mentions Arreola's pleasure in expensive objects: "Es impresionante la catolicidad de sus intereses, y enorme, desmedida, la alegría con que todo lo vive: [. . .] las cosas de lujo [como] prendas de vestir, encuadernaciones, muebles, cristales *art-nouveau*, buenos vinos (sobre todo franceses)" (The catholicity of his interests impresses, and his enormous, boundless, joy with everything that he lives: . . . the luxury items [like] clothing, bookbindings, furniture, art nouveau glass, fine wines [especially French ones]) (Alatorre, "Juan José" 87).

47. I first heard this anecdote in 2010, when I was conducting a series of interviews with Mexican writers born in the 1970s. An alarmed Vivian Abenshushan and a disturbed Alberto Chimal mentioned the event when I interviewed them separately. In 2005, Arreola's humiliation also appeared in a blog post by a third writer of this generation, Bef (Bernardo Fernández), who remembered "el lamentable paso del maestro Juan José Arreola [. . .] reducido a un payaso amariconado en sus tristes intervenciones en la TV nacional (¿alguien lo recuerda en duelo dialéctico con Thalía?)" (the regrettable misstep by *maestro* Juan José Arreola . . . reduced to a faggy clown on his sad appearances on national TV [does anyone remember him in a dialectical duel with Thalía?]) (Fernández, "25 razones"). Jorge F. Hernández, in an interview from 2008 published in *Revista UNAM*, blames Arreola for allowing the circumstances that facilitated the argument: "Juan José Arreola se expuso a que Thalía se burlara de él, pero fue porque aceptó salir en la tele tanto hablando de futbol y en lugar de que eso fuera reconocido como algo que finalmente promueve la lectura, en realidad fue una trampa" (Juan José Arreola exposed himself so that Thalía could make fun of him, but it was because he agreed to appear on television so often talking about soccer and instead of having that recognized as something that promotes reading, it was actually a trap) (Hernández, "Entrevista"). Writers born in the 1960s and 1970s clearly took great interest in this anecdote, perhaps because it demonstrated the power of televised media to humiliate a literary celebrity. Many of Arreola's peers write about the event. For instance, in Carballo's memoir he remembers that Arreola transformed after the 1970s into a caricature of his earlier smooth-talking dandy. This decline coincided with his attempt to garner mass-audience appeal on TV (*Ya nada* 265). In contrast, Alatorre defended Arreola's appearances on television, in part because he appeared with him, for eight months, in 1978 and 1979. Alatorre preferred not to judge Arreola's more extensive participation on television, although he alluded to one of the "greater scandals," that of Thalía's remark (Alatorre, "Juan José" 87).

48. Domínguez Michael recalls that one morning near the day of the latter's death, President Zedillo pushed Paz's wheelchair, and the poet made some remarks in defense of the deceased father of Emilio Azcárraga Jean, heir to the Televisa empire (*Octavio Paz* 563).

49. Monsiváis explains in careful biographical logic the roots of Novo's self-aware reactionary perspective: "Para Novo, la Revolución es antes que nada la muerte del tío a manos de salvajes, y esto fomenta a grados extremos su conservadurismo; también, la Revolución, origen de las instituciones, es la única salida de los jóvenes escritores" (For Novo, the Revolution is first and foremost the uncle's death at the hands of savages, and that encourages to extreme degrees his conservatism; also, the Revolution, the origin of the institutions, is the only way out for the young writers") (*Salvador Novo* 21). Novo's negative reputation finds a defender in Domínguez Michael, who observes that at least at the beginning of his nonfiction writing, Novo "no era tan reaccionario ni tan conservador como lo pinta la leyenda" (was not as reactionary nor as conservative as legend paints him) ("Cliente").

50. At first glance, Novo's and Arreola's double connection with democratic values and glamorous personalities might seem nonsensical. But scholars of glamour have little trouble locating the link with democracy. Gundle writes that the appeal of glamour by the twentieth century "was most powerful to those who lay outside the realm of privilege and success" (389). Gundle remains cynical about the power of glamour to effect actual social change, however. For a highly readable exploration of the roots of glamour, which are not connected to democracy, see Joan DeJean's study of seventeenth-century Paris under Louis XIV, *The Essence of Style*.

51. Alí Chumacero appears not to have finished high school or college, though he started both. He explains in an interview: "[N]o terminé la preparatoria y nunca pude. [. . .] Nunca logré inscribirme en la Universidad. Fui expulsado de la Autónoma de Guadalajara, acusado de comunista. [. . .] Pero asistí desde ese momento, al llegar [en la Ciudad de México], a la Escuela de Filosofía de la Facultad de Filosofía y Letras. [. . .] En [el Centro] Mascarones [de la UNAM], todavía, donde fui un discípulo muy cercano del doctor José Gaos, el gran maestro al que tanto debe la cultura mexicana" (Azar, "Alí Chumacero"). (I didn't finish high school and I never could. . . . I never managed to enroll at the University. I was expelled from the Autonomous [University] of Guadalajara, accused as a communist. . . . But I attended after that, when I arrived [in Mexico City], the School of Philosophy and Letters [at the UNAM]. . . . At [the UNAM's Centro] Mascarones, still, I was a very close disciple of Dr. José Gaos, the great expert to whom Mexican culture owes so much.) On a different level of incomplete studies, René Avilés Fabila reports that people attribute a PhD to him even though he did not finish his dissertation: "Hice los estudios del posgrado [en ciencias políticas] en París, en la Sorbonne, pero no redacté la tesis doctoral" (I did the coursework for the graduate degree [in political science] in Paris, at the Sorbonne, but I didn't write the dissertation) (CME Avilés Fabila 94). Note that López Velarde, the poet of the excessively accessible "La suave patria," actually finished his university degree—like the institutional persona non grata Salvador Novo after him. If Novo denied even making typos, López Velarde was an all-around perfect student. As Guillermo Sheridan's biography reminds us, the turn-of-the-twentieth-century poet not only acquired a law degree but earned such outstanding grades that the

faculty excused him from the professional exam (*Un corazón adicto* 113). Carlos Fuentes also completed his university studies and worked as a lawyer before making it as perhaps Mexico's first professional writer. Interestingly, in 2016 Volpi's *Examen de mi padre* defends his decision to focus on law studies and take literature courses only as an auditor as a Mexican tradition, perhaps without knowing that not all his heroes finished the degree: "creía que ésta [mi vocación literaria] debía pasar por el estudio de las leyes, como hicieron Paz, Fuentes o Pitol antes que yo" (I thought that it [my literary vocation] should pass through the study of law, just as Paz, Fuentes or Pitol did before me) (91).

52. The network of important personalities who supported Alatorre's academic reputation seems almost entirely male. In the thirty-five-page interview that records the conversation between fellow scholars Jean Meyer and Antonio Alatorre, only two women's names appear, those of Sor Juana Inés de la Cruz and Lourdes Arizpe (Meyer 139).

CHAPTER 7

Epigraphs: He [Salvador Elizondo] and Juan García Ponce, Víctor Flores Olea, Vicente Rojo and myself were born in the same year. I don't list the women's names out of discretion and because they always tell me that it's a mistake to say one's own age.—Poniatowska, "Salvador Elizondo."

Don't even think about asking me my age, don't even think about it . . .—María Conesa speaking with Elena Poniatowska, "¡Ay, ay, ay," 29.

1. In a four-hour conversation with Reyes Razo, Rulfo told the reporter, "Yo soy contador privado. Estudié en Guadalajara" (I am a private accountant. I studied in Guadalajara) (6). This statement is a lie, according to biographer Barrientos del Monte. Barrientos del Monte corrects Rulfo's mistruth about his qualifications: "Lo de 'contador' se lo creyeron muchos, cosa que no fue cierta. En realidad al final de la secundaria [. . .] tomó algunos cursos que tenían que ver con la materia, pero nunca se tituló como tal" (The "accountant" story convinced a lot of people, but it wasn't true. Actually, at the end of middle school . . . he took a few classes related to the subject, but he was never accredited as such) (9n2). The emotional tension such a lie causes appears on a video recording from 1977 of the Spanish television show *Entrevista a Fondo* (In-depth interview), with host Joaquín Soler Serrano. Twenty-three and a half minutes into the conversation, at the very instant that Soler Serrano mentions the accounting studies, Rulfo fishes a cigarette packet out of his suit jacket. By the time Rulfo begins to affirm the fib, he is smoking. Soler Serrano is proud to have dug up a little-known "fact" of Rulfo's biography, and Rulfo obliges his interlocutor's professional expertise by repeating the lie, which makes both of them look good (Soler Serrano). If the hypochondriac tendencies are not enough, Rulfo's compulsive reach for a cigarette must surely indicate the stresses involved in the lying performance. For more data, see Reina Roffé's review of Rulfo's consistent lie about his age, among others (19–20, 24).

2. In 1949, on the occasion of his wedding, Rulfo claimed to be twenty-nine, though he was thirty; he was, in fact, older than the bride by eleven years and not a mere decade (Barrientos del Monte 39). On the birth certificate for his son in 1952, Rulfo also claimed to be thirty-three and his wife, Clara, only ten years younger than he.
3. During our interview, Martha Domínguez Cuevas meditated on changes in application procedures that, in the context of the Centro Mexicano de Escritores, evolved from requiring few documents to demanding a birth certificate or voter's registration card. The voter registration card (*credencial de elector*) came into existence in 1992. The irony does not escape me that the voter registration card itself was developed to ensure more democratic elections, and yet in the context of grant applications it curtails the would-be freedom to decide one's age category.
4. Other men also lie about age. Carlos Fuentes removed one year from his age in his grant application for the Centro Mexicano de Escritores, although his motives for claiming that he was twenty-seven when he was actually twenty-eight remain hazy ("Carlos Fuentes"). Perhaps he forgot his age? Fuentes's application, as Aguilar Sosa notes, juxtaposes an incorrect birth year—1929 instead of the accurate 1928—with a plea for an adjustment from the bachelor to the married man rate for the grant, since he will marry on January 6, 1956 ("Carlos Fuentes"). Melo's autobiography lists members of his generation in proud terms and claims that one man, Juan José Gurrola, actually increased his age, for unknown reasons (Melo 43).
5. Vasconcelos, along with the general notion of the mature male writer, appears in the previously mentioned all-male Iconografía series. The cover photos for these oversized illustrated albums include a "mature" José Vasconcelos in an image from 1943, when he would have been about sixty-one; Agustín Yáñez in a portrait perhaps taken during the 1960s, when he was in his sixties, but before his hair turned entirely gray; Daniel Cosío Villegas in an image taken around 1958, when he was sixty or so; and Jaime García Terrés in a photograph from 1982, at about age fifty-eight; Carlos Pellicer in a picture that may date from the 1940s, when he was in his forties or perhaps early fifties. Men can age visibly without falling off the book cover.
6. A meticulous statistical study of the film industry, published in 2004, found that women are nominated for and win acting Oscars at a significantly younger age than men; moreover, at the time of that study youth was the most powerful criterion for predicting females who will win the Best Actress award, while "middle age" best predicted male Best Actor winners (Lincoln and Allen 616). It would be interesting to know if women screenwriters receive recognition later than men writers, or if that category also privileges women's youth. The same analysis of the "double jeopardy" effect in Hollywood—the financial punishment of being a woman and of being an aging woman—finds that in the late twentieth century, the term "older" tended to be used to describe male actors over the age of forty and female actors over the age of thirty (616). In 2016, a separate examination of 2,000 films with English-language dialogue affirmed the ongoing gender and age bias. When correlating a given actor's age with the amount of dialogue he or she

delivers, the study found that women actors over age forty speak "substantially" less than men actors over forty; in fact, compared to the decreasing dialogue available to aging women actors, "for men, it's the exact opposite: there are *more roles* available to older [men] actors" (Anderson and Daniels).

7. Race also affects the dynamic. In New Spain, for instance, the legal system viewed the "Indians" as perpetual minors, regardless of their biological age (Fisher 191). Yet, among slaves sold in Central Mexico a certain level of physical maturity brought the highest prices. Notarial records from Puebla and Mexico City slave markets from the period 1600 to 1700 show that the financial value of slaves "rose from infancy, peaked just before reaching 30 years of age, and only truly depreciated at 40" (Seijas and Sierra Silva 321). The viceroyalty treated age differently even for the more privileged. As historian Sonya Lipsett-Rivera reminds us, under colonial law males and females "did not reach full legal maturity until the age of twenty-five, although, unless emancipated (by marriage for example), they remained subject to their father's authority indefinitely" (60). Ways of breaking the *patria potestad*, as the father's power was known, included "the children's marriage or taking of religious vows, the father's death or civil death, the father's imprisonment or heresy, and finally, if the father married incestuously" (63).
8. The data on English-language writing student Jerri Orson has been lost to history.
9. Treviño had earned certain literary fame as a cultural journalist, and the evaluators probably also knew that she had two children, born in 1953 and 1954, with the painter Alberto Gironella. The three judges gave Treviño the grant for 1964–65, and Rulfo, true to his remarkably feminist habits, as seen in the archive, commented only on Treviño's work (17). Arreola scribbles the third opinion on the shared notecard: "Un buen tema, propuesto por una persona de capacidad evidente" (A good topic, proposed by a person of evident ability) (17). Given the context of Shedd's remark, Arreola's meaning remains unclear here. What is "evident" ability? Does Arreola refer to Treviño's publication record or to her attractive self-presentation? Or both?
10. In her biography of Nellie Campobello, Clara Guadalupe García recognizes the complicity necessary for Campobello's false thirtieth birthday party: "ella apagó treinta velitas sin que nadie sospechara que en realidad tenía cuarenta" (she blew out thirty little candles without anyone suspecting that in reality she was forty) (105).
11. Sara Potter observes that Surrealist artists' "female lovers or wives were generally much younger than their male partners," and yet these women (or "girls") never remained sufficiently young; the women formed "part of an ever-rotating roster, as they were frequently traded in for newer, younger models" (75).
12. In an unauthorized biography of Monsiváis, Braulio Peralta also mentions Omar García as only the last in a number of partnerships (201). In so many respects, Monsiváis's elderly love of cats and his domestic disarray sets him up to repeat the later-in-life patterns familiar from the women writers judged as *locas* (crazy), like Elena Garro and Guadalupe Amor. However, Monsiváis can play the same hand and win—the same hand except for the woman card, of course. I cannot cite a sin-

gle report describing the bodies of elderly men authors, such as Paz or Fuentes, as stinking or mired in unsightly decay, in contrast to the publications on Garro and her daughter. (For more on Helena Paz Garro, see Morelos; Atala; or Cabrera. For Garro and Amor, see my book *Femmenism.*) For more on Monsiváis's cats, I can cite Jaime Avilés, who describes a visit to Monisváis's home; after Sabina Berman and her friend leave, Monsiváis opens thirty-eight cans of Whiskas for "su manada de felinos en medio de un hedor insoportable" (his herd of cats amid an unbearable stench) ("Tres años sin Monsiváis").

13. During our interview, Domínguez Cuevas remembered a conversation that she, Montemayor, and Alí Chumacero shared in one of their monthly gatherings for a meal: "Entonces Alí, pues Alí era muy picardiento, [y] dice, 'Mira, este pendejo se casa. Se casa. Yo nada más con una me he casado. He tenido veinte mil, pero solamente con una me he casado. Pero ése se divorcia, se casa, le cuesta dinero, luego tiene que mantener a los hijos y se mete en un montón de problemas. Ya le dije que de aquí en adelante no se vuelve a casar.' Y ya no se vuelve a casar. Ya tuvo a sus amigas, a sus amantes y cambiaba pero ya no se casó y con la última que fue con la que murió." (Then Alí, well Alí was very ornery, [and] he says, "Look, this asshole gets married. He gets married. I only married one. I've had twenty thousand [lovers], but only one whom I've married. But he gets divorced, gets married, it costs him money, then he has to support the children, and he gets into a ton of problems. I already told him that from here on he doesn't marry again." And he didn't remarry. He had his women friends, his lovers, and he changed [them] but he didn't marry again and with the last one he died.)

14. The standards of youth-oriented culture privilege "vigor, health, novelty, and a youthful appearance," and therefore aging seems doomed to a bad rep insofar as the old are left to embody the inverse qualities (Mintz 331).

15. The slang and pastimes that Rulfo cites in Mastretta's defense harness youth culture, and informality guides several paragraphs of praise, written by hand on small pieces of stationery, which begin as if in the middle of a thought shared with Mastretta: "una vida sin policías, ni jueces, ni enfermedades ni castigos; ni fábricas, ni trabajos; sin iglesias; en fin, una vida hecha para hacer el amor entre dulces y caramelos, sin otras obligaciones que ir a ver una película de Buñuel de vez en cuando, o buscar su 'aliviarme' con distintos cuates o cuatachas de la 'onda' en lo que proponen la autora escribir" (a life without police, or judges, or illnesses or punishments; or factories, or jobs, or churches; in short, a life made to make love between candies and caramels, without any more obligations than going to see a Buñuel film once in a while, or looking for her "release" with various guys or gals from the "wave" in terms of what the author proposes to write) (CME Rulfo 64-1). Still, Rulfo isolates key terms in quotation marks, such as the youth group of the "onda," perhaps in order to demonstrate that he knows his distanced place on the age continuum in relation to the youthful dreamers. Possibly, the point in common between Rulfo and Mastretta is not so much youth aesthetics but a shared interest in heterosexual romance, a salient plot device in Rulfo's own *Pedro Páramo.*

16. Without Jaime Sabines, who won at the unusually advanced age of 38, the average age among men grant winners drops to 26.5, and the median remains at 27.
17. Sally Chivers develops this point in terms of film in *The Silvering Screen*, where she correlates agedness with illness: "Looking old means *being* old, which, in this discourse, means being ill. To age visibly means to admit ill health" (8).
18. Nevertheless, Agustín denies his youthful reputation by boasting that it has taken fifty years to earn his age: "Tengo mis 50 años más bien cumplidos que las arañas, cabrón. Me ha costado 50 años tenerlos. Y me siento muy contento con ellos" (I've put in a hard 50 years, bastard. It took me 50 years to have these. And I feel very happy with them) (L. E. Ramírez 25).
19. Jiménez-Sandoval allegorizes the age difference, with Mariana's modern womanhood set against Carlitos's boyish Mexican fascination with the economic model of the United States (438).
20. Mintz writes that the term *adulthood* is a relative newcomer to the English language, dating only to the 1860s and 1870s (xi). The term *adultez* is rarely used in Spanish, although with new awareness of age discrimination and the boom in children's consumption, including the boom in children's literature begun in the 1980s and 1990s, the term seems to be growing in popularity. Indeed, the Google Ngram Viewer shows a fairly steady and relatively dramatic rise in the frequency of the term *adultez* in Spanish-language sources across the twentieth century. The definition of adulthood and old age, as well as a far-off future, continues to change. A commemorative edition of *Las batallas en el desierto* issued in 2011 changes the father's age from forty-two to forty-eight and switches the unthinkable year of the future from 1980 to 2000 (Saborit).
21. Interestingly, Patrick Dove echoes that age-based national allegory in his reading of *Pedro Páramo*. Dove advances a parallel with Paz's thought on Mexican national immaturity and states that Juan Preciado's journey to find his father is "strikingly reminiscent of the Pazian analogue between nascent nation and adolescent" (93).
22. Kahneman summarizes findings that show that a bad mood sparks different, more critical forms of cognition than a good mood (69). Other twenty-first-century social scientists agree with this principle and propose that critical reasoning skills benefit from close attention to details, as analytic attention sharpens under a mood "at least a notch below happy" (Kashdan and Biswas-Diener 105). Literary critics themselves may think best when under the influence of a bad mood.
23. *Pedro Páramo* is so serious, if by *serious* we mean *pessimistic*, that Nuala Finnegan calls the novel a "relentless negative depiction of the failures of postrevolutionary Mexico" ("Voice"). Similarly, Stephanie Merrim speculatively traces the resonance of existentialism in *Pedro Páramo*, a connection that she suspects is likely since "anguish, bad faith, and alienation . . . suffuse the text" (310).
24. Scholars of Pacheco's poetry sometimes emphasize affect over the cool. Victoria Carpenter views the violence of Mexican history as an affective event that Pacheco's poetry helps preserve in collective memory, because strong emotions in the relevant text "contain the emotional cycle of anger, grief, and shame," with different versions

of a poem emphasizing selectively one or another of these emotions (471). Possibly, Pacheco's poetry defies the cool preferred throughout *Las batallas en el desierto.*

25. A less clinical description of this depressive quality appears in Laura García-Moreno's study of melancholy in *Pedro Páramo.*
26. Fernando Valerio-Holguín's article in *Revista de Literatura Mexicana Contemporánea* takes the bolero in the context of Pacheco's novella so seriously that he concludes that the songs are a means of creating sexual identity for Carlitos, who constructs his love for Mariana as both individual subjectivity and collective experience (26). Robert Weis's concise article on Bimbo bread in Mexico constitutes a brief and delightful read on this subject of kitsch processed food in *Las batallas en el desierto.*
27. Yvette Jiménez de Báez in an article from 1989 points out that the breakdown of the family is central to all of Rulfo's work, which suggests that the point about Pedro's dysfunction applies to the whole of the oeuvre (577). Patricia Reagan reminds us that Debrah Cohn made a similar point in an article published in 1998 (32). This pessimistic view of relationships may extend even to Rulfo's photographs. Amit Thakkar describes the striking isolation of figures in the portraits of people whom Rulfo did not know and hypothesizes a visual principle of isolationist thresholds: "This isolation is connected to exclusion" ("Studium"). In a related project, Paulina Millán emphasizes the reserved, literally distanced approach that Rulfo adopted on contemplating strangers: "when he did photograph men or women he did not know, he never did this from the front—his models are never looking at the camera; he always captured them from a distance, in profile or crouching down." In this sense, Rulfo's photos seem museum-ready: a study of subjects already begging for study because they were aesthetically observed.
28. Alejandro Zamora anticipates my perspective here and writes elegantly that Carlitos's schoolmates have absorbed the adult narrative of hatred that surrounds them: "integran ese odio a su vida de niños en forma de batallas en el desierto: de rechazos, de burlas, de discriminaciones reales" (they integrate that hatred into lives as children in the form of battles in the desert: rejections, jokes, real discrimination) (154). He astutely continues, "Dicho de otro modo, son niños que ya son un poco sus padres, un poco adultos" (To put it another way, they are children who are already a little bit their parents, already a little bit adults). Cynthia Steele shares this opinion and notes that Pacheco's short stories often cover this same thematic of "childhood as a training ground for alienation and corruption" (90).
29. See also María Paz Oliver on the scant criticism dedicated to Fadanelli; she notes that *Lodo* marks a prizewinning exception in Fadanelli's largely popular oeuvre (78). Paz Oliver studies *Lodo* as a novel of digression.
30. Younger brother Alfredo Mancini studied for a master's in legal science at the University of California, Los Angeles, and the older Huberto took classes on pathology at Stanford University.
31. Alfredo repeats an official stance here that appears, for instance, in President Peña Nieto's National Plan for Development, proposed for the five-year period of 2013

to 2018. The plan sets the third of five national goals as the creation of a "Mexico with Quality Education," and the proposed pedagogical orientation emphasizes the notion of productiveness—meaning more a mechanical arts than a liberal arts education.

32. In an essay from *Insolencia* about the contemporary intellectual force of statistics, Fadanelli complains, "Las estadísticas se han convertido en religión para aquellos que tienen pereza de pensar y sirven a cualquiera que las interprete según la orientación de sus propios intereses. Estamos saturados de estadísticas sin sentido, movedizas, alejadas de cualquier acepción de lo complejo" (166–67). (Statistics have become a religion for those too lazy to think, and they serve anyone who interprets them according to the orientation of his/her own interests. We are saturated with meaningless statistics, quicksand, far removed from any sense of the complex.) To handle the complexity that Fadanelli admires, thinkers must engage in the opposite of the "lazy" who prefer the "religion" of percentages. In defense of literature, Fadanelli acknowledges that thanks to the famous and deceased authors' contribution there is such a role as writer, but worries that continued activity is of dubious import in the face of a small reading public: "Y a pesar de la aparente importancia de la literatura, desde hace muchos años los escritores contemporáneos sobreviven a expensas de la histórica celebridad de sus abuelos. Creo que nunca antes en la literatura se había dependido tanto del pasado para encontrarle un poco de sustancia a las cosas. Gracias a la tradición que los soporta (a expensas de la fama que poseen Kafka, Bellow o Tolstoi) los escritores aún pueden pasearse por ahí sin pudor aunque en la actualidad no se les lea: extraño reconocimiento. Acaso porque el *mercado*, en su acepción más pueril, se encuentra saturado de libros y la confusión reinante en la comunicación, sumada a la triste ausencia de lectores, no permite a cada quien tomar el lugar que le corresponde" (18). (And in spite of the apparent importance of literature, for a long time now contemporary writers survive at the expense of their grandfathers' historical celebrity. I think that never before in literature have we depended so much on the past to find some small substance in things. Thanks to the tradition that supports them [at the expense of the fame that Kafka, Bellow, or Tolstoy possess] writers can still walk around out there shamelessly although in today's world no one reads them: strange acknowledgment.) It is tempting to suspect that the lack of change in authors' performance discourages the public's renewed attention to writers.

33. Since the 1990s, Fadanelli has created a series of mediocre adult protagonists, of which Domingo is only one. Fadanelli begins *¿Te veré en el desayuno?* (Will I see you at breakfast?) (1999) with the italicized warning "*La siguiente es la historia de cuatro personas cuyas vidas no merecían haber formado parte de novela alguna*" (*The following is the story of four people whose lives do not deserve to have formed part of any novel*) (7). He also develops the aesthetic in short stories. In "¿Acaso creen que soy un imbécil?" (Maybe they think I'm an idiot?) from the collection *Compraré un rifle* (I'll buy a rifle) (2004), the character Heberto admits his averageness: "Sí, era un hombre mediocre y no le tenía miedo a esa palabra, es más, el ser un mediocre

no tenía gran importancia porque si lo pensaba bien nunca había conocido a un hombre virtuoso y, exceptuando a Dios, no daría la mano a cortar por nadie" (62). (Yes, he was a mediocre man and wasn't afraid of that word, what's more, being mediocre wasn't terribly important because if he thought it over carefully he had never met a virtuous man and, excepting God, he wouldn't stick his hand in the fire for anyone.) Even Fadanelli's most critically celebrated fiction champions the mediocre. The protagonist of *Lodo*, Benito Torrentera, pitilessly assesses his own impotence when it comes to achievement: "Y en esto quisiera ser muy claro: siempre he sido un hombre de mediana inteligencia, incapaz de llevar ningún vicio hasta el extremo. Soy en general un hombre mediocre y no me da pena confesarlo. No soy inteligente ni vicioso" (26). (And in this I would like to be very clear: I have always been a man of medium intelligence, incapable of carrying any vice to the extreme. I am in general a mediocre man and I'm not embarrassed to confess it. I am neither intelligent nor vice ridden.)

34. In an essay from *Insolencia*, Fadanelli playfully proposes the novel as a science that hinges on ambiguity and something beyond the easy rules of formal logic: "Me gustaría imaginarme a la novela como una ciencia . . . de los juicios morales que se adivinan, no que se comprueban; que se ponen en marcha y no que se veneran" (I would like to imagine the novel as a science . . . whose moral judgments are guessed at, but not proven; that are set into motion and that are not venerated) (117).
35. For more analysis of the trope of vagrancy in Fadanelli's work, see Sergio Gutiérrez Negrón. For thought on the place of Fadanelli's protagonists within Mexican confinements, see Paul Goldberg, who notes that, in *Lodo*, Benito ends up caught in the same civilization/barbarism binary that his initial distance from rural settings and indigenous peoples insists upon, with Benito located safely in the civilized category; after all, before committing a double homicide out of jealousy over Eduardo, Benito identifies himself mainly as an underpaid philosophy professor in Mexico City (143). Serrato Córdova also employs the civilization/barbarism binary to discuss the lettered city in *Hotel DF* as under siege from the barbaric violence unleashed by the illicit drug trade (127).
36. In her dissertation, Karen Frazier takes on Fadanelli's *Hotel DF* as a *novela negra* (hardboiled detective novel). Frazier recognizes the misogyny of Fadanelli's oeuvre and comments that *Hotel DF* "seems a bit more subdued than some of his other works in terms of the prevalence of the degraded treatment of women," though the novel still includes "relationships that are defined by the sexual, physical, and emotional abuse of the female partner" (122–23).

CONCLUSION

Epigraph: "Joan Rivers, Live at the Apollo."

1. The call for applications as contained in the documentation of the case required that applicants be under thirty years of age (CME Torres Villarreal 16). This call was published in such places as the newspaper *Excélsior* and the website for Cona-

culta, as the file on Torres Villarreal shows, and thus the argument on behalf of the Centro implies that the applicant should have known better than to attempt to hold a grant when biological demands as a fertile woman would have prevented her from complying with the widely publicized stipulations (8).

2. Alongside the discussion of her regrettable decision, it seems appropriate to remember Domínguez Cuevas's sacrifice and effort. A grant winner from the Centro, Carmen Boullosa, recalls Domínguez Cuevas as a maternal figure who ran the day-to-day operations of the place: "Era una persona lindísima y además era como una figura materna porque éramos tan jóvenes [. . .]. Ella estaba en el segundo piso todo el tiempo en su escritorio. Vivía dedicada al Centro Mexicano de Escritores. Ella era el alma del Centro Mexicano de Escritores. Ella regañaba a Rulfo. Ella regañaba a Elizondo [. . .]. Era una autoridad. Era una autoridad muy sólida, muy linda, muy cálida. Una gente preciosa. [. . .] Le tuve mucho cariño a Martha. Era una mujer muy mayor de otra generación, de otra cultura. Era la secretaria y era muy férrea. Muy férrea. Si alguien no entregaba la material, si no llegaba a la reunión, no se pagaba la beca. Le gustaba ejercer la autoridad" (Boullosa, personal conversation). (She was a lovely person, and besides, she was like a maternal figure because we were so young. . . . She was on the second floor the whole time at her desk. She lived dedicated to the Mexican Center for Writers. She was the soul of the Mexican Center for Writers. She scolded Rulfo. She scolded Elizondo. . . . She was an authority. She was a very solid, very lovely, very warm authority. A beautiful person. . . . I had a lot of affection for Martha. She was a quite older woman from another generation, from another culture. She was the secretary, and she was strong. Very strong. If someone didn't turn in material, if they didn't come to the meeting, the scholarship wasn't paid to them. She liked to exercise authority.)

3. According to Patrick Iber, the more specific reasons were economic: "The CME's closure came in 2005 after reductions in the budget that came from the Secretaría de Educación Pública combined with its failure to secure support from the Fundación Telmex, which did not get assurances from the government that its contribution would be tax exempt" (270).

BIBLIOGRAPHY

"#Ropasucia." *La Tempestad*, 8 Mar. 2017. www.latempestad.mx/ropasucia/. Accessed 17 May 2017.

"La #Ropasucia se lava en México." Cultura. *i-D*, 27 Nov. 2015. i-d.vice.com/es_mx/article/la-ropasucia-se-lava-en-mxico. Accessed 17 May 2017.

Abelardo Hernández, Juan. *Octavio Paz: El poeta que hiló su tiempo*. Mexico City: Conaculta; Random House Mondadori, 2008.

Abenshushan, Vivian. "Defensa del vividor como artista." *Hoja por hoja*, 16 Feb. 2009. Reprinted on *Salon Kritik*, the website of Guillermo Fadanelli, 8 Oct. 2017. salonkritik.net/08–09/2009/02/_defensa_del_vividor_como_arti.php4. Accessed 16 Feb. 2009.

Abenshushan, Vivian, Rodolfo Fonseca, and Gerardo Rod. *Crónicas de la infancia*. Salvador Novo. Colección Poesía e Infancia. Mexico City: SM Ediciones, 2003.

Abrams, Dennis. "Women Buy Books, Men Review Them." *Publishing Perspectives*, 13 Apr. 2014. http://publishingperspectives.com/2015/04/women-buy-books-men-review-them/. Accessed 11 Aug. 2015.

Adán sin fronteras. Directed by Fernando J. Navarro, written by Isabel Maceiras. Cana 22 Televisión Metropolitana, 2004.

Agencia EFE. "A Pacheco se le caen los pantalones minutos antes de recibir el Cervantes." *20 minutos*, 23 Apr. 2010. www.20minutos.es/noticia/686260/0/pacheco/caen/pantalones/. Accessed 25 Nov. 2015.

Aguilar, Enrique. *Elías Nandino: Una vida no/velada*. Mexico City: Grijalbo, 1986.

Aguilar Galván, Carlos. "Entrevista con Héctor Gómez: Salvador Novo desde el escenario." *El Gallo Ilustrado*, *El Día*, 28 Aug. 1994, 2–3.

Aguilar Sosa, Yanet. "Antología de poesía mexicana crea polémica." Letras. *El Universal*, 10 June 2016. www.eluniversal.com.mx/articulo/cultura/letras/2016/06/10/antologia-de-poesia-mexicana-crea-polemica. Accessed 20 Mar. 2017.

———. "Un asomo al alma de Salvador Elizondo." Confabulario. *El Universal*, 11 Mar. 2015. www.eluniversal.com.mx/articulo/cultura/artes-visuales/2015/11/3/un-asomo-al-alma-de-salvador-elizondo. Accessed 16 Apr. 2016.

———. "Carlos Fuentes: El origen de *La región más transparente*." Sección Cultura. *El Universal*, 12 May 2013. archivo.eluniversal.com.mx/cultura/71785.html. Accessed 14 Feb. 2016.

———. "Elizondo, a 10 años de su muerte." Press release, Fondo de Cultura Económica. www.fondodeculturaeconomica.com/Editorial/Prensa/Detalle.aspx?seccion=Detalle&id_desplegado=78343. Accessed 16 Apr. 2016.

———. "En busca de la historia formativa de Monsiváis." *El Universal*, 18 June 2012, 23.

———. "Fundación Juan Rulfo censura a la UNAM." *El Universal*, 7 Apr. 2017. www.eluniversal.com.mx/articulo/cultura/letras/2017/04/6/fundacion-juan-rulfo-censura-la-unam. Accessed 8 Apr. 2017.

———. "Monsi, misógino elegante, no un machín cualquiera." *El Universal*, 7 May 2013, E12.

———. "Vicente Leñero, el joven escritor." Confabulario. *El Universal*, 2 June 2013. confabulario.eluniversal.com.mx/vicente-lenero-el-joven-escritor/. Accessed 16 Apr. 2016.

Agustín Yáñez: Iconografía. Edited by Olivia Ramírez Ramos. Image research by María Luz, Casal Pagés, and Gabriel Yáñez. Biobibliography by Alberto Enrique Perea. Mexico City: Fondo de Cultura Económica, 2014.

Alarcón, Óscar. *Veintiuno: Charlas con 20 escritores*. Puebla, Mexico: Nitro/Press and Benemérita Universidad Autónoma de Puebla, 2012.

Alatorre, Antonio. "Juan José Arreola." *Letras Libres*, Oct. 1999, 84–87. http://www.letraslibres.com/mexico/juan-jose-arreola. Accessed 30 July 2016.

———. *La migraña*. Mexico City: Fondo de Cultura Económica, 2012.

Alfonso Reyes: Iconografía. Image research, bibliography, and text selection by Xavier Guzmán Urbiola, Héctor Perea, and Alba C. de Rojo. Mexico City: Fondo de Cultura Económica, El Colegio de México, 1989.

Allen, Woody, and Marshall Brickman, writers. *Annie Hall*. MGM, 1977. *Daily Script*. http://www.dailyscript.com/scripts/annie_hall.html. Accessed 6 Aug. 2015.

Almaraz, Alejandro. "Retratos del poder." *Alejandro Almaraz*, 2007–2017. alejandroalmaraz.com.ar/es/work/5/retratos-del-poder#4. Accessed 4 Aug. 2015.

Amor, Guadalupe. "La solitaria." In *Galería de títeres*. Mexico City: Fondo de Cultura Económica, 1959. 99–100.

Anderson, Danny J. "Creating Cultural Prestige: Editorial Joaquín Mortiz." *Latin American Research Review* 31, no. 2 (1996): 3–41.

Anderson, Hannah, and Matt Daniels. "Film Dialogue from 2,000 Screenplays, Broken Down by Gender and Age." *The Pudding*, Apr. 2016. pudding.cool/2017/03/film-dialogue/. Accessed 3 May 2017.

Arcq, Teresa. "María Izquierdo, pintora moderna." In *María Izquierdo del Museo de Arte Moderno*. Mexico City: Museo de Arte Moderno, INBA, 2013.

Aristegui Noticias, "'Mariquita' y 'La Vestida,' las palabras que Fox le dijo a Labastaida en 2000." YouTube video. 7 Mar. 2013. www.youtube.com/watch?v=WZ86Yt_oLgc. Accessed 11 June 2018.

Arráncame la vida. Sinopsis. Planeta de Libros. Grupo Planeta 2017. www.planetadelibros.com.mx/libro-arrancame-la-vida/154777. Accessed 30 Dec. 2017.

Arreola, Juan José. *Ramón López Velarde: El poeta, el revolucionario*. 1988. Mexico City: Alfaguara, 1997.

Arreola, Orso. *El último juglar: Memorias de Juan José Arreola*. Mexico City: Diana, 1998.

Asad, Talal. "Free Speech, Blasphemy, and Secular Criticism." In *Is Critique Secular? Blasphemy, Injury, and Free Speech*, edited by Asad. Berkeley: Townsend Center for the Humanities, University of California Press, 2009. 20–63.

Ascencio, Esteban. *Me lo dijo Elena Poniatowska*. 1997. Mexico City: Laberinto, 2014.

Atala, Alejandra. "Su habitación propia: Crónica de un encuentro con Helena Paz Garro, primera parte." In *Voz de la tribu: Revista de la Secretaría de Extension de la UAEM [Universidad Autónoma del Estado de Morelos]*, 2015, 2:67–69.

Atamoros, Noemí. "La Fundación Alica de Nayarit ofreció gran homenaje al poeta Alí Chumacero." Sección B. *Excélsior*, 11 Nov. 1997. CME Chumacero, File 49-1: 54, 55.

Atwood, Margaret. *Payback: Debt and the Shadow Side of Wealth*. Toronto: Anansi Press, 2008.

Augé, Marc. *Everyone Dies Young: Time Without Age*. Translated by Judy Gladding. New York: Columbia University Press, 2016.

Ávila, Sonia. "Año, 1954. Pedro Páramo, en anticipos." *Excélsior*, 21 Sept. 2014, 3.

———. "El museo imaginario de Octavio Paz." *Excélsior*, 9 Sept. 2014, 5.

Avilés, Jaime. "Tres años sin Monsiváis." El Canario Temerario. *El Financiero*, 21 June 2013, 39.

Azar, Héctor. "Alí Chumacero: En los andamios de la creación." *Excélsior*, 20 Aug. 1988. CME Chumacero, File 49-2: 146.

———. "El Centro Mexicano de Escritores." *El Universal*, 13 Aug. 1981. CME Azar, File 16-2: 97.

Barajas, Rafael (El Fisgón). *La princesa Selenita*. Mexico City: Era, 2014.

Barrantes-Martín, Beatriz. "Transformaciones seculares en la Ciudad de México: *Las batallas en el desierto* de José Emilio Pacheco." *Taller de Letras* 34 (2004): 25–37.

Barrera, Reyna. *Salvador Novo: Navaja de la inteligencia*. Mexico City: Plaza y Valdés, 1999.

Barrientos del Monte, Fernando. *Juan Rulfo: El regreso al paraíso*. Guadalajara: Universidad de Guadalajara; Jalisco: Editorial Universitaria, 2007.

Beckman, Ericka. *Capital Fictions: The Literature of Latin America's Export Age*. Minneapolis: University of Minnesota Press, 2013.

———. "*Pedro Páramo* and 'Permanent Primitive Accumulation.'" Paper presented at the Latin American Studies Association Conference, San Juan, Puerto Rico, 2015. www.academia.edu/12762219/Pedro_PpercentC3percentA1ramo_and_Permanent_Primitive_Accumulation—LASA_paper. Accessed 10 May 2018.

———. "Unfinished Transitions: The Dialectics of Rural Modernization in Latin American Fiction." *Modernism/modernity* 23, no. 4 (2016): 813–32.

Bell, Lucy. "The Death of the Storyteller and the Poetics of (Un)Containment: Juan Rulfo's *El llano en llamas*." *Modern Language Review* 107, no. 3 (2012): 815–38.

———. "Photography, Punctum and Shock: Re-Viewing Juan Rulfo's Stories." *Bulletin of Hispanic Studies* 91, no. 4 (2014): 437–52.

Bellatin, Mario. *Las dos Fridas*. Mexico City: Conaculta, 2009.

Benavie, Arthur. *Drugs: America's Holy War*. New York and London: Routledge, 2009.

Benítez Torres, César. "Salvador Novo y la TV." Pantalla Casera. *unomásuno*, 18 Jan. 1994.

Berlant, Lauren. "The Subject of True Feeling: Pain, Privacy, and Politics." In *Cultural Pluralism, Identity Politics, and the Law*, edited by Austin Sarat and Thomas R. Kearns. Ann Arbor: University of Michigan Press, 1999. 49–84.

Berman, Sabina. "Pensar con el pene." Opinion. *Proceso*, 16 Apr. 2017. www.proceso.com.mx/482556/pensar-con-el-pene. Accessed 19 Apr. 2017.

Biagioli, Mario. "Tacit Knowledge, Courtliness, and the Scientist's Body." In *Choreographing History*, edited by Susan Leigh Foster. Bloomington: Indiana University Press, 1995. 69–81.

Biron, Rebecca E. *Murder and Masculinity: Violent Fictions of Twentieth-Century Latin America*. Nashville: Vanderbilt University Press, 2000.

Boldy, Steven. *A Companion to Juan Rulfo*. Woodbridge, UK: Tamesis, 2016.

Bordo, Susan. *The Male Body*. New York: Farrar, Straus and Giroux, 1999.

Boullosa, Carmen. *Cuando me volví mortal*. Mexico City: Cal y Arena, 2010.

———. "Dead Souls." *Nation*, 5 June 2006, 25–28.

———. "Más acá de la nación." *Revista de Estudios Hispánicos* 46 (2012): 55–72.

———. Personal interview. 22 Nov. 2016.

Bowden, Charles, and Molly Molloy, eds. *El Sicario: The Autobiography of a Mexican Assassin*. New York: Nation Books, 2011.

Bowskill, Sarah E. L. *Gender, Nation, and the Formation of the Twentieth-Century Mexican Literary Canon*. London: Modern Humanities Research Association, W. S. Maney & Son, 2011.

Bradu, Fabienne. "La vida que vale: Autobiografías mexicanas." *Literatura Mexicana* 22, no. 2 (2011): 183–201.

Brandes, Stanley. "Drink, Abstinence, and Male Identity in Mexico City." In *Changing Men and Masculinities in Latin America*, edited by Matthew C. Gutmann. Durham: Duke University Press, 2003. 153–76.

Bretón, Salvador. "Entrevista con José Agustín: De *La tumba* a *La vida con mi viuda*." *El Universo del Búho*, 22 May 2011, 5–17.

Brown, Brené. *Daring Greatly: How the Courage to Be Vulnerable Transforms the Way We Live, Love, Parent, and Lead*. New York: Gotham Books [Penguin], 2012.

Brown, Wendy. *Undoing the Demos: Neoliberalism's Stealth Revolution*. New York: Zone Books, 2015.

Brugnolo, Stefano, and Laura Luche. "Los muertos que no mueren en *Pedro Páramo* y en *Cien años de soledad*." *Taller de Letras* 46 (2010): 126–48.

Bucio, Érika P. "Eternizan a Monsiváis en el Museo de Cera." *Reforma*, 26 Jan. 2013, 19.

———. "Va biblioteca de Monsiváis a La Ciudadela." *Reforma*, 10 Mar. 2012, 19.

Bunker, Steven B. *Creating Mexican Consumer Culture in the Age of Porfirio Díaz*. Albuquerque: University of New Mexico Press, 2012.

Burgin, Angus. *The Great Persuasion: Reinventing Free Markets since the Depression*. Cambridge, MA: Harvard University Press, 2012.

Burns, David D. *Feeling Good: The New Mood Therapy*. 1980. Rev. and updated. Preface by Aaron T. Beck. New York: Avon Books, 1999.

Butler, Judith. *Gender Trouble: Feminism and the Subversion of Identity*. New York and London: Routledge, 1990.

Cabrera, Rafael. "Helena Paz Garro, la vida entre dos fuegos." *Animal Político*, 31 Mar. 2014. www.animalpolitico.com/2014/03/helena-paz-garro-la-vida-entre-dos-fuegos/. Accessed 12 July 2016.

Cain, Susan. *Quiet: The Power of Introverts in a World That Can't Stop Talking*. New York: Crown, 2012.

Callahan, David. *The Givers: Wealth, Power, and Philanthropy in a New Gilded Age*. New York: Alfred A. Knopf, 2017.

Calomiris, Charles W., and Stephen H. Haber. *Fragile by Design: The Political Origins of Banking Crises and Scarce Credit*. Princeton: Princeton University Press, 2014.

Calvillo, Ana Luisa. "El inicio psicodélico de José Agustín en 1968." sábado. *unomásuno*, 15 Nov. 1997, 22–23.

Camacho, Fernando. "Recupera la beca la joven Ninett Torres Villarreal." *La Jornada*, 25 Sept. 2004. CME Torres Villarreal, 22.

Camacho Olivares, Alfredo. "Soy un tigre sin jaula: Alí Chumacero." *Excélsior*, 19 Oct. 1996, 9-B. CME Chumacero, File 49-1: 25.

Campo, Xorge del. "La narrativa joven de México." *Studies in Short Fiction* 8, no. 1 (1971): 180–98.

Campos, Isaac. *Home Grown: Marijuana and the Origins of Mexico's War on Drugs*. Chapel Hill: University of North Carolina Press, 2012.

Carballo, Emmanuel. "Prólogo." In *Marco Antonio Montes de Oca*, by Marco Antonio Montes de Oca. Mexico City: Empresas Editoriales, 1967. 5–12.

———. "Prólogo." In *Salvador Elizondo*, by Salvador Elizondo. Mexico City: Empresas Editoriales, 1966. 5–12.

———. "Prólogo." In *Tomás Mojarro*, by Tomás Mojarro. Mexico City: Empresas Editoriales, 1966. 5–10.

———. "Prólogo." In *Vicente Leñero*, by Vicente Leñero. Mexico City: Empresas Editoriales, 1967. 5–12.

———. "Salvador Novo." In *Diecinueve protagonistas de la literatura mexicana del siglo XX*. Mexico City: Empresas Editoriales, 1965. 229–62.

———. *Ya nada es igual: Memorias (1929–1953)*. 1994. Mexico City: Fondo de Cultura Económica, 2004.

"Carlos Fuentes." *Wikipedia*, 13 Oct. 2015. en.wikipedia.org/wiki/Carlos_Fuentes. Accessed 25 Dec. 2015.

Carlos Pellicer: Iconografía. Introduction by Carlos Monsiváis. Image and bibliographical research by Alba C. de Rojo. Mexico City: Fondo de Cultura Económica, 2003.

Carpenter, Victoria. "'Y el olor de la sangre manchaba el aire': Tlatelolco 1521 and 1968 in José Emilio Pacheco's 'Lectura de los "Cantares Mexicanos."'" *Bulletin of Hispanic Studies* 95, no. 4 (2018): 451–74.

Carreño, Manuel Antonio. *Manual de urbanidad y buenas maneras para uso de la juventud de ambos sexos en el cual se encuentran las principales reglas de civilidad y etiqueta que deben observarse en las diversas situaciones sociales. Precedido de un breve tratado sobre los deberes morales del hombre.* 38th ed. [1932]. Mexico City: Editorial Patria, 1983.

Carruthers, Bruce G., and Laura Ariovich. *Money and Credit: A Sociological Approach.* Cambridge, UK, and Malden, MA: Polity Press, 2010.

Casi Divas. Directed by Issa Lopéz. Columbia Pictures, 2008.

Castañeda, Jorge G. *Mañana Forever? Mexico and the Mexicans.* New York: Alfred A. Knopf, 2011.

Castellblanch, Ramón. "Gender Equity in Mexico." Letters to the Editor. *New York Times*, 9 May 2017, A22. www.nytimes.com/2017/05/08/opinion/gender-equity-in-mexico.html?emc=edit_tnt_20170509&nlid=27776096&tntemail0=y&_r=0. Accessed 10 May 2017.

Castillo, Debra A., and Stuart A. Day. "Introduction: A New Kind of Public Intellectual?" In *Mexican Public Intellectuals*, edited by Castillo and Day. New York: Palgrave Macmillan, 2014. 1–13.

"Centro Mexicano de Escritores." In *Enciclopedia de la literatura en México.* Fundación para las Letras Mexicanas. www.elem.mx/institucion/datos/308. Accessed 11 May 2017.

"Centro Mexicano de Escritores: Bases del concurso, 1975–1976, XXV aniversario." Mexico City, 1975.

"Centro Mexicano de Escritores: XXVII Concurso Nacional, 1978." Mexico City, 1978.

Chivers, Sally. *The Silvering Screen: Old Age and Disability in Cinema.* Toronto: University of Toronto Press, 2011.

"Clementina Díaz y de Ovando." *Wikipedia*, 17 Sept. 2016. es.wikipedia.org/w/index.php?title=Clementina_Díaz_y_de_Ovando&oldid=93703561. Accessed 11 Oct. 2016.

CME Agustín Ramírez, José. Archive Centro Mexicano de Escritores. Box 31, File 178-2. Fondo Reservado of the Biblioteca Nacional de México, Universidad Nacional Autónoma de México, Mexico City.

CME Aridjis, Homero. Archive Centro Mexicano de Escritores. Box 1, File 8. Fondo Reservado of the Biblioteca Nacional de México, UNAM, Mexico City.

CME Arreola, Juan José. Archive Centro Mexicano de Escritores. Box 2, Files 10-1, 10-2, 10-3. Fondo Reservado of the Biblioteca Nacional de México, UNAM, Mexico City.

CME Avilés Fabila, René. Archive Centro Mexicano de Escritores. Box 3, File 12-1. Fondo Reservado of the Biblioteca Nacional de México, UNAM, Mexico City.

CME Ayala Blanco, Jorge. Archive Centro Mexicano de Escritores. Box 3, File 15. Fondo Reservado of the Biblioteca Nacional de México, UNAM, Mexico City.

CME Azar, Héctor. Archive Centro Mexicano de Escritores. Box 4, Files 16-1, 16-2. Fondo Reservado of the Biblioteca Nacional de México, UNAM, Mexico City.

CME Bonifaz Nuño, Rubén. Archive Centro Mexicano de Escritores. Box 6, File 29. Fondo Reservado of the Biblioteca Nacional de México, UNAM, Mexico City.

CME Boullosa, Carmen. Archive Centro Mexicano de Escritores. Box 6, File 30. Fondo Reservado of the Biblioteca Nacional de México, UNAM, Mexico City.

CME Carrasco Teja, Alfredo. Archive Centro Mexicano de Escritores. Box 8, Files 42, 43. Fondo Reservado of the Biblioteca Nacional de México, UNAM, Mexico City.

CME Carrión Bogard, Ulises. Archive Centro Mexicano de Escritores. Box 4, File 45. Fondo Reservado of the Biblioteca Nacional de México, UNAM, Mexico City.

CME Castillo Macías, Germán. Archive Centro Mexicano de Escritores. Box 9, File 47. Fondo Reservado of the Biblioteca Nacional de México, UNAM, Mexico City.

CME Chumacero, Alí. Archive Centro Mexicano de Escritores. Box 9, Files 49-1, 49-2. Fondo Reservado of the Biblioteca Nacional de México, UNAM, Mexico City.

CME Cross, Elsa. Archive Centro Mexicano de Escritores. Box 10, File 51. Fondo Reservado of the Biblioteca Nacional de México, UNAM, Mexico City.

CME Dávila, Amparo. Archive Centro Mexicano de Escritores. Box 11, File 56. Fondo Reservado of the Biblioteca Nacional de México, UNAM, Mexico City.

CME Díaz y de Ovando, Clementina. Archive Centro Mexicano de Escritores. Box 11, File 59. Fondo Reservado of the Biblioteca Nacional de México, UNAM, Mexico City.

CME Dolujanoff, Emma. Archive Centro Mexicano de Escritores. Box 11, File 60. Fondo Reservado of the Biblioteca Nacional de México, UNAM, Mexico City.

CME Fuentes, Carlos. Archive Centro Mexicano de Escritores. Box 15. File 75-1. Fondo Reservado of the Biblioteca Nacional de México, UNAM, Mexico City.

CME Galindo, Sergio. Archive Centro Mexicano de Escritores. Box 16. File 77-1. Fondo Reservado of the Biblioteca Nacional de México, UNAM, Mexico City.

CME García Ponce, Juan. Archive Centro Mexicano de Escritores. Box 17. File 82-2. Fondo Reservado of the Biblioteca Nacional de México, UNAM, Mexico City.

CME Guzmán, Humberto. Archive Centro Mexicano de Escritores. Box 19, File 100. Fondo Reservado of the Biblioteca Nacional de México, UNAM, Mexico City.

CME Leñero, Vicente. Archive Centro Mexicano de Escritores. Box 21, File 110-2. Fondo Reservado of the Biblioteca Nacional de México, UNAM, Mexico City.

CME Mastretta, Ángeles. Archive Centro Mexicano de Escritores. Box 24, File 130. Fondo Reservado of the Biblioteca Nacional de México, UNAM, Mexico City.

CME Parra Ramírez, Gabriel. Archive Centro Mexicano de Escritores. Box 29, File 167. Fondo Reservado of the Biblioteca Nacional de México, UNAM, Mexico City.

CME Robles, Martha. Archive Centro Mexicano de Escritores. Box 34, File 192. Fondo Reservado of the Biblioteca Nacional de México, UNAM, Mexico City.

CME Rulfo, Juan. Archive Centro Mexicano de Escritores. Box 35, File 203-1. Fondo Reservado of the Biblioteca Nacional de México, UNAM, Mexico City.

CME Sabido, Miguel. Archive Centro Mexicano de Escritores. Box 37, File 205. Fondo Reservado of the Biblioteca Nacional de México, UNAM, Mexico City.

CME Sabines, Jaime. Archive Centro Mexicano de Escritores. Box 37, File 206-1. Fondo Reservado of the Biblioteca Nacional de México, UNAM, Mexico City.

CME Torres Villarreal, Ninett. Archive Centro Mexicano de Escritores. Box 41, File 239. Fondo Reservado of the Biblioteca Nacional de México, UNAM, Mexico City.

CME Tovar, Juan. Archive Centro Mexicano de Escritores. Box 42, File 241. Fondo Reservado of the Biblioteca Nacional de México, UNAM, Mexico City.

CME Treviño, Ana Cecilia. Archive Centro Mexicano de Escritores. Box 42, File 243. Fondo Reservado of the Biblioteca Nacional de México, UNAM, Mexico City.

CME Vallarino Almada, Roberto. Archive Centro Mexicano de Escritores. Box 42, File 248. Fondo Reservado of the Biblioteca Nacional de México, UNAM, Mexico City.

CME Volpi Escalante, Jorge Luis. Archive Centro Mexicano de Escritores. Box 44, File 260. Fondo Reservado of the Biblioteca Nacional de México, UNAM, Mexico City.

Cobin, John. "Taxes on Books in Chile." *Escape America Now*, 10 May 2012. escapeamericanow.info/taxes-on-books-in-chile/. Accessed 20 Apr. 2017.

Cohen, Sandro. "Huberto Batis, pornotólogo." *Sandro Cohen Blogspot*, 25 July 2007. sandrocohen.blogspot.mx/2007/07/huberto-batis-pornontlogo.html. Accessed 26 July 2016.

———. "Martha Robles *dixit*." *unomásuno*, 6 Nov. 1993. CME Robles, 17.

Cohn, Deborah N. *The Latin American Literary Boom and U.S. Nationalism During the Cold War*. Nashville: Vanderbilt University Press, 2012.

———. "Paradise Lost and Regained: The Old Order and Memory in Katherine Anne Porter's Miranda Stories and Juan Rulfo's *Pedro Páramo*." *Hispanofilia* 124, no. 1 (1998): 65–86.

"Colegio de México." *La Jornada*, 8 Sept. 2014, 20.

Coloroso, Barbara. *The Bully, the Bullied, and the Bystander: From Preschool to High School—How Parents and Teachers Can Help Break the Cycle of Violence*. Updated ed., 2003. HarperCollins ebooks, 2010.

"Concede Corte amparo para uso recreativo de la mariguana." *Diario de México*, 11 Apr. 2018. www.diariodemexico.com/concede-corte-amparo-para-uso-recreativo-de-la-mariguana. Accessed 14 May 2018.

"Concluyen las celebraciones por el centenario de Octavio Paz." *Filias*, *Milenio*, 2 Dec. 2014, 10.

Covey, Stephen R. *The Seven Habits of Highly Effective People: Restoring the Character Ethic*. 1989. New foreword and afterword. New York: Free Press, 2004.

Crowston, Clare Haru. *Credit, Fashion, Sex: Economies of Regard in Old Regime France*. Durham: Duke University Press, 2013.

Daniel Cosío Villegas: Iconografía. Image research and text selection by Alba C. de Rojo. Biography and bibliography by Adolfo Castañón. Mexico City: Fondo de Cultura Económica, 2001.

Dargis, Manohla. "Report Finds Wide Diversity Gap Among 2014's Top-Grossing Films." Critic's Notebook. *New York Times*, 5 Aug. 2015. Accessed 6 Aug. 2015.

Deb, Sopan, and Marina Franco. "'Penis Seat' Causes Double Takes on Mexico City Subway." *New York Times*, 31 Mar. 2017. www.nytimes.com/2017/03/31/world/americas/penis-seat-mexico-city-harassment.html. Accessed 11 May 2018.

Debroise, Olivier. *Mexican Suite: A History of Photography in Mexico*. Austin: University of Texas Press, 2001.

De Grazia, Edward. *Girls Lean Back Everywhere: The Law of Obscenity and the Assault on Genius*. New York: Random House, 1992.

DeJean, Joan. *The Essence of Style: How the French Invented High Fashion, Fine Food, Chic Cafés, Style, Sophistication, and Glamour*. New York: Free Press, 2005.

Delman, Edward. "Is Smoking Weed a Human Right? Why the Mexican Supreme Court Thinks the Answer Is Yes." *Atlantic*, 9 Nov. 2015. www.theatlantic.com/international/archive/2015/11/mexico-marijuana-legal-human-right/415017/. Accessed 12 Apr. 2016.

Los demonios del Edén. Directed by Alejandra Isla. Instituto Mexicano de Cinematografía, Producciones Volcán, 2007.

Díaz-Guerrero, Rogelio. "Psicología del mexicano." In *Anatomía del mexicano*, selected and with a prologue by Roger Bartra. Mexico City: Plaza y Janés, 2002. 281–87.

Diener, Ed, and Robert Biswas-Diener. *Happiness: Unlocking the Mysteries of Psychological Wealth*. Malden, MA: Blackwell, 2008.

Diners Club advertisement. *El Heraldo de México*, 7 July 1972, 2C. CME Azar, File 16-2: 115.

Docter, Mary. "José Emilio Pacheco: A Poetics of Reciprocity." *Hispanic Review* 70, no. 3 (2002): 373–92.

Domínguez Cuevas, Martha. *Los becarios del Centro Mexicano de Escritores, 1952–1997*. Mexico City: Aldus, Cabos Sueltos, 1999.

———. Personal interview. 23 July 2016. Xalapa, Veracruz.

Domínguez Michael, Christopher. "Cliente de su ingenio: Salvador Novo (1904–1974)." Convivio. *Letras Libres*, Dec. 2004. www.letraslibres.com/mexico-espana/cliente-su-ingenio-salvador-novo-1904–1974. Accessed 21 July 2016.

———. *Octavio Paz en su siglo*. Mexico City: [Aguilar] Penguin Random House Grupo Editorial México, 2014.

———. "Prólogo." In *Camaradas: Soledad*, by Rubén Salazar Mallén. Mexico City: Conaculta, 2010. 9–35.

———. *William Pescador*. Mexico City: Era, 1997.

Domínguez-Ruvalcaba, Héctor. *Modernity and the Nation in Mexican Representations of Masculinity: From Sensuality to Bloodshed*. New York: Palgrave Macmillan, 2007.

Dove, Patrick. "Reflections on the Origin: Transculturation and Tragedy in *Pedro Páramo*." *Angelaki* 6, no. 1 (2001): 91–110.

Dowd, Maureen. "The Women of Hollywood Speak Out." *New York Times*, 20 Nov. 2015. www.nytimes.com/2015/11/22/magazine/the-women-of-hollywood-speak-out.html?hp&action=click&pgtype=Homepage&clickSource=story-heading&module=second-column-region®ion=top-news&WT.nav=top-news. Accessed 20 Nov. 2015.

Dowd, Nancy. *The Man Question: Male Subordination and Privilege*. New York: New York University Press, 2010.

Dowd, Nancy E., Nancy Levit, and Ann C. McGinley. "Feminist Legal Theory Meets Masculinities Theory." In *Masculinities and the Law: A Multidimensional Approach*, edited by Frank Rudy Cooper and Ann C. McGinley. Foreword by Michael Kimmel. New York: New York University Press, 2012. 25–50.

Dowdy, Michael. "'Of the Smog': José Emilio Pacheco's Concussive Poetics of Mexico City." *Hispanic Review* 79, no. 2 (2011): 291–316.

Durán, Manuel. *Genio y figura de Amado Nervo*. Buenos Aires: Editorial Universitaria de Buenos Aires, 1968.

Edsall, Thomas B. "When the President Is Ignorant of His Own Ignorance." Opinion. *New York Times*, 30 Mar. 2017. www.nytimes.com/2017/03/30/opinion/when-the-president-is-ignorant-of-his-own-ignorance.html?action=click&pgtype=Homepage&clickSource=story-heading&module=opinion-c-col-right-region®ion=opinion-c-col-right-region&WT.nav=opinion-c-col-right-region&_r=0. Accessed 30 Mar. 2017.

Efraín Huerta: Iconografía. Image research, prologue, chronology, and text selection by Emiliano Delgadillo Martínez. Mexico City: Fondo de Cultura Económica, 2014.

Elizondo, Salvador. *Autobiografía precoz*. 1966. Mexico City: Editorial Aldus, 2000.

———. *Camera lucida*. 1983. 3rd ed. Mexico City: Fondo de Cultura Económica, 2001.

———. *Salvador Elizondo*. Prologue by Emmanuel Carballo. Mexico City: Empresas Editoriales, 1966.

Enrigue, Álvaro. *Valiente clase media: Dinero, letras y cursilería*. Barcelona: Editorial Anagrama, 2013.

"En sólo dos años se convirtió en escritor." *Proceso*, 13 May 2000. www.proceso.com.mx/183270/en-solo-dos-anos-se-convirtio-en-escritor. Accessed 5 July 2016.

Epple, Juan Armando. "De Santa a Mariana: La Ciudad de México como utopía traicionada." *Revista Chilena de Literatura* 54 (1999): 31–42.

Espinosa, Jorge Luis, III. "Luisa Josefina Hernández: Fueron pocos los escritores de México que no pasaron alguna vez por el CME." *unomásuno*, 19 Feb. 1994, 24.

Estrada, Oswaldo. "Tragos amargos y ebrios encargos: Metáforas de la bebida en *El llano en llamas* de Juan Rulfo." In *Aguas santas de la creación*. Mérida: Dirección Cultural del Ayuntamiento de Mérida, UC Mexicanistas Intercampus Research Program, 2010. 207–22.

Faber, Sebastiaan. *Exile and Cultural Hegemony: Spanish Intellectuals in Mexico, 1939–1975*. Nashville: Vanderbilt University Press, 2002.

Fadanelli, Guillermo. "¿Acaso creen que soy un imbécil?" In *Compraré un rifle*. Barcelona: Anagrama, 2004. 59–69.

———. *Al final del periférico*. Mexico City: Penguin Random House, 2016.

———. "Breve diccionario de autores anómalos." Terlenka. *El Universal*, 13 Feb. 2012, E13.

———. *Clarisa ya tiene un muerto*. 2000. Mexico City: Ediciones B, 2012.

———. *Educar a los topos*. Barcelona: Anagrama, 2006.

———. *Elogio de la vagancia*. Mexico City: Mondadori, 2008.

———. *En busca de un lugar habitable*. 2006. Oaxaca: Almadía, 2012.

———. *El hombre nacido en Danzig*. Mexico City: Almadía; Conaculta, 2014.

———. *Hotel DF*. Mexico City: Mondadori, 2010.

———. *Insolencia: Literatura y mundo*. Oaxaca: Almadía, 2012.

———. "Interroguen a Samantha." In *Compraré un rifle*. Barcelona: Anagrama, 2004. 15–22.

———. *Lodo*. Madrid: Debate, 2002.

———. *Malacara*. Barcelona: Anagrama, 2007.

———. "Mi mamá me mima." In *El día que la vea la voy a matar*. 1992. Mexico City: Moho, 2010. 25–29.

———. *Mis mujeres muertas*. Mexico City: Random House Mondadori, 2012.

———. "Mi tía Clarita." In *El día que la vea la voy a matar*. 1992. Mexico City: Moho, 2010. 38–49.

———. "Monsiváis." Terlenka. *El Universal*, 15 June 2015, E13.

———. "Muebles, de un lugar a otro." In *Más alemán que Hitler*. 2001. Mexico City: Cal y Arena, 2009. 23–30.

———. *Para ella todo sueña a Frank Pourcel*. 1998. Mexico City: Ediciones B, 2012.

———. *¿Te veré en el desayuno?* 1999. Oaxaca: Almadía, 2009.

"Fallece la historiadora Clementina Díaz y de Ovando, miembro de Academia Mexicana de la lengua." *SinEmbargo*, 19 Feb. 2012. http://www.sinembargo.mx/19-02-2012/155374. Accessed 7 Oct. 2017.

Federal Bureau of Investigation. JFK Assassination System Identification Form. Mary Ferrell Foundation, Assassination Archives and Research Center, NARA Record Number 124-10220-10481, pp. 1–5. https://www.maryferrell.org/showDoc.html?docId=129794#relPageId=1&tab=page. Accessed 25 Sept. 2017.

Fernández, Bernardo (Bef). "25 razones para no ver la televisión (mexicana)." *Monorama* (blog). 10 Aug. 2005. http://monorama.blogspot.com/2005/08/25-razones-para-no-ver-la-televisin.html. Accessed 6 Oct. 2017.

———. *Uncle Bill*. Mexico City: Sexto Piso, 2014.

Fernández, Claudia, and Andrew Paxman. *El Tigre: Emilio Azcárraga y su imperio Televisa*. Mexico City: Grijalbo; Penguin Random House Grupo Editorial México, 2013.

Fernández, Marcial. "Yo soy el último mohicano de la inteligencia: Roberto Vallarino." *unomásuno*, 16 Oct. 2001. CME Vallarino Almada, 6.

Fernández, Sergio. "Historia de un corazón promiscuo." In *Ensayo literario mexicano*, selected by John S. Brushwood, Evodio Escalante, Hernán Lara Zavala, and Federico Patán. Edited with prologue and notes by Federico Patán. Mexico City: Universidad Nacional Autónoma de México; Universidad Veracruzana; Aldus, 2001. 91–109.

Filipovic, Jill. "The All-Male Photo Op Isn't a Gaffe. It's a Strategy." Opinion. *New York Times*, 27 Mar. 2017. www.nytimes.com/2017/03/27/opinion/the-all-male-photo-op-isnt-a-gaffe-its-a-strategy.html?_r=0. Accessed 8 Oct. 2017.

Fineman, Stephen. *Organizing Age*. New York: Oxford University Press, 2011.

Finnegan, Nuala. Introduction to *Rethinking Juan Rulfo's Creative World: Prose, Photography, Film*, edited by Dylan Brennan and Nuala Finnegan. London: Modern Humanities Research Association and Routledge, 2016. Ebook.

———. "Voice, Authority, and the Destruction of Community in *Cré na Cille* (The Dirty Dust) by Máirtín Ó Cadhain and *Pedro Páramo* by Juan Rulfo." In *Rethinking Juan Rulfo's Creative World: Prose, Photography, Film*, edited by Dylan Brennan and Nuala Finnegan. Cambridge: Modern Humanities Research Association and Routledge, 2016. Ebook.

Fisher, Andrew B. "Keeping and Losing One's Head: Composure and Emotional Outbursts as Political Performance in Late-Colonial Mexico." In *Emotions and Daily Life in Colonial Mexico*, edited by Javier Villa-Flores and Sonya Lipsett-Rivera. Albuquerque: University of New Mexico Press, 2014. 168–97.

Fishman, Lois R. "Searching for Juan Rulfo." *Américas* 36, no. 7 (1984): 28–33.

Fornäs, Karin Becker, Erling Bjurström, and Hillevi Ganetz. *Consuming Media: Communication, Shopping, and Everyday Life*. Oxford: Berg, 2007.

Fraiman, Susan. *Cool Men and the Second Sex*. New York: Columbia University Press, 2003.

Franco, Jean. "El viaje al país de los muertos." In *La ficción de la memoria: Juan Rulfo ante la crítica*, edited with a prologue by Federico Campbell. Mexico City: Era/Coordinación de Difusión Cultural UNAM, 2003. 136–55.

Frazier, Karen Marie. "Neoliberal Noir: Bearing Witness to Systemic and Subjective Violence in Mexico." Dissertation, University of Michigan, 2016.

Friedman, Megan. "What Dr. Christine Blasey Ford and Anita Hill Saw During Their Hearings Was Eerily Similar: Many, Many Men." *Elle*, 27 Sept. 2018. www.elle.com/culture/career-politics/a23493926/christine-blasey-ford-anita-hill-hearings-photos/. Accessed 27 Oct. 2018.

Friis, Ronald J. *José Emilio Pacheco and the Poets of the Shadows*. Lewisburg, PA: Bucknell University Press, 2001.

Fudacz, Jamie. "Between Place and Non-Place: The Fictions of Guillermo Fadanelli." *Interférences littéraires/Literaire interferenties* 13 (2014): 117–32.

Fuentes, Carlos. *La muerte de Artemio Cruz*. 1962. Barcelona: Bruguera, 1982.

———. *Myself with Others: Selected Essays*. New York: Farrar, Straus and Giroux, 1988.

———. "Tiempo mexicano." 1959. In *Anatomía del mexicano*, selected with a prologue by Roger Bartra. Barcelona: Plaza y Janés, 2002. 257–65.

Fuentes La Roche, Cristina, and Rodolfo Mendoza, eds. *Carlos Fuentes y la novela latinoamericana*. Photographs by Daniel Mordzinski. Xalapa: Universidad Veracruzana, 2013. 44–46.

Gamboa, Federico. *Santa*. Mexico City: Grijalbo, 1979.

Gámez, Silvia Isabel. "El feminismo de Monsi." *Reforma*, 9 May 2013, 23.

———. "Las interpretaciones de la novela no se agotan: Un páramo de enigmas." *Reforma*, 14 Mar. 2015, 16.

García, Clara Guadalupe. *Nellie: El caso Campobello*. Mexico City: Cal y Arena, 2000.

García, Jacobo G. "Entrevista: Elena Poniatowska, 'No tengo más que preguntas sobre las cosas.'" *El Mundo*, 18 Apr. 2014. www.elmundo.es/cultura/2014/04/18/534ff4e4e2704e2e468b4572.html. Accessed 9 Mar. 2017.

García Beraza, Felipe. "Juan Rulfo en el Centro Mexicano de Escritores." 1983. CME Rulfo, 134–39.

García Márquez, Gabriel. "Nostalgia de Juan Rulfo." *Araucaria* 33 (1986). Reprinted as "60 años de Pedro Páramo," *Arcadia* 9 (Apr. 2015). www.revistaarcadia.com/libros/articulo/proposito-60-anos-pedro-paramo/43997. Accessed 9 Mar. 2017.

García-Moreno, Laura. "Melancolía y desencanto en *Pedro Páramo*." *Revista Canadiense de Estudios Hispánicos* 30, no. 3 (2006): 497–519.

García Peña, Lilia Leticia. "'Normales' y estigmatizados: Los símbolos de la estigmatización social en Juan Rulfo." *Espiral: Estudios sobre Estado y Sociedad* 22, no. 64 (2015): 41–66.

García Ramírez, Sergio. "Celestino Porte Petit Candaudap." In *Nuestros maestros*. Vol. 2. Mexico City: Universidad Nacional Autónoma de México, 1992. 217–21.

García Tsao, Leonardo. "Sólo con tu pajero." Espectáculos. *La Jornada*, 22 June 2001, 15.

Garibay, Ricardo. *Cómo se gana la vida*. Mexico City: Editorial Joaquín Mortiz, 1992.

———. *Fiera infancia y otros años*. 1982. Mexico City: Conaculta, 1994.

Garmabella, José Ramón. "Veo un México enfermo, incongruente, ruinoso: Avilés." *Excélsior*, 9 Nov. 2003, 10-A, 11-A, 15-A. CME Avilés Fabila, 10–11.

Garrigan, Shelley E. *Collecting Mexico: Museums, Monuments, and the Creation of National Identity*. Minneapolis: University of Minnesota Press, 2012.

Garza, José. "La poesía, para escucharse más que leerse: Chumacero." *La Jornada*, 15 Oct. 1997. CME Chumacero, File 49-1: 53.

Ghosh, Amitav. *The Great Derangement: Climate Change and the Unthinkable*. Chicago: University of Chicago Press, 2016.

Gimme the Power. Written and directed by Olallo Rubio. DVD. Mexico City: Amateur Films, 2012.

Giry, Stéphanie. "An Odd Bird." *Legal Affairs: The Magazine at the Intersection of Law and Life*, Sept. 2002. https://www.legalaffairs.org/issues/September-October-2002/story_giry_sepoct2002.msp. Accessed 27 Sept. 2017.

Global Gender Gap Report 2016. "Rankings." World Economic Forum. reports.weforum.org/global-gender-gap-report-2016/rankings/. Accessed 10 May 2017.

Goldberg, Paul. "La conciencia globalizada: Comportamiento y consume en *Lodo* de Guillermo Fadanelli." *Hispanic Journal* 26, nos. 1–2 (2005): 137–49.

Goldman, Francisco. *The Interior Circuit: A Mexico City Chronicle*. New York: Grove Press, 2014.

———. *Say Her Name*. New York: Grove Press, 2011.

Goldsmith, Kenneth. *Uncreative Writing: Managing Language in the Digital Age*. New York: Columbia University Press, 2011.

Gómez Jiménez, Jorge. "La extraña muerte de Natasha Fuentes." *JorgeLetralia: Notas marginales sobre literatura y temas afines*, 26 Aug. 2005. jorgeletralia.net/2005/08/26/la-extrana-muerte-de-natasha-fuentes/. Accessed 12 July 2016.

Gonzales, Michael J. "Imagining Mexico in 1910: Visions of the Patria in the Centennial Celebration in Mexico City." *Journal of Latin American Studies* 39, no. 3 (2007): 495–533.

González, Isabel. "SCJN determina que expresiones 'puñal' o 'maricón' fomentan la discriminación." *Excélsior*, 7 Mar. 2013. www.excelsior.com.mx/nacional/2013/03/07/887690. Accessed 5 Apr. 2016.

González, Keri. "Memorias entrecruzadas: *La amortajada* y *Pedro Páramo*." *Cuadernos Americanos* 25, no. 3 (2011): 89–111.

González Boixó, José Carlos. "Aclaraciones de Juan Rulfo a su novela *Pedro Páramo*." In *Pedro Páramo*, by Juan Rulfo. 2002. 24th ed. enl. Madrid: Cátedra, 2012. 247–51.

———. "Cronología de la 'Historia.'" In *Pedro Páramo* by Juan Rulfo. 2002. 24th ed. enl. Madrid: Cátedra, 2012. 181–90.

———. "Introducción." In *Pedro Páramo*, by Juan Rulfo. 2002. 24th ed. enl. Madrid: Cátedra, 2012. 11–54.

González G., Susana. "Adquirió empresa de Carlos Slim otros ocho inmuebles en el Centro Histórico." *La Jornada*, 21 Oct. 2007. http://www.jornada.unam.mx/2007/10/21/index.php?section=capital&article=030n1cap. Accessed 12 Apr. 2015.

González Rodríguez, Sergio. "*Barracuda* en Moho" and "Escalera al Cielo." *El Ángel*, *Reforma*, 8 Feb. 1998, 1.

———. *El hombre sin cabeza*. Barcelona: Anagrama, 2009.

———. "Novísimas amistades." Cartas a Minerva. *Excélsior*, 26 July 1991, 1, 8.

González Suárez, Mario. *De la infancia*. Mexico City: Tusquets, 1998.

Graeber, David. *Debt: The First 5,000 Years*. Brooklyn: Melville House, 2011.

———. *The Utopia of Rules: On Technology, Stupidity, and the Secret Joys of Bureaucracy*. Brooklyn: Melville House, 2015.

Graff Zivin, Erin. *Figurative Inquisitions: Conversion, Torture, and Truth in the Luso-Hispanic Atlantic*. Evanston: Northwestern University Press, 2014.

Greenblatt, Stephen. *Hamlet in Purgatory*. 2011. Enl. ed., with a new preface by Greenblatt. Princeton: Princeton University Press, 2013. Kindle ed.

Gregory, Alice. "A History of Classical Music (the Women-Only Version)." *New York Times*, 2 Dec. 2016. www.nytimes.com/interactive/2016/12/02/arts/music/01womencomposers.html. Accessed 3 Dec. 2016.

Griselda Álvarez: Imágenes en el tiempo. Edited by Francisco Blanco Figueroa, Guillermina Araiza Torres, and Agustín Herrera Reyes. Colima City: Universidad de Colima, 2007.

Guerrero, Javier. "Correspondencias secretas: Carlos Reygadas lee a Juan Rulfo." *Revista Internacional d'Humanitats* 16 (2013): 33–52.

Guilbert, Georges-Claude. *Madonna as Postmodern Myth: How One Star's Self-Construction Rewrites Sex, Gender, Hollywood, and the American Dream*. Jefferson, NC: McFarland, 2002.

"Guillermo Fadanelli." *Wikipedia*, 30 Nov. 2015. es.wikipedia.org/w/index.php?title=Guillermo_Fadanelli&oldid=87435244. Accessed 11 Oct. 2016.

Gullette, Margaret Morganroth. *Aged by Culture*. Chicago: University of Chicago Press, 2004.

———. *Agewise: Fighting the New Ageism in America*. Chicago: University of Chicago Press, 2011.

Gundle, Stephen. *Glamour: A History*. Oxford: Oxford University Press, 2008.

Gunn, Drewey Wayne. "'The Beat Trail to Mexico,' from American and British Writers in Mexico, 1556–1973." In *Adventures into Mexico: American Tourism Beyond the Border*, edited by Nicholas Dagen Bloom. Lanham, MD: Rowman & Littlefield, 2006. 77–87.

Gutiérrez, Alejandro, and Armando Ponce. "Indignarse ante los grandes hoyos negros." *Proceso*, 27 Apr. 2014, 60–65.

Gutiérrez, Laura G. *Performing Mexicanidad:* Vendidas y cabareteras *on the Transnational Stage*. Austin: University of Texas Press, 2010.

———. Personal interview. 3 Mar. 2017.

Gutiérrez, Manuel. "Beyond the Verbal and Visual Divide: How the Visual Arts Are Shaping the Production, Promotion, and Consumption of Literature in Contemporary Mexico." Paper presented at the Annual Meeting of the Modern Language Association, New York, Jan. 2018.

Gutiérrez Negrón, Sergio. "El peligro del ludita: Vagancia, humanismo y técnica en la ensayística de Guillermo Fadanelli." *Revista de Estudios Hispánicos* 48 (2014): 449–70.

Guzmán, Humberto. "La literatura de la onda y *Mester*." *Excélsior*, 24 June 1990. CME Tovar, 114–15.

Haas, Tanni, ed. *The World's Richest Man: Carlos Slim in His Own Words*. Chicago: Agate Imprint, 2014.

Hanish, Laura D., Alison Hill, Sherri Gosney, Richard A. Fabes, and Carol Lynn Martin. "Girls, Boys, and Bullying in Preschool: The Role of Gender in the Development of Bullying." In *Bullying in North American Schools*, edited by Dorothy L. Espelage and Susan M. Swearer. New York: Routledge, 2004. 132–46.

Haraway, Donna J. *Staying with the Trouble: Making Kin in the Chthulucene*. Durham: Duke University Press, 2016.

Haro, Blanca. "La voz de las escritoras mexicanas: María Luisa Mendoza." *La Mujer de Hoy* 8, no. 175 (1969).

Harris, Christine R., Noriko Coburn, Doug Rohrer, and Harold Pashler. "Two Failures to Replicate High-Performance-Goal Priming Effects." *PLoS ONE* 8, no. 8 (2013): e72467. doi:10.1371/journal.pone.0072467. Accessed 17 Mar. 2017.

Herbert, Julián. *Álbum Iscariote*. Mexico City: Era; Conaculta, 2013.

———. *Canción de tumba*. 2011. Mexico City and Barcelona: Random House Mondadori, 2012. Translated by Christina MacSweeney as *Tomb Song* (Minneapolis: Gray Wolf Press, 2018).

———. "Mi nombre es Ixca Cienfuegos." In *Carlos Fuentes y la novela latinoamericana*, edited by Cristina Fuentes La Roche and Rodolfo Mendoza. Photographs by Daniel Mordzinski. Xalapa: Universidad Veracruzana, 2013. 44–46.

Hernández, Jorge F. "Octavio Paz: La mente lúcida que hace falta comprender nuestra realidad: Entrevista con Jorge F. Hernández." *Revista Digital Universitaria* 9, no. 9 (2008). www.revista.unam.mx/vol.9/num10/art79/art79.pdf. Accessed 27 Oct. 2018.

Hernández, Juan. "Homenaje en memoria de Héctor Azar, hoy en el Palacio de Bellas Artes." *unomásuno*, 17 Oct. 2000. CME Azar, File 16-3: 172.

Hillman, D. C. A. *The Chemical Muse: Drug Use and the Roots of Western Civilization*. New York: St. Martin's Press, 2008.

"Himno Nacional Mexicano." *Wikipedia*, 22 June 2016. en.wikipedia.org/wiki/Himno_Nacional_Mexicano. Accessed 11 July 2016.

Hind, Emily. "El bárbaro doctorado del Norte: Entrevista con Luis Felipe Lomelí." *Confluencia* 32, no. 1 (2016): 208–23.

———. "Classism, *Gente Decente* and Civil Rights: From Suffrage to Divorce and Privileges in Between." In *Modern Mexican Culture: Critical Foundations*, edited by Stuart Day. Tucson: University of Arizona Press, 2017. 184–202.

———. "Entrevista a Guillermo Fadanelli." *A Contra Corriente* 14, no. 1 (2016): 306–30.

———. *Femmenism and the Mexican Woman Intellectual from Sor Juana to Poniatowska: Boob Lit*. New York: Palgrave Macmillan, 2010.

———. *La Generación XXX: Entrevistas con veinte escritores mexicanos nacidos en los 70, de Abenshushan a Xoconostle*. Mexico City: Eón, 2013.

Holson, Laura M. "Susan Cain Instigates a 'Quiet Revolution' of Introverts." *New York Times*, 25 July 2015, ST10. www.nytimes.com/2015/07/26/fashion/susan-cain-instigating-a-quiet-revolution-of-introverts.html. Accessed 29 Dec. 2017.

Huerta, David. "La neblina de la literatura." Libros y otras cosas. *El Universal*, 1 Apr. 2015, E14.

Hyman, Louis. *Borrow: The American Way of Debt*. New York: Vintage Books, 2012.

———. *Debtor Nation: The History of America in Red Ink*. Princeton: Princeton University Press, 2011.

Iber, Patrick. "The Cold War Politics of Literature and the Centro Mexicano de Escritores." *Journal of Latin American Studies* 48, no. 2 (2016): 247–72.

Idalia, María. "Martha Robles presentó sola su propio libro." Sección B. *Excélsior*, 21 Nov. 1996. CME Robles, 10.

Illouz, Eva. *Cold Intimacies: The Making of Emotional Capitalism*. Cambridge: Polity Press, 2007.

Instituto de Investigaciones Bibliográficas. Facebook post, 15 Oct. 2015. https://www.facebook.com/BiblioNacMex.HemeroNacMex.IIBUNAM/posts/974375029268459. Accessed 30 Aug. 2017.

Irwin, Robert McKee. "The Legend of Jorge Cuesta: The Perils of Alchemy and the Paranoia of Gender." In *Hispanisms and Homosexualities*, edited by Sylvia Molloy and Robert McKee Irwin. Durham: Duke University Press, 1998. 29–53.

———. *Mexican Masculinities*. Minneapolis: University of Minnesota Press, 2003.

———. "La pedo embotellado: Sexual Roles and Play in Salvador Novo's *La estatua de sal*." *Studies in the Literary Imagination* 33, no. 1 (2000): 125–32.

Jaime García Terres: Iconografía. Introduction by José Emilio Pacheco. Image research and bibliography by Alba C. de Rojo. Poems selected by Rafael Vargas. Mexico City: Fondo de Cultura Económica; Universidad Nacional Autónoma de México; El Colegio Nacional, 2003.

Jaimes, Héctor. "Ética y 'modernidad líquida': *Fricción* de Eloy Urroz y *Lodo* de Guillermo Fadanelli." *Revista de Estudios Hispánicos* 49 (2015): 25–44.

James, Lawrence. *The Middle Class: A History*. London: Little, Brown, 2006.

Jamison, Leslie. "Grand Unified Theory of Female Pain." In *The Empathy Exams: Essays*. Minneapolis: Graywolf Press, 2014. 185–218.

Janzen, Rebecca. *The National Body in Mexican Literature: Collective Challenges to Biopolitical Control*. New York: Palgrave Macmillan, 2015.

Jiménez de Báez, Yvette. "Destrucción de los mitos, ¿posibilidad de la Historia? *El llano en llamas* de Juan Rulfo." In *Actas del IX Congreso de la Asociación Internacional de Hispanistas 18–23 agosto 1986*. Vol. 2. Berlin: Verveurt, 1989. 577–90; Alicante: Biblioteca Virtual de Miguel de Cervantes, 2016. www.cervantesvirtual.com/obra/destruccion-de-los-mitos-posibilidad-de-la-historia-el-llano-en-llamas-de-juan-rulfo-/. Accessed 10 May 2018.

Jiménez-Sandoval, Saúl. "Capitalismo, deseo y el anti-Edipo en *Las batallas en el desierto*." *Mexican Studies/Estudios Mexicanos* 27, no. 2 (2011): 431–48.

"Joan Rivers, Live at the Apollo, Part 2." YouTube video. Posted by ArseRaptor, 29 Aug. 2009. https://www.youtube.com/watch?v=WXEt2gYcweQ. Accessed 11 Aug. 2015.

Jörgensen, Beth. "*Tinísima*: Elena Poniatowska's Tina Modotti." In *Literatura Mexicana/Mexican Literature*, papers presented at a conference held 6–7 Nov. 1992, edited by José Miguel Oviedo. Philadelphia: University of Pennsylvania, 1993. 22–33.

"José Emilio Pacheco (1939–2014) legó una poesía viva." *Excélsior*, 30 June 2014, 5.

José Revueltas: Iconografía. Image research, prologue, chronology, and selection of texts by José Manuel Mateo. Mexico City: Fondo de Cultura Económica, 2014.

José Vasconcelos: Iconografía. Introduction by Alonso Lujambio. Prologue by Héctor Vasconcelos. Image research, introductory note, and selection of texts by Rafael Vargas and Xavier Guzmán Urbiola. Mexico City: Fondo de Cultura Económica, 2010.

Juan Rulfo, Página Oficial. Nota biográfica. 2001. juan-rulfo.com/cronologia_galeria_19.htm. Accessed 10 Jan. 2018.

"Juan Rulfo, Premio Nacional de Letras, Lector Patológico." Cultural section. *El Sol de México*, 17 Sept. 1982, D-1, D-7.

Kahneman, Daniel. *Thinking, Fast and Slow*. New York: Farrar, Straus and Giroux, 2011.

Kashdan, Todd, and Robert Biswas-Diener. *The Upside of Your Dark Side: Why Being Your Whole Self—Not Just Your "Good" Self—Drives Success and Fulfillment*. New York: Hudson Street Press, 2014. Kindle ed.

Klein, Axel. *Drugs and the World*. London: Reaktion Books, 2008.

Klein, Richard. *Cigarettes Are Sublime*. Durham: Duke University Press, 1993.

Knight, Alan. "La Revolución Mexicana: Su dimensión económica, 1900–1930." In *Historia económica de México: De la Colonia a nuestros días*, edited by Sandra Kuntz Ficker. Mexico City: Secretaría de Economía; Colegio de México, 2010. 473–99.

"Las Ladies of Polanco.MOV." YouTube video. Posted by by tizitto68, 22 Aug. 2011. https://www.youtube.com/watch?v=6QCrGKm8mg4. Accessed 22 Sept. 2017.

"Las Ladies of Polanco—Noticiero con López Dóriga." YouTube video. Posted by duni410, 24 Aug. 2011. https://www.youtube.com/watch?v=ymTcwgIqUnQ. Accessed 22 Sept. 2017.

Lee, Susan Savage. "The Cost of Dreams of Utopia: Neocolonialism in Juan Rulfo's *Pedro Páramo* and Cormac McCarthy's *All the Pretty Horses*." *Confluencia* 30, no. 1 (2014): 152–70.

Lemus, Rafael. *Contra la vida activa.* Versus Round 9. Mexico City: Tumbona Ediciones, 2008.

Leñero, Vicente. *Vicente Leñero.* Prologue by Emmanuel Carballo. Mexico City: Empresas Editoriales, 1967.

Lenson, David. *On Drugs.* Minneapolis: University of Minnesota Press, 1995.

León, Francisco. "Christopher Domínguez Michael: Algo más que un crítico literario." El Semanario Cultural. *Novedades,* 30 June 2002, 3–4.

Lerner, Susan. "A Conversation with Jonathan Franzen." *Booth: A Journal,* 13 Feb. 2015. booth.butler.edu/2015/02/13/a-conversation-with-jonathan-franzen/. Accessed 20 Jan. 2015.

Levine, Caroline. *Forms: Whole, Rhythm, Hierarchy, Network.* Princeton: Princeton University Press, 2015.

Lincoln, Anne A., and Michael Patrick Allen. "Double Jeopardy in Hollywood: Age and Gender in the Careers of Film Actors, 1926–1999." *Sociological Forum* 19, no. 4 (2004): 611–31.

Lipsett-Rivera, Sonya. "Model Children and Models for Children in Early Mexico." In *Minor Omissions: Children in Latin American History and Society,* edited by Tobias Hecht. Madison: University of Wisconsin Press, 2002. 52–71.

"List of Countries by Literacy Rate." *Wikipedia,* 12 Feb. 2017. en.wikipedia.org/wiki/List_of_countries_by_literacy_rate. Accessed 18 Feb. 2017.

"Literatura: Muere sorpresivamente hija del escritor Carlos Fuentes." Espectáculos. *Emol,* 25 Aug. 2015. www.emol.com/noticias/magazine/2005/08/25/193361/literatura-muere-sorpresivamente-hija-del-escritor-carlos-fuentes.html. Accessed 12 July 2016.

Livas, Irene. *Alfonso Reyes para niños.* Introduction by Alejandra Rangel. Mexico City: Consejo para la Cultura de Nuevo León, 1999.

Loaeza, Guadalupe. *Las yeguas desbocadas.* Mexico City: Planeta, 2016.

Lomelí, Luis Felipe. Personal interview. 25 Aug. 2015.

Lomnitz, Claudio. *Deep Mexico, Silent Mexico: An Anthropology of Nationalism.* Minneapolis: University of Minnesota Press, 2001.

———. *The Return of Comrade Ricardo Flores Magón.* New York: Zone Books, 2014. Kindle ed.

Long, Ryan. "The Institution of Fiction: From Yáñez, Rulfo, and Fuentes to Pitol and Del Paso." In *A History of Mexican Literature,* edited by Ignacio Sánchez del Prado, Anna M. Nogar, and José Ramón Ruisánchez Serra. Cambridge: Cambridge University Press, 2016. 260–77.

Lozano, Brenda. *Cuaderno ideal.* Mexico City: Alfaguara, 2014.

Luis Cardoza y Aragón: Iconografía. Introduction by David Huerta. Image research by Alba C. de Rojo. Mexico City: Fondo de Cultura Económica, 2004.

Luiselli, Valeria. "Because Night Has Fallen and the Barbarians Have Not Come." In *México 20: New Voices, Old Traditions.* Translated by Christina MacSweeney. Forewords by D. B. C. Pierre and Cristina Rivera Garza. London: Pushkin Press, 2015. 137–49.

———. *La historia de mis dientes.* Illustrations by Daniela Franco. Mexico City: Sexto Piso, 2013. Translated by Cristina MacSweeney as *The History of My Teeth* (Minneapolis: Coffee House Press, 2015).

Luna, Ilana. *Adapting Gender: Mexican Feminisms from Literature to Film*. Albany: SUNY Press, 2018.

Lynam, Jessica. "Betrayal, Infatuation and Abandonment in *Las batallas en el desierto* by José Emilio Pacheco." *Caribe: Revista de Cultura y Literatura*, 14, no. 1 (2011): 43–60.

Maccoby, Michael. "El carácter nacional mexicano." In *Anatomía del mexicano*, selected and with a prologue by Roger Bartra. Mexico City: Plaza y Janés, 2002. 243–56.

Mahieux, Viviane. "The Chronicler as Streetwalker: Salvador Novo and the Performance of Gender." *Hispanic Review* 76, no. 4 (2008): 155–77.

Malinowski, Bronislaw. "On Phatic Communication." 1923. In *The Discourse Reader*, edited by Adam Jaworski and Nikolas Coupland. 2nd ed. New York: Routledge, 2006. 296–98.

Manjarrez, Héctor. *Útil y muy ameno vocabulario para entender a los mexicanos*. Mexico City: Grijalbo, 2011.

Manley, Mark. "400 Pueblos." http://www.markmanleyphotography.com/documentary/400-pueblos/du02/. Accessed 26 Sept. 2017.

Mantilla Osorno, Adolfo. "Una genealogía del cuerpo masculino en el arte mexicano." In *El hombre al desnudo: Dimensiones de la masculinidad a partir de 1800*. Mexico City: INBA, 2014. 44–55. Published in conjunction with the exhibition of the same name, shown at the Museo Nacional de Arte, Mexico City, 6 Mar. to 17 June 2014.

Maristain, Mónica. "10 autores inconfundiblemente mexicanos y para los cuales su país ha sido y es un motivo siempre elocuente de escritura." *Sinembargo.mx*, 16 Sept. 2012. www.sinembargo.mx/16-09-2012/365774. Accessed 25 Oct. 2016.

Martin, Douglas. "Stephen R. Covey, Herald of Good Habits, Dies at 79." Obituaries. *New York Times*, 17 July 2012, A22. www.nytimes.com/2012/07/17/business/stephen-r-covey-herald-of-good-habits-dies-at-79.html. Accessed 9 Apr. 2016.

Martin, Gerald. "Vista panorámica: La obra de Juan Rulfo en el tiempo y en el espacio." In *Toda la obra: Juan Rulfo*, edited by Claude Fell. 1992. Madrid: Signatarios del Acuerdo Archivos ALLCA XX, 1997. 573–650.

Martínez, José. *Los secretos del hombre más rico del mundo: Carlos Slim*. Mexico City: Océano, 2011.

Martínez Malo, Jesús R. "La locura contenida." In *Pensar a Cuesta*, edited by Francisco Segovia. Mexico City: Fractal; Conaculta, 2005. 31–61.

Mastretta, Ángeles. *Arráncame la vida*. 1985. 21st ed. Mexico City: Cal y arena, 1993.

McCann, Matt. "Great Men (Mostly) Through History." Lens: Photography, Video, and Visual Journalism. *International New York Times*, 3 Aug. 2015. lens.blogs.nytimes.com/2015/08/04/great-men-mostly-through-history/. Accessed 4 Aug. 2015.

McCarthy, Ellen. "Guy Talese Can't Name a Single Female Writer Who Inspired Him. Thankfully, Twitter Has a Few Suggestions." Arts and Entertainment. *Washington Post*, 2 Apr. 2016. www.washingtonpost.com/news/arts-and-entertainment/wp/2016/04/02/gay-talese-cant-name-a-single-woman-writer-who-inspired-him-thankfully-twitter-has-a-few-suggestions/?tid=sm_tw&utm_term=.b69e47fe3132. Accessed 15 May 2017.

McDonnell, Myles. *Roman Manliness:* Virtus *and the Roman Republic*. Cambridge and New York: Cambridge University Press, 2006.

Melo, Juan Vicente. *Juan Vicente Melo*. Prologue by Emmanuel Carballo. Mexico City: Empresas Editoriales, 1966.

Mendieta y Nuñez, Lucio, and María Elena de Anda. *Vida y obra de Amado Nervo*. Mexico City: Instituto Mexicano de Cultura, 1979.

Mendoza Mociño, Arturo. "Guillermo Fadanelli: A los hombres la juventud no les va bien." *Reforma*, 3 May 1997, 3C.

Merrill, Dennis. *Negotiating Paradise: U.S. Tourism and Empire in Twentieth-Century Latin America*. Chapel Hill: University of North Carolina Press, 2009.

Merrim, Stephanie. "The Existential Juan Rulfo: *Pedro Páramo*, Mexicanness, and the Grupo Hiperión." *Modern Language Notes* 129, no. 2 (2014): 308–29.

"Mesa redonda, 'Novo y el Teatro.'" *Excélsior*, 23 Aug. 1994, 5-B.

"Mexicanos, ciclistas y ¡desnudos!" Noticias. *Univisión*, 14 June 2014. www.univision.com/noticias/noticias-de-mexico/mexicanos-ciclistas-y-desnudos-fotos. Accessed 3 Mar. 2017.

Meyer, Jean. "Palabras de vida: Una conversación con Antonio Alatorre." *Istor: Revista de Historia Internacional* 11, no. 44 (2011): 98–140.

Mignolo, Walter. "Delinking: The Rhetoric of Modernity, the Logic of Coloniality, and the Grammar of De-Coloniality." *Cultural Studies* 21, nos. 2–3 (2007): 449–514.

Millán, Paulina. "A Journey Through Juan Rulfo's Photography." Translated by Helena Buffery. In *Rethinking Juan Rulfo's Creative World: Prose, Photography, Film*, edited by Dylan Brennan and Nuala Finnegan. London: Modern Humanities Research Association and Routledge, 2016. Ebook.

Miller, Geoffrey. *Spent: Sex, Evolution, and Consumer Behavior*. New York: Viking, 2009.

"Miller v. California." *Wikipedia*, 9 Jan. 2017. https://en.wikipedia.org/wiki/Miller_v._California. Accessed 1 Mar. 2017.

Mintz, Steven. *The Prime of Life: A History of Modern Adulthood*. Cambridge, MA: Belknap Press of Harvard University Press, 2015.

Miranda, Catalina. "Entrevista: Huberto Batis 25 años en el suplemento *sábado* de *unomásuno* (1977–2002)." In Miranda, *Huberto Batis 25 años*, 23–172.

———. *Huberto Batis 25 años en el suplemento* sábado *de* unomásuno *(1977–2002)*. Introduction, interviews, journalistic anthology, and appendixes by Miranda. Mexico City: Editorial Ariadna, 2005.

———. "Introducción: Huberto Batis, el maestro y editor." In Miranda, *Huberto Batis 25 años*, 11–22.

Mohr, Melissa. *Holy Shit: A Brief History of Swearing*. Oxford: Oxford University Press, 2013.

Molina, Javier. "EU es el país de lo supuestamente práctico donde no se valora la cultura: José Agustín." *unomásuno*, 12 Jan. 1979, 19. CME Agustín Ramírez, 112.

———. "No fue mi meta ser escritor: Galindo." *unomásuno*, 4 Aug. 1984, 20. CME Galindo, 31.

Monsiváis, Carlos. *Carlos Monsiváis*. Prologue by Emmanuel Carballo. Mexico City: Empresas Editoriales, 1967.

———. *El estado laico y sus malquerientes*. Mexico City: Universidad Nacional Autónoma de México; Random House Mondadori, 2008.

———. "Jorge Cuesta: Las libertades de la inteligencia." In *Jorge Cuesta*. Mexico City: Editorial Terra Nova, 1985. 9–24.

———. "José Emilio Pacheco: 'Aprendimos que no se escribe en el vacío.'" *Nexos* 31, no. 378 (2009): 50–57. www.nexos.com.mx/?p=13144. Accessed 10 May 2018.

———. *Salvador Novo: Lo marginal en el centro*. Mexico City: Era, 2000.

———. *Yo te bendigo, vida: Amado Nervo, crónica de vida y obra*. Mexico City: Gobierno del Estado Nayarit; Hoja Casa Editorial, 2002.

"Monsiváis, inmortalizado." *La Crónica de Hoy*, 26 Jan. 2013, 17.

Montes de Oca, Marco Antonio. *Marco Antonio Montes de Oca*. Prologue by Emmanuel Carballo. Mexico City: Empresas Editoriales, 1967.

Montes García, Enrique. "No escribí más porque fui un poeta oscuro y perdido." Nacional. *Siempre!*, 12 Dec. 1996, 28–29. CME Chumacero, File 49-1: 10.

Moorhead-Rosenberg, Florence. "Message in a Bottle: Tricks of Time in *Las batallas en el desierto*, by José Emilio Pacheco." *Rocky Mountain Review of Language and Literature* 53, no. 1 (1999): 11–28.

Mora, Sergio de la. *Cinemachismo: Masculinities and Sexuality in Mexican Film*. Austin: University of Texas Press, 2006.

Morales, Dionicio. "Marco Antonio Montes de Oca: Zedillo, política, poesía (II)." *Excélsior*, 14 Aug. 1994. CME Montes de Oca, 40.

Morales Carrillo, Alfonso. "El ácarata y las estrellas." In *Semo Fotografía, 1894–1981*, edited by Emma Cecilia García Krinsky. Mexico City: SINAFO–Fototeca Nacional del INAH, 2001. 60–85.

Morelos, Rubicela. "Fallece Helena Paz Garro, a los 74 años. Su final fue solitario y triste: Investigadora." Cultura. *La Jornada*, 31 Mar. 2014. www.jornada.unam.mx/2014/03/31/cultura/a09n1cul. Accessed 12 July 2016.

Moreno-Brid, Juan Carlos, and Jaime Ros. *Development and Growth in the Mexican Economy: A Historical Perspective*. Oxford: Oxford University Press, 2009.

Moretti, Franco. *The Bourgeois: Between History and Literature*. London: Verso, 2013.

Moss, Mark. *The Media and the Models of Masculinity*. Lanham, MD: Rowman & Littlefield, 2011.

"Muere Natasha Fuentes Lemus, hija de Carlos Fuentes." *Letralia, Tierra de Letras* 10, no. 129 (2005). letralia.com/129/0822fuentes.htm. Accessed 12 July 2016.

Mulvey, Laura. "Visual Pleasure and Narrative Cinema." *Screen* 16, no. 3 (1975): 6–18.

Musacchio, Humberto, ed. *México: 200 años de periodismo cultural*. 2 vols. Mexico City: Conaculta, 2012, 2013.

Nandino, Elías. *Juntando mis pasos*. Guadalajara: Aldus, 2000.

Natter, Tobias G., and Elisabeth Leopold, eds. *Nude Men: From 1800 to the Present Day*. Vienna: Leopold Museum, 2012.

Nettel, Guadalupe. *El cuerpo en que nací*. Barcelona: Anagrama, 2011.

———. *Octavio Paz: Las palabras en libertad*. Translated by Eduardo Berti. Mexico City: Taurus; Penguin Random House Grupo Editorial Mexico, 2014. Kindle ed.

"Nobel Prize Facts." https://www.nobelprize.org/nobel_prizes/facts/. Accessed 25 Oct. 2016.

Novo, Salvador. "Cartas a un Amigo de Salvador Novo." *El Heraldo de México*, 10 May 1972. Also in the file "Novo, Salvador. No. 2 (1959–1973)," 71. Centro de Documentación Literaria, Mexico City.

———. "Cartas a un Amigo de Salvador Novo." *El Heraldo de México*, 25 Apr. 1973. Also in the file "Novo, Salvador. No. 2 (1959–1973)," 112. Centro de Documentación Literaria, Mexico City.

———. *La estatua de sal*. Prologue by Carlos Monsiváis. 1998. Mexico City: Fondo de Cultura Económica, 2008. 13–72.

———. *Material de lectura: Salvador Novo en el centenario del autor*. Poesía Moderna, no. 55. Selected with notes by Carlos Monsiváis. Mexico City: Universidad Nacional Autónoma de México, 2004. www.materialdelectura.unam.mx/index.php?option=com_content&task=view&id=125&limitstart=1. Accessed 8 Aug. 2015.

Oliveira, L. M. *Árboles de largo invierno: Un ensayo sobre la humillación*. Oaxaca: Almadía, 2016.

O'Meara, Jennifer. "What 'The Bechdel Test' Doesn't Tell Us: Examining Women's Verbal and Vocal (Dis)Empowerment in Cinema." *Feminist Media Studies* 16, no. 6 (2016): 1120–23.

Ontiveros, José Luis. "René Avilés Fabila." *Robinson Literario*. CME Avilés Fabila, 21.

Oropesa, Salvador A. *The Contemporáneos Group: Rewriting Mexico in the Thirties and Forties*. Austin: University of Texas Press, 2003.

Ortega, Julio, ed. *Carlos Fuentes en el siglo XXI: Una lectura transatlántica de su obra*. Xalapa: Universidad Veracruzana, 2015.

———. *Transatlantic Translations: Dialogues in Latin American Literature*. Translated by Philip Derbyshire. London: Reaktion Books, 2006.

Ortuño, Antonio. "Elizondo: Una remembranza *S.nob*." *Letras Libres*, 8 Feb. 2008. www.letraslibres.com/mexico-espana/elizondo-una-remembranza-snob. Accessed 20 Feb. 2017.

Osorno, Diego Enrique. "Carlos Slim: Señor de México." In *Alguien limpia un fusil en su cocina: Retratos de señores y rebeldes*. Monterrey: Universidad Autónoma de Nuevo León, 2011. 135–47.

———. *Slim: Biografía política del mexicano más rico del mundo*. Mexico City: Debate, 2015.

———. "¿Qué trama el señor Gael?" *Gatopardo*, Mar. 2012, 74–85, 100–103.

Ostrower, Francie. *Why the Wealthy Give: The Culture of Elite Philanthropy*. Princeton: Princeton University Press, 1995.

Pacheco, José Emilio. *Las batallas en el desierto*. 1981. 12th ed. Mexico City: Era, 1993.

Pacheco, Laura Emilia. *José Emilio Pacheco: A mares llueve sobre el mar*. Illustrations by Mario Rosales. Colección Así Ocurrió: Instantáneas de la historia. Mexico City: SM, 2014.

Paint the Revolution: Mexican Modernism, 1910–1950. Edited by Matthew Affron, Mark A. Castro, Dafne Cruz Porchini, and Renata González Mello. Philadelphia: Philadelphia Museum of Art; Mexico City: Museo del Palacio de Bellas Artes; in association with Yale University Press, 2016. Published in conjunction with the exhibition at the Philadelphia Museum of Art, 25 Oct. 2016 to 8 Jan. 2017.

Palapa Quijas, Fabiola. "Murió la escritora y académica Clementina Díaz y de Ovando." *La Jornada*, 20 Feb. 2012. http://www.jornada.unam.mx/2012/02/20/cultura/a10n1cul. Accessed 12 Aug. 2017.

Palaversich, Diana. "Las trampas del sexo: Dos caras del realismo sucio." *La palabra y el hombre*, no. 126 (2003): 193–201.

Palhares, Lucilia de. "El cronista de la ciudad enjuicia a los escritores mexicanos hoy y antaño." *Novedades*, 15 June 1976. CME Rulfo, 48.

Palou, Pedro Ángel. *El fracaso del mestizo*. Mexico City: Ediciones Culturales Paidós, 2014.

Pantoja, Óscar, and Felipe Camargo. *Rulfo: Una vida gráfica*. Bogotá: Rey Naranjo Editores, 2014.

Paso, Fernando del. *Memoria y olvido: Vida de Juan José Arreola (1920–1947)*. Mexico City: Conaculta, 1994.

"Pasos hacia la igualdad de género en México, 2007." Instituto Nacional de las Mujeres, Dirección de Estadística, August 2007. http://cedoc.inmujeres.gob.mx/documentos_download/100894.pdf. Accessed 10 May 2018.

Paz, Octavio. *El camino de la pasión: López Velarde*. Mexico City: Planeta, 2001.

———. *El laberinto de la soledad. Postdata. Vuelta a El laberinto de la soledad*. 1950. 2nd ed. Mexico City: Fondo de Cultura Económica, 1993.

———. *Xavier Villaurrutia en persona y obra*. Illustrations by Juan Soriano. 1978. Mexico City: Fondo de Cultura Económica, 1990.

Paz Avendaño, Reyna. "Con lectura de poemas, música y video rinden homenaje a José Emilio Pacheco." *La Crónica de Hoy*, 1 July 2014, 19.

Paz Oliver, María. *El arte de irse por las ramas: La digresión en la novela latinoamericana contemporánea*. Leiden and Boston: Brill Rodopi, 2016.

Peguero, Raquel. "La pintura de Montes de Oca, poesía para vivir: Octavio Paz." Cultura. *La Jornada*, 9 Feb. 1994, 28. CME Montes de Oca, 49.

Peláez Máximo, Patricia Isabel. "Los estudios no matan las pasiones: Tendencias estéticas en *Lodo*, de Guillermo Fadanelli." In *Nada es lo que parece: Estudios sobre la novela mexicana, 2000–2009*, edited by Miguel Guadalupe Rodríguez Lozano. Mexico City: Universidad Nacional Autónoma de México, 2012. 55–68.

Pellicer, Juan. "Economía poética de *Pedro Páramo* de la Revolución a la Cristiada." *Literatura Mexicana* 21, no. 2 (2010): 197–202.

Pengelly, Martin. "Gay Talese in Twitter Storm after Failing to Name Inspirational Female Writers." Books. *Guardian*, 2 Apr. 2016. www.theguardian.com/books/2016/apr/02/gay-talese-twitter-female-writers. Accessed 22 Apr. 2016.

Penrose, Brian. "Soft vs. Hard: Why Drugs Are Not Like Eggs." In *Cannabis: Philosophy for Everyone; What Were We Just Talking About?*, edited by Dale Jacquette. Foreword by Rick Cusick. Malden, MA: Wiley-Blackwell, 2010. 162–72.

Peralta, Braulio. *El clóset de cristal*. Mexico City: Ediciones B, 2016.

Petrich, Blanche. "'Mi gober, tú eres el héroe': Kamel Nacif a Mario Marín." *La Jornada*, 14 Feb. 2006. www.jornada.unam.mx/2006/02/14/index.php?section=politica&article=005n1pol. Accessed 8 Oct. 2017.

Petrol del Dr. Torrel, de París, advertisement. *El Mundo Ilustrado*, 31 Jan. 1904.

Piccato, Pablo. *The Tyranny of Opinion: Honor in the Construction of the Mexican Public Sphere*. Durham: Duke University Press, 2010.

Piñón, Alida. "Entrevista: Omar García, pareja de Carlos Monsiváis." *El Universal*, 18 June 2011, E17.

———. "Monsiváis, cronista y protagonista." *Excélsior*, 11 Aug. 2010, 8.

Pitol, Sergio. *Sergio Pitol*. Prologue by Emmanuel Carballo. Mexico City: Empresas Editoriales, 1966.

Plan Nacional de Desarrollo, 2013–2018. Diario Oficial de la Federación, 20 May 2013. pnd.gob.mx/. Accessed 10 Nov. 2014.

"Plaza Río de Janeiro." *Wikipedia*. 28 Jan. 2017. es.wikipedia.org/wiki/Plaza_R%C3%ADo_de_Janeiro. Accessed 3 Mar. 2017.

Ponce, Amando. "Ocho jóvenes obtuvieron las becas Novo; el Centro Mexicano de Escritores en peligro." *El Proceso*, 25 June 1983. www.proceso.com.mx/136407/ocho-jovenes-obtuvieron-las-becas-novo-el-centro-mexicano-de-escritores-en-peligro. Accessed 11 May 2017.

Poniatowska, Elena. "¡Ay, ay, ay, mi querido capitán! María Conesa." In *Palabras cruzadas*. Mexico City: Era, 2013. 27–52.

———. "Los cafés de París: Deux Magots, Flore, Lip, Closerie des Lilas." In *Jardín de Francia*. Mexico City: Fondo de Cultura Económica, 2008. 96–97.

———. *Dos veces única*. Mexico City: Planeta, 2015.

———. "En recuerdo de Carlos Monsiváis." *La Jornada*, 4 May 2011, 5a.

———. "El más inquietante de los escritores mexicanos: Salvador Elizondo." In *Palabras cruzadas*. Mexico City: Era, 2013. 381–95.

———. "*Monsi* después de *Monsi*." *La Jornada*, 20 June 2011, 10a.

———. "No te vayas, Carlos Fuentes." In *Carlos Fuentes y la novela latinoamericana*, edited by Cristina Fuentes La Roche and Rodolfo Mendoza. Photographs by Daniel Mordzinski. Xalapa: Universidad Veracruzana, 2013. 70–76.

———. "Salvador Elizondo: IV y última." *La Jornada*, 8 Apr. 2006. www.jornada.unam.mx/2006/04/08/index.php?section=opinion&article=a05a1cul. Accessed 7 June 2018.

———. *Sansimonsi*. Illustrations by Rafael Barajas. Mexico City: Ediciones Uache, 2013.

———. "Su majestad el rey Juan Carlos me pide permiso: Lola Beltrán." In *Palabras cruzadas*. Mexico City: Era, 2013. 247–72.

Popovich Karic, Pol. "El momento inicial de *Pedro Páramo*." *Contexto* 15, no. 17 (2011): 15–33.

Potter, Sara A. "Disturbing Muses: Gender, Technology, and Resistance in Mexican Avant-Garde Cultures." Dissertation, Washington University in St. Louis, 2013.

Pountain, Dick, and David Robins. *Cool Rules: Anatomy of an Attitude*. London: Reaktion Books, 2000.

Quiet Revolution. Website for *Quiet: The Power of Introverts in a World That Can't Stop Talking*, by Susan Cain. www.quietrev.com/quiet-the-book/. Accessed 29 Dec. 2017.

Quiroz Arroyo, Macarena. "La juvenil cantante Thalía se expresó fuerte, en contra del escritor Juan José Arreola." *Excélsior*, 3 June 1991. CME Arreola, 110.

Race, Kane. *Pleasure Consuming Medicine: The Queer Politics of Drugs*. Durham: Duke University Press, 2009.

Ramírez, Luis Enrique. "José Agustín: Escritor joven, muchacho eterno." Cultura. *La Jornada*, 25 Aug. 1994, 25, 27.

Ramírez, Santiago. "Psicoanálisis del mestizaje." In *Anatomía del mexicano*, selected and with a prologue by Roger Bartra. Mexico City: Plaza y Janés, 2002. 237–42.

Rashkin, Elissa J. *The Stridentist Movement in Mexico: The Avant-Garde and Cultural Change in the 1920s*. Lanham, MD: Lexington Books, 2009.

———. *Women Filmmakers in Mexico: The Country of Which We Dream*. Austin: University of Texas Press, 2001.

Reagan, Patricia E. *Deconstructing Paradise: Inverted Religious Symbolism in Twentieth-Century Latin American Literature*. Lanham, MD: Lexington Books, 2016.

"Reconoce UNAM a destacadas universitarias." *Excélsior*, 8 Mar. 2018. www.excelsior.com.mx/nacional/2018/03/08/1225110. Accessed 17 May 2018.

Reiner, Andrew. "Teaching Men to Be Emotionally Honest." *New York Times*, 4 Apr. 2016. www.nytimes.com/2016/04/10/education/edlife/teaching-men-to-be-emotionally-honest.html?_r=0. Accessed 17 Apr. 2017. First published as "The Masculine Mystique," *Education Life*, 10 Apr. 2016, ED11.

Reisman, David, with Nathan Glazer and Reuel Denney. *The Lonely Crowd: A Study of the Changing American Character*. 1961. Abridged ed., with a new preface. New Haven: Yale University Press, 1969.

Restall, Matthew. *Seven Myths of the Spanish Conquest*. New York: Oxford University Press, 2003.

"Resultados 2015." In *Sistema Nacional de Creadores de Arte*. Secretaría de Cultura, Fondo Nacional para la Cultura y las Artes. foncaenlinea.cultura.gob.mx/resultados/resultados.php. Accessed 2 Aug. 2016.

"Resultados 2016." In *Sistema Nacional de Creadores de Arte*. Secretaría de Cultura, Fondo Nacional para la Cultura y las Artes. foncaenlinea.cultura.gob.mx/resultados/resultados.php. Accessed 2 Aug. 2016.

Reyes Razo, Miguel. "Juan Rulfo: He vuelto a escribir . . . voy despacio, pero lleva trazos de lo que yo quería crear." *El Universal*, 11 Feb. 1977, 6.

Reynebeau, Marc. "'*Je ne sais quois*': Some Reflections on the Study of Charisma." In *Charismatic Leadership and Social Movements: The Revolutionary Power of Ordinary Men and Women*, edited by Jan Willem Stutje. New York: Berghahn Books, 2012. 155–63.

Ribas-Casasayas, Alberto. "El tirano indigente: *Pedro Páramo*, deuda y necropolítica." *A Contracorriente* 14, no. 3 (2017). acontracorriente.chass.ncsu.edu/index.php/acontracorriente/article/view/1559. Accessed 10 May 2018.

Rivera Garza, Cristina. *Había mucha neblina o humo o no sé qué*. Mexico City: Penguin Random House, 2016.

———. "Oddly/Curiosamente." In *Carlos Fuentes y la novela latinoamericana*, edited by Cristina Fuentes La Roche and Rodolfo Mendoza. Photographs by Daniel Mordzinski. Xalapa: Universidad Veracruzana, 2013. 77–82.

Robbins, Bruce. *Upward Mobility and the Common Good: Toward a Literary History of the Welfare State*. Princeton: Princeton University Press, 2007.

Roffé, Reina. *Juan Rulfo: Biografía no autorizada*. Prologue by Blas Matamoro. Madrid: Fórcola, 2012.

Ronell, Avital. *Crack Wars: Literature, Addiction, Mania*. Lincoln: University of Nebraska Press, 1992.

Rosales Maldonado, Iván J. "Tú puedes ser beneficiado . . . Becas para escritores." *Uni-Verso: El Periódico de los Universitarios* (Universidad Veracruzana) 3, no. 88 (20 Jan. 2003). https://www.uv.mx/universo/88/infgral/infgral13.htm. Accessed 5 July 2016.

Rosas, Tania, and Vanessa Alemán. "Exigen juicio político contra juez que amparó a 'Porky.'" *Excélsior*, 30 Mar. 2017. www.excelsior.com.mx/nacional/2017/03/30/1154990l9. Accessed 19 Apr. 2017.

Rossell, Daniela. *Ricas y famosas: México, 1994–2001*. Afterword by Barry Schwabsky. With English translation by Luis Gago. Madrid: Turner, 2002.

Rubio Rossell, Carlos. "Vivir para contarlo." Temas. *Mercurio*, 16 Apr. 2014. revistamercurio.es/temas/vivir-para-contarlo/. Accessed 9 Mar. 2017.

Ruisánchez Serra, José Ramón. *Historias que regresan: Topología y renarración en la segunda mitad del siglo XX mexicano*. Mexico City: Universidad Iberoamericana; Fondo de Cultura Económica, 2012.

———. "Literaturas del bien, contraescrituras del mal: El caso Fadanelli." *Revista de Literatura Mexicana Contemporánea* 12, no. 29 (2006): 75–81.

Ruiz-Poveda Vera, Cristina. "The Ineffable in Contemporary Ibero-American Cinema: Memory, Death, and Spiritual Journeys." Dissertation, University of Florida, 2018.

Rulfo, Juan. *Pedro Páramo*. Translated by Margaret Sayers Peden. Foreword by Susan Sontag. New York: Grove Press, 1994.

———. *Pedro Páramo*. Edited by José Carlos González Boixo. 24th rev. ed. Madrid: Cátedra, 2012.

Ruiz, Bernardo. Email message to author, 9 July 2015.

Ruiz, Eduardo. "El reverso del 'milagro mexicano': La crítica de la nación en *Las batallas en el desierto* y *El vampiro de la colonia Roma*." *Ciberletras* 26 (2011). www.lehman.cuny.edu/ciberletras/v26/ruizeduardo.htm. Accessed 10 May 2018.

Ruiz, Ramón Eduardo. *Mexico: Why a Few Are Rich and the People Poor*. Berkeley: University of California Press, 2010.

Ruy Sánchez, Alberto. *Octavio Paz: Cuenta y canta la historia*. Illustrations by Ángel Campos. Colección Así Ocurrió: Instantáneas de la historia. Mexico City: SM, 2014.

Ryan, Michael, and Douglas Kellner. *Camera Politica: The Politics and Ideology of Contemporary Hollywood Film*. Bloomington: Indiana University Press, 1988.

Sabido, Miguel. Personal interview. 22 July 2016. Mexico City.

Saborit, Antonio. "Metamorfosis de *Las batallas en el desierto.*" *Nexos* 34, no. 408 (2011): 93–94. www.nexos.com.mx/?p=14604. Accessed 10 May 2018.

Sada, Daniel. *El lenguaje del juego.* Barcelona: Anagrama, 2012.

Saint-Amour, Paul K. *Tense Future: Modernism, Total War, Encyclopedic Form.* New York: Oxford University Press, 2015.

Sainz, Gustavo. *Gustavo Sainz.* Prologue by Emmanuel Carballo. Mexico City: Empresas Editoriales, 1966.

"Salvador Novo: Su musa callejera." In *Contribuciones al pensamiento social mexicano.* Coordinación Centro Mexicano de Estudios Sociales/Debate-Reflexión-Propuestas. Mexico City: Cenzontle Grupo Editorial, 2005. 141–46.

Sánchez, Fernando Fabio. *Artful Assassins: Murder as Art in Modern Mexico.* Translated by Stephen J. Clark. Nashville: Vanderbilt University Press, 2010.

Sánchez Ambriz, Mary Carmen. "Con M de Monsi." La Crítica: Libro. *Milenio,* 20 May 2013, 40.

———. "Mis lectores son las mujeres: René Avilés Fabila." *Siempre!,* 22 Aug. 2001, 38–39.

Sánchez Prado, Ignacio M. "La incesante paradoja del ensayo joven." *Letras Libres,* no. 140 (Aug. 2010): 82–83.

———. "Juan Rulfo: El clamor de la forma." In El llano en llamas, Pedro Páramo *y otras obras (En el centenario de su autor),* edited by Pedro Ángel Palou and Francisco Ramírez Santacruz. Madrid: Iberoamericana; Frankfurt am Main: Vervuert, 2017. 171–201.

———. "Nación y castración: *El bachiller* de Amado Nervo." In *Entre hombres: Masculinidades del siglo XIX en América Latina,* edited by Ana Peluffo and Ignacio M. Sánchez Prado. Madrid: Iberoamericana; Frankfurt am Main: Vervuert, 2010. 275–88.

———. "Pacheco, o los pliegues de la historia." *Torre: Revista de la Universidad de Puerto Rico* 9, no. 33 (2004): 391–99.

———. *Screening Neoliberalism: Transforming Mexican Cinema, 1988–2012.* Nashville: Vanderbilt University Press, 2014.

Sándel, Alberto, and León Felipe Barrón, eds. *El libro de los espejos: Encuentros con Salvador Elizondo.* Xalapa: Instituto Literario de Veracruz / Mexico City: Secretaría de Cultura, 2016

———. "Los sueños de Eurídice y Orfeo I: Entrevista con Paulina Lavista." In *El libro de los espejos: Encuentros con Salvador Elizondo,* edited by Alberto Sándel and León Felipe Barrón. Xalapa: Instituto Literario de Veracruz / Mexico City: Secretaría de Cultura, 2016. 77–90.

———. "Los sueños de Eurídice y Orfeo II: Entrevista con Paulina Lavista." In *El libro de los espejos,* edited by Sándel and Barrón. 185–98.

Sandoval, Adriana. Prologue to *Santa,* by Federico Gamboa. Mexico City: Fondo de Cultura Económica, 2006. 9–15.

Sassen, Saskia: *Expulsions: Brutality and Complexity in the Global Market.* Cambridge, MA: Belknap Press of Harvard University Press, 2014.

Saul, Heather. "Tamara de Anda: Trolls Target Mexican Journalist in Westminster Attack Hoax." *iNews: The Essential Daily Briefing,* 22 Mar. 2017. inews.co.uk/news/

uk/westminster-bridge-attack-journalist-mexico-targeted-hoax-claiming-missing/. Accessed 17 May 2018.

Savage, Charlie. "A Judge's View of Judging Is on the Record." *New York Times*, 14 May 2009. http://www.nytimes.com/2009/05/15/us/15judge.html. Accessed 13 Aug. 2015.

Schulz, James H., and Robert H. Binstock. *Aging Nation: The Economics and Politics of Growing Older in America*. Westport, CT, and London: Praeger, 2006.

Scott, Joan Wallach. *Only Paradoxes to Offer: French Feminists and the Rights of Man*. Cambridge, MA: Harvard University Press, 1996.

Sedgwick, Eve Kosofsky. "Epidemics of the Will." In *Incorporations*, edited by Jonathan Crary and Sanford Kwinter. New York: Zone Books, 1992. 582–95.

Seijas, Tatiana, and Pablo Miguel Sierra Silva. "The Persistence of the Slave Market in Seventeenth-Century Central Mexico." *Slavery & Abolition: A Journal of Slave and Post-Slave Studies* 37, no. 2 (2016): 307–33.

Selisker, Scott. "The Bechdel Test and the Social Form of Character Networks." *New Literary History* 46 (2015): 505–23.

Serrato Córdova, José Eduardo. "La ciudad letrada y la ciudad sitiada: El caso de *Hotel D.F.*, de Guillermo Fadanelli." In *2010 y alrededor del festejo . . . : Estudios sobre novela mexicana*, edited by Miguel Guadalupe Rodríguez Lozano. Mexico City: Universidad Nacional Autónoma de México, 2016. 115–30.

Shariff, Shaheen. *Confronting Cyber-Bullying: What Schools Need to Know to Control Misconduct and Avoid Legal Consequences*. Cambridge: Cambridge University Press, 2009.

Sheridan, Guillermo. "Carta de amor con faltas de lenguaje." Minutario. *El Universal*, 13 May 2014, E11.

———. *Un corazón adicto: La vida de Ramón López Velarde*. Image research by Xavier Guzmán Urbiola. Mexico City: Fondo de Cultura Económica, 1989.

Smith, Benjamin T. "Public Drug Policy and Grey Zone Pacts in México, 1920–1980." In *Drug Policies and the Politics of Drugs in the Americas*, edited by Beatriz Caiuby Labate, Clancy Cavnar, and Thiago Rodrigues. Cham, Switzerland: Springer, 2016. 33–51.

Smith, Stephanie Jo. *Gender and the Mexican Revolution: Yucatán Women and the Realities of Patriarchy*. Chapel Hill: University of North Carolina Press, 2009.

Smith, Stacy L., Marc Choueiti, and Katherine Pieper. "Inequality in 700 Popular Films: Examining Portrayals of Gender, Race, and LGBT Status from 2007–2014." Media, Diversity, and Social Change Initiative. Harnish Foundation, University of Southern California, n.d.

———. "Inequality in 900 Popular Films: Examining Portrayals of Gender, Race/Ethnicity, LGBT, and Disability from 2007–2016." Media, Diversity, and Social Change Initiative. Annenberg Foundation, University of Southern California, n.d.

Soler Serrano, Joaquín. "Juan Rulfo: Entrevista a fondo." *A Fondo, con Joaquín Soler Serrano*, Radiotelevisión Española, 7 Apr. 1977. YouTube video. Posted by Miguel Angel Herrera, 29 Apr. 2012. www.youtube.com/watch?v=V74yJztkx-c. Accessed 8 Oct. 2017.

Sommers, Joseph. "Entrevista con Juan Rulfo." *Siempre!*, 15 Aug. 1973, 6–7. Cited on *Ciudad Seva*. www.ciudadseva.com/textos/teoria/opin/rulfo2.htm. Accessed 20 July 2016. Reprinted in Sommers, "Los muertos no tienen tiempo ni espacio (un diálogo con

Juan Rulfo)," in *La ficción de la memoria: Juan Rulfo ante la crítica*, selected and with a prologue by Federico Campbell (Mexico City: Era, 2003). 517–21.

Sorais Castañeda G., Claudia. "Representación y configuración de un canon: El Premio Bellas Artes de Poesía Aguascalientes a través de sus jurados." Paper presented at the Coloquio 50 años del Premio Bellas Artes de Poesía Aguascalientes, Aguascalientes, Mexico, 2 May 2018.

Soto van der Plas, Christina. "Beginnings of José Emilio Pacheco." In *Mexican Literature in Theory*, edited by Ignacio Sánchez del Prado. New York: Bloomsbury, 2018. 159–76.

Soto Viterbo, Felipe. *La conspiración de las cosas*. Mexico City: Mondadori, 2012.

Speckman Guerra, Elisa. *¿Quién es un criminal? Un recorrido por el delito, la ley, la justicia y el castigo en México (desde el virreinato hasta el siglo XX)*. Illustrations by Alejandro Magallanes. Mexico City: Ediciones Castillo, 2006.

Stacomb advertisement. "¿Es usted un hombre a la moderna?" *El Universal Ilustrado*, 24 May 1928. In *México: 200 años de periodismo cultural, 1911–1960*, vol. 2, edited by Humberto Musacchio. Mexico City: Conaculta, 2012. 96.

Stallaert, Christiane. "Cruzar la frontera del encanto: Juan Rulfo en el sistema mundial de las letras." *Herméneus* 19 (2017): 335–63.

Stearns, Peter N. *American Cool: Constructing a Twentieth-Century Emotional Style*. New York: New York University Press, 1994.

Steele, Cynthia. "Commodification and Desire in the Wasteland: *Las batallas en el desierto* (1981), by José Emilio Pacheco." In *Politics, Gender, and the Mexican Novel, 1968–1988: Beyond the Pyramid*. Austin: University of Texas Press, 1992. 88–109.

Steinem, Gloria. "Women Have 'Chick Flicks.' What About Men?" Opinion. *New York Times*, 2 Mar. 2017. www.nytimes.com/2017/03/02/opinion/gloria-steinem-women-have-chick-flicks-what-about-men.html. Accessed 3 Mar. 2017.

Street, John. "The Celebrity Politician: Political Style and Popular Culture." In *The Celebrity Culture Reader*, edited by P. David Marshall. New York and London: Routledge, 2006. 359–70. Originally published in *Media and the Restyling of Politics*, edited by John Corner and Dick Pels (London: Sage, 2003). 85–98.

Susman, Warren I. *Culture as History: The Transformation of American Society in the Twentieth Century*. New York: Pantheon Books, 1973.

Taibo, Benito. *Cómplice*. Mexico City: Planeta, 2015.

———. *Persona normal*. Mexico City: Planeta, 2011.

Tenenbaum, Barbara. *The Politics of Penury: Debts and Taxes in Mexico, 1821–1856*. Albuquerque: University of New Mexico Press, 1986.

Thakkar, Amit. *The Fiction of Juan Rulfo: Irony, Revolution, and Postcolonialism*. London: Tamesis, 2012.

———. "Irony and the Priest in Fragment 14 of Juan Rulfo's *Pedro Páramo*." *Bulletin of Hispanic Studies* 83, no. 3 (2006): 203–24.

———. "Studium and Punctum in Juan Rulfo's 'Puerta del cementerio de Janitzio.'" In *Rethinking Juan Rulfo's Creative World: Prose, Photography, Film*, edited by Dylan Brennan and Nuala Finnegan. London: Modern Humanities Research Association and Routledge, 2016. Ebook.

Tortajada Quiroz, Margarita. *Frutos de mujer.* Mexico City: Conaculta, INBA, 2001.

Trejo Fuentes, Ignacio. "En el homenaje a René Avilés Fabila." *Siempre!*, 21 Mar. 2004, 65.

"Trolls Target Journalist over Harassment Case." *Mexico News Daily*, 25 Mar. 2017. mexiconewsdaily.com/news/trolls-target-journalist-over-harassment-case/. Accessed 11 May 2018.

Tucker, Duncan. "Oxfam Study Highlights Mexico's Drastic Wealth Inequality Crisis." *Latin Correspondent*, 26 June 2015. latincorrespondent.com/2015/06/oxfam-study-highlights-mexicos-drastic-wealth-inequality-crisis/. Accessed 19 July 2016.

Tugend, Alina. "Peeking at the Negative Side of High School Popularity." Your Money. *New York Times*, 18 June 2010. www.nytimes.com/2010/06/19/your-money/19shortcuts.html. Accessed 26 Apr. 2017.

Turkle, Sherry. *Alone Together: Why We Expect More from Technology and Less from Each Other.* New York: Basic Books, 2011.

Tyler, George R. *What Went Wrong: How the 1% Hijacked the American Middle Class . . . and What Other Countries Got Right.* Dallas: Benbella Books, 2013. Kindle ed.

Universal Declaration of Human Rights. United Nations. http://www.un.org/en/universal-declaration-human-rights/. Accessed 6 Oct. 2017.

"El universo de Juan Rulfo: A propósito de *Pedro Páramo* (1955)." Coordinación Nacional de Literatura, 20 Aug. 2015. http://www.literatura.bellasartes.gob.mx/articulos.html. Accessed 29 Sept. 2017.

Unnever, James D., and Dewey G. Cornell. "Bullying, Self-Control, and ADHD." *Journal of Interpersonal Violence* 18, no. 2 (2003): 129–47.

Usi, Eva. "Xavier Velasco, el chico terrible de la literatura mexicana." *DW*, 12 Oct. 2014. http://www.dw.com/es/xavier-velasco-el-chico-terrible-de-la-literatura-mexicana/a-17988715. Accessed 22 Dec. 2015.

Valencia, Norman. *Retóricas del poder y nombres del padre en la literatura latinoamericana: Paternalismo, política y la forma literaria en Graciliano Ramos, Juan Rulfo, João Guimarães Rosa y José Lezama Lima.* Madrid: Iberoamericana; Frankfurt am Main: Vervuert, 2017.

Valerio-Holguín, Fernando. "Identidad musical y estructuras de sentimientos: *Las batallas en el desierto* de José Emilio Pacheco." *Revista de Literatura Mexicana Contemporánea* 17, no. 50 (2011): 21–27.

Valis, Noël. *The Culture of Cursilería: Bad Taste, Kitsch, and Class in Modern Spain.* Durham: Duke University Press, 2002.

Vallarino, Roberto. "Salvador Novo diez años después de su muerte." In *Catorce perfiles.* Mexico City: Coordinación de Difusión Cultural, Dirección de Literatura, Universidad Nacional Autónoma de México, 1997. 135–41.

Vallarino Almada, Roberto. "René Avilés Fabila verá reeditada su obra completa." *unomásuno*, 19 Sept. 2001. CME Avilés Fabila, 28.

Vanden Berghe, Kristine. "Parecidos estilísticos entre Nellie Campobello y Juan Rulfo." In El llano en llamas, Pedro Páramo *y otras obras (En el centenario de su autor)*, edited by Pedro Ángel Palou and Francisco Ramírez Santacruz. Madrid: Iberoamericana; Frankfurt am Main, Vervuert, 2017. 301–25.

Vargas, Jorge A. *Mexican Law for the American Lawyer.* Durham: Carolina Academic Press, 2009.

Vargas, Rafael. *Octavio Paz, entre la imagen y el nombre.* Mexico City: Conaculta, 2010.

Vargas Betancourt, Margarita. Email message to author, 25 Sept. 2017.

Velasco, Xavier. "La agonía del *chic* y el retorno del naco vengador." In *Luna llena en las rocas: Crónicas de astronautas y licántropos.* 2005. 3rd ed. Mexico City: Alfaguara, 2007. 65–72.

———. *La edad de la punzada.* Mexico City: Alfaguara, 2012.

———. *Éste que ves.* Mexico City: Alfaguara, 2006.

Velázquez, Carlos. *La marrana negra de la literatura rosa.* Mexico City: Sexto Piso, 2010.

Venegas, Ricardo. "El guía de los escritores noveles." *La Jornada Semanal,* 14 Nov. 2010. http://www.jornada.unam.mx/2010/11/14/sem-venegas.html. Accessed 5 July 2016.

Ventura, Abida. "Reflexionan sobre influencia británica en Paz." *El Universal,* 14 Apr. 2015, E11.

Verani, Hugo J. "Disonancia y desmitificación en *Las batallas en el desierto* de José Emilio Pacheco." *Hispamérica* 14, no. 42 (1985): 29–40.

Villa-Flores, Javier. *Dangerous Speech: A Social History of Blasphemy in Colonial Mexico.* Tucson: University of Arizona Press, 2006.

Villalobos-Ruminott, Sergio. *Heterografías de la violencia: Historia, nihilismo, destrucción.* Adrogué, AR: Ediciones La Cebra, 2016.

Villegas, Eduardo. "La pequeña lección de Orlando." In *Primer encuentro de escritores del Norte.* Ciudad Victoria, TM: Instituto Tamaulipeco para la Cultura y las Artes, 2012. 235–46.

Villela, Víctor. "Arreola, un taller continuo." sábado. *unomásuno,* 6 Apr. 1997. CME Arreola, 49.

Villoro, Juan. "Carlos Monsiváis: La multitud de uno solo." *Cultura y arte de México,* no. 12 (June 2011): 4–6.

Vital, Alberto. *Noticias sobre Juan Rulfo: 1784–2003.* Mexico City: Editorial RM, 2003.

Volek, Emil. "*Pedro Páramo* de Juan Rulfo: Una obra aleatória em busca de su texto y del género literário." *Revista Iberoamericana* 61, no. 150 (1990): 35–47.

Volpi, Jorge. *Examen de mi padre.* Mexico City: Penguin Random House, 2016.

Vossler, Molly. "Men Dominate UF's List of Highest-Paid Faculty; University Officials Say They're Working to Address the Disparity." *Alligator,* 2 Dec. 2016. http://www.alligator.org/news/campus/article_8eadbf10-b853-11e6-ad7a-1b583144dfdb.html. Accessed 5 Dec. 2016.

Waldron, John V. "Reinscribing Poetry's Potential: José Emilio Pacheco Reads Ramón López Velarde." *Hispanófila* 154 (2008): 59–72.

Walkowitz, Rebecca L. *Born Translated: The Contemporary Novel in an Age of World Literature.* New York: Colombia University Press, 2015.

Way, Niobe. *Deep Secrets: Boys' Friendships and the Crisis of Connection.* Cambridge, MA: Harvard University Press, 2011.

Weimer, Daniel. *Seeing Drugs: Modernization, Counterinsurgency, and U.S. Narcotics Control in the Third World, 1969–1976.* Kent, OH: Kent State University Press, 2011.

Weis, Robert. "Por la verdad del Osito Bimbo: Los intelectuales de élite, la cultura nacional y la industrialización de la comida en México." *Brújula* 1 (2002): 94–103.

Wendling, Mike, and Kayleen Devlin. "Grenfell 'Miracle Baby': Why People Invent Fake Victims of Attacks and Disasters." *BBC Trending*, 29 June 2017. www.bbc.com/news/blogs-trending-40419479. Accessed 11 May 2018.

Wentzell, Emily A. *Maturing Masculinities: Aging, Chronic Illness, and Viagra in Mexico.* Durham: Duke University Press, 2013.

Whitmore, Alice. "Subterranean Mexican Blues: Guillermo Fadanelli and the Genesis of Trash Literature." *Journal of Iberian & Latin American Research* 23, no. 2 (2017): 104–21.

Williams, Gareth. *The Mexican Exception: Sovereignty, Police, and Democracy.* New York: Palgrave Macmillan, 2011.

Wolcott, James. "The Hung and the Restless." *Vanity Fair*, Mar. 2012, 200, 207.

Wolfenzon, Carolyn. "*Batallas en el desierto*: La inversión del melodrama cinematográfico como estrategia crítica sobre la Revolución Mexicana." *Confluencia* 28, no. 1 (2012): 46–60.

Wolfson, Gabriel, and Jorge Aguilar Mora, eds. *Se acabó el centenario: Lecturas críticas en torno a Octavio Paz.* Puebla, Mexico: Fundación Universidad de las Américas, Puebla, 2015.

World Bank. Population data. https://data.worldbank.org/indicator/SP.POP.TOTL. Accessed 3 Aug. 2015.

Wouters, Cas. *Informalization: Manners and Emotions since 1890.* Los Angeles: Sage Publications, 2007.

Zaldívar Lelo de Larrea, Arturo. "Amparo directo en revisión 2806/2012." Secretary Javier Mijangos y González. www.miguelcarbonell.com/artman/uploads/1/Sentencia_amparo_en_revisi_n_2806-2012.pdf. Accessed 5 Apr. 2016.

———. "Amparo en revisión 237/2014." Secretaries Arturo Bárcena Zubieta and Ana María Ibarra Olguín. Collaborators Guillermo Kohn Espinosa and Miguel Oscar Casillas Sandoval. www.estevez.org.mx/wp-content/uploads/2016/05/14002370-002-2780-2.pdf. Accessed 5 Apr. 2016.

Zamora, Alejandro. "Hacia una infancia de nuestra historia nacional: *Las batallas en el desierto*, de José Emilio Pacheco." *Revista de El Colegio de San Luis* 1, no. 2 (2011): 148–61.

Zelizer, Viviana A. *The Purchase of Intimacy.* Princeton: Princeton University Press, 2005.

Zunz, Olivier. *Philanthropy in America: A History.* 2011. Princeton: Princeton University Press, 2014.

INDEX

ABOUT THE AUTHOR

Emily Hind is an associate professor of Spanish at the University of Florida. Hind has published two books of interviews with Mexican writers, as well as a book of criticism, *Femmenism and the Mexican Woman Intellectual from Sor Juana to Poniatowska: Boob Lit*.